THE FRENCH REVOLUTION
AND WHAT WENT WRONG

THE FRENCH REVOLUTION AND WHAT WENT WRONG

Stephen Clarke

CENTURY

Published by Century in 2018

1 3 5 7 9 10 8 6 4 2

Century
20 Vauxhall Bridge Road
London SW1V 2SA

Century is part of the Penguin Random House group of companies whose addresses can be found at global.penguinrandomhouse.com.

Penguin
Random House
UK

First published by Century in 2018

www.penguin.co.uk

A CIP catalogue record for this book is available from the British Library.

ISBN 9781780895512

Typeset in 13/15 pt Ehrhardt MT Pro
by Integra Software Services Pvt. Ltd, Pondicherry

Printed and bound by Clays Ltd, St Ives PLC

Penguin Random House is committed to a sustainable future for our business, our readers and our planet. This book is made from Forest Stewardship Council® certified paper.

'In general, may we not say that the French Revolution lies in the heart and head of every violent-speaking, of every violent-thinking French Man?'

> Thomas Carlyle (1795–1881), Scottish writer, in
> *The French Revolution: A History* (1837)

'Toute révolution qui n'est pas accomplie dans les moeurs et dans les idées échoue.'
'Any revolution that does not have sufficiently complete morals and ideas will fail.'

> François-René de Châteaubriand (1768–1848),
> French writer and politician, in his *Historical, Political and Moral Essay on Revolutions Ancient and Modern* (1797)

'La révolution est comme Saturne – elle dévore ses enfants.'
Revolution is like [the Roman god] Saturn – it devours its children.'

> Pierre Victurnien Vergniaud (1753–93), French politician
> who pronounced the death sentence on Louis XVI in January 1793
> and was himself guillotined ten months later

Fluctuo nec mergor. To all those responsible, merci.

Contents

INTRODUCTION
(AND JUSTIFICATION)

I must start by stressing that I am not a French-style royalist. People who seriously hope that France will one day be ruled again by the descendants of Louis XVI or his relatives are usually so anti-democratic that they regard a British monarch as a dangerous leftie – and a heretical Protestant.

Many of these modern-day French monarchists also believe that anyone who can't trace their ancestry back to Asterix the Gaul should be deported from France.

For obvious reasons, I am definitely not one of those.

Having said that, there is a lot of romantic nonsense talked and written about the French Revolution – mainly by the French themselves.

Listening to these revo-mantics, one would think that in the space of a few weeks in 1789, every powder-faced *aristo* was forced to donate his or her wealth to the starving masses; every lazy landowner was dispossessed in favour of a worthy producer of handmade goat's cheese; and a despotic king and his free-loading wife were displaced (and then humanely dispatched) to make way for a benign bunch of philosophy-reading demo-crats who gave *Liberté, Égalité* and *Fraternité* to everyone in France.

But almost all of that is almost entirely false. And the aim of this book is to explain why.

Liberté, Égalité and *Fraternité* may have been the initial aims of the Revolution, but for several years the reality was more like Tyranny, Megalomania and Fratricide. And what the French rarely acknowledge, or even realize, is that guillotining royals and *aristos* was not at all what their revolutionaries originally intended. The fact is that even during the storming of the Bastille, almost no one in France was calling for King Louis XVI to be deposed, let alone decapitated.

The truth is that even before 14 July 1789, a revolution had taken place, and a new, egalitarian Constitution was being drafted by a more or less democratically elected parliament (if male-only suffrage can be called democratic). This Constitution overtly reaffirmed Louis XVI's position as head of state. He was far from happy with some of the changes being imposed upon him, but he accepted them, and began to work with the new government on creating a reined-in, English-style monarchy.

What was more, once his wife Marie-Antoinette had been forced to stop spending the GDP on parties and necklaces, and the aristocrats were no longer able to tax their peasant tenants to death, Louis XVI was very popular with the average *Français* and *Française*. He was the star guest at the ceremony to mark the first anniversary of Bastille Day, during which a mass oath of allegiance was sworn to both king and nation.

Louis XVI's attendance at the ceremony was heartily cheered by the Parisian crowds – the same people who had spent much of the previous summer rioting. Most ordinary citizens felt that, without the stalling tactics of the aristocrats, Louis would have given them fairer taxation and even a measure of political influence years earlier. This was why in 1790, the King was still seen by the general population as a potential benefactor, a figure of hope.

That same year, an author and former soldier called Antoine Rigobert Mopinot published a project to erect a statue of Louis XVI in Paris, 'to transmit to future generations the happy revolution that has revitalized France under [his] reign'.[1] Mopinot

---

[1] This is a quotation from Mopinot's proposal to erect the statue. See the Select Bibliography on page 535 for the policy on giving sources for quotations and other information in this book.

went on to assert that the new regime 'ensures the continuing prestige and stability of the French throne, and gives the French nation complete freedom to observe its laws, with the support of royal power'. He was expressing the general view at the time that there was no contradiction between revolution and royalty. In 1792, Mopinot was still in possession of an unsevered neck, and was again pitching his project to the post-revolutionary parliament, so no one can have thought that his desire to celebrate Louis XVI's continued existence was particularly subversive.

However, by 1793 this process of peaceful reform had come to a brutal end, and France was charging down the perilous path of civil war, dictatorship and mass public executions. It is estimated that 300,000 French men, women and children were killed by their compatriots, many of them in the most barbarous way imaginable (drowning and bayonetting were especially popular), during the 'Terreur' that followed the fall of the constitutional monarchy. And the tragic fact was that by the end of it all, the poorest and most oppressed sections of the population were left even worse off than they had been in 1789.

All of which suggests that something went disastrously wrong with France's Revolution…

PART I

Pourquoi la Révolution?

'*Le peuple français vous accuse d'avoir commis une multitude de crimes pour établir votre tyrannie, en détruisant sa liberté.*'
'The French people accuse you of having committed a multitude of crimes to establish your tyranny, thereby destroying liberty.'

Accusation put to Louis XVI during his trial in
December 1792

Chapter 1

CREATING EUROPE'S GRANDEST PALACE

'*Ce palais immense dont la façade du côté des jardins est ce qu'il y a de plus beau dans le monde, et dont l'autre façade est dans le plus petit et le plus mauvais goût.*'

'This immense palace, of which the façade looking out over the gardens is the most beautiful thing in the world, while the other façade is in the meanest and the worst taste.'

Voltaire (1694–1778), French writer and philosopher

I

In the modern French psyche, everything changed in 1789. So much so that Louis XVI's reign, and that of every king before him, is known as the 'Ancien Régime' – the 'Former Regime'.

This wasn't a name Louis XVI chose for himself, obviously. He had no inkling that his regime was going to be 'former'. It is a label coined after the Revolution, to describe what went before, and it is still used today when talking about pre-1789 France, even though the country has had plenty of different systems of government since. In the twenty-first century, France is governed by the so-called 'Fifth Republic', explicitly admitting that there have been at least four other Anciens Régimes.

'Ancien' has a second meaning – ancient. And the French monarchy certainly was that, arguably going back as far as

Charlemagne in the eighth century. But the element that caused its downfall was newer. At the time of the Revolution, the class of all-powerful, over-privileged, complacent aristocrats who infuriated the French so much that *'aristo'* is still an insult today had only existed for a couple of centuries at most. They had moulded themselves into a kind of glass ceiling that prevented any hope of social mobility for the 'lower' classes, and also formed a barrier between the King, Louis XVI, and his people. There had been aristocrats before that, of course, but they began to evolve into their mutant form sometime in the sixteenth century, in one specific location in France.

In purely physical terms, the most visible cause of resentment amongst poor French people before the Revolution was the mind-bogglingly immense palace of Versailles. It was an oasis of absurd luxury and scarcely believable excess situated 20 kilometres outside Paris, a flagrant symbol of the distance that the French monarchy and its courtiers had placed between themselves and ordinary people.

In the 1780s, a common sight in the impoverished suburbs and villages around Paris was a carriage-load of drunk aristocratic revellers, their wigs askew and their powdered noses in the air, driving back to Versailles after a night out on the town, just as dawn was breaking and the poor were embarking on another day's underpaid, overtaxed toil.

By 1789, the palace of Versailles was on the wane, as was the town that had grown up around it to house the thousands of people whose ambition was to be received at court or just to make money out of the royals and their hangers-on. The glory days of the seventeenth and early eighteenth century were over, and Versailles was a sordid shadow of the place that the Sun King, Louis XIV, had turned into a vast temple to his own glory, populated by thousands of his worshippers.

Louis XIV's great-great-great-grandson Louis XVI had got rid of the worst excesses of royal etiquette, and was even trying to clamp down on his wife Marie-Antoinette's notorious shopping habit. Even so, by the enforced end of Louis XVI's reign,

Versailles was still a sort of malignant growth on the body of France that large sections of the population wanted to amputate.

But who had created this microcosm of obscene privilege, and who had enabled it to become so bloated?

II

Before the sixteenth century, French kings did not have a settled court. They wandered constantly from château to château, keeping an eye on their properties and reminding the locals who was in charge by showing off their expensive armour and, just as importantly, by collecting taxes. The royal entourage consisted mainly of immediate family and a small army of soldiers, some of whom were there to guard the tax collectors.

This began to change under François I, who reigned from 1515 to 1547. François was a contemporary of England's Henry VIII, and similar in looks and lifestyle. Even though they weren't exactly of the 'make love not war' school (Henry invaded France, for example, and François grabbed chunks of Italy), they were Renaissance men and aspired to a life of leisure, culture and comfort. François I allowed more women into his entourage (not just as conversation partners, of course), so that his court became less military, more refined and more stylish.

He began to develop a royal life centred on dancing, feasting and generally showing off. There was still plenty of medieval jousting, and the King would risk serious injury by challenging knights to duels with lances, but these tournaments were mainly designed to emphasize that François was the alpha male at the head of a glittering court that outshone all other mortals.

This was the dawning of Louis XIV's notion of the Sun King, an absolute monarch who ruled by divine right and was therefore worthy of being treated like a god. It was François I who decreed that the man of highest rank present at court should hand the King his shirt when he got out of bed every morning. The ritual was a bizarre mixture of honour and obligation, a system of enslaving members of the royal entourage that Louis XIV would expand into a whole lifestyle.

Under François I, it became a powerful social motivation amongst the aristocracy to be admitted into the King's inner circle, and staying there required style, money and flattery. Anyone who failed to show enough deference, who spoke ill of the King or his family, or who simply didn't cut the royal mustard, could be banished from court, meaning that their noble titles would count for nothing (except wealth and a pleasant château, of course).

The poet Jean Dupuys wrote a cautionary verse about this growing desire to be seen at François I's court:

> *Vous qui avez le vent à gré,*
> *Et qui savez flatter la cour,*
> *Gardez-vous bien que le degré*
> *A descendre ne vous soit court.*

> (You who are in favour,
> And know how to flatter the court,
> Beware of how steep
> And sudden your fall might be.)

Given that the King was the focus of court life, it was natural that his minions should come to him and not vice versa, and so François became more sedentary, and built or expanded some of France's finest châteaux as venues for his life of luxury: Amboise, Blois and Chambord on the Loire; Saint-Germain-en-Laye in the hunting forest west of Paris; and Fontainebleau to the south. He also renovated the Louvre, the royal palace in the centre of Paris, demolishing some of its darker medieval sections. As yet there was no Versailles.

This addiction to parties and palace-building, as well as costly wars against England, Italy and the Habsburg Empire, quickly emptied France's coffers, so François doubled the tax on agricultural harvests (*la taille*, or cut, deriving from the notches on the counting sticks used before most of the population could read), and tripled the tax on salt (*la gabelle*, from an Italian word for a levy), both of which would loom large in 1789. He also introduced duties on moving goods from one French province to another, as well as reforming the tax-collection system so that he could get his hands on his subjects' money more efficiently.

Even this wasn't enough, though, and François I was forced to sell royal lands and some of his crown jewels. He also borrowed from French noblemen, at least one of whom, Jacques de Beaune, paid the ultimate price for asking to be reimbursed. De Beaune was the *intendant des finances*,[1] the head of France's treasury, and François I had him executed for corruption, even though poor Beaune proved his innocence at his trial.

In short, by using the nation's purse as his personal entertainment budget, François I was laying down the foundations of the bloated court of Versailles, and perhaps of the Revolution itself. In 1548, just a year after François's son Henri II inherited the throne, there was a minor uprising in the southwest of France over the salt tax. It began in the countryside, spread to Bordeaux, and only ended when Henri sent two armies to crush the rebellion and execute 140 people – not just the ringleaders, but also the local officials who had been slow to stem the first stirrings of revolt. The King's aim was clear – his people had to understand that resistance to royal rule was useless.

III

Perhaps as an attempt to improve the social climate, 50 years later King Henri IV created a very new type of French monarchy, one that would not have been out of place in modern Scandinavia. If Henri IV had had a bicycle, he would have

---

[1] This was a precarious job. The treasurers of French Kings Philippe IV, Philippe V, Philippe VI, Charles IV and Charles VI all ended up hanging from the notorious mass gibbet at Montfaucon, a hill in the north of Paris which is now host to the HQ of the French Communist Party.

ridden it, Swedish-style, around the streets of Paris – carefully avoiding the open sewers, of course.

Politically, he was a moderate compared to later kings. Having switched religions several times himself, in 1594 he gave Protestants the right to worship freely – much to the fury of the Catholic establishment.

After mopping up a minor religious civil war (largely fomented by Spanish Catholics), Henri IV settled down to become a man of peace, which was a huge relief to his taxpayers. And when he did go into battle, he was a benign victor, ordering that successfully besieged cities should not be pillaged – a risky strategy because the right to rape, murder and rob had long been one of the perks of the combatant's trade. As a result, Henri spent much of his reign trying to suppress violent gangs of frustrated, unemployed soldiers who terrorized the French countryside.

At court – mainly at the Louvre in Paris – Henri IV was so relaxed about etiquette that once, when his food taster forgot his job description and drank a whole glass of wine, Henri joked: 'At least you could have drunk to my health.' (A century later, at the height of Louis XIV's tyrannical Versailles, the offender would probably have been banished to a trading post halfway up the Mississippi, with a quip about enjoying excess liquid.)

Henri IV was no saint, but he was no hypocrite either. When accused of being too fond of hunting, gambling, womanizing, banqueting and dancing, he replied: 'As long as one doesn't go too far, that should be said in praise rather than disapproval.' And unlike later monarchs, his courtiers were under no obligation to lose to him at cards and dice, and he would often gamble away small fortunes.[2]

No one really disapproved of Henri IV's frivolities, mainly because he was known to spend long hours with his ministers,

---

[2] Luckily for Henri IV, the number of courtiers wanting to come and win his money was limited. At this time the aristocracy seems to have undertaken a population-control scheme. Men were so quick to pick an argument that during Henri IV's 21-year reign, around 14,000 noblemen are thought to have been killed in duels. A poker night at the palace would have turned into a massacre.

and never to shirk work. The results of this dedication to duty were visible to every Parisian, because Henri oversaw extensive modernization of the city, including the construction of a major new river crossing, the Pont-Neuf.

He also promised to help the poor, saying that every family should have *'une poule au pot'* – 'a chicken for the pot'. To facilitate the transport of produce, he launched an ambitious scheme to connect France's three coastlines – the Mediterranean, the Atlantic and the Channel. The plan included the 57-kilometre-long Canal du Briare, linking the Rivers Loire and Seine, a spectacular engineering project that gave work to some 18,000 men.

Conscious of his popularity, Henri IV would often venture outside his palace with only a minimal team of bodyguards. He would tour Paris on horseback or on foot, meeting and greeting his subjects, and enjoying the bustle of street life. He was as unlike the Sun King Louis XIV – or even modern French presidents – as can be imagined.

And this was precisely the reason why the Henri IV model of monarchy didn't catch on in France. It was during one of his unprotected outings, riding in a carriage with only four guards, that Henri was stabbed through the right lung by a religious fanatic, and died before he could be rushed back the few hundred yards to the Louvre.

His assailant, François Ravaillac, took rather longer to die. He was given a gruesomely detailed death sentence:

> His nipples, arms, thighs and the fat of the legs shall be squeezed in a clamp, his right hand that held the knife with which he committed the regicide shall be burnt with hot sulphur, and a mixture of molten lead, boiling oil, pitch, hot resin, wax and sulphur will be poured on the parts that have been clamped. Then his body will be stretched and quartered by four horses.

Sadly for Ravaillac, he was a muscular man, and the execution took all day, including the time wasted while one of the exhausted horses was replaced.

But even this extreme punishment, watched by a large crowd of mesmerized Parisians, was no comfort to the royal family, and future French kings deemed it wiser to distance themselves from knife-wielding plebs. It is probably no coincidence that Henri IV's successor, Louis XIII, began to convert a poky little castle in Versailles into a royal haven.

IV

In the early seventeenth century, no one could have imagined that Versailles would one day become Europe's most glamorous palace, or provoke a revolution. Louis XIII's first equerry, the Duc de Saint-Simon, described it as 'the saddest and most ungracious of places, with no view, no water and no land, because it is all airless quicksand and marshes'. The only building of any size there was a castle, surrounded by stagnant ponds and accessible from the nearest village by a rutted track.

But this seems to have been exactly what Louis XIII loved about it. Becoming king in 1610 at the early age of eight, he seized power from his mother, the Regent, when he was 15, only for her to start a civil war against him. After her army was defeated, he was persuaded to reconcile the warring factions in France by accepting her back at court. With a disgruntled old queen on the rampage in his royal palaces at the Louvre, Fontainebleau and Saint-German-en-Laye, it was hardly surprising that he began to seek refuge elsewhere.

The young Louis XIII would often ride out from Paris to hunt in the forest close to the old castle, which belonged to the Archbishop of Paris, Jean-François de Gondi. At the end of a day chasing deer, rather than returning to the Louvre, Louis would impose his company on the lucky clergyman, along with a few friends and a small group of servants.

Louis became so fond of the place that in 1624 he bought 117 *arpents* (an *arpent* was a measure comprising 220 'king's paces', or 71.46 metres) of land from 16 landowners, on a small plateau outside the village of Versailles, where he built a modest hunting lodge for himself and a few male companions.

To counter rumours of 'immoral' male-only antics, Louis invited his mother Marie de Médicis and his wife Anne d'Autriche (despite her name she was a Spanish princess – it was her mother who was Austrian) to dine there in November 1626. The household was run so modestly that Louis served the meal himself. But he then spoilt the mood of mixed domesticity by sending both ladies back to their bedchambers in Paris. This was a men's club, he said, and he preferred it that way: 'A large number of women would spoil everything.' Which did nothing to dispel the rumours about gay goings-on.

Of course, a modest hunting lodge to a French king was a palace to ordinary people. The first royal building there consisted of a main house with two small wings. According to a detailed inventory made in 1630, it had 26 rooms. The King's apartments on the first floor consisted of a *cabinet* (his den), a bedroom, dressing room (which also contained his personal commode, the *chaise percée*) and a reception room.

All the King's rooms were hung with tapestries. Those in his bedroom depicted the story of Marc Antony and Cleopatra, while the theme in his *cabinet* was goddesses. The furniture was relatively simple. There were two hard-backed wooden chairs, six silk-covered wooden stools, a large table, and a leather rug. Louis XIII wanted to sleep in royal comfort, however, so his bed was topped with three cotton-stuffed mattresses.

The *cabinet* had a sideboard, two chests, a table with two silver candelabras and a leather-topped writing desk. It wasn't only a workroom, because its central feature was a billiard table. Here Louis also kept his chess and backgammon sets, his roulette wheel and other games such as a *jeu de l'oie* (a board game) and *jonchets* (pick-up sticks) – enough amusements for some exciting boys-only nights in the country.

The other rooms were mainly bedchambers for the King's close male friends, all of them aristocrats, and simple monastic-like cells for the guards. There were also two rooms full of mattresses for last-minute guests.

The only woman allowed to spend any time there was the wife of the full-time concierge.

Louis XIII was so happy with his hideaway that he decided to opt for exclusive ownership of the whole area. In April 1632, he bought the archbishop's property, which was listed in the sale agreement as 'an old ruined château, several farm buildings, arable land, meadows, woods, chestnut groves, ponds and other outbuildings'. The price was 60,000 *livres tournois*, the equivalent of about 4,000 months of a worker's salary, paid in pieces of 16 *sous*. Twenty *sous* made one *livre*, which meant that the archbishop came away with a heap of 75,000 coins, probably made of silver.

Louis also bought out other landowners in the area, and created gardens around his 'lodge', but he never raised Versailles above what a scornful contemporary referred to as 'a small house of a gentleman living on ten to twelve thousand *livres* per year'. To give an idea of how disdainful this comment was, 12,000 *livres* represented about half the salary later paid to the lucky servant whose duty was to carry the *chaise percée* of the next monarch, Louis XIII's son Louis XIV, in and out of his bedroom every morning. And it was this next Louis who decided to lift Versailles out of obscurity.

V

When Louis XIV came to the throne in 1643, he was only four years old. His father had died young, partly of the effects of Crohn's disease, and partly of the 1,200 enemas and 250 laxative purges prescribed by his doctors to cure it. Louis XIV's mother, Anne d'Autriche, had never approved of her husband's Versailles bolthole, so at first the future Sun King was kept in the dark about it.

Louis XIV's troubled childhood became decidedly dysfunctional when he was still only 12 and under his mother's regency.

First, parliament rebelled against the Crown, and a rebel army put up barricades in Paris, forcing the court to flee to Saint-Germain-en-Laye, 20 kilometres west of the Louvre. Then two of Louis XIV's cousins (and potential claimants to the throne), the Princes de Condé and de Conti, turned against him, and a sporadic civil war raged for three years.

At one point in the period of unrest known as 'la Fronde' ('the Sling', a mocking name given to the rebels who were likened to children flinging stones), Louis XIV and his mother were captured by a Parisian mob and held prisoner in the Palais-Royal. Luckily for the royal captives, seventeenth-century mobs were less fond of beheadings and lynchings than their eighteenth-century equivalents.

The years of rebellion only came to an end when Conti was imprisoned and the people got tired of Condé's rebel army pillaging the countryside. So it wasn't until 1653 that Louis XIV could finally settle down and begin evolving into a tyrannical, absolutist monarch.

Louis XIV was 15 when he emerged from his mother's regency, and it was hardly surprising that he should look around for a way of keeping parliament, the Parisians and the nobles under the royal thumb. He knew that as things stood, any nobleman wanting to cause trouble just had to whip up the people of Paris to his cause. Louis XIV saw that he needed to domesticate the court, and crush any thoughts of revolution or dissent beneath the sheer weight of his power. He was to be the Roi Soleil, the Sun King – because no one dares to question the movements of the sun.[3]

Gradually, Louis XIV conceived the ingenious idea of moving himself permanently out of range of riotous mobs, while imprisoning his aristocrats (many of whom served in parliament) in luxury. The core of his idea was that he would make it obligatory

---

[3] Copernicus's and Galileo's theory that the Earth revolves around the sun and not vice versa had still not been fully accepted, mainly thanks to the Church's determined opposition.

to attend court, or at least so desirable that to stay away would feel like social exile. Once he had entrapped the nobles, a rigid code of etiquette would regiment their every move, and the dress code would be so outlandish that the richest *aristos* would have to bankrupt themselves to keep up. He would have aristocrats feeding him, dressing him, even wiping his bottom – and they would fight, or even pay, for the privilege of doing it.

It was a fiendish plan that would eventually bring down both the nobility and the monarchy, but for more than a century, it worked spectacularly well.

Louis XIV introduced phase one of his scheme by saying that he owed it to his family, the Bourbons,[4] to build a new palace in their honour. The Louvre, Fontainebleau, Saint-Germain-en-Laye, Blois, Amboise and all the rest were very chic, but Louis wanted a home of his own. He also owed it to France to prove that it was the most powerful country in Europe, he said. This he would do by building the most fabulous palace that Europe had ever seen, with him as the most fabulous ruler.

By now the young Louis XIV had discovered his father's hunting lodge in the forest of Versailles, and had begun using it as a love nest. When he was 22, he started an affair with a maid of honour in his brother's household. The lucky girl was a teenager called Louise de la Vallière. Not that the affair was very flattering. At the outset, young Louise was meant to be a cover for the more passionate affair that the King was enjoying with his brother's wife, Henrietta (who was, incidentally, the daughter of King Charles I of England). To make things even more complicated, Henrietta was said to be using Louis XIV to escape

---

[4] Bourbon whiskey was originally made in Bourbon County, Kentucky, an area named in gratitude for France's help during the American War of Independence. Bourbon biscuits, originally called 'Creolas' when they were launched in 1910, were rebranded with the name of the French royal family in the 1930s. They were created by the English biscuit company, Peek Freans, who also invented the Garibaldi biscuit (a homage to the general of the same name).

from the clutches of her own lover. Even before the royal court reached the peak (or trough) of its debauchery under Louis XV, sexual matters amongst courtiers were pretty torrid.

Unexpectedly, Louis XIV soon became attached to young Louise de la Vallière, and would ride out to Versailles once or twice a week for a romantic rendezvous. Typically though, these were not furtive midnight excursions. Louis would go to Versailles with a dozen or so close friends, all dressed in identical costumes as a sort of code – one that everyone quickly deciphered.

Louis XIV tired of Louise after four pregnancies in five years,[5] but his affection for Versailles didn't wane, and he began to put on lavish entertainments there, inviting France's greatest comic playwright, Molière, to stage several plays, including the premiere of one of his most famous works, *Tartuffe*.

It was in the 1660s that Louis decided to turn his former love nest into a permanent home – and the gilded cage of all his courtiers. He set his architect, Louis Le Vau, the master of French classicism, to work, and seems to have given him a simple brief: 'Make it VERY, VERY BIG.'

Le Vau offered Louis XIV two building plans: either demolish the old château and start again, or expand the existing buildings into the gardens at the rear. Like many homeowners, Louis chose extension over demolition, and in 1668, Le Vau's workmen began turning the former hunting lodge into Europe's largest palace, with 2,300 rooms.

The central area, which surrounded Louis XIII's original château, consisted mainly of the King and Queen's accommodation. Their apartments were built around a courtyard in which only the highest-ranking nobles and members of the

---

[5] Her first two babies died in infancy, but the second two survived and were legitimized as members of the royal Bourbon family. One of them, Marie-Anne, came in useful in royal politics. Louis XIV later married her off to the son of his cousin and former enemy the Prince de Conti.

royal family were allowed to park their carriages. There was also a chapel (which sounds intimate but was actually a vast, gold-and-marble cathedral), buildings in the forecourt for ministers, and long north and south wings, much of which were given over to cramped accommodation for those honoured with the right to reside in the palace – a convenient privilege when it came to changing costume several times a day for different ceremonies.

At the heart of the project was the Grand appartement for Louis XIV himself, a seven-room collection of generously sized *salons*. The most luxurious of these was the salon Apollon, or Apollo Room, with its painted ceiling depicting Louis as a sun god on his chariot. The four seasons, the hours (all of them feminine, reflecting the King's favourite pastime), and the rest of the universe gravitated around him. Modesty was not one of his faults. Originally, the Apollo Room sported a 2.6-metre silver throne, but even Louis XIV eventually found this a bit extravagant, and in 1689 he had it and other pieces of silver furniture melted down to pay for a war against the League of Augsburg.

One of Louis XIV's favourite *salons* in the apartment was his billiard room, the salon de Diane (dedicated to the goddess of hunting). The King was skilled with a billiard cue, and he had a balustrade constructed so that women could look down on the table and applaud his good shots. Inevitably, the salon de Diane became known as the 'applause room'.

This Grand appartement was by no means a private space. Louis XIV lived most of his adult life as the star of a royal pantomime, and performed every bodily function except sexual intercourse in front of an audience. During the daytime, most of his *salons* would be awash with courtiers, visitors, advisors and attendants. The same went for the Queen's apartment, a mirror image of his own – Louis and she would eat their evening meal before a carefully selected audience in the Queen's antechamber, and the Queen even gave birth six times while courtiers looked on.

The most famous room in the new palace was the Grande galerie, since renamed the galerie des Glaces[6] (the gallery of mirrors and not, as some French children mistakenly believe, the gallery of ice creams). This magnificent, 73-metre reception area stretched for almost the whole width of the new palace, its windows looking out over the gardens, a view that was reflected in the 357 mirrors on the opposite wall.

This was where courtiers and the public waited for a glimpse of the King, and where diplomats would be forced to parade on their way to a royal audience. Accordingly, the whole theme of the decor was Louis XIV's genius and France's prestige. The ceiling was conceived as a sort of *arc de triomphe* glorifying the Sun King, with paintings depicting his military victories (such as his personal command over the troops who captured Maastricht in 1673) and allegories representing his political achievements – 'Order re-established in finances, 1662', 'Protection given to the arts, 1663' and other such grandiose titles.

The mirrors themselves were a message to the world that France now surpassed even Venice in its skill at glassmaking. In the seventeenth century, huge faultless mirrors were the height of technological achievement. The equivalent today might be a gallery of gigantic 3-D movie screens showing films that celebrate France's food, wine and nuclear power stations, with built-in odour-producing cells that allow visitors to smell the food and the radioactive emissions. In 1919 the galerie des Glaces, with its gold-encrusted statues and crystal chandeliers, was still considered intimidating enough to be chosen as the venue for the signature of the Treaty of Versailles, the agreement that was designed to scare the Germans off war forever. And the room is still used by modern French presidents to

---

[6] Readers may be wondering why 'Grande galerie' and 'galerie des Glaces' have capital letters in apparently illogical places. The reason is that this book uses the spellings of French proper names given in the Larousse online encyclopedia, larousse.fr.

receive official guests, proving that Louis XIV's notion of self-aggrandizement has never been surpassed.

By 1682 the palace was close enough to completion[7] for Louis XIV to move the whole of his court and his government out from Paris to Versailles. In the meantime, he had been a very regular visitor to the building site – like every homeowner, he knew that builders take far too many breaks unless you keep an eye on them.

VI

Louis XIV also made sure that a whole new town grew up around the burgeoning palace. For a start, some 1,500 staff were to be accommodated in houses constructed on top of the old village of Versailles, after the previous residents – disposable rustics – had been evicted.

Louis gave away 500 free plots of land to his favourite aristocrats, and granted building permits to everyone else. He went as far as declaring that that houses in Versailles would be *'insaisissables'*, that is, they could not be seized by debtors or the courts. This was a great favour to the many noblemen and -women with gambling addictions, and especially to those who would be forced to overspend on clothes, wigs and the general expense of courtly life. Louis knew that they would need to borrow fortunes to be able to stay at court, and might then be harassed by creditors. Some would probably have to sell their Paris homes to finance their new lifestyles. But at least they could hang on to their Versailles house, even if they had borrowed money to build it and never repaid the loans.

Not that these new properties were entirely safe. Several aristocratic courtiers saw their new mansions demolished on Louis XIV's orders to make way for two immense stable blocks and a huge Orangerie which, in 1686, caused the visiting ambassador

[7] In fact, Louis XIV did not declare himself satisfied with Versailles until 1710, more than 40 years after construction work began. Sadly for him, by then he had less than five more years to enjoy it.

of Siam to remark that: 'The King's fortune must be very big if he builds such a marvellous home for his orange trees.'

The ambassador was right – Louis XIV had ambitious plans for his plants. He commissioned his gardener, André le Nôtre, to impose a look of total artificiality on the 830 hectares of parkland, using angular lawns and flowerbeds, dancing fountains and a 1.6-kilometre-long cruciform lake. The palace grounds were to symbolize the triumph of Louis XIV over nature.

Like the galerie des Glaces, the gardens were designed to show off the best of French technology. The 2,000-odd fountains, waterfalls and water spouts were to be powered by hydraulic energy, using a large reservoir built above the level of the fountains, and connected to a network of buried pipes. Some of this water was pumped in from the River Seine, ten kilometres away.

Louis XIV followed every step of this huge gardening project, at one point sending a memo to Jean–Baptiste Colbert,[8] the man in charge of executing Le Nôtre's plans, telling him: 'You must make the Versailles pumps work well, especially those at the top reservoir, so that when I arrive, they don't break down all the time and upset me.'

When a 200-kilometre network of pipes, aqueducts and diverse watercourses was completed in the late 1680s, Versailles possessed the biggest water system in Europe. Not only did the château have running water, a rare commodity, but with one turn of a tap, simple gravity would produce spectacular displays of water jets in its gardens. It was scarcely an exaggeration to say that the city of Paris was less well supplied with water than the King's private home. (Much later, Parisians would say the same thing about bread, and start rioting.)

The gardens took as long as the palace itself to complete, and at times mobilized more than a thousand workers, including whole regiments of soldiers who were drafted in to transport 150,000 plants and countless tons of fertile soil, turning the

---

[8] Bizarrely, Colbert was also the man in charge of the navy. He seems to have been Louis XIV's Monsieur Eau.

former 'stinking ponds' and boggy marshes into Europe's most sophisticated green space.

Today, the grounds are still spectacular and often crowded with visitors, but they are uneventful compared to Louis XIV's day. Then, there would have been masses of finely dressed courtiers strolling, loitering, eating or using the more secluded areas of shrubbery for various bodily functions. Louis himself watched over the gardens as keenly as he did the palace, and would walk there very regularly. The fountains were only in full spout when he was present – as he approached, the water features along his route would be turned on; as soon as he was out of sight of a particular fountain, it was to be switched off. When he was inside the château, only the fountains visible to him would be active. Again, the Sun King was showing that he controlled the elements.

Throughout his reign Louis XIV was constantly suggesting improvements to his grounds, the most outrageous of which was to create a 'royal fleet' of boats for his Grand Canal.

The Grand Canal, explicitly rivalling Venice's waterway, was impressive enough on its own: its east–west 'trunk' was 1,650 metres long, and the north–south crossbar 1,000 metres. It was 60 metres wide. Seen from the windows of the galerie des Glaces, looking downhill across the gardens, it seems immense – to the modern eye, every bit as long as an airport runway. To seventeenth-century viewers, it would have been the hugest garden feature imaginable, stretching away almost to the horizon thanks to a trick of sloping perspective.

Along the central 'trunk' of the canal there were three large octagonal basins where Louis XIV's garden fleet was moored. These boats included a dozen or so gondolas, four of them donated by the city of Venice and crewed by genuine Venetian gondoliers. There were also rowing barges up to 13 metres long, the largest being designed to hold the King, a small orchestra and a team of rowers. Louis XIV also commissioned several scale models of merchant vessels and warships big enough for a crew of a dozen men.

This miniature royal fleet even included a 13-metre galley complete with 32 cannons. It was a model of the large oar-powered ships used by the French navy until the middle of the eighteenth century, usually rowed by chained, branded convicts. To ensure complete authenticity, the galley in the gardens of Versailles was actually rowed by prisoners sent from Marseille.

Outside the realm of his gardens, Louis XIV's naval policy was to expand France's fleet of galleys, so much so that Jean-Baptiste Colbert, his Navy Minister, sent out a message to the country's magistrates: 'His Majesty desires to renew his stock of galleys and boost the number of galley slaves, so his intention is that you condemn the greatest possible number of convicts to them.'[9] Although these prisoners were often guilty of relatively minor crimes, the galley was usually, in effect, a death sentence, thereby saving Louis the cost of building new prisons. The inclusion of a giant model galley in his new palace gardens, rowed by real prisoners, might well have been a none-too-subtle message to any courtiers or Versailles townspeople harbouring thoughts of rebellion.

Louis XIV's pleasure boats were often built in the grounds at Versailles, being assembled from wooden parts pre-shaped at naval boatyards. As well as carpenters and wood carvers, the boats required upholsterers for the taffeta-covered seats, curtain makers for the gold and silver drapes, and painters to apply gold leaf and to colour in the royal standards that were carved into the wood. The palace's boatyards were located in a village near the canal that housed boatbuilders, maintenance men and several dozen sailors, most of whom had been recruited in France's ports. As the number of real gondoliers imported from Venice grew (to 13 in 1681), this inland harbour had more boats and inhabitants than some of France's real fishing villages, and was christened la Petite Venise.

---

[9] This punishment was so common that even today, when French people are complaining that a job is too tough or complicated, they will say *'quelle galère!'* – 'what a galley!' or *'je rame'* – 'I'm rowing'.

All the sailors, gondoliers and galley slaves would be mobilized for Louis XIV's water festivals, when the Grand Canal would look like a miniature Mediterranean, a calm sea of gilded gondolas, ornately carved barges and sailing ships, with the wigs, silks and satins of their aristocratic passengers glowing in the light from torches and the flash of (blank) cannon fire, often accompanied by music written for the occasion, such as the *Trumpet Concerto for Parties on the Canal of Versailles* by Michel Richard Delalande.

On these occasions, the fleet's movements would be choreographed by Louis XIV in person, but he was much more than an admiral. With his total mastery of the waters of Versailles, he was presenting himself as the source of life itself. It was exactly this kind of arrogance that would provoke the Revolution a century later.

What's more, Louis XIV's overt sovereignty over the elements extended beyond water. With his gigantic firework parties, he gave fire; by remodelling Versailles from a swamp-bound hunting lodge into Europe's finest castle, shipping whole hillsides of soil to create its gardens, he had dominated the Earth; and of course as the Sun King, he symbolically provided light and a physical focus to French society.

Most crucially of all, though, Louis XIV also controlled time.

Chapter 2

ENSLAVING THE ARISTOCRACY

'Avec un almanach et une montre, on pouvait à trois cent lieues de lui dire avec justesse ce qu'il faisait.'
'With an almanac and a watch, one could, even at a distance of 300 leagues, say exactly what he was doing.'

> Said of Louis XIV by Louis de Rouvroy,
> Duc de Saint-Simon (1675–1755), in his memoirs

I

At the end of the seventeenth century, Louis XIV's court consisted of about 10,000 people, almost all of them constantly clamouring for royal attention. The Italian writer Primi Visconti, who spent eight years at Louis XIV's court, wrote that the spectacle of the King emerging from his palace for a tour of the grounds reminded him of 'the queen bee when she goes out into the fields with her swarm'.

Some of these drones would be asking for a serious favour – the 1996 French film *Ridicule*, for example, tells the credible story of a young nobleman, with the wonderfully aristocratic name Grégoire Ponceludon de Malavoy, who has to jump through a succession of protocol hoops to beg Louis XIV for a grant so that he can drain the marshes on his land and save his peasant tenants from malaria.

More often, though, the petitioners would be jostling in the corridors of Versailles in the hope of obtaining an honour such as the right to hold the King's candlestick while he went to bed – a job that they would be willing to pay for.

Performing the most menial tasks for the King and his courtiers were about 7,000 servants, all of them permanently guarded (or kept under control) by some 4,000 infantrymen and 4,000 cavalry. On an average day when Louis XIV was in residence, there might be a crowd of 15,000 people flowing around the palace and the grounds – all of them living according to the King's timetable.

When the Duc de Saint-Simon wrote of Louis XIV that 'with an almanac and a watch, one could, even at a distance of 300 kilometres, say exactly what he was doing' he did not disapprove. He found this predictability and stability reassuring. At least you knew where you were with Louis XIV – literally. Just as the sun determines what time of day it is, the Sun King decided what all his courtiers and the members of the royal family – all his most credible rivals for power – were doing at any given time.

From dawn till dusk and into the night, life at Versailles was centred on Louis XIV's movements and desires. The rigorous palace schedule meant that everyone's attention was focused on what was happening in ten minutes' time, an hour later, that evening, or the next day. Courtiers had to change clothes, move from room to room, wait around, be ready to appear before the monarch. They had to learn the rules of behaviour for each different ceremony, and spend vast amounts of money on exactly the right costumes for each one. No ambitious prince or nobleman had time or money left for raising a revolutionary army. In any case, their plotting skills were exercised trying to work out how to beat a rival to a key post at court, or even how to get admitted to a specific event. Weeks might be wasted starting a malicious rumour or plotting to trick someone into a faux pas. At Versailles, etiquette was the opium of the aristocracy.

If you were invited to attend court at Versailles, it was impossible to refuse, even if it meant moving out of your château or spacious Paris mansion and into a cramped apartment at the palace. If you weren't at Versailles, you were nobody. If you didn't know the rules of etiquette, you were an uncultured slob. Everywhere outside Versailles was a dead zone. As the nineteenth-century writer Stendhal put it, 'Louis XIV's masterpiece was to create the boredom of exile.'

II

A look at the Sun King's typical daily routine suggests that attendance at court wasn't exactly exciting, either.

At seven o'clock, his *valet de chambre* got up from a camp bed in Louis XIV's room (the King usually slept alone, behind the curtains of a four-poster), and returned at seven fifteen with servants to open the shutters. If it was cold enough (which it often was, with the palace's large windows and high ceilings), attendants called *feutiers* (from the French *feu*, for fire) would light a fire. At seven thirty precisely, the *valet de chambre* went to the royal bedside and announced, '*Sire, voilà l'heure.*'

The *premiers gentilshommes de la chambre* (first gentlemen of the bedchamber) would then enter and open the royal bed curtains. The *premiers gentilshommes* were a team of four, each man being on duty for one year in a four-year cycle. This annual changeover didn't happen just because opening the bed curtains was too exhausting. It was a highly sought after position amongst French noblemen. The *premier gentilhomme* on duty was in charge of the budget for the King's bedroom, so he could siphon off money from the purchase of candles, curtains, sheets, etc. He also had the power to invite people into the royal bedroom or – equally important – exclude them. Influence was the most valuable currency at Louis XIV's Versailles and the *premier gentilhomme* possessed enough of it to stuff a mattress.

Once the bed curtains were successfully drawn, the *premier médecin* (first doctor) entered the room. He would give Louis a quick check-up, and maybe pass on a piece of Versailles gossip (especially if he had been bribed to do so by some intriguer). At the same time, musicians – usually violinists and oboe players – would pipe up one of the King's favourite tunes beneath his bedroom window.

At 8.15 a.m., it was time for the *entrée familière* – not a meal but the entrance by selected members of the royal family – and the *grande entrée* of Louis XIV's closest servants – the *grand chambellan* (Godefroy-Maurice de la Tour d'Auvergne), his longest-serving and most intimate advisor, keeper of his seal, second in rank when receiving ambassadors, and – a key role – the man who would hand the King his shirt in the morning (as long as no high-ranking royal was present).

With the *grand chambellan* came the *grand maître*, head of Louis XIV's household, and the *maître de la garde-robe* (master of the wardrobe). The *grand chambellan* would bring a small font so that Louis could bless himself, before a 15-minute religious service was held for all those in the room.

By now, the King had been awake for an hour, but he was still not out of bed. At eight thirty his hairdresser (*valet du cabinet des perruques*) would enter, to shave Louis (every other day) and choose his headgear for the early part of the morning – his *perruque du lever*, or 'getting-up wig'. Louis would now rise, put on a dressing gown and slippers, and go to sit by the fireplace to be coiffed.

After a few minutes, the *seconde entrée* would be announced, and a new crowd of people would crush in. They included an 'ordinary' doctor and surgeon, secretaries, readers, the silver-ware keeper (*contrôleur de l'argenterie*), more wardrobe valets, and other carefully selected *gentilshommes*.

By this time, Louis might well be perched on his commode, or *chaise d'affaires*, but no one would bat an eyelid, or a nostril. The monarch was a public personage, as visible as the sun itself, and his bowel movements would always be observed by an uncritical audience of highly fortunate witnesses. The privilege of watching Louis defecate was reserved for people who had been granted the necessary certificate, called a *brevet d'affaires*, which cost around 200,000 *livres*, the equivalent during Louis XIV's reign of the price of about 1,000 houses in an average French town – payable to the King, of course. The man with the honour of carrying the commode in and out of the bedroom and emptying it, the *porteur de chaise d'affaires*, had paid Louis 20,000 *livres* for the job. The salary was only 600 *livres* per year, but it was hereditary, so over the generations it was an investment. In short, Louis XIV was living proof that where there's muck there's brass.

Once the royal stools had been recorded and approved by the doctors, and the commode taken away, the *huissier* (bailiff) at the door could begin to announce the lucky 'people of quality' who had been selected to attend the *grand lever*, or 'grand getting-up' – including women. This entry ceremony was performed in strict order of protocol, so that no mere *marquis* could elbow in front of a *duchesse*. By 9 a.m. the room often contained about 50 people, and was so full that a lesser noble could hardly get through the door, and almost certainly could not see Louis XIV. But at least they were present, and their name had been called out across the crowd of wigs.

Next, the people who could actually see the King were allowed to watch him having his breakfast, usually one or two cups of *bouillon* (broth) or herbal tea – which had been tasted beforehand to check for poisons, and individually announced on arrival in the room as though they were guests: *'Le bouillon du Roi!'*

Invigorated by this light refreshment, Louis would take off his own dressing gown and nightshirt, and remove the lucky charms he wore in bed – which were mainly religious relics. According to his second wife, Madame de Maintenon, one of these was 'from the real cross, and apparently authenticated by the best [experts]'.

To cover up the royal nudity, the person of highest rank would give the King his shirt. Resorting to some rare self-sufficiency, Louis would tie his own tie before selecting two handkerchiefs from three offered to him, perhaps adding an element of suspense for his spectators.

He then prayed again, kneeling by his bed. Despite rumours of dissolute goings-on at court, Louis XIV himself always tried to impose religious order at Versailles, and would even check up on who was observing Lent. If he heard reports of any courtier eating meat during the fasting season, the unfortunate aristocrat might be deselected from the *grand lever* crowd – a humiliating demotion.

After his personal moment of prayer, Louis XIV would lead a procession though the galerie des Glaces towards his chapel, attended by his cortège of close servants and courtiers, for a ten o'clock mass. This was when most courtiers got their first daily glimpse of the King, and throngs of France's chicest *aristos* in their finery would line the route, hoping to say a word in the royal ear or catch his eye. Women would often hold a candle to look devout – but also to provide soft lighting for their faces.

Daily mass was obligatory for all Louis XIV's closest entourage. After all, he was monarch by divine right, so everyone had to pay homage to the source of his power. As the satirist Jean de la Bruyère put it, describing the crowds in the chapel: 'The people worship the King and the King worships God.'

Louis XIV was unquestionably devout, but he made sure that his daily religious routine was never boring by constantly commissioning new music for the services from the royal composer Lully or rivals for his post. Morning mass at Versailles was where the country's best new music was to be heard.

Only after mass would Louis finally go to his office, the *cabinet de travail*, having taken more or less three hours to get up. Despite this apparent inefficiency, the whole government of France happened in that office, mainly in morning sessions. As Louis XIV said, *'L'État, c'est moi.'* ('I am the state.')

Given that he celebrated mass every day, Louis seems to have thought it unnecessary to observe the Sabbath, and worked on Sundays, when he usually held his Council of State. On Tuesdays and Saturdays, he presided over the Council of Finances, and on Wednesdays a second Council of State. Mondays, Thursdays and Fridays were flexible, and would be given over to urgent matters of state, or to meetings with his architects and gardeners. Building work continued during most of his lifetime, and the renovation of Versailles was given the same importance as politics.

Nevertheless, Louis took his country's political affairs seriously – the proof of this was that during his councils, ministers were actually allowed to sit down in his presence. Elsewhere in the palace everyone had to remain standing while Louis XIV was in view – even his own brother could only sit if expressly instructed to do so by the King.

At 1 p.m. Louis walked back to his bedroom, his route again lined by courtiers hoping to be noticed. Getting a prime spot between the *cabinet* and the bedroom was a huge honour because if you had a request – a relative to be promoted, a marsh to be drained, an invitation to be obtained – now was the time to put your case. Everyone knew that if first impressions worked, the lucky courtier might receive a private audience, and if their pitch was good enough, the King might grant them the funds and the royal seal of approval for their project.

For this to work, you had to look good – Louis might notice a tall or particularly well dressed man and stop to ask one of his attendants who this person was. But looks weren't enough. The object of the King's attention then had a few seconds during which to impress, preferably with a piece of quotable flattery. The diarist and courtier Saint-Simon said that shameless obsequiousness was the only way to approach Louis XIV: 'The crudest [pieces of flattery] were well received, and the most degrading were enjoyed even more.'

Louis XIV liked to feed people a line to see how quick-witted they were. He once famously asked the painter Charles Le Brun, 'Do you not think I have aged?' Le Brun came back with, 'Sire, all I see are a few more campaigns on Your Majesty's forehead.' Not exactly flattering, but highly effective because Louis loved to be thought of as a successful general. It was surely no coincidence that Le Brun became director of the Royal Academy of Painting and Sculpture and one of the men hired for the interior decoration of Versailles.

Similarly, the playwright Jean Racine was asked to go to Holland to watch the King's army at work, presumably to get inspiration for one of his grandiose plays in which rulers battle for supremacy. Rashly, Racine didn't go, and on his return to Versailles, Louis confronted him: 'Didn't you want to go and watch a siege?', to which Racine quipped that he had ordered a new set of campaign outfits from his tailor, but 'when he delivered them, the towns that Your Majesty was besieging had been taken'. A piece of repartee that saved Racine – and his career – from royal disfavour.

Sometimes these attempts at flattery would go wrong, because even Louis XIV had his limits. The Duc d'Uzès became a laughing stock at court for repeating the same barely credible flattering remark at every occasion. The King once asked Uzès when his wife's baby was due, and the duke replied absurdly: 'Oh, Sire, whenever Your Majesty wishes.' While watching a scientific experiment, Louis was pleased with the chemist's servile 'Sire, these two gases will now have the honour of decomposing before Your Majesty,' but less impressed when Uzès added: 'If Your Majesty will permit it.' Worst of all, though, when the Queen asked Uzès what time it was, he told her: 'The time that Your Majesty wishes.' It sounds as though she set him up just to create some gossip.

Louis XIV's lunch, called *dîner*,[1] was eaten in his bedroom, alone – if you don't count the horde of spectators. Again, a select crowd of courtiers would be allowed in to stand and watch the King eating at his small square table, where he would tuck in to soup (often taking three or four bowls), ham, mutton, game, hard-boiled eggs, salad, fruit and *pâtisseries*.

The dishes sound simple enough, but the chefs were as keen to impress as everyone else at Versailles. The King's cooks

[1] Calling the midday meal 'dinner' is a lot less vulgar than some Brits would have us believe.

invented delicacies like *filets de cerf aux perdreaux truffés* (fillets of venison with truffle-stuffed partridges), and would sometimes flavour his food with violets. The gardeners also had to raise their performance and provide perfect seasonal produce – at the height of Louis XIV's reign, his gardens grew seven varieties of melon and six of strawberries. Of course, when Louis favoured a certain fruit or vegetable, everyone in Versailles had to follow suit, and the town's shopkeepers would take full advantage – during a craze for peas in the 1660s, prices went up to 130 *livres* per pound, almost a year's salary for an average worker.

The food at Versailles was subject to etiquette every bit as rigid as the rules guiding the palace's human residents. Each dish was brought from the kitchen accompanied by a dozen or so attendants – and any courtier seeing the convoy would have to bow to the King's meal. Different dishes and drinks would have their own processions because they came from separate departments in the King's kitchens, which were housed in a vast building that Louis XIV had constructed on the site of the church of the old Versailles village. The kitchens preserved a holy aspect, because the building contained a chapel dedicated to St Roch, who was believed to protect against epidemics and bad food – the patron saint of salmonella and unrisen soufflés. Six priests served in this chapel, blessing the dishes and those who prepared them.

The kitchen workers and waiters numbered about 500. For example, it took three people just to pass Louis XIV a glass of wine. The *gentilhomme* with the honour of serving the King at table would call out *'à boire pour le Roi!'* ('a drink for the King'). The *chef d'échansonnerie-bouche* (head wine server) would then give the *gentilhomme* a golden tray carrying a glass and two flasks – one of wine, the other of water to dilute it. The two men, followed by the *aide de gobelet échansonnerie-bouche* (assistant goblet and wine server) would bow before the King's table, and then pour a little mixture of wine and water into cups for tasting. If none of the three tasters collapsed foaming at the mouth, the *gentilhomme* would then give the King the two flasks, and Louis would mix his own drink in his glass.[2]

The whole rigmarole with the flasks and glasses had to be repeated every time the King wanted a refill, because the drinks were kept on a chest of drawers set against the wall.

After his *dîner*, the King got changed (again, watched by a few courtiers), and then went about his afternoon activities. These he decided upon almost at the last minute, only giving his orders in the morning, and thereby obliging the courtiers who were to be honoured by his presence to rush off and put on their walking, riding or hunting outfits – while also keeping people on tenterhooks to see who would be invited.

In younger life, Louis XIV would go shooting in the park at least twice a week and hunt deer on horseback in the nearby forest at least once. He was by all accounts an excellent marksman – the Duc de Saint-Simon wrote that 'there was no better shot than he' (although in French, the word *tireur* was also a crude double entendre). Louis XIV could bag 250 birds in a single day. This was not surprising, though, as 2,000 pheasants and 5,000 partridges might be released from the royal pheasant house to ensure that the King would not be frustrated.

Louis XIV would often give the dead birds to ladies present, who would wear the bloody corpses on their belts as trophies, and return to the palace still showing these gruesome signs of royal favour.

The King's afternoon riding expeditions provided slightly different opportunities to stain his courtiers' clothing. Legend has it that Louis XIV was blessed with an abnormally large (or patient) bladder, and could ride for hours without stopping.

---

[2] As readers of modern detective fiction will have spotted, there was a loophole in this elaborate security etiquette – a clever poisoner only had to put a drop of arsenic directly into the King's glass. But then Agatha Christie was a long way off, and this ceremony was more about etiquette than a real fear of poisoning.

Naturally, while he rode, everyone else in his party had to ride. There were no comfort breaks unless Louis himself took one, and because he rarely did so, any courtier whose bladder was bursting had a painful choice – either cork it or wet themselves in the saddle. A quick stop behind a tree – however discreet – would be noticed and the offender banished from future hunting parties.

On clement afternoons, Louis also loved to promenade around his gardens, which, as we have already seen, would come to life before his eyes. Fountains would spring up as he walked, and hats would come off – he was the only person permitted to cover his head when he was present. Music would also start up, because music, along with flattery, was one of Louis XIV's true loves, and just like flattery, he wanted to hear it everywhere he went. Louis himself played the lute, harpsichord and guitar (brilliantly, of course, according to his courtiers).

On his walks, Louis was either accompanied by strolling musicians or would come across small orchestras posted at strategic points around the grounds. When performing in windy weather, the court composer Jean-Baptiste Lully would have to increase the number of musicians in his ensemble so that they could make themselves heard.

Naturally, every orchestra, marching band and choir at Versailles had to play the King's favourite songs, adding still more layers to the repetitive tedium of the courtiers' lives. Elisabeth-Charlotte, the German wife of Louis XIV's gay brother Philippe d'Orléans, once described a typical concert at court as 'a tune from an old opera that we have heard a hundred times before'. And she was an avowed *admirer* of Louis XIV.

The King would return to the palace at about 5 p.m. and change clothes again, donning his most flamboyant costume and largest wig of the day, before visiting his queen or official mistress for a little tête-à-tête.

Three times a week, between seven and ten in the evening, Louis held his *'appartement'*. This was the courtiers' favourite time of day, because the King hosted entertainments accompanied by a generous buffet of ice creams and *pâtisseries* at which everyone would help themselves. It was all very relaxed, with Louis mingling, talking about that day's hunting, listening to music, dancing, watching card games and playing billiards.

Even so, with Louis present, relaxation was a relative concept. Betting was allowed at court, although forbidden in Paris, and it was a dangerous pursuit at Versailles, because players were willing to raise the stakes to ruinous levels just to attract the King's attention. When they hit a losing streak, their fate would be sealed if Louis joined the game while they were trying to win their money back, because it was not polite to beat the King.

Playing billiards against Louis XIV provided another excellent chance to flaunt one's talent for obsequiousness. It was said, for example, that a politician called Michel Chamillart was made Secretary of State for War and Minister of Finance purely thanks to his skill at losing to Louis at billiards. Chamillart was notoriously bad at both jobs and was dubbed by a wit as 'a hero at billiards, a zero at the ministry'.

The worst thing about these 'informal' evenings, though, was that in hot weather, the huge crowd would create such a hammam that ice creams would melt instantly and bewigged, overdressed courtiers would suffer heat exhaustion.

In fact, Louis himself often couldn't stand the heat, and would frequently leave these evening entertainments to his son (also called Louis, though destined never to reign, because he died of smallpox in 1711 before he could inherit the throne). The King, meanwhile, might be with his mistress enjoying his own overheated *soirée*.

The evening entertainments over, Louis XIV would retire to his antechamber from 10 to 11p.m. to eat his *souper*, a formal meal for which he would be seated in an armchair and watched by courtiers, including a row of especially favoured people who were allowed to stand behind him. Again, musicians might well be playing in the background.

Louis would sometimes use a meal like this to cause ructions at court. On 5 January 1685, for example, the diarist the Marquis de Sourches noted that: 'The King gave a *souper* for the ladies. But they were only a small number, to the great displeasure of those who were not invited.' Louis XIV was a master of divide and rule.

After supper, it was back to the bedroom with the same elite group who had attended his *lever*. The ceremony was the same as in the morning, only performed backwards, and with extra prayers. The only new element in the evening was the ceremony of the candlestick. The chaplain would hand it to the *premier valet de chambre*, who would carry it over to the King's armchair. Louis would then select one of his courtiers to take off one glove and hold the candlestick while he got undressed.

The King climbed into his bed, the curtains were drawn, the *premier valet de chambre* would lie down on his camp bed, and everyone else would leave the room knowing that at seven o'clock the next morning, it would all begin again. If they were very lucky, tomorrow they would be invited to watch the King eat, maybe even from behind his chair; they might get the chance to utter some self-abasing flattery, lose at billiards, and hear the same tune for the thousandth time; and if they were amongst the most favoured in the realm, they might even get to watch the Sun King perform a bowel movement.

III

The elite in the King's bedroom weren't the only courtiers at Versailles to be subjected to waste products. When Louis XIV was in residence, the palace was so crowded that bodily functions became an embarrassing problem. According to an inventory of royal furniture, between 1664 and 1705 there were about 350 *chaises de commodité* (commodes) kept in *garde-robes à chaise* (literally, 'chair wardrobes') all over the building – but this was not enough to cope with the crowds, and not always convenient when courtiers were waiting at a key spot for the King to pass by. Hence the many stories of chic French aristocrats disappearing into bushes in the gardens, peeing in staircases or behind curtains, or getting servants to hold chamber pots and vases so that they could relieve themselves whenever they needed to. It is said that some men would go into bedrooms and use shaving and washing bowls – an unpleasant surprise for the occupant who later returned to their room to freshen up.

Even the clergy got in on the act – it was said that the aged Bishop of Noyon (who was also an aristocrat) was once caught short while alone on the upper level of the chapel at Versailles, and urinated over a balustrade. The guard on duty below heard the sudden cascade and rushed over to see a man of the cloth with his cloth hitched up. The guard quickly reported the matter to Louis XIV's valet. Louis, though, had a soft spot for the old bishop, who was often present for his evening prayers, and did nothing to punish this desecration.

The palace must have reeked, especially on hot days, so that standing in smelly corridors, next to urine-soaked curtains, while bursting to use a *chaise*, in the vague hope of catching the King's eye, must have been a source of constant humiliation for the crème de la crème of civilized French society. Most of all, though, one has to pity the servants whose job it was to lift the collecting bowls out of all the *chaises de commodité* and empty their contents into 30–odd cesspits dotted about the grounds.

On top of all this, the prospect of being in Louis XIV's presence became less and less enticing as his reign went on.

It is often said that Louis XIV never bathed because his doctors believed that washing was dangerous. There was a widely held theory at the time that hot water could enter the body via the pores and poison it. One of Louis XIV's physicians, Théophraste Renaudot, said that 'bathing exterminates the body and fills the head with vapours'.[3] Then again, water

---

[3] In other respects, Renaudot was a more modern doctor. He opened a dispensary in Paris that was free for the poor and expensive for the rich. Because of this, his name has been given to a French public-health charity,

quality was not always perfect, so there might have been something in this theory, especially in cities like Paris where until the nineteenth century most household water came direct from the River Seine, which was also the main sewer.

However, the stories about Louis XIV's body odour are often exaggerated. As we saw when discussing his fountains, some of the water piped into Versailles came from springs, so the quality could be relatively good. Louis himself loved swimming in rivers when he was a young man, and took frequent baths when he was older. In the 1670s he built himself a 'bathing apartment' with a tub that would be replenished by a small army of servants carrying jugs of hot water from a nearby boiler room.

Accounts of how often Louis XIV bathed tend to vary according to the strength of the writer's belief in an absolute monarchy, but it is likely that he would have wanted to wash off the smell, sweat and blood after hunting – meaning that he would have bathed several times per week in younger life.

Not all Louis XIV's courtiers followed his example. Many aristocrats believed in the dangers of washing, and would content themselves with a quick morning swab of the face and hands with a cloth moistened with water or vinegar – only the visible parts of the body had to look clean. To reduce body odours, they had creams and strong perfumes (musk and patchouli were favourites), and the better-off aristocrats who had rooms at the palace could change their shirts and undergarments several times a day. Even so, with the mix of body odours and perfumes, the crowded corridors of Versailles would definitely have set the nostrils twitching.

Despite the many portraits depicting Louis XIV as a demi-god, in later life his physical presence was far from pleasant. Like many people of the time, his dental hygiene left much to be desired, so that from the age of 38, in the late 1670s, his teeth

---

the Institut Renaudot. He also published a newspaper that featured job adverts, in an explicit attempt to ease poverty and unemployment.

began giving him serious problems. In 1678, one of his doctors, Antoine d'Aquin, noted that the King's 'right cheek and gum were swollen, and the abscess, having suppurated ... was lanced and pus was withdrawn'.

By 1685, d'Aquin was reporting that a botched operation to have teeth removed from Louis XIV's upper left jaw 'sometimes caused a flow of bad-smelling purulent matter'. The doctor described 'a hole in this jaw which, every time he drank or gargled, let the water enter his nose, from which it flowed like a fountain'. One has to pity the lucky courtiers chosen to observe the royal meals.

The hole was eventually cauterized after an agonizing session with red-hot irons and no anaesthetic, but thereafter, Louis was apparently a victim of 'a strong, almost cadaverous odour when he blew his nose'.

By the time he was 47, Louis XIV had lost all his upper teeth but one, while all his lower teeth were partially rotten. This was just after his second marriage, to Madame de Maintenon. Never can 'you may now kiss the bride' have sounded so threatening. Not that the ceremony would have included those words – it was held in secret and was by all accounts a sombre mass.

In short, Louis XIV became a sort of *Picture of Dorian Gray* in reverse. The royal portraits stayed eternally glamorous[4] while the real man lost his teeth and emitted cadaverous odours – and his courtiers were obliged to pretend it wasn't happening.

IV

The question is, why did this daily regime of tyranny and pretence not provoke a rebellion amongst the courtiers?

Were none of these proud aristocrats – some of whom traced their families back to Charlemagne or William the Conqueror,

[4] A notable exception is Antoine Benoist's extraordinary *Portrait of Louis at 68, Seven Years before His Death*, still on display at Versailles. Half-picture, half-sculpture, it is astonishingly convincing, and shows a saggy-jawed, hook-nosed and decidedly morose Louis. Even more astonishing, Benoist was one of the King's official artists and created the unflattering image with royal permission.

or who were members of other European royal families – sick of the stench and the self-degradation? And why was there no Versailles revolution against the crushing boredom?

Surely it would only have taken direct action by a few influential figures, supported by Louis XIV's ambitious younger brother, Philippe d'Orléans, to have put an end to the whole absurd 'emperor's new clothes' regime. If a few hats had been defiantly kept on heads in the gardens of Versailles, a few aristocratic backsides planted on seats while the King was dining, or groans of disgust heard when he sat on his commode, then the spell would have been broken. The rebellious nobles could have convinced the Parisian mob that things were going to change, malcontents everywhere would have refused to pay their abusive local tax collectors, and Louis XIV's sun would have set.

But it didn't happen.

There seem to have been several reasons why Versailles never became unbearable for Louis XIV's courtiers – at least, not until the very end of his reign, when he was ill and increasingly under the sway of his religious wife.

For a start, boredom breeds gossip, and the aristocrats at Versailles spent their days and nights starting, passing on and elaborating salacious rumours about each other. The young wife of an aged duke was pregnant? Bets would be taken on who was the real father, especially after the baby was born and illicit resemblances could be alleged.

The King's various *coucheries* also provided plenty of entertainment, though he was so open in his infidelities that remarks about his mistress would mainly be jealous backbiting rather than moral accusations.

Not even the Queen, Marie-Thérèse, escaped the Versailles rumour mill – when she gave birth to a daughter in 1664, witnesses at the delivery remarked that the newborn girl was dark-skinned. One of the ladies-in-waiting, Madame de Motteville, described the baby as *'une mauresse'*, 'a black North African'. To scotch rumours, the doctors blamed the infant's dark complexion on the long labour and even on the Queen's fondness for chocolate (she had started the fashion for drinking it in Paris), but there was so much gossip that 40 days later, some courtiers refused to believe the report that the baby had died. A few years afterwards, it was suggested that a young black servant girl at Versailles was the daughter, who had been hidden away. There were also stories that the girl was the fruit of an encounter between Louis XIV and a Caribbean maid.

Yet the rumours at court weren't all sexual tittle-tattle. With Louis governing France from one room at Versailles, courtiers felt flattered to be at the heart of national affairs. Today, French politicians seem to love nothing better than being filmed or photographed in hushed conversation with each other, under-lining their status as members of an in-the-know in-crowd. At Louis XIV's court it was no different.

Courtiers could see and hear the King giving out orders, watch foreign ambassadors arrive and judge how they had been received, or witness ministers and generals being appointed and dismissed. In his diaries, the Marquis de Sourches constantly noted rumours that today would be thought of as security leaks. On 11 March 1690, for example, de Sourches talked about the *'rumeur'* that 'twelve thousand of the Holy Roman Emperor's best troops on the Rhine had left for Hungary' (this retreat by France's enemy in the Nine Years War was good news), though he added that 'perhaps the number was not so great and, osten-sibly, the truth was that he had only marched away five or six thousand'. Clearly everyone was openly swapping hearsay about troop movements.

This story is accompanied by a long list of newly appointed army officers (all of them aristocrats), complete with their family background, because being selected for one of the King's elite regiments was confirmation of the family's noble status.

Sourches wrote similar entries for decades, especially during Louis XIV's frequent wars, suggesting that the corridors of Versailles constantly echoed to the sound of official proclamations and only semi-hushed revelations. Insider knowledge like that is the basis of modern politicians' whole careers, and must have fascinated the thousands of aristocrats in seventeenth-century Versailles.

Another reason why the nobility tolerated the Sun King's blinding self-aggrandizement was baser: money. There were fortunes to be made and lost at Versailles, and not just from gambling.

The idea of selling state jobs wasn't new. It was created by Henri IV in 1604, but Louis XIV turned it into a growth industry that earned him a fortune. When he created the post of *percepteur des taxes d'enlèvement d'ordures à Paris* (collector of taxes to pay for rubbish collection), for example, it was sold for a vast sum – 75,000 *livres*. The new recruit was guaranteed to cream off his percentage of the tax, and had the power to hold whole Parisian neighbourhoods to ransom if they didn't pay up. Louis, meanwhile, received not only the 75,000 *livres* and his share of the taxes, but also an annual payment from the tax collector so that he could keep his job. It was win-win-win.

As bathing in hot water became more fashionable (or less risky) towards the end of Louis XIV's reign, he decided to raise money by making it necessary to buy a licence to set up a high-class bathhouse – a sort of seventeenth-century urban spa – where the well-off residents of most major towns in France could pay a small fortune to wash, get a shave, have their wig powdered and deloused, and even undergo minor operations.

These licences sold so well that in 1689 Louis issued an edict creating 200 more. The 200 existing spa owners, known technically as the *barbiers-perruquiers-baigneurs-étuvistes* (barbers-wigmakers-bathers-steamroom operators) were horrified at the idea of so much competition – and certain that the market would not support so many of these spas – so they clubbed together and paid the King a 'voluntary contribution' of 100,000 *livres* to have the edict withdrawn. This was the equivalent of 1,000 years' salary for a common soldier or coachman, so the earnings at stake must have been immense.

Just like a modern free-market economy, the aristocrats knew that some of the profits from Louis XIV's lucrative jobs and licences would trickle down to them. The problem was that to stand a chance of cashing in, they had to bow and scrape to the King. Invitations to join him at his second home at the nearby château de Marly were as sought-after as tickets to a World Cup final. Courtiers would mutter a two-word plea – *'Sire, Marly?'* – as he passed them in the gardens or the corridors, and the going rate to get one's name on the guest list by other means was apparently 6,000 *livres*, payable to the Princesse d'Harcourt, a cousin by marriage of Louis XIV. The aristocrats paid up, partly so that they would be perceived as influential members of the in-crowd, but also for the opportunity to earn their cash back.

Sometimes Louis even made people's mere presence at Versailles a blatant moneymaking scheme. In 1681 he organized a national lottery, nominally in aid of the poor, and obliged his courtiers to be generous, though this time he was offering large prizes in return. Participants bought as many tickets as they could afford, wrote their name on them, and put them in collecting boxes, with some gamblers trying to improve their chances by scribbling flattering messages to the King on the outside of their folded ticket. One was apparently inscribed with a clever, obsequious pun: 'One Louis can make my fortune' (a Louis was a coin as well as the King's name).

The take-up was massive, with collection boxes arriving from all around the country – though there were complaints that some provincial boxes had not arrived in time for the draw. In any case, it came as no surprise when a ticket belonging to Louis XIV won the main prize of 100,000 *livres*. Sportingly, or because he thought that such obvious cheating would scupper future lotteries, he refused to accept his winnings, and put the money back in the pot. But, coincidentally or not, other large prizes were won by Louis XIV's son, brother, wife and several other prominent courtiers.

In short, it was very worthwhile for aristocrats to stay on at Versailles, within range of all this money. But not everyone at court had the cash to buy a job, an audience with the King, or even enough hats to keep up with fashion. So, predictably, some

courtiers resorted to theft. There were unimaginably rich pick-
ings at the palace, and everyone knew that the jewellers in town
never asked where sellers had obtained the diamonds, brooches
or odd pieces of gold and silverware that they were peddling.

One evening, a skilful blade cut a large diamond button from
the dress of Marie-Adelaïde de Savoie, the mother of the future
King Louis XV, taking a neat square of material with it. She
didn't notice anything until it was too late, and when she
reported her loss, news was put about that the perpetrator must
have been a common gatecrasher, no doubt to preserve the
court's reputation.

At a ball on 11 December 1697, the Chevalier de Sully caught
a young nobleman trying to steal a jewel from his outfit. The
King was informed, but nothing was done in order to protect
the thief's family's name. The young man was simply exiled
from court, which was considered punishment enough. Even
so, the young criminal knew that with a little well-placed flattery, bribery or (if really necessary) bravado on the battlefield,
the exile could be rescinded.

Money flowed down through Versailles society in other forms,
too. Any dishes served to the King that he didn't finish were
resold in town by the *serdeaux* – as their name suggests, they
were originally the King's water servers, but later became more
general servants, often from noble families, whose job was to
clear away the tables after a meal or party. Along one side of the
place d'Armes in Versailles, just outside the palace entrance,
market stalls would sell royal dishes, often untouched, to townspeople or down-on-their-luck courtiers who were looking for a
cheap meal. Not surprisingly, *serdeau* was another job title that
had to be bought.

Thanks to Louis XIV, the whole town of Versailles became an
El Dorado, with canny residents able to make fortunes from the
palace run-off. Chief amongst these were the hotel and inn
owners providing board, lodging and prostitutes for the permanently incoming tide of builders, craftsmen, merchants, con

artists and hangers-on. By 1700 the huddle of streets around the palace contained more than 100 hotels and inns.

Surprisingly, the fortune hunters who were most at risk were those who worked in the rag trade – any kind of tailor, seamstress, shoemaker, milliner, wigmaker or haberdasher.

They might have been expected to prosper the most, because fashions at court were so absurd that no garment could be bought ready-made. At the start of Louis XIV's reign, for example, men's garters and shoes were swathed in so many ribbons that courtiers were in real danger of somersaulting down staircases – Louis himself popularized the use of the walking stick to counter this. Naturally, vast stocks of ribboned garters had to be hand-sewn, and the walking sticks had to be personalized with jewels or gold handles as a mark of rank. Louis also decreed from time to time that certain courtiers would be allowed to wear a certain colour, so that new uniforms had to be ordered at top speed.

Women at the palace were encumbered with heavy dresses consisting of three skirts – *la modeste, la friponne* (or 'mischievous', because a lover might lift it) and *la secrète*. At court, they had to wear a train, the length of which depended on their rank – these could reach 12 feet (the French didn't start measuring in metres until the Revolution) for a duchess, up to 44 feet for the Queen.

Under obligation to wear these customized costumes, both male and female courtiers spent half their lives getting measured and fitted, and begging the best cloth cutters and needleworkers to give priority to their new outfit. But this didn't help the workers themselves, and the most frequent bankrupts in the town of Versailles were tailors.

This was because, despite the huge demand for clothes and accessories of all sorts, the nobles rarely paid in full for the finery they ordered. A shopkeeper who sold a pair of shoes, a cane or gloves might be able to demand cash, but large, complicated creations would be supplied on credit, and bills would often be ignored. And even if the courtiers were sued for payment, ultimately they were protected, thanks to Louis XIV's decree making their houses inviolable property. If a Versailles aristocrat pleaded cash-poverty, no creditor could force him or her to sell their valuable mansion, so that a nobleman or -woman with huge debts could stay at court, living on credit, and angling for the glance or word from the King that might make him or her rich for life – or for generations.

Meanwhile, the tailors they bankrupted would have to pawn the tools of their trade, which would be bought by another fortune hunter.

In short, Louis XIV created a self-perpetuating market economy based on the notion of his own glory. It was totally corrupt but highly efficient. The proudest aristocrats in France would obey his every whim in the hope of earning prestige and its associated cash. This probably explains why, after the troubles at the start of his reign, Louis never entertained any doubts about the justi-fication for his absolutist regime.

In a way, though, his self-confidence was a mistake, because by rewarding aristocrats for self-abasing obedience, Louis XIV seems to have sown the seeds for the demise of the monarchy.

After all, if you were an aristocrat who had been forced to humiliate yourself, and then pay a fortune, to land a lucrative job, you would be more than keen to hang on to it. If that job involved wielding power as, say, a tax collector or a judge, *and* making a rich living out of corruption, this keenness would become an obsession. And if you had also bought the right to pass your job on to future generations of your family, staying in your position of power would become your entire dynastic *raison d'être*.

So Louis XIV might have thought he was enslaving his aris-tocracy, but he was in fact giving it a very good reason to bite the royal hand that fed it. Thanks to Louis XIV, the aristocracy could feed itself, and had less reason to show allegiance to the monarch. What's more, taxing the less fortunate had now become the aristocrat's whole way of life.

This was the situation that would cripple Louis XVI's attempts to reform French society before 1789, and that would end up sending him and many aristocrats to the guillotine.

Louis XIV was so sure of his unshakeable authority that he once even felt comfortable enough to joke about a riot. When his first grandson was born in 1682, the people of Versailles came to the palace to celebrate, but things quickly got out of hand. Building work was still going on, and the mob began to tear down wooden scaffolding and set light to it, throwing tarpaulins and old clothes on to the celebratory bonfire to get it really roaring.

Anxious courtiers advised Louis XIV to send soldiers to disperse the mob and put out the flames, but the King quipped: 'Let them carry on, as long as they don't burn us.'

It would be another century before his joke would turn sour.

Chapter 3

MORAL AND FINANCIAL BANKRUPTCY

'La naissance n'est rien où la vertu n'est pas.'
'Birth is nothing where there is no virtue.'
Molière (1622–73), French playwright, in Dom Juan

I

The gangrene of the leg that killed Louis XIV in 1715 spread throughout Versailles almost immediately.

Rotting slowly on his deathbed, Louis XIV received the future king, his five-year-old great-grandson. The dying 76-year-old had outlived two generations of heirs, and, with the wisdom of melancholic hindsight, told the boy to avoid war at all costs, because 'it is the ruin of peoples'.

In French *'la ruine'* is usually financial, and Louis XIV knew what he was talking about, because the decade-long Spanish War of Succession, during which France had fought against practically the whole of Europe, had emptied the country's coffers. Taxes, already heavy, had become crippling – though not for the nobility, of course, who didn't pay tax. Meanwhile, French farmers and agricultural labourers, some of the poorest in Europe, were losing 10 per cent of their harvest to their (usually noble) landlord, another 10 per cent to the Church (which didn't pay tax), a percentage of all produce they transported across toll bridges (which usually belonged to an aristocrat), as well as paying levies on salt and alcohol, and giving workdays for whatever projects the King wanted doing, but which might also benefit the local *aristo*. Urban workers weren't much better off – they escaped the taxes on harvests, but their basic wage was far lower than that of workers in London and Amsterdam, for example.

Overall, Louis XIV's advice to his great-grandson was coming a little too late. He was leaving his country in deep financial *ruine*.

Almost the only reason why the people of France didn't rise up in the last years of Louis XIV's reign, apart from the threat of brutal repression, was that some two million people, almost 10 per cent of the population (at the poorer end of the social ladder, naturally), died in the winter famines of 1693 and 1709. The people just didn't have the energy or the numbers for a revolution.

After this cataclysmic end to the longest reign in French history, the new king, the infant Louis XV, and more particularly his regent, Louis XIV's nephew Philippe d'Orléans,[1] had a great opportunity to usher in an era of peaceful growth under a less crippling tax regime and a fairer system of government.

At first, Philippe showed good intentions. He wrote an open letter to his provincial tax collectors announcing that he intended to introduce a fairer system of taxation. Philippe also restored the right of parliament to contest a royal law – the *droit de remontrance* – which Louis XIV had abolished in 1673.

Symbolically, Philippe abandoned Versailles. The great symbol of royal decadence and profiteering was emptied almost overnight, and the new Finance Minister, Adrien de Nouailles, even suggested burning it down, though that might have been to fumigate the place after poor Louis XIV's slow death from advancing gangrene of the leg.

---

[1] This was the son of the Philippe d'Orléans, younger brother of Louis XIV, mentioned earlier.

The Palais-Royal in central Paris became the seat of government, while the infant King Louis XV was sent to live in the château de Vincennes, just outside the eastern fringes of the capital.

Leaving Versailles suggested that the royal family had finally recognized that their life of flagrant decadence was over.[2]

All in all, the post-Sun King era seemed to be starting promisingly. But you don't grow potatoes on an ornamental rose bush, and 41-year-old Philippe quickly showed that he was a typical product of his royal upbringing, a lover of sex parties and gambling who was totally disconnected from the everyday realities of running an economy.

The Palais-Royal became the scene of even more outrageous decadence than Louis XIV had ever managed. Philippe's *'soupers'* ('suppers') became notorious, usually ending up – or even starting off – as orgies. In his memoirs, the Duc de Saint-Simon wrote that the Regent spent his suppers 'in very strange company. His mistresses [the Regent had five or six, and enjoyed playing them off against each other], sometimes an opera girl, often Madame du Berry [Philippe's own daughter], and a dozen men.' Saint-Simon lists a few revellers' names, before adding 'men he [the Regent] had just met, a few ladies of dubious virtue, and unknowns who shone by their wit or debauchery … They drank, became heated, talked loudly and dirtily, outdid each other's impieties, and when they had made enough noise and got drunk enough, they went to bed.'

The rumours of an incestuous relationship between Philippe and his daughter were rife, and the fact that he was having affairs with half a dozen women was public knowledge, but Philippe didn't seem to care. Saint-Simon said that 'the scandal surrounding this public harem, and the depravity and impiety of his suppers, was extreme and spread everywhere.'

[2] In 1789, one of the first acts of the revolutionaries would be to impose the same gesture, forcing the King and Queen to move into Paris, where everyone could keep tabs on their lifestyle and spending.

Unjustly perhaps, it was Philippe's daughter, who nowadays would be seen as a victim of abuse, who became the biggest figure of hatred in Paris. She was grossly overweight, which was bad enough in sophisticated Parisians' eyes (as well as those who couldn't afford to eat and drink as much as her), and was nicknamed *'La Jouflotte'* ('Fat cheeks'). It was rumoured that she would sleep with any available man, including most of the male servants and guards at her home at the palais du Luxembourg in Paris. When she cut off public access to the Luxembourg gardens, the city's satirists dropped any finesse from their usual wit, and turned grossly insulting. It was alleged that she had done this so that she could cavort about naked, and in his memoirs, the Comte de Maurepas quotes a song of the time that went:

> They've closed the door to the Luxembourg gardens,
> It's fat Jouflotte's fault,
> She would have done better, the tart,
> To close the hole nearest her backside,
> Where all her guards get to play.

Not exactly subtle, even if it did rhyme in French:

> On nous a fermé la porte
> Du jardin du Luxembourg.
> C'est la grosse Joufflotte
> Qui nous a joué ce tour.
> Elle eût mieux fait, la bougresse,
> De boucher le trou
> Le plus voisin de ses fesses,
> Par où ses gardes font joujou.

The Regent Philippe's daughter was the ultimate victim of his debauchery, and died in 1719 aged only 23. When a postmortem was performed, she was found to be pregnant for the seventh time, just three months after a miscarriage. One of her last acts was to reopen the Luxembourg gardens to the public.

II

The French have never been convinced by the Anglo-Saxon view that their political leaders need to be squeaky-clean sexually,[3] so sex addiction and even incest didn't prevent Philippe d'Orléans running the country.

But Philippe's detractors were convinced that his behaviour endangered the country. Saint-Simon says that during the infamous *soupers*, the palace was 'so heavily barricaded that it was useless to try and get to the Regent, no matter what kind of problem arose. I don't mean just the unexpected affairs of an individual, but matters which might have endangered the state.' Saint-Simon can't have been the only person in Paris to channel his moral disapproval through concerns about state security.

Saint-Simon also thought that Philippe's lackadaisical attitude to life meant that even if he put in relatively long working hours compared to other members of the royal family – he sometimes worked all morning and then until five in the afternoon – he wasted a lot of time:

> A thousand private affairs, as well as government business that he could have dealt with in half an hour, and then taken a firm decision, were prolonged, either through weakness or because of his terrible desire to cause divisiveness. He would sometimes admit that his favourite maxim was the toxic 'divide and rule'. Most matters revealed his defiant attitude to everything and everybody.

Philippe was not the ideal leader, then. It was a case of personality over politics, with a dysfunctional personality at the helm.

[3] In the mid-nineteenth century, the Emperor Napoléon III oversaw an economic boom and commissioned most of Paris's famous boulevards while carrying on an energetic campaign of public adultery. Even the more sedate Jacques Chirac, President of France from 1995 to 2007, was a tireless skirt-chaser whose brief encounters earned him the affectionate nickname 'Monsieur five minutes including a shower'. It doesn't stop him being remembered as a decent president.

Perhaps it was out of sheer indolence that Philippe pursued a strategy of peacemaking – apart from a short war with Spain between 1718 and 1720 caused by suspicions that the Spanish wanted to claim the French throne. Even this war involved little French action outside of a brief incursion across the Pyrenees, and a bout of skirmishing over ownership of Florida. Nothing very costly for the taxpayer.

In a spectacular turnaround, Philippe actually signed an alliance with France's traditional enemy, England, which was a major money-saver in terms of land and sea battles not fought. He even turned his back on the traditional Auld Alliance by withdrawing French support for the Stuart pretenders – a sure way to make peace with London.

However, Philippe's biggest downfall was economic, and probably linked to the aristocratic love of gambling that had been nurtured amongst the courtiers at Louis XIV's Versailles.

In 1715, seeing that Louis XIV had left France in dire need of money, Philippe d'Orléans did what many people in his position might do, if they didn't have an efficient government to advise them against it – he contacted an old friend who seemed to be very handy at accumulating cash.

In Philippe's case, this was a Scotsman called John Law.

Despite his moral-sounding name, Law was a conman and gambler who had been deported by several European countries – including France. During Louis XIV's reign, the Scotsman had introduced a card game, faro, to Versailles, where it had become immensely popular amongst the richest courtiers – including Philippe d'Orléans – because it was relatively easy for the banker/dealer to cheat. Often, of course, that banker was Law himself, and it didn't take very long for the losers to complain that Law's winning streaks were getting too frequent. Eventually, Louis XIV signed his deportation order.

The question is: when Philippe d'Orléans invited the card cheat Law to return to France *and become his chief financial advisor*, was it a sign of desperation? Or was it a canny sense that

Law might be able to wheedle cash out of the aristocrats, as he had done before at the card table?

In any case, the scheme that Law came up with was so bold, and generated so much financial activity, that he has inspired swindlers ever since, right down to the American Bernie Madoff, whose fraudulent schemes cost his investors an estimated $18 billion, and who in 2009 was sentenced to 150 years in prison.[4]

Law's scheme was legal enough. It was based on the theory that money breeds money. At the beginning of the eighteenth century, most money in France was stagnating. It was locked away in aristocrats' safes or in banks, in the form of gold and silver coins or jewellery. The rich lived off interest, off the taxes from their tenants, or bribes generated by the jobs they had bought.

Law explained to Philippe d'Orléans that this cash could be put to use to generate wealth amongst the population at large. For example, aristocratic Parisian A has 1,000 *livres* and gives it to his mistress. The mistress spends her money on a diamond ring; the jeweller buys champagne; the wine seller gets himself a wig and a suit; the tailor has to pay for treatment against syphilis; the quack gets his horses reshod; and so on, until a large chunk of the money ends up back in the pocket of aristocratic Parisian A in the form of taxes or bribes. But meanwhile everyone has benefited.

In a way, it was the system that Louis XIV had been using at Versailles by letting his cooks and servants sell off his half-eaten meals, by selling jobs that would allow the incumbent to accept bribes, or by letting thieves get away with jewel theft.

Law launched his system in 1716. He set up a Banque générale, which began issuing a new currency of paper banknotes, underwritten by royal silver and gold, and by Philippe's official

---

[4] Strangely, Madoff is scheduled for release on 14 November 2139, which implies that he will get an automatic 20 years off for good behaviour – not that this can give him much cause for celebration.

patronage. The new banknotes caught on so well that in 1718 Law was allowed to change the name of the bank to the Banque royale. However, even then the fraud had begun, because the face value of its banknotes already outweighed its bullion.

Nevertheless, money was circulating, and wealth was trickling out of the aristocracy into a new and growing bourgeoisie. As Saint-Simon put it in his memoirs: 'People rushed to change their lands and houses into paper.' The Regent himself was doing his best to get the paper money into circulation by doling it out as gifts to his friends, relations and political allies. What was more, according to Saint-Simon, 'in the evening, his mistresses and cronies ... grabbed it [paper money] out of his pockets, because all these gifts were in notes, which were worth their weight in gold, and were even preferred to it.'

At the same time, Law set up companies aimed at making a fast buck out of France's colonies. His Compagnie d'Occident (Company of the West) was given exclusive trading rights between France and Louisiane, which comprised much more than the modern state of Louisiana – it stretched right up the Mississippi from the Gulf of Mexico to the Great Lakes and west as far as French settlers had roamed into Wyoming, Colorado and Texas.

By vastly overstating the wealth of minerals, timber and furs to be had in Louisiane, and by shipping out thousands of poor, press-ganged 'settlers', most of whom would die of starvation or be massacred by Spanish troops and Native Americans, Law's company began attracting investors and selling worthless swampland.

The Compagnie d'Occident did so well that Law was given permission to repeat his exploits and set up a worldwide operation under the propitious-sounding name Compagnie perpétuelle des Indes orientales. He merged this with the Banque royale, and even contrived to lend the state a billion of his paper *livres*. Public confidence in Law's business acumen was so great that in the first three months of 1720, the price of shares in the company rose from 500 to 20,000 *livres*, a 40-fold increase.

Predictably, with share prices so absurdly high, some people began to decide that it might be time to cash in on their investment. A few of them made vast sums of money, especially thanks to some blatant insider dealing. A grandson and a godson of Louis XIV, both young men in their twenties, were well informed enough to convert millions of *livres* of banknotes into gold before the rush started. But after these huge payouts to the in-crowd, the defaults began, leading to a frantic run on the paper currency.

In Paris, the bank at Palais-Royal announced that it would open at 6 a.m. on 17 July to give coins in exchange for one ten-*livre* note per person, a relatively small denomination, but enough to buy a couple of sheep at market. The trouble was that Parisians have never been keen on queuing, and as soon as the gates to the bank courtyard opened, the crowd surged forward, killing five or six people at the front of the line.

The bodies of three victims were being carried out into the place du Palais-Royal when, by an ironic coincidence, Law's carriage was passing by. He wasn't in it, but his coachman began to swear at the crowd blocking his way, and these insults were met with a volley of stones. An angry mob followed the coach back to Law's house in the nearby Marais and started lobbing stones through the windows. According to some reports, 17 people were killed when the rioters were dispersed by armed soldiers.

After this, other attempts were made to set up counters on market days to change small notes, but they soon fizzled out, and on 20 July, Law's bank was declared 'semi-bankrupt'. It had one billion *livres'* worth of banknotes in circulation, and only 322 million in hard bullion.

Confiscating the assets of a few prominent people accused of slandering the bank, and exiling some vocal critics to the colonies, did nothing to restore public confidence. Law even converted to Catholicism to improve his image. In desperation, he resorted to making it illegal for households to own more than

500 *livres'* worth of precious metals, the idea being to remove every alternative to paper money. Homes were raided, and privately owned gold, silver and jewels were seized. After the first raids, people started burying their heirlooms – Saint-Simon said that many old people took the location of their hiding places to their graves so that the French countryside was probably littered with buried treasure. He concluded: 'It was only thanks to a miracle rather than an effort of government ... that such terrible measures did not produce revolutions ... and that so many millions of people made penniless or dying of hunger uttered nothing more than sighs and complaints.'

Even so, these 'sighs and complaints' were enough to have the seizures of precious metals suspended, and in October 1720 the whole French banking system collapsed, leaving about two million French people with worthless pieces of paper. Law blamed the Regent, saying that the system would have worked if Philippe d'Orléans hadn't used the bank's capital as his personal pocket money. Saint-Simon, a generally conservative man who used to meet Law regularly, seems to have agreed to a certain extent, saying that: 'If we had confined ourselves to his [Law's] bank, and used it wisely, we could have doubled the nation's resources and made its commerce, and that between individuals, infinitely simple.' But, Saint-Simon added, such a bank could only work in a republic, or a monarchy like Britain, where the powers of state and Crown were separated, so that 'finances are governed solely by those who supply them'. In France, he said, 'a king, and under his name, a mistress, a minister, or favourites' would find such a bank 'an easy lure', the proof being that the Regent 'without limit or distinction ... doled out money with both hands'.

Law escaped from the fiasco with his freedom – he fled to Brussels in December 1720, and thence to Venice, where he died in poverty nine years later. Philippe d'Orléans emerged with a kind of immortality – Law's speculative new town in Louisiane, virtually the only thing to survive the financial collapse, was named La Nouvelle-Orléans in Philippe's honour.

III

As Saint-Simon had said, this mismanagement of the economy could easily have caused revolution. In five years, Philippe had led France from state bankruptcy to private, individual ruin. He had even helped to cheat his own social class out of a sizeable share of its previously untouchable store of wealth.

Revolution still didn't come, however, for two main reasons.

First, in a rare show of financial intelligence, the Regent appointed a team of Paris financiers called Pâris (with an accent)[5] to audit the accounts and make sure that the small investors didn't lose out when Law's system collapsed. Everyone who had invested less than 400 *livres* – about a quarter of a million people – got all their money back. About 20 per cent of the others also received full or partial refunds. Only really big investors (those who weren't friends or relatives of the Regent, anyway) and anyone accused of forging share certificates and banknotes, lost their whole fortune – and 185 people who had managed to make profits were prosecuted for speculating, thereby bringing in fines of 187 million much-needed *livres*.

Inflation had hit everyone – Saint Simon estimated that the price of everyday goods was multiplied by six when the run on paper money started – but small payments had always been made in hard metal coinage, so the poorest section of the population had been protected from total bankruptcy. In fact, Law's schemes hadn't hurt the peasant and working classes half as much as Louis XIV's taxes.

In any case, the economic hardship clearly wasn't painful enough to provoke the mass rioting that the rise in the price of bread would cause in 1789. And amongst the poor, who had nothing much to lose, the general attitude to the state's financial collapse in 1720 was probably 'serves you rich idiots right'.

The second reason why nationwide revolution didn't come after Law's downfall was that an uprising would have needed

[5] Amusingly, perhaps, *pari* also means bet.

support from someone in the ruling classes. Power was still in the hands of a small aristocratic elite – the bourgeoisie had not yet expanded in number, wealth and influence, as it would later in the century. And for the time being, the aristocrats didn't want to undermine the system that kept them at the top of the social pile, especially because the regime was about to change anyway, as soon as Louis XV was old enough to rule. By 1720, at the precocious age of ten, the infant King had taken to attending government meetings alongside the Regent, albeit silently. A new, potentially manipulable monarch was about to take the throne.

What was more, the aristocrats had recently seen what happened to anyone who rocked the royal boat.

In 1718, there had been an uprising of sorts in Brittany, the so-called 'Conspiration de Pontcallec'. Nominally, this was a revolt against excessive taxation and an attempt to declare Breton independence.

In 1717, after the Regent's initial promise to reduce income tax, he had decided to do the opposite. In the early eighteenth century, people were apparently still shocked by their leaders' broken promises, and the Bretons declared that they weren't going to pay the two million *livres* that was demanded of them. Their self-appointed spokesman was a local noble, Chrysogone Clément de Guer, alias the Marquis de Pontcallec, by all accounts a cruel landlord who tyrannized his tenants and lived mainly off tobacco smuggling. In other words, not a man personally troubled by taxation.

The King of Spain, Philip V, a grandson of Louis XIV with his eyes on the French throne, saw an opening and sent missives to Brittany promising to ship in an army of 2,000 Irish mercenaries. On the strength of this, Pontcallec began recruiting his own troops. But bad weather delayed the Spanish fleet, so that only one ship arrived, with a paltry cargo of 300 soldiers. Seeing that their cause was hopeless, one of the Breton nobles advised the Irishmen to get back on their boat and leave; he, meanwhile, revealed the plot to the governor of Brittany, who brought in an army of 15,000 royal troops to quash the rebellion before it began.

Meanwhile, the man who might have been a national figurehead for an uprising was arrested. This was Louis-Auguste de Bourbon, the Duc du Maine, an illegitimate (and afterwards legitimized) son of Louis XIV and his mistress Madame de Montespan. Louis-Auguste had been designated in Louis XIV's will as the rightful regent, before Philippe d'Orléans, a fully legitimate royal, had persuaded parliament to appoint him instead. Suspected of plotting with Philip V of Spain, Louis-Auguste was taken away in a carriage and locked up in the château de Doullens, in the far north of France. There, according to Saint-Simon, he spent most of his time 'praying, often prostrate ... and behaved towards [his jailer] like a very young schoolboy towards his master ... Any sudden noise or unusual movement made him go pale and fear death.' And this was a man four years older than the Regent Philippe d'Orléans – not exactly the ideal candidate to lead a revolutionary army. When Louis-Auguste was eventually released, he quickly set about worming his way back into favour with the royal family.

When the Breton revolt collapsed, the rebel leader Pontcallec went into hiding disguised as a peasant, but he was apparently so unpopular with the tenant classes that he was betrayed, and ultimately beheaded in Nantes along with four co-conspirators and the effigies of 16 others who had escaped. *Pour décourager les autres*, the judges who were sent to Nantes by the Regent ordered that all the conspirators' assets should be seized (thus neatly replacing the lost income taxes) and their families' noble rank be withdrawn. Saint-Simon also mentions a more bizarre punishment: their woodland was cut down to a height of nine feet. This can't have been for the timber – surely the bottom nine feet were amongst the most valuable – and must have been a symbolic beheading of their hunting forests.

The executions of Pontcallec and his followers were carried out in Nantes, the capital of Brittany, on the same morning that the sentence was passed, 26 March 1720, while a large army occupied the city and cannons were pointed at its walls. It was a lesson in how to repress a revolt – and how *not* to organize one.[6]

For all these different reasons, in 1720 the French people refrained from revolution. They seemed to be content to have a single scapegoat, the Regent, Philippe d'Orléans. In May of that year, just as Law's financial system was unravelling, the city of Marseille was hit by an outbreak of the plague. It raged throughout the summer, killing about 40,000 people in Marseille itself (almost half the population) and 100,000 more in Provence as a whole. The general consensus was that this disaster was a direct result of Philippe's debauchery, the divine retribution for his *irréligion*.

So when Louis XV, now a much more mature 12 years of age, was crowned in 1722, the French again looked forward to a fresh new start.

How wrong they were.

[6] Bertrand Tavernier's 1975 film, *Que la fête commence*, tells the story of Pontcallec's uprising, though very much from a 1970s French perspective, with plenty of screen time devoted to the naked female flesh at Philippe d'Orléans's orgies.

Chapter 4

LOUIS XV, THE WORST OF BOTH WORLDS

'If the French Kingship had not, by course of Nature, long to live, he of all men was the man to accelerate Nature.'

Thomas Carlyle (1795–1881), writing about
Louis XV in *The French Revolution: A History* (1837)

I

As soon as he was old enough to do so, Louis XV proved that he had learnt little or nothing from his predecessors' mistakes. His long reign – 51 years not counting the regency – was to combine a return to Louis XIV's excesses at Versailles with a taste for Philippe d'Orléans-style debauchery. The new Louis's long career of self-indulgence, coupled with his mismanagement of the aristocracy, was to bring the monarchy to its knees, effectively getting it into position for the *coup de grâce* at the end of the century.

Like the Regent before him, the young Louis XV began modestly enough. As soon as he was crowned, he declared that Versailles would be the official venue of his court, but instead of migrating there permanently, he decided to spend only between 140 and 200 days a year at the palace, and he cut the number of courtiers and servants from 10,000 at the time of Louis XIV to only 4,000-odd. This was still a sizeable crowd, but it marked a symbolic change in emphasis. Versailles was no longer a solar system; it was more of an asteroid shower.

At the age of 15, Louis XV married a 22-year-old Polish princess, Marie, who bore twin princesses (the first of their ten children) less than two years later. In 1729, still aged only 19, Louis and Marie produced a son and heir. The young king's dynastic duty was done.

In an attempt to free himself from political intriguers, Louis XV decided to rule almost alone alongside an ageing bishop who had been his private tutor ever since he was six. This was the 72-year-old Antoine-Hercule de Fleury, who was appointed Minister of State.

Rule by a king and a bishop was monarchy at its most absolutist, but the old clergyman, who had started his career as a young priest, brought a breath of fresh air to government. He cut spending and thereby helped to restore confidence in the currency, settling the country's finances into a period of relative stability. He encouraged merchants to import cheap raw materials like cotton and transform them into valuable exports like clothes, harnessing and increasing the skills that would become one of the staples of France's economy of the future. He also instigated a programme of road-building that provided work for the impoverished labouring class as well as creating a new network of trade routes.

In foreign affairs, Fleury helped Louis XV keep his promise to his great-grandfather to be a peacemaker. Fleury maintained cordial relations with both Britain and Spain, reducing the need for military spending and therefore avoiding unpopular new taxes. The satirical writer Voltaire, by nature an anti-authoritarian, had only kind words for Fleury, saying that he possessed the virtues of 'gentleness, a sense of equality, [and] a love of order and peace'.

Even in his private life, Fleury showed exceptional restraint for the times. As a bishop, he was entitled to a large income from taxes, but he spent most of it on the poor of his diocese.

Sadly, old Fleury died in 1743, taking his spirit of moderation and careful management with him. Even so, at the beginning of Louis XV's reign, the French people really felt that their young monarch was going to get the country back on its feet. As for the King himself, it soon became clear that he was much happier lying down.

At Versailles, Louis XV had been quick to rebel against some of his great-grandfather's grossest absurdities: he was, for example, adamant that he would not be performing bowel movements in public. He had a commode installed in an alcove in his new, smaller bedroom at the palace, a break from the theatre that Louis XIV's bedchamber had been.

The new King still performed a public *lever* (getting out of bed and dressing), but from his early twenties, this would often happen after he had crawled home after a night in a woman's bed, or from a dance that he had attended until dawn.

Almost as soon as he had produced a male heir to the throne (Frenchwomen never got the right to become monarchs), Louis XV began to live a double life, respecting the more visible elements of palace etiquette but not letting it hamper his extra-curricular activities. Soon, rumours about his dissolute lifestyle began to circulate freely, especially because Louis was inadvertently creating a horde of gossipers who wanted to dish the dirt on him.

By reducing the number of courtiers at Versailles, and by loosening the stranglehold of daily rituals there, Louis XV might have seemed like a modernizer. But this was not the case. Perversely, whittling down the number of hangers-on at court only had the effect of making the elite more elite. In order to reduce the number rationally, Louis became stricter about the definition of nobility. To remain at court, aristocrats had to prove that their family had been of noble birth since 1400, and Louis ordered his official genealogists to write up registers of those who qualified. In doing so, he redefined the nobility as the old medieval knight class, the 'flower of France' – not that they had won themselves much glory at battles like Crécy and Agincourt.

The cut-off date of 1400 was even stricter than that required by French tradition. It was in 1604 under the pragmatic Henri IV that the so-called *noblesse de robe* (nobility of the gown) had been created, officializing the status of men ennobled when taking on a public post, usually as a judge or state administrator. In return for their promotion and the right to pass on the job and its financial rewards to their heirs, these new nobles had to pay an annual fee to the King.

Members of the *noblesse de robe* were looked down upon by the older *noblesse d'épée* (nobility of the sword), who, as their name suggests, had usually been given titles after military service. In fact, by tradition, officer rank in the army was only open to members of the *noblesse d'épée*.

But Louis XV went even further, limiting his courtiers to the even older *noblesse d'ancienne extraction*, whose titles were so ancient that no one really knew why they were noble unless they bore the name of a battle.

Aristocrats were accustomed to being listed and defined – decades earlier, Louis XIV had ordered a register to be drawn up, though all he wanted to do was to cut out tax evasion by families falsely claiming to be noble, and he didn't care when a dynasty had earned or bought its title.

Now, however, Louis XV was ordering his genealogists to give a royal slap in the face to men who had won battles for Louis XIV, as well as those who had simply been filling the royal coffers by paying the annual subscription for their job title since 1604. It was a stark message to anyone with social ambitions – know your place – and it came at exactly the wrong time for the monarchy, which needed to broaden its support, not set the ambitious, rising classes against it.

It was also a warning to the country's administrators, who felt entitled to their highly lucrative jobs, that the monarchy felt no innate solidarity towards them. They would have to stand up to the royal family if they wanted to hold on to their money, status and power. And this was exactly what they did in 1749, when Louis XV tried to introduce a 5 per cent income tax on the clergy and the aristocracy, who had previously been exempt from taxes. The provincial parliaments (which were controlled by the local nobility) and the clergy encouraged riots against the reform, and Louis was forced to back down.

The lesson was clear: it was possible for the privileged classes to beat off the King's attempts to introduce even a small measure of social equality. But the full repercussions of this defeat would not be felt until the last few years of Louis XV's reign. For the moment, there was a shaky, top-heavy, status quo.

II

Amongst the *noblesse* at court, the climate of snobbery became so intense that it began to permeate the language. Like British MPs referring to the House of Commons as 'this place' or actors refusing to name the Scottish play, courtiers would never mention the name of Versailles, preferring to call it *'ce pays-ci'* ('this country'). Anyone using the V-word was looked down on as an outsider.

Champagne was not referred to by the truly chic as champagne – it had to be called *vin de Champagne*. Even coins got new names (appropriately, given the trauma that the currency had just gone through) and a *louis d'or* was known to courtiers as a *'louis en or'*. Pronunciations changed, too – it became vulgar to pronounce the last syllables of some words – *sac* (bag), for example, became *sa*. It was all getting too effete for words.

Of course, if someone was beautiful or brilliant, he or she could break through the firewall of snobbery. This was especially true of women who wanted to sleep with Louis XV. Most famous of these was his long-term official mistress, Madame de Pompadour, the daughter of a government bureaucrat who had been forced to abandon his family and go into exile after being accused of selling black-market food during a minor famine in 1725. Unfortunately for his daughter, his faults went even deeper than his conscience – his surname was Poisson. The future lover of Louis XV was born Jeanne-Antoinette Fish.

In a fairly typical French story, Jeanne-Antoinette was rumoured to be the illegitimate daughter of her mother's lover, a vastly wealthy royal tax collector called Charles François Paul Le Normant de Tournehem, who married off the young, good-looking Jeanne-Antoinette to his nephew. Now head of a rich household, she began to host literary *salons* in Paris and to act in theatrical *soirées* at her husband's nearby château – which happened to be in a royal hunting forest.

Louis XV had preserved the royal tradition of hunting almost every day except Sunday, and was a regular visitor to his forests all around Paris. Whenever he travelled out to the woodland near Jeanne-Antoinette's château, she would go for a carriage ride in the grounds and pop out from behind a tree as the King rode by.

She was careful to dress in bright colours, usually blue and pink, but even without the bright colours, Jeanne-Antoinette's charms were highly noticeable: one of Louis XV's huntsmen wrote that she was 'svelte, relaxed, supple and elegant', and had 'a perfectly formed nose, a charming mouth, very beautiful teeth, the most delicious smile' and eyes that 'lent themselves to all types of seduction'.

This attention-seeking wasn't only Jeanne-Antoinette's idea. Her uncle-in-law (and possible biological father) was anxious to restore the reputation of some financier friends of his who had been disgraced during the John Law fiasco (see above, Chapter 3). This band of old bankers therefore decided that the svelte and supple young Jeanne-Antoinette would become Louis XV's mistress. Jeanne-Antoinette was delighted. Her husband, who was apparently very much in love with his vivacious wife, had no say in the matter.

At last, during one of her gawdy apparitions, Louis noticed her, and sent her a deer that he had hunted. At the time, it was considered an honour to receive a large bloody animal carcass from an admirer. As we saw earlier, Louis XIV was liberal with gifts of dead birds.

In February 1745, Jeanne-Antoinette, now known by her married name, Madame d'Étiolles, was invited to a masked ball celebrating the wedding between Louis XV's son and a Spanish princess. Jeanne-Antoinette was disguised as Diana the huntress, and quickly ensnared a certain male yew tree who apparently invited her to climb into his branches. Soon afterwards, her marriage was annulled and she was living on the second floor of the palace of Versailles, just above the King's own apartments, the two sets of rooms linked by a 'secret' staircase.

This adultery was all very open because by now the mother of Louis XV's children, Marie, had decided that ten pregnancies were enough, and had given up her place in his bed to young pretenders. She had withdrawn into a life of prayer, etiquette and charitable good works that would endear her to the people long after Louis XV had ruined his own, and the Crown's, reputation.

The arrival of a black marketeer's daughter as official mistress to the King was a bourgeois bombshell to his snobbish courtiers. As well as being low-born, she spoke vulgar French, and never mastered the courtiers' jargon or refined accent. Luckily for the gossips, her maiden name, Poisson, was a gift. In Paris, street singers began to entertain the crowds with satirical songs about her, nicknamed *'poissonades'*. One of these compared her to a fishwife:

> *Si la cour se ravale,*
> *De quoi s'étonne-t-on?*
> *N'est-ce pas de la Halle*
> *Que nous vient le Poisson?*

> (If the tone at court is being lowered,
> Why is anyone surprised?
> Isn't it from the market hall
> That we get fish?)

Another songster was even more brutal, calling her *'une bâtarde de catin'* – 'a bastard slut'. Perhaps it was this bitchiness that encouraged the King to compensate by lavishing gifts – and a title – on his common-born mistress. In June 1745 he made her a *marquise* by buying her the estate and associated noble title of Pompadour in central France.[1] A year later, he bought her another château at Crécy just outside Paris – she had it completely renovated, with frescoes by the country's most fashionable artist, François Boucher, and rebuilt the nearby village to make it look more picturesque. Louis XV even gave her six hectares of the royal grounds at Versailles and had a 'hermitage' built for her so that she could escape the sneers of his courtiers. (Of this refuge, more later.)

Despite being a *bourgeoise* interloper with no real right to be at court, Jeanne-Antoinette, now officially known as Madame de Pompadour, came to dominate her royal lover's life. He was prone to sudden mood swings, and if a minister or advisor began to depress the King with bad news or a request for complicated advice, she would order the public servant out of the room and turn the conversation to frivolities. And Louis would acquiesce.

His increasing indifference about protocol (ironic after his initial insistence on having only the most noble of nobles at court) became so bad that even royals could be insulted with no comeback. At a supper in 1745, the Princesse de Conti, a granddaughter of Louis XIV, went into a dining room to find that there were no seats available. No one stood up to let her sit down, and she stormed out, saying that she had never seen *'des gens si malhonnêtes'* ('such ill-bred people').

Thanks to jealous aristocratic gossips and satirical songs, this kind of behaviour became public knowledge, and the general perception was that Louis XV was losing control of his own palace – and all because he was thinking with his trousers.

---

[1] After Jeanne-Antoinette's death in 1760, Louis XV took back the château at Pompadour and, rather appropriately, turned it into a horse stud.

III

By 1752, Jeanne-Antoinette's charms were no longer enough to enthral her royal lover, but she was determined not to lose her privileged place at the palace. She therefore set herself up as his procurer. With the aid of the King's head valet, Dominique Lebel, she began to provide the middle-aged monarch with an inexhaustible supply of sexual entertainment.

For Jeanne-Antoinette, the vital thing was that none of the girls should replace her as official mistress, so they had to be vetted. No witty, intelligent, over-ambitious beauties would be allowed in the King's bed. They had to be simple sex objects – and preferably far too young to be seen with Louis in public. Because of their reduced status, and age, they were known as the King's *petites maîtresses* – little mistresses.

As a venue for the vetting, Jeanne-Antoinette installed a sort of brothel-antechamber in the so-called 'Parc-aux-Cerfs' ('Deer Park') area of Versailles – an apt name given that she had met the King during a deer hunt, and then dressed up as a huntress to snare him. Here, prostitutes from Paris would be checked over for signs of excess intelligence or ambition (and presumably disease), before being smuggled into the King's bedroom as his after-dinner treat.

The most famous of these was Marie-Louise O'Murphy, who in 1752 was immortalized lying naked on a divan by the painter François Boucher, her pink buttocks and smooth thighs splayed, apparently just before or after a visit from a lover. Casanova was a huge fan of the painting, and said of it that: 'The skilful artist painted her legs and her thighs so that the eye could not help desiring to see more.' Louis XV seems to have agreed wholeheartedly with Casanova (on more things than art).

Mademoiselle O'Murphy was a fairly typical visitor to the Parc-aux-Cerfs. She was the daughter of a petty criminal and a prostitute, both of Irish immigrant stock, and a sister to three prostitutes who had once followed the French army to Flanders. She was only one of many young girls who modelled for Boucher, a painter known as a supplier of mild pornography to the art-loving aristocracy.

Casanova boasted that he had shown Boucher's painting to Louis XV, who then asked to see the model in the flesh, but in fact a copy of the picture belonged to Jeanne-Antoinette's brother, a more likely source of female company for the King. In any case, on the strength of her portrait, young Marie-Louise was taken out to the Parc-aux-Cerfs and became a regular visitor there between 1752 and 1755. She gave birth to a daughter, almost certainly Louis XV's child, in 1754, when she was just 16.

It is easy to imagine the jaded King looking forward to his nightly amusements – and his subjects did a lot of imagining. Louis XV was widely perceived as a man who expended all his energies on these dalliances, forgetting his duty and pulling the monarchy down to unprecedented levels of depravity.

The song quoted above making fun of Jeanne-Antoinette's maiden name contains some lines about this royal negligence:

> *Jadis c'était Versailles*
> *Qui donnait le bon goût;*
> *Aujourd'hui la canaille*
> *Règne, tient le haut bout.*

> (Once it was Versailles that
> Set standards of good taste;
> Today it is the riff-raff
> Who reign, who have the upper hand.)

Another song gave a detailed criticism of the whole of Louis XV's government and all his policies at home and abroad. It had a refrain that went:

> *Ah le voilà, ah le voici,*
> *Celui qui n'en a nul souci.*

(There he is, here he is,
The man without a care in the world.)

The song showed that Louis XV was increasingly seen as a worthless king who fiddled with his mistresses while France burned.

In the past, people had baulked at, or even rebelled against, Louis XIV's taxes, and disapproved of some of his excesses, but they had never looked down on him. This scorn for a king was a royal novelty – and a dangerous one.

IV

Louis XV's negligence was also having a visible impact on Versailles. Courtiers with rooms in the palace took to throwing their rubbish out of the window into the park. One of the biggest fountains in the grounds, the bassin de Neptune, built by Louis XIV's great architect Le Nôtre, was used as a dump by the kitchen staff. An ornamental lake, the pièce d'eau des Suisses, was turned into a laundry.

Thieves would steal lead from the massive network of water pipes that criss-crossed the gardens, vandals would break statues, and courtiers were not safe from common criminals entering the château itself – it was a far cry from the days when the aristocrats could be sure that the hand picking their pocket would be neatly manicured.

This climate of *laissez-faire* almost cost Louis XV his life.

In the early evening of 5 January 1757, the King came down a stairway lined with his guards, on his way out of the palace of Versailles. He was about to climb aboard a carriage when a man sprang out of the shadows and tapped him on the shoulder. When Louis didn't turn round, the attacker stabbed him in the side with an eight-centimetre blade. Bleeding profusely, the King was led back up the stairs, asking his attendants, 'Why would anyone want to kill me? I've never hurt anyone.' In his bedroom, he declared that he was about to die, and then passed out.

As was the custom at the time, a surgeon did his best to help the wounded King on his way off this mortal coil by bleeding him further, but luckily for Louis, he regained consciousness during the treatment, and had the strength to tell his wife Marie: '*Je suis assassiné*' ('I am murdered') – perhaps a reference to the surgeon.

Meanwhile, the attacker had been seized by the guards. Robert-François Damiens was a 41-year-old former valet at a Jesuit school, a job he had lost when he broke the vow of celibacy, who had thereafter worked as a servant in the homes of some of Louis XV's most virulent opponents in the *noblesse de robe*.

Damiens had rented a sword and hat to make himself look noble, and entered the palace along with other people seeking a royal audience. He had then awaited his chance to push through the line of guards, and stabbed Louis.

The King's assailant was taken to the Bastille and tortured, and swore first that he had accomplices, and then that he had acted alone. It was assumed that he had been sent either by a faction of the clergy or by the parliamentarians whom Louis was still trying to tax. According to Louis XV's Foreign Secretary, the Marquis d'Argenson, Damiens showed no remorse at all, and told his interrogators that 'the King governed badly, and it would have been a great service to the country to kill him.'

Louis XV initially called for mercy for his attacker, but then issued a statement which must have sounded ironic coming from such an unpopular king: 'Our people, to whom our life belongs as much as it does to ourselves, demand vengeance for the crime against the life that we desire to preserve for the sake of their happiness.'

Damiens was duly tried and sentenced to the punishment dished out to regicides (even those who didn't manage to kill a king): he was to be torn into four pieces by horses after a whole list of barbarous public tortures. Hearing the sentence, Damiens quipped, 'It's going to be a rough day.'

On 28 March, Damiens was taken to the place de Grève in Paris (now the place de l'Hôtel-de-Ville). On a scaffold, in front of a horrified crowd, with pincers attached to his nipples, arms and legs, he had molten lead, boiling oil, hot resin and sulphur poured on him, and his right hand burnt off, before being attached to four horses and slowly dismembered. It took over two hours and he didn't die until all four limbs had been pulled off. The crowd, usually bloodthirsty at executions, booed the 16 executioners, who themselves were horrified by what they were forced to do.[2]

As for Louis XV, he was quickly back on his feet. The wound was not deep, but he told his entourage that 'it is deeper than you think – it strikes at my very heart.'

What he meant, of course, was that he took the attack as a sign that the people didn't love him. In this, he was right. The Marquis d'Argenson wrote that: 'It was noticed in Paris that the good bourgeois expressed a lot of pain at this attack [on the King], but the lower classes stayed mute.' There were constant fears of another attempt on the King's life or that of his heir, and Argenson predicted that: 'In the end our fearful princes will have to live like tyrants, constantly distrusting the French people.'

They ought to have heeded his warning.

V

It wasn't only Louis XV's sexual antics that turned the people against him. He had quickly forgotten old Cardinal de Fleury's calls for austerity, and embarked on some wild spending.

As well as giving lavish parties and balls, he would organize huge celebrations for any family occasion, like the masked ball for his son's wedding where he had picked up Jeanne-Antoinette – and as we have already seen, he spent a fortune on land and

---

[2] Damiens was the last man to be executed in this way – the next people to commit regicide would be congratulated by the state.

houses for her. Similarly, when he decided that he no longer wanted to see his *petite maîtresse* O'Murphy after three years of regular service, he gave the teenager a parting gift of 200,000 *livres* – ten times the annual salary that Fleury had received as Minister of State. Louis XV's priorities were clear – three years of sex was worth ten of government.

To celebrate the birth of one of his grandsons in 1751, Louis XV commissioned a firework display at Versailles costing an almost obscene 664,000 *livres*. If this wasn't costly enough, a stray rocket fell on the roof of the stables, causing damage that cost 157,599 *livres* to repair.

After several mainly peaceful years under the influence of Fleury, Louis XV also got France embroiled in costly wars.

He intervened in the Austrian War of Succession, which was mainly an excuse for the whole of Europe to take sides and fight for supremacy. Typically, Louis XV supported the armies who wanted to stop a woman, Maria Theresa,[3] becoming ruler of Austria on the grounds that females should not aspire to such high rank. She won, and became Archduchess of Austria and Queen of Hungary.

This war opposed France with Britain, Austria, Holland and Russia, amongst others, and forced Louis to lay out huge sums of money on his army and navy. His troops enjoyed some success – memorably (in French minds, at least) beating the British at the Battle of Fontenoy in 1745 – but he inexplicably gave away almost all his territorial gains in the subsequent peace treaty in 1748, prompting the furious French to complain that the war had all been for nothing. They coined a new idiom: *'bête comme la paix'*, 'as stupid as peace'. Though they would soon come to regret that.

The only compensation for Louis XV was that in 1744, on his way to join his army in the east of France, he had fallen ill with dysentery and almost died, at which point his more patriotic

---

[3] This was the mother of Marie-Antoinette, whom Louis XV would later choose as the wife of his grandson and heir, the future Louis XVI.

subjects had prayed for him, and dubbed him 'Louis le Bien-Aimé' – 'Louis the Well-Loved'. It was a name that he would vainly try to cling on to for the next 30 years.

The unresolved issues from the Austrian War of Succession were largely to blame for the next great conflict, the Seven Years War of 1756–63, during which Britain and France again went toe-to-toe, along with most of the rest of Europe, resulting in a massive cost in lives, money and territory. This time France was amongst the biggest losers, and ended up handing over some of its most prestigious colonies to Britain, including all but a corner of Canada, all its American colonies east of the Mississippi, Pondicherry (its main trading post in India) and several of its Caribbean islands.[4]

These territorial losses robbed France of essential earnings from its colonies, which it desperately needed to pay off the cost of war. Louis XV borrowed money as well as imposing two waves of the *vingtième* (twentieth), the 5 per cent tax that had caused a rebellion amongst the previously tax exempt in 1749. This time, the *noblesse de robe* let the tax measure through, perhaps because they realized that the nation really did need the money, so that between 1756 and 1763 income tax on all sections of the population tripled.

Losing wars and tripling income tax have never helped any leader's popularity ratings, and Louis XV was no exception.

[4] For more details on France's humiliations – and Britain's ethnic cleansing of French colonies – during the Seven Years War, see *1000 Years of Annoying the French*.

Chapter 5

A GLIMMER OF ENLIGHTENMENT

'Aucun homme n'a reçu de la nature le droit de commander les autres.'
'No man has received from Nature the right to command others.'
Denis Diderot (1713–84), French philosopher and writer,
in his *Encyclopédie*, published between 1751 and 1772

I

While the monarchy was edging its way towards the guillotine, some truly positive things were happening in France. Louis XV's reign saw huge advances in the sciences, and the emergence of some of the greatest writers in the French language. This was the siècle des Lumières – the Age of Enlightenment.

Cartography was one of Louis XV's favourite sciences, and he commissioned a 180-page map of France, the most accurate ever produced, from the cartographer César-François Cassini, an undertaking that took some 30 years to complete. Cassini and his son began by triangulating the coast and the main transport routes of France; then the rest of the country was filled in over a period of some 60 years by the succeeding generations of the Cassini family. The result was astonishingly accurate, and a real scientific triumph for France.

Initially, Louis XV had promised to payroll the whole project, and even when he ran out of cash during the Seven Years War, he helped Cassini to set up a private company financed by subscribers (one of the first among them being the official royal mistress, Jeanne-Antoinette de Pompadour). Louis also gave Cassini the rights to sell the maps – all in all, he was behaving like a royal patron at his productive best.

On a similarly geographical theme, Louis XV was also a supporter of the navigator Louis-Antoine de Bougainville, who fought in the unsuccessful French campaign to hang on to Canada and then sailed around the world, setting up the first colony in the Falkland Islands (which were quickly snatched from him by the Spanish).

In 1766 Louis XV entrusted Bougainville with a mission to (amongst other things) explore the Pacific Ocean looking for 'valuable metals and spices', to 'examine the lands, trees and main productions; bring back samples and drawings of everything he [Bougainville] considers noteworthy' and 'note as many places as possible that might serve as stop-overs for ships … and anything that might be useful for navigation'. In essence, Louis XV wanted to know everything about the vast expanse of ocean between the west coast of the Americas and the east of Africa.

Bougainville fulfilled his mission. The navigator and his team discovered new plant species (including the flower that would bear Bougainville's name), mapped countless useful atolls, and even inadvertently gave France the honour of providing the first female circumnavigator of the globe. After several months at sea, Bougainville discovered that one of his deckhands, Jean Bart, was actually a woman, the lover of the expedition's botanist. She was put ashore in Mauritius, but had already sailed around the world.

During his various missions to the South Seas, Bougainville was a serious rival to the Englishman James Cook, who was so keen to destroy the Frenchman's reputation that he blamed French sailors for tarnishing the earthly paradise of Tahiti by giving the grass-skirted girls syphilis. But when Bougainville published his *Voyage autour du monde* (*Voyage around the World*) in 1771, no one gave a thought to sexually transmitted diseases. The whole of Europe was fascinated by his depiction of *'le paradis polynésien'* and its scantily clad maidens whose families thought it polite to let the visiting sailors enjoy unlimited casual sex.[1]

Louis XV was also a keen follower of developments in watch-making, which was of course a vital part of the developing science of navigation. At the time, even the best watches were only accurate to about half an hour. Not a great problem in a world quiet enough for several reliable church clocks to be within earshot of any town-dweller, but still something of an embarrassment for what was meant to be a precision science.

Louis gave patronage to several of the best watchmakers in Europe, paying them generous salaries as royal *horlogiers* (clock-makers) and attracting some of the most skilled craftsmen on the continent to Paris. One of these was the Swiss-born Ferdinand Berthoud, who came to France in 1745. In 1761 he began building his first marine chronometer to aid the calcula-tion of longitude. At the same time, a Paris-born clockmaker, Pierre Le Roy, made several advancements in clock mecha-nisms, including a vital invention that would stop marine chro-nometers becoming unreliable as temperatures changed during long voyages, causing the metal parts to expand and contract.

Louis XV ordered tests of these French discoveries aboard navy ships, enabling France to lead the field for several years – or at least to keep abreast of their rivals, the British, who, with typical pragmatism, were borrowing the French technology and making it more practical.

However, Louis XV's interest in clockmaking was by no means completely scientific. He also loved watches as jewels,

[1] Louis XV must have thought that, at last, someone had provided scien-tific proof that his ideal social model was natural.

and was just as excited by advances in watch miniaturization as he was in measuring longitude. When a young watchmaker called Pierre-Augustin Caron[2] published a paper on making almost flat watches (embossed with plenty of jewels, of course), Louis XV invited him to court and commissioned a miniature timepiece for his mistress, Jeanne-Antoinette de Pompadour. The resulting watch was just one centimetre in diameter and set on top of a ring. It was wound up by turning the bezel (head) of the ring, and set using a tiny key.

As well as being an impressive piece of diamond-encrusted bling, the watch was an almost miraculous work of precision engineering, the equivalent at the time of shrinking mobile phones from bricks to credit-card holders in the 1990s (though of course they have since expanded again into slices of toast). The existence of such a small, accurate watch made France a world leader in sophistication, a place where technology and beauty could be combined to create modern miracles. (But only, of course, if you were very, very rich.)

Botany was another of Louis XV's passions. Admittedly this was encouraged in him by Jeanne-Antoinette de Pompadour when he stopped sleeping with her – she thought he needed a hobby. But Louis threw himself into botany with almost the same energy that he was devoting to having sex with young prostitutes, and from 1759 to 1774, he supervised and funded the creation of a botanical garden at Versailles containing around 4,000 species – the biggest in Europe. (The British didn't start developing Kew Gardens until the 1770s.)

He commissioned open-air plantations, tropical greenhouses and even a canal for aquatic species, and put together a team of botanists who were sent on plant-gathering expeditions to Africa, Asia Minor, Mexico and throughout Europe (including

---

[2] Caron would later buy an aristocratic title, de Beaumarchais, before falling out with the establishment and taking revenge in two satirical plays, *The Barber of Seville* and *The Marriage of Figaro*. See Chapter 10.

of course those accompanying Bougainville to the Pacific). They brought back little-known plants like coffee, pineapples and cherries, as well as collecting and protecting rare species from all over France, including every variety of native strawberry.

The Versailles botanists, headed by a modest man called Bernard de Jussieu who invented a new way of classifying flowering plants but didn't bother to publish it, also carried out important experiments to improve food crops, discovering that potatoes grown by the Germans were more efficient than French varieties (*quelle surprise*), and developing cures for cereal diseases in an attempt to ward off France's frequent famines.

It was a noble scientific enterprise that couldn't possibly have a downside – except in Louis XV's hands. Typically, he managed to create one critical flaw, albeit accidentally and posthumously.

The new buildings around his botanical garden included the aforementioned 'hermitage' intended for his mistress, Jeanne-Antoinette. It was a square construction with sides of 23 metres that contained 'only' about 20 main rooms, as well as kitchens, bathrooms and a warren of tiny servants' bedrooms. A bijou cottage by Versailles standards. But this was the Petit Trianon that would later be converted by Marie-Antoinette into a fantasy farm where she would gambol with lambs and pretend to be a peasant – a piece of role pay that would disgust the French public and knock one of the final nails into the royal family's coffin.

II

Under Louis XV's patronage, France also created the greatest compendium of knowledge in the western world, Denis Diderot's *Encyclopédie*,[3] *ou Dictionnaire raisonné des sciences, des*

---

[3] The word 'encyclopaedia' was invented in the sixteenth century, and means something like 'well-rounded education'. It was a neat example of an abbreviation, a combination of the ancient Greek words for 'circular' and 'child-rearing', *enkyklios* and *paideia*.

arts et des métiers (a *métier* is a trade or craft), published in Paris in instalments between 1751 and 1772. The first volume features a dedication in capital letters: 'Avec Approbation et Privilège du Roi' – 'with the King's approval and favour'.

Initially intended as a translation of the *Cyclopaedia*, published in two volumes in 1728 by the English writer Ephraim Chambers, the French editor/publisher Diderot expanded the work into a 35-volume megalith, including 12 volumes of illustrations. Diderot commissioned 68,000 entries from about 160 contributors, as well as writing some himself.

Given the huge scope of the work, Diderot stooped to a fair amount of plagiarism from existing scientific books, and stole whole volumes of illustrations. He admitted that some of the entries were 'weak, mediocre and even outright bad', but his priority was to get this wealth of knowledge and opinion into the public arena. The result was the most complete description of the known universe that had ever been attempted, starting with a five-page essay on the uses of the letter A in the French language and ending with a description of Zzuéné, a city in ancient Egypt.

The *Encyclopédie* included entries on all aspects of the sciences, on geography, the arts and language, as well as opinion pieces on religion, war, slavery (especially the need to abolish it, at a time when France was battling to hold on to its Caribbean sugar plantations) – and on politics.

The most telling of these political essays is probably the one-page entry on 'monarchy', on page 636 of volume 10 ('*Mame-Mz*'). It starts out neutrally enough, giving a factual description of a regime in which 'sovereign power ... resides indivisibly in one man called a king, monarch or emperor'. It is interesting to see that these 'modern' French thinkers discounted influential monarchs like Elizabeth I of England, Mary, Queen of Scots (who was half-French) and especially Catherine the Great, who had been on the Russian throne for three years in 1765 when this volume was published. In the 1750s, supposedly the most enlightened men in France had not seen the light about the equality of the sexes.

After the simple definition of monarchy, the description gets more controversial, and the author ('D. J.', alias Louis de Jaucourt, who wrote almost a quarter of the whole *Encyclopédie*) declares that: 'Unlike a republic, a monarchy is not based on principles of good morality' (an obvious dig at Louis XV's failings). A monarchy is a self-serving regime, he continues, because 'the virtues shown are less about one's duty to others than one's duty to oneself' – a startlingly modern version of John F. Kennedy's famous 'ask not what your country can do for you'.

Then comes a lucid breakdown of how power was exercised by the absolutist French monarchy:

> Since it is only from the monarch that one may receive wealth, honours and rewards, the desire to deserve them sustains the throne ... If the monarch is virtuous, and dispenses rewards and punishments justly, everyone is keen to deserve his bounty, and his reign is a golden age. If the monarch is not virtuous ... it degenerates into baseness and slavery.

D. J. goes on, helpfully, to list different ways in which a monarchy can fall: if public servants are showing misplaced loyalty to the King rather than to the country; if a monarch tries to intimidate his people, or encourages them to have children just to provide more taxpayers; or even if the King becomes too frivolous – another below-the-belt stab at Louis XV.

The timing of volume 10's publication was a stroke of incredible luck. In the month it appeared, December 1765, the heir to the throne, Louis XV's son Louis Ferdinand, died prematurely, leaving Louis XV's 11-year-old grandson to be groomed as the future Louis XVI. The *Encyclopédie*'s definition of monarchy ends with a warning:

> Someone will tell the subjects of a monarchy on the brink of falling: 'A prince is born to you who will restore it [the

monarchy] in all its glory. Nature has blessed this successor with a wealth of virtues and qualities that will delight you; you just have to assist him in their development.' Alas! People, I fear that the hopes you are given will be disappointed. Monsters will choke this beautiful flower at its birth; their poisonous breath will extinguish the goodness from this heir to the throne ... They will fill his soul with errors, prejudice and superstition ... They will infect this tender shoot with the spirit of domination that possesses them. These are the main causes of the decadence and fall of the most flourishing monarchies.

In short, D. J. was telling his readers not to believe all the hype when a fresh face comes to the throne – the subtext being 'look what became of the infant Louis XV'. If Diderot and his fellow authors had simply picked up volume 10 and hit Louis XV over the head, they couldn't have been more provocative.

After this swipe at the crown, one might have expected the entry for *'Révolution'* to say something along the lines of 'meet you all outside the Bastille on 14 July', but it is decidedly muted. It even states that Cromwell's takeover in Britain had 'no valid religious pretext' – so the *Encyclopédie* seems to have taken the orthodox French Catholic line.

Similarly, at *'République'* (also signed 'D. J.'), there are stark warnings about abuses of power even after a monarchy has fallen. If a republic is too big, he warns, an over-powerful governing body can 'ravage the state' and 'destroy each citizen with its demands'. 'There are great fortunes and therefore no moderation,' he adds, and 'the common good is sacrificed to a thousand vested interests.'

D. J. prefers small, Greek-style city republics where the leaders are a close-knit community and have to respect the wishes of their fellow citizens. Perhaps he thought that the French monarchy might be replaced by the republics of Paris, Lyon, Bordeaux, Strasbourg and Marseille, with more rural versions in places like Brittany and Normandy. If so, he was something of a prophet, because one result of the French Revolution would be the division of the country into its *départements*, each with its own *président*. The difference he didn't foresee was that once a French republic was firmly established, it would retain a monarch-style national president who lives in a palace and looks down with regal detachment on the plebs below.

Overall, the *Encyclopédie* was the biggest stage on which the philosophers commonly known as the 'Lumières' analysed their world, both through a definition of abstract ideas and a detailed examination of history – and one thing that their reasoning condemned was the abuse of power and privilege under Louis XV. Of course they could not say this outright. They knew that the royal and religious censors would study any entries likely to be controversial. Sometimes Diderot tried to bamboozle the censors by making criticisms under an apparently neutral entry. For example, the *Encyclopédie* gives a factual treatment to France's Franciscan monks (the *'Cordeliers'*), but mocks them savagely at the entry for *'Capuchon'* (hood), making fun of a 100-year schism in the order over the shape of their hoods.

Chief amongst the censors was the Church, which rightly felt itself under attack. After all, it had long been opposed to scientific explanations for apparently divine phenomena. Only a century earlier, Galileo had been tried by the Inquisition and forced to recant his heretical theory that the Earth revolved around the Sun.

Riffling suspiciously through the *Encyclopédie*, the French clergy was furious to see a reminder under *'Église'* (Church) that 'Jesus Christ founded the Church in a state of poverty', compared to the modern Catholic Church's wealth of land and money. The *Encyclopédie* also criticized the idea of imposing any punishment other than excommunication for heresy, thereby undermining centuries of burnings and only slightly less fatal forms of torture.

It was perhaps not surprising that Diderot's great work was anti-establishment. In 1749, after starting work on the *Encyclopédie*, he was arrested and imprisoned for three months in the château de Vincennes, to the east of Paris. This was where Louis XV had spent the first few months waiting to accede to the throne, but the conditions of Diderot's confinement were less luxurious. He was charged with 'impiety', based on sections of his book *Lettres sur les aveugles à l'usage de ceux qui voyent* (*Letters on the Blind, Intended for Those Who Can See*) in which he discussed perception and the need to question everything around us, including religious faith. At one point his book suggests that it is just as absurd to accept the Christian view of the universe as it is to mock a pagan for believing that the world is held up by an elephant standing on a tortoise's back[4] – not the kind of argument that went down well with eighteenth-century French bishops. Eventually, Diderot was only released from his cell after intense lobbying by booksellers and aristocratic bibliophiles.

As soon as the first two volumes of the *Encyclopédie* were published, the clergymen whispering in the King's ear about morality convinced him and his Council of State to ban the books as an attack on religion. The ban was soon lifted, though, and the volumes continued to appear at a rate of about one per year, with the bigots combing each new publication for outright heresy or political subversion.

In 1757, they saw their chance. Louis XV had been severely shaken by the attempt on his life (see above, Chapter 4), and was afraid of troublemakers. Despite his sympathy for the sciences, he was willing to listen to accusations that the *Encyclopédie* was fomenting instability. The would-be assassin Damiens had been caught with an unusual amount of cash in his pocket (one *louis* – not a fortune, but a suspicious sum for an out-of-work servant), and it was easy to allege that he had been paid by subversive, irreligious elements. Royal approval for the *Encyclopédie* was therefore withdrawn and Pope Clement XIII listed the book in

---

[4] Diderot was writing more than two centuries before Terry Pratchett would invent his Discworld, perched on the back of four elephants who are standing on a turtle.

the Church's official *Index Librorum Prohibitorum*, alongside such great names as Copernicus, Erasmus and Martin Luther.[5]

From then on, volumes of the *Encyclopédie* were published under a Swiss banner, even though Louis XV's royal printer, André le Breton, was producing them in Paris, where they were widely available under the counter. This was not unusual. In the eighteenth century, there was a huge market for seditious books in France, where dangerous ideas were the equivalent of Swedish films in 1950s England, or rock music in the Soviet bloc.

Combining the new taste for science with a growing desire for anti-establishment satire, the *Encyclopédie* was a huge success, selling around 24,000 copies, including pirate copies and abridged editions. From the 1750s onward, France was flooded with science-based sedition.

The *Encyclopédie* could have been a beacon for the world, calling attention to the enlightened, modern-thinking regime of Louis XV. But with the aid of his powerful religious advisors, Louis turned the authors against him, so that each new volume contained brilliantly argued denouncements of state-sanctioned bigotry and despotism. Instead of harnessing the power of the Lumières, the establishment had become their self-appointed victim.

III

Sadly for the monarchy, Louis XV's reign was also a golden age of satirical writing.

Charles Louis de Secondat, Baron de la Brède et de Montesquieu (usually known as Montesquieu to save breath and ink), had been writing satire while Louis XV was still a child. His *Lettres persanes* (*Persian Letters*), published in 1721, were critiques of France in the form of 161 postcards home from two supposedly naive Persian travellers. Alongside

[5] Authors later added to the *Index* include Gustave Flaubert, Charles Baudelaire, Victor Hugo and Graham Greene.

harmless caricatures of snobbish ways of dressing and speaking, and affectionate remarks about Frenchwomen, there were also vitriolic attacks on the monarchy and religious oppression. Unsurprisingly, the book had to be published anonymously and imported from Amsterdam.

Montesquieu's other great anti-establishment book was *De l'esprit des lois* (*On the Spirit of Laws*) published in 1748 – also anonymously – in Geneva and Amsterdam. It contains a carefully reasoned attack on absolutist monarchy and an idealistic defence of republicanism. It also lambasts any hypocritical Christian attempt to defend slavery, naively asking the reader why God would not have attributed a soul to black bodies as well as white. It even condemns Europeans for 'exterminating' Native Americans.

Not surprisingly, Montesquieu was given the accolade of being added to the Pope's *Index Librorum Prohibitorum* in 1751, but died soon afterwards. Even so, his books lived on, not least as lengthy quotations in the *Encyclopédie*'s political entries. And by the time the Revolution came, his ideas were being bandied about as established truths – though not all his pleas for benevolent, democratic rule would be listened to.

But probably the most famous of the subversive French thinkers snapping at Louis XV's heels was Voltaire – real name François-Marie Arouet. Voltaire was a member of the French establishment, the son of a man who collected the tax on spices, and who got rich on his commission. Voltaire was groomed to succeed his father in the lucrative job, but was barely out of his teens when he discovered that he could have a lot more fun showing off his acerbic wit in Paris's chic literary *salons*.

However, the young Voltaire chose the wrong butt for his jokes. Accused of writing an insulting poem about the Regent, Philippe d'Orléans, he was exiled to the provinces (a heinous punishment at the time). On his return to Paris, he repeated his offence, and, when arrested, complained to the police that the Regent deserved it: 'He exiled me because I let the public know that his daughter is a whore.' This earned him 11 months in the Bastille.

Members of well-to-do families were often sent to the Bastille – a nobleman could have anyone who annoyed him locked up simply by requesting a so-called *'lettre de cachet'* ('letter with the royal seal'). Sometimes, fathers would do this to protect their own wayward sons who were in danger of committing a capital crime like treason or sodomy. It was not exactly a bread-and-water, chained-to-the-dripping-walls imprisonment, but it was a humiliating exile from public life, and an abuse of power, and Voltaire's stay in the notorious prison turned him into a lifelong anti-authoritarian.

Still aged only 23, he dropped his family name Arouet, which sounded like *à rouer* – to be thrashed – or *un roué* – the nickname for an immoral crony of the Regent – and adopted the more modern-sounding Voltaire.

It didn't take the rebranded satirist long to get himself sent to the Bastille yet again. Enjoying real success with his plays, and becoming something of a star at the *salons*, the skinny, nakedly ambitious young wit began to get up the noses of Paris's aristocrats. One evening at dinner, Voltaire was delighting the company with his observations when a boorish nobleman butted in. This was Guy-Auguste de Rohan-Chabot, Chevalier de Rohan, Comte de Chabot (in those days, French aristocrats carried the whole of their family tree around with them in their names), who was known as a crooked moneylender. He asked who the loud commoner was.

Voltaire replied: 'He is a man who does not drag a great name about with him, but who honours the name he bears.' It was a neat slap in the face to the snobbish loan shark, who promptly had Voltaire beaten up by his servants, while Rohan himself looked on. When Voltaire boasted that he was taking fencing lessons in order to challenge the cowardly Rohan to a duel, the nobleman panicked and obtained a *lettre de cachet*. Voltaire was back at the Bastille for a month, then banished from France, unable to return without Louis XV's permission.

It was an exile that would cost the French monarchy dear.

It was 1726, and Voltaire crossed the Channel to England. Here, over the next three or four years, he was to write a book that, alongside the *Encyclopédie* (which Diderot was just starting to compile), would begin to eat away at the root of the monarchy as efficiently as the gangrene in Louis XIV's leg.

Hard as it is to believe, Voltaire found early-eighteenth-century England astonishingly democratic. This was a corrupt nation where MPs could get elected for life by buying enough land in a so-called 'pocket borough' (later more accurately dubbed a 'rotten borough'), a country where whole villages and their occupants belonged to the local squire, and whose capital city teemed with urban poor. But Voltaire was taken under the wing of a common-born merchant called Everard Falkener, who would later become Britain's ambassador to Turkey, a posting that would have been reserved for a nobleman under Louis XV's regime. Through Voltaire's fog-tinted lenses, Falkener became a symbol of British upward mobility. And with Everard's encouragement, Voltaire threw himself into the game of social advancement, bringing out a private edition of one of his plays, *Henriade*, about France's King Henri IV, and making himself a tidy profit of £2,000. Voltaire never lost this taste for gambling, investing and lending money to friends to start up business ventures, and would later go on debt-collecting tours around Europe.

In London, Voltaire met two of his literary heroes: Alexander Pope, author of the gently satirical *Rape of the Lock*, a poem in which a frivolous nobleman steals ('rapes') a lock of a society girl's hair; and the Anglo-Irish Jonathan Swift, whom Voltaire saw as a model of anti-establishment writing, not knowing perhaps that Swift's best-selling *Gulliver's Travels* had had its more seditious passages cut out by its publisher to avoid arrest.

In any case, Voltaire donned the mantle of the freethinking London satirist, and started writing what would become *Lettres écrites de Londres sur les Anglois[6] et autres sujets* (*Letters Written from London on the English and Other Subjects*).

---

[6] *Anglois* instead of *Anglais*. In eighteenth-century French word endings, '*ai*' was commonly written '*oi*'. Hence the French name François.

The book was, more or less, a series of love letters about Britain purportedly written to a French friend, in much the same vein as Montesquieu's *Lettres persanes*. Voltaire waxed lyrical about religious freedom in Britain at a time when the clergy still held France in the grip of its jewelled gloves. He took an overt swipe at hypocritical French clergymen: 'The priests here [in England] are almost all married. And the awkward manners they acquired at university, coupled with their limited contact with women, means that most bishops make do with their own wife.'

Voltaire praised the British tax system, which was based on income rather than social status, and the entrepreneurial spirit that allowed British businessmen to rise up in society alongside the aristocrats.

Worst of all from Louis XV's point of view, Voltaire took up Montesquieu's anti-absolutist banner, calling for the monarch's power to be reined in by an elected parliament:

> England is the only nation on Earth that has managed to limit the power of kings by resisting them, and has finally established a wise system of government in which the ruler is all-powerful when it comes to doing good, and has his hands tied if he attempts to do evil.

According to Voltaire, France needed a British-style monarchy. It was time for Louis XV's creaky defence of the ancient French status quo to end.

This was incendiary stuff, far more dangerous than a poem about the Regent's slutty daughter. Written in Voltaire's punchy, witty style, it was bound to capture the French imagination. The only thing that wasn't punchy was the long title, so Voltaire changed it to *Lettres philosophiques* – which was also pretty provocative given that at the time 'philosophical' was considered by the Church as the opposite of 'religious'.

In 1728, before he had finished writing the book, Voltaire was given leave to return to France. He decided it was wiser to sneak in, and entered the country disguised as an Englishman. While putting the final touches to his text and working out how to publish it without earning a return trip to the Bastille, he lay low for a few years and put together a rainy-day fund in case he needed to escape again.

Finally in 1734, *Lettres philosophiques* was published and, within days, confiscated copies were being burnt outside the Palais de Justice in Paris. The ban naturally guaranteed the book's success, and it was said that even illiterate people bought it just for the titillation of owning such forbidden literary fruit.

Voltaire had fully anticipated the scandal, and the book was published anonymously, mainly abroad. But his witty style was as recognizable as his opinions, and the police raided his Paris apartment in search of evidence against him. They found nothing conclusive, but under Louis XV no proof was necessary – all it took to get yourself thrown in the Bastille was to be annoying – so Voltaire found himself the target of yet another *lettre de cachet*, which he avoided by hiding out at the château of his lover, the mathematician Émilie du Châtelet, 250 kilometres away in far-flung eastern France.

No one came looking for him, but the authorities knew a dangerous enemy when they saw one, and Voltaire was destined to spend most of the rest of his life in exile from Paris, trying to redeem himself. Just a year after the publication of *Lettres philosophiques*, he signed a pledge avowing his 'complete submission to the religion of his fathers', and was told that he could return to Paris if he wanted – but that the *lettre de cachet* still stood, meaning that he might find himself being dragged out of bed by the police.

The risk was too great, and Louis XV never signed the pardon that would have allowed Voltaire to return to take his place in Europe's capital of freethinking. Even so, Voltaire kept up a barrage of books, letters and pamphlets defending his ideas, especially his hatred of religious intolerance. He made sure that, unlike the *Encyclopédie*, his texts were short and affordable. He even called one of them his *Portable Philosophical Dictionary* and wrote in the introduction that readers didn't need to plough through it all from A to Z – the idea was that 'anywhere one opens it, one will find food for thought'. He was the consummate communicator. If he were alive today he would be posting one-minute satirical rants on YouTube.

All in all, from the monarchy's point of view, Louis XV was probably wise to keep such a virulent critic at a distance. Voltaire would have to wait until 1778, and the more forgiving attitude of the young Louis XVI, before he could return to Paris. By then the 83-year-old writer was dying of prostate cancer, and had only a few months to live.

So it was a noble gesture on Louis XVI's part to allow such a living symbol of subversion to come home. Though, as we shall see, giving apparent royal approval to hard-hitting satire was something that the monarchy would come to regret.

IV

Other writers of the period also deserve a mention here, all of whom would have claimed that they wrote to demand drastic reform, if not outright revolution, and that they wanted to free France of religious bigotry and censorship.

These include Jean-Jacques Rousseau, whose theory that nature was in essence good, and that uneducated peasants were therefore inherently noble, would be dramatically disproved when roving bands of the rural poor started tearing aristocrats limb from limb during the Revolution.

However, far more interesting in terms of their impact on the monarchy were Sade and Beaumarchais – the first an outlaw and pornographer, the second a satirist and sometime courtier at Versailles: two very different men who had an equally damaging effect on Louis XV's reputation.

To his fans, the Marquis de Sade was a resistance fighter against sexual repression and literary censorship. To the modern legal system, he would be a paedophile, kidnapper, rapist and murderer who boasted about his exploits in print. But more than anything, Sade was a logical product of Louis XV's regime – an amoral aristocrat who thought he could live out his deranged sexual fantasies with total impunity because of his social position. The regime censored him, but only in the way that a factory owner might try to cover up evidence that he was polluting the water table.

Donatien Alphonse François de Sade came from a noble family that could trace its title back to the thirteenth century. He was born in 1740, in one of the biggest palaces in Paris, the hôtel de Condé, home of the Prince de Condé, who was a grandson of Louis XIV via a royal mistress. Sade's mother was a lady-in-waiting to the Prince's wife.

The infant *marquis* (the title given to the son of a count)[7] therefore grew up at the heart of the French establishment. In his novel *Aline et Valcour* (a comparison between a cannibalistic African nation and a South Sea paradise), Sade later admitted that all this 'luxury and abundance' had made him feel superior as a child, so that he became 'haughty, despotic and irascible' – though why he needed to confess this is not clear, because such sentiments were absolutely normal for someone of his class.

At 14 Sade joined the King's light cavalry, whose officers all came from France's oldest noble families, before transferring to a regiment nominally headed by the infant brother of Louis XVI, Louis Stanislas, the future King Louis XVIII (the puppet monarch who would be placed on the throne after the fall of Napoleon in 1814). Sade saw action against Prussia, and one of his officers described him as 'very disturbed, but very brave'.

While in uniform, Sade began to make a name for himself by frequenting brothels and seducing actresses. Again, this was typical of his class, but his bad reputation scared off several

[7] The title could also be acquired in other ways. For example, Kings Louis XIV and XV sometimes dubbed their mistresses *'marquise'*. Kings also granted the title *'marquis'* to men when giving them land in return for some favour or achievement.

aristocratic brides, and he eventually had to marry the daughter of a rich tax official so that he could keep up a façade of respectability while he pursued his sexual hobbies.

Consorting with prostitutes – even very young ones – was not illegal, and neither was picking up poor girls in the street and persuading them to do sexual favours in return for 'charity', so Sade would have been able to carry on regardless if he hadn't strayed into more dangerous territory.

In 1763, a fan-maker called Jeanne Testard agreed to spend the night with Sade in Paris, and quickly regretted it. Afterwards she rushed to the police to complain. In her statement, she said that Sade had called the Virgin Mary a 'bastard', and had boasted that he had put communion wafers into a woman's vagina and then penetrated her, shouting, 'If you're God, avenge yourself!' Jeanne herself had seen him masturbate over a crucifix, and he had ordered Jeanne to defecate on a statue of Christ (which she had refused to do). She said Sade had invited her to meet in a church the following Sunday so that they could repeat his sexual ritual with communion wafers.

Apparently, Jeanne wasn't the only girl to complain, and Louis XV ordered Sade to be locked up in the dungeons at the château de Vincennes. Thanks to his influential family, though, the young nobleman was soon released.

After this, Sade seems to have toned down his activities – or paid the girls enough to buy their silence – and his next arrest didn't come until Easter Sunday 1768, when he kidnapped a 36-year-old widow called Rose Keller.

Following her husband's death, Rose had been reduced to begging, and Sade picked her up and offered her a job as the concièrge of a house in the village of Arcueil, just outside Paris. What she didn't know was that the house was a secret bachelor pad that Sade kept as a venue for his orgies.

He took Rose there in a carriage with the curtains drawn so that she wouldn't know where she was going, and when they arrived, he locked her in a bedroom while he went downstairs to party with some prostitutes. Returning an hour later, he was dressed in a butcher's apron. He forced the terrified Jeanne to strip at sword point, and then tied her up and whipped her. After treating her wounds with a lotion, he left her overnight, returning next day to masturbate and whip her again, threatening to kill her if she didn't stop screaming. Again, he treated her wounds with his lotion and left her, but this time she managed to escape through a window and appeal for help. Despite offers from Sade to pay Rose off, the horrified villagers fetched a police lieutenant who arrested him.

Of course, Sade's family did their best to stifle the affair, claiming that he could not be tried by an ordinary judge because his alleged crimes were 'not covered by the law'. The case therefore went before a royal court, where everyone expected Sade to be let off. After all, his defence was watertight: she was a prostitute, he had paid her, and the only reason he had whipped her was that he had wanted to test the efficiency of his lotion. Aristocrats could thrash commoners whenever they wanted, as Voltaire had discovered to his cost (see section III above). Sade himself had once beaten up a coachman for daring to demand payment. Case closed, it seemed.

However, Rose Keller had also made allegations of blasphemy, and it was these that earned Sade his prison sentence – a six-month stint in the château at Saumur on the Loire.

The rest of Sade's life was a series of close shaves and imprisonments. In 1772 he held an orgy at which he served cake laced with a beetle-based aphrodisiac. It was said that some of the guests died of poisoning. Sade was sentenced to death for sodomizing girls during the orgy, but escaped to Italy – with a nun. In 1774 he hired five 'very young' girls as servants and was sued by their parents for kidnapping. In 1777 the father of another kidnapped girl shot at Sade while rescuing his daughter from the *marquis*'s clutches.

Rumours about what Sade did with his young 'servants' were so lurid that his mother-in-law issued a *lettre de cachet* against him for his own good. She knew that if he came to trial again, he would probably end up on the blasphemer's bonfire. It was during his long period in detention from 1777–90, mainly at the Bastille, that Sade committed his long career to paper, in books like *The 120 Days of Sodom*, the story of four noblemen (including a bishop) who lock 46 young prisoners of both sexes in a castle where they carry out every imaginable sexual experiment before killing their victims.

He also wrote more sober works, like his *Dialogue between a Priest and a Dying Man*, in which the latter excuses his amorality by saying that he was 'corrupted by nature', and argues calmly against the existence of God.

Sade claimed to be one of the freethinking Lumières – *'Je suis philosophe'* – an atheistic thinker along the lines of Diderot, Voltaire and their contemporaries (from whom he borrowed most of his philosophical arguments). But Sade's interpretation of freedom seems to have been very much an establishment one: as a rich nobleman, he claimed the right to do whatever he wanted to anyone poor enough to accept ritual abuse in exchange for money. In essence, it was a (much) more violent version of what Louis XV was doing with the young girls provided for his amusement at Versailles. The Marquis de Sade was simply a perverse exaggeration of the accepted standards of the time, the ugly face of the absolutist monarchy and its unshakeable prejudices.

Even though he was imprisoned by both Louis XV and XVI, in the French public imagination, Sade must have been a reminder of what the idle rich could do to the poor, as long as they were more discreet, and less blasphemous, about it than the *marquis* had been.

Sade was the ugly grimace behind the face powder, and yet another blemish on the monarchy's rapidly worsening complexion.

V

Beaumarchais, meanwhile, started out at the opposite end of the social spectrum to Sade. But like Sade, he only seems to have discovered his passion for freethinking and democracy after committing a crime and ending up in prison.

Pierre-Augustin Caron de Beaumarchais first came to Louis XV's attention as a brilliant watchmaker in the 1750s (see section I above). As humble Monsieur Caron, he had been one of the low-born but handsome high achievers who managed to break through the barrier of snobbery surrounding Versailles. Once he had caught Louis XV's eye with his miraculously miniature watch, he wormed his way further into the royal family by becoming the harp teacher to four of the King's daughters – Caron had also invented a mechanism that made the harp's foot pedal work more smoothly.

Now a regular at Versailles, Caron made friends with one of the King's financial advisors, Joseph Pâris Duverney – one of the men who had helped Louis XV clear up the mess after collapse of the economy in 1720. Pâris let Caron in on lucrative investments that paid well enough for the ladies' harp teacher to buy himself a job as a *secrétaire du Roi* – and the noble title that went with it.

The new suffix to his name, de Beaumarchais, was a passport to even higher social advancement. Under the patronage of Louis XV's cousin, Louis-François de Bourbon-Conti, the ex-harpist acquired yet another royal job as *lieutenant général des chasses* – one of the men responsible for running the King's hunt.

Now noble and comfortably off, Beaumarchais had time to develop his literary career. He had always written – he claimed to have created the anti-establishment character of Figaro when he was only nine years old – but for the moment, he began to put on plays with titles like *Jean Bête à la foire* (*Stupid John at the Fair*) that made fun of the uncultured French proles he would champion in his later, more famous plays. He was the witty court jester writing in-jokes for the Versailles in-crowd.

In 1770, though, Beaumarchais seems to have grown over-confident. When his financial mentor Joseph Pâris Duverney died, leaving a fortune to Beaumarchais, the family contested the will. An investigator called Louis-Valentin Goëzman was put on the case, and Beaumarchais decided that the court case could be won with a bribe. Goëzman's wife accepted a watch and a small sum of money – apparently too small, because Goëzman submitted a report suggesting that Beaumarchais was guilty of forging the will, a crime that was punished with a fine.

By this time, Beaumarchais was already in prison after getting in a fight with a (slightly more noble) nobleman who accused the interloper of stealing his mistress. Behind bars, his only weapon was his pen, and he took to writing satirical pamphlets against Goëzman, helping to create a literary genre of the time, the *mémoire judiciaire* or legal memoir, in which accuser and accused could battle out their court case via the printing press and the literary *salon*, throwing 'anonymous' insults and allegations at each other. Public opinion would side with the wittier pamphleteer, and judges, who were members of the chattering classes, would be tempted to do the same, especially if the pamphlet sold well enough to finance a decent bribe.

Beaumarchais had already been prosecuted for his forgery, but thanks to his four acerbic *mémoires*, Goëzman lost his job. This didn't help Beaumarchais much, though – Louis XV read the pamphlets and was so incensed by these attempts to pervert the course of justice, as well as the forgery of a courtier's will, that Beaumarchais was stripped of his money and civil rights. He was back to zero.

To redeem himself, in early 1774 Beaumarchais (he managed to hang on to his name) agreed to work for the King on another literary matter.

A notorious pimp and blackmailer called Charles Théveneau de Morande (note the 'de' – this was yet another rogue aristocrat) was threatening to publish salacious (and partially true) rumours about Louis XV's new mistress, Madame du Barry. These weren't hard to invent – Jeanne du Barry was the illegitimate daughter of a seamstress and a monk, and had enjoyed a successful career as a high-class prostitute, passing through several noble hands before, at the age of 25, netting the dream sugar daddy, the then

58-year-old king. She was something of a figure of fun at Versailles – even more straight-talking than Madame de Pompadour before her, with an even stronger lower-class accent. It is said that she once told Louis XV that he had knocked over a cup with the line: 'Hey, France, your coffee is buggering off!'

The blackmailer Morande had run away to London to escape imprisonment for previous crimes, and was in dire need of money. He therefore chose a sure-fire hit title for his work – *The Secret Memoirs of a Public Woman, or Research into the Adventures of Madame la Comtesse du Barry from the Cradle to the Royal Bed, Enriched with Anecdotes and Incidents Relating to the Plot and Noble Actions of the Duc d'Aiguillon* (a reference to a boast by said duke that he had bedded the King's mistress). It wasn't exactly catchy, but it was certainly catch-all, and Louis XV knew that the book would be a bestseller.

Morande was demanding 1,000 *louis* in cash plus a life pension of 4,000 per annum – vast sums that would keep him a lot more comfortably than pimping. Louis XV dispatched Beaumarchais to London to negotiate. A more efficient dictator might have sent a messenger with a poisoned dagger, but Beaumarchais was simply instructed to hand over a heap of coins and make promises about future income. In return, Morande had the unpublished books burned in a brick oven at St Pancras, closing one of the most profitable literary deals of the century.

This success naturally began to *encourager les autres* like wildfire, and it suddenly became fashionable to write scurrilous rumours about the royal family in the hope of cashing in, either through blackmail or book sales. Thanks to Louis XV's bad reputation, almost anything was believable, and, adding irony to irony, Louis was forced to allow Beaumarchais to hire Morande to combat the trend, with only partial success.

The scurrilous *mémoire*, the genre that Beaumarchais had helped to create, became the literary sensation of the period, a sort of eighteenth-century gutter press. Suddenly it was highly profitable to dash to the printer and publish any titbit of gossip about the royal family – true, false or anywhere in between.

In this way, as Louis XV's reign came to an end, public opinion was being manipulated by endless pieces of fake news, most of them alleging immoral goings-on at Versailles. It was a very twenty-first-century climate, in fact, with truth taking second place to unfounded allegation, and there was no reason why things should change after Louis XV's death. Just a few years later, Marie-Antoinette was to fall victim to probably the biggest, and most damaging, wave of scandal ever to hit the monarchy. And some of the most savage *mémoires* written against her would be by one Pierre-Augustin Caron de Beaumarchais.[8]

But for the time being, it was still Marie-Antoinette's grand-father-in-law, Louis XV, who was battling vainly against the tide of semi-libellous allegations being published against him, thrusting his popularity even deeper into the gutter.

VI

Towards the end of his life, Louis XV tried to introduce a daring piece of social reform that would have freed France from the stranglehold of privileged power. Well, one of the strangleholds, anyway.

As we have already seen, in eighteenth-century France, the courts of justice were generally far from just. Judges, the most powerful members of the *noblesse de robe*, made fortunes from the bribes nicknamed 'spices' (*'épices'*) that they received in return for favourable verdicts, and even if they were flagrantly corrupt, they could not be removed. In short, they had what the French today consider the ideal employment contract – the boss couldn't tell them what to do, and couldn't fire them no matter how bad they were at their job. Even better for them, but worse for France, having paid the King to be appointed to a job for life, the judges could bequeath their position and its noble rank to their heirs.

[8] Under Louis XVI Beaumarchais would also write, and get permission to produce, his most provocative play, *The Marriage of Figaro*. See Chapter 10.

In a period of rule by the privileged, local corruption in the courts might not have bothered the King too much as long as it didn't harm his friends or family, but these judges also presided over the regional parliaments that could oppose or block laws made by the royal ministers in Versailles. They were the people who had stood up to Louis XV in 1749 when he first tried to tax the nobility.

This parliamentary veto on royal laws was called the *droit de remontrance*, or right of remonstration. Thanks to this power, the judges liked to think of themselves as British-style parliamentarians, a force for democracy, despite the fact that they were corrupt, self-interested, unelected snobs. (In fact, many British MPs at the time were also corrupt, self-interested snobs, but at least they had been elected, albeit often by fixing elections.)

In any case, the French judges formed an immovable bedrock of power outside the King's (or the people's) control. They wielded this power to oppose any measure that attacked privilege in France, claiming that they were defending freedom when in reality they were only safeguarding their own income and that of their cronies.

Louis XV wasn't the first king to try and rein them in. Louis XIV had limited the *droit de remontrance* after regional parliaments had played a role in the rebellion against him, the so-called 'Fronde' (see Chapter 1), but his immediate successor, Philippe d'Orléans, had restored it in return for their support in making him regent.

In 1763, Louis XV launched a new assault on the bastion of judiciary power, and tried to impose a tax to pay for the ruinous Seven Years War. The Breton parliament refused. This time, Louis XV was determined not to back down. On trumped-up charges involving two anonymous letters 'verified by handwriting experts', Louis had the chief judge of the Breton parliament, a man called Louis-René de la Chalotais, locked up in the Bastille. The rogue judge's son and four other parliamentarians were also arrested, and their case became a public *cause célèbre*, with Voltaire himself stepping in and inventing the heroic legend of Chalotais denied pen and ink, having to write pleas for help from his cell with a toothpick and vinegar.

In the end, under pressure from the judiciary and the massed ranks of the philosophers, who were idealistic about parliamentary democracy, Louis XV had Chalotais exiled to Saintes, a pleasant town near the Atlantic coast. But the King had finally decided that enough was enough.

In 1766, Louis XV arrived unannounced at a session of the Paris parliament to call the judges to order. He gave a speech, assuring them that: 'Remonstrations will always be received favourably when they are suffused with the moderation that characterizes the judiciary and the truth' – Louis must have been biting his tongue when he put 'judiciary' and 'truth' in the same sentence. But he went on to warn that if the parliaments abused their position, 'confusion and anarchy will take the place of legitimate order, and the scandalous spectacle of a rivalry to my sovereignty would reduce me to the sad necessity of using all the power that I have received from God to protect my people.'

Louis XV was renowned for his cold formality in public, and the speech must have sounded like a chilling threat – mess with the absolute monarch of France and you're messing with the creator of the universe.

Louis was as good as his word. After years of stalemate and fruitless negotiation, in 1770, he ordered his chancellor, René Nicolas Charles Augustin de Maupeou (usually called just Maupeou, for obvious reasons) to end the judges' omnipotence. According to a royal edict, the regional parliaments would be allowed to 'remonstrate' only once with a royal bill, and would have to let it pass the second time. If they tried to avoid the issue by refusing to come to a decision, they would have their personal assets confiscated.

Being French, when threatened by the ruling class the parliaments naturally went on strike. After ignoring several calls to reconvene, all the Paris parliamentarians received home visits from armed soldiers who forced them at gunpoint to decide between accepting the King's ruling or going into exile. Almost all of them chose exile – a mass defiance of royal sovereignty and a provocative signal to their colleagues in the rest of the country.

In reprisal, Maupeou abolished the hereditary right to sit in parliament, replacing the Paris *parlement* with a body of paid administrators, and announcing that similar changes would be phased in in the regions. At the same time, Maupeou declared that from now on, court cases would be completely free of charge, and overseen by judges appointed by the Crown.

This was a fundamental reform of France's social structure, even more radical than emptying the House of Lords and con-fiscating all the wigs and gowns at the Old Bailey, because these French lords had derived both their titles and their income from their jobs. At a stroke, a whole tier of the aristocracy had had all its privileges, including its lucrative income from bribes, revoked, and poor people knew that they now had a chance of standing up for their legal rights. It was a French revolution.

Naturally, the judges didn't go down without a fight. Supported by power-hungry members of Louis XV's own family, by the rest of the aristocracy, and by troublemaking pamphleteers like Beaumarchais, who was still smarting at the humiliation imposed on him by Louis XV over the Goëzman affair, the judges fought back.

It was easy to find lines of attack. Wasn't this ageing, lecher-ous king incapable of understanding serious matters of state? And wasn't he under the thumb of his strumpet of a mistress, Madame du Barry, who was out to avenge the aristocratic snubs she had suffered since her arrival at Versailles?

The answer to those questions was a partial yes.

Louis XV didn't want to be bothered with the day-to-day mechanics of 'his' reforms, and left it all to Maupeou while he continued to enjoy the pleasures of life at Versailles. But his royal pride was genuinely piqued by the judges' refusal to bow to their sovereign, and he really did recognize the need for his government to make laws without the interference of a corrupt gang of self-serving judges.

It was true that he let Madame du Barry wage her personal campaigns against anyone who annoyed or insulted her – for example, she had undermined the King's faith in his Minister of War and Foreign Affairs, the Duc de Choiseul, whose friends had published pornographic stories about her. Louis subsequently sent Choiseul into exile, a political mistake because he was popular amongst ordinary people.

But the strongest accusation made against Louis XV was that by replacing the parliamentarians with royal employees, he was revealing himself as a tyrant. Even if ordinary people would gain by this reform, the judges claimed that the King was removing democratic rights. Wanting their old absolute power back, the parliamentarians managed to stir up public feelings against absolute monarchy, making Louis even more unpopular than ever.

They generally did this anonymously, or via pamphlets, because anyone openly challenging the King was bound for the Bastille. When addressing Louis directly, they were more diplomatic. One appeal cited past kings who had been more tolerant towards them, including the fifteenth-century Louis XI, who once promised parliamentarians that 'in his lifetime he would not force them to do anything against their conscience'.[9]

In the spirit of the times, new rumours about Louis XV began to circulate. These now went far beyond stories about juvenile prostitutes. According to one story that a courtier heard, and apparently believed, the King had a secret hoard of millions in cash, and was deliberately causing anarchy in France before doing a bunk.

[9] The judges were conveniently forgetting that, in reality, Louis XI had been a centralizer whose motto when issuing orders was: 'Let me be the first to learn your news,' meaning: 'I want to control every stage of the process.'

Another rumour sprang up, alleging that Parisians were stealing children so that Louis XV could bathe in their blood to cure his leprosy. This story caused minor rioting. In the eighteenth century, much like today, few ordinary people asked for proof that a piece of scurrilous news was true. Goodwill towards Louis XV had sunk so low that they would believe almost anything.

It was a tragic irony: Louis XV's decision to strip away a layer of abusive privilege from French society, and ensure that a poor citizen had as much chance of winning a court case as a rich aristocrat (well, almost – favouritism would never be abolished completely), caused him to be seen by increasing numbers of his subjects as an enemy of democracy.

It was true that he had replaced the parliamentarians by his own men, but there was almost certainly more chance of unbiased government under the royal appointees than the corrupt judges.

And overall, Louis XV's rule had not been as harmful to ordinary people as that of the 'great' King Louis XIV. His sex life had been a PR disaster for the monarchy, and his nickname 'Louis le Bien-Aimé' had been inaccurate for most of his reign, but he had done his best to limit taxation by avoiding war. The main exception was the ruinous Seven Years War of 1756–63, but that had been provoked when the Brits started grabbing French possessions in America. Since then, Louis XV had been all for peace. In fact the final straw that precipitated his minister Choiseul's sacking was not a pornographic pamphlet about Madame du Barry. Louis had discovered that Choiseul was preparing a war against Britain, and exploded with rage: 'Monsieur, I told you that I wanted no wars!'

At the end of his reign, Louis XV's attempts to do good weren't limited to preserving the peace. He genuinely seems to have been feeling the need to go out on a positive note. To repent for his sinful lifestyle, he allowed his youngest daughter, Louise, to become a Carmelite nun (well, she was 32 and unmarried), presumably so that she would use her influence on the one judge that Louis had not sacked.

VII

In 1774, after almost 60 years on the throne, Louis XV's own reputation was in ruins, but – astonishingly, perhaps – even he had not really shaken the foundations of the monarchy itself. The *philosophes* had spent decades hammering away at established religion, privilege and royal absolutism, but even the most virulently philosophical writer of the time, Voltaire, was still in favour of the monarchy per se – he simply wanted its powers to be subject to the control of a democratic parliament. The most radical rethink of the main issues of the time, Diderot's *Encyclopédie*, stopped short of condemning the monarchy outright, even after the book had lost its royal seal of approval and been more or less banned by royal censors. Revolution, as in removal of the royal family, was not in the air.

All everyone seems to have wanted is for Louis XV himself to vacate the throne. After his death from the effects of smallpox on 10 May 1774, officials were so afraid that his funeral cortège through Paris would be met by people throwing rotten vegetables (or worse) that the carriage carrying his remains left Versailles at night and drove around the western edges of Paris to the traditional burial site at the basilica of Saint-Denis, just north of the city. Over the next few days, it was said that no one mourned Louis XV, and that everyday life went on as normal, except for parties celebrating the departure of the immoral old tyrant.

But Voltaire wrote a glowing eulogy that he published on 25 May. In this, he praised Louis XV for his modern, scientific mind, even saying that 'all his servants confess that there has never been a kinder master, and all those who worked for him attest to his amiable nature ... His memory will be dear to us, because his heart was good.'

Voltaire's text alludes to the King's immorality and unfortunate habit of letting court squabbles get out of hand, but concludes that 'France will owe him an eternal debt for abolishing the venal judiciary ... For what Louis XV established, and for what he did away with, we owe him our gratitude.'

In fact, that wasn't the actual conclusion of Voltaire's eulogy, because the eccentric old philosopher used Louis XV's death as an excuse to sing the praises of inoculation against smallpox. But he gave his public-health campaign a monarchist flavour, saying 'let inoculation guarantee us the survival of our new king, our princes and princesses!'

Voltaire was being obsequious towards the royals in the hope of ending his exile from Paris, but he also seems to have been summing up the general mood amongst the French: Louis XV has gone at last. Things can only get better. The King is dead; long live the King.

People had thought the same when old Louis XIV died in 1715. Exhausted by over-taxation, they had been glad to see the back of him. This time, though, there was a difference. Even if people didn't want to see the monarchy toppled, they no longer felt innate respect for their sovereigns. There was no more awe. Nevertheless, it was still possible that a successful new king could restore the old majesty.

A modern parallel would be 1997 in Britain, when public opinion rounded on the Queen for her perceived heartlessness after the death of the 'people's princess', Diana. The Queen and the royal family as a whole (except for young Princes William and Harry) were seen as aloof. Republicanism reared its head in the tabloids. But the Queen quickly showed that she understood what was at stake – she went live on TV to express her sorrow, and joined the mourning masses as they heaped their floral tributes outside Kensington Palace. Subsequently she relaunched the monarchy's brand, becoming first the nation's grandmother, then the screen partner of James Bond, a player of internet pranks alongside Prince Harry, and of course the star of great national pageants whenever another jubilee year came around, or a photogenic prince got married or had a baby. The Queen understood that as long as the monarchy is in place, it can save its reputation.

When, on 26 April 1774, Louis XV showed the first symp-toms of smallpox and took to his bed at Versailles, the French monarchy was still on its feet, and very few people in France seriously wanted it to fall. It was like an exhausted relay runner, holding out the baton for the next pair of hands, confident that a new, younger member of the team would take up the challenge and run the following leg of the race.

This was the 19-year-old Louis XVI – whose first act as king would be to drop the baton.

Chapter 6

LOUIS XVI AND MARIE-ANTOINETTE ARE AN EARLY FLOP

'Nous régnons trop jeune.'
'We reign too young.'

Louis XVI (1754–93, reigned 1774–92)

I

Even before Louis XVI came to the throne in 1774, many people were convinced that he had condemned the monarchy to its doom.

In April 1770, the 15-year-old Prince, then called Louis Auguste, was married by proxy in a Viennese church to an Austrian, Maria Antonia Josepha Joanna, who was a year younger than him. Many courtiers at the palace of Versailles opposed the match. Not only was the girl foreign (known by her enemies as *'l'Autrichienne'*),[1] she was a mere archduchess. Surely, the snobs asked, Louis XV could have found a true princess for his grandson? Was this not one step down the slippery social ladder towards the calamitous situation whereby a prince

---

[1] A crude pun: the French name for a female Austrian sounds like *'l'autre chienne'*, which could be translated as 'that bitch'.

of the realm might one day marry, say, a kindergarten assistant, a salesman's daughter, or a foreign actress?

This xenophobic nickname was in fact another example of anti-royal fake news. Certainly, Maria Antonia was from Vienna, but she was 50 per cent French, with an Austrian mother, Maria Theresa, a French father, François de Lorraine, and two French grandparents, Léopold, Duc de Lorraine, and Élisabeth-Charlotte d'Orléans (a granddaughter of Louis XIII). In fact, '*l'Autrichienne*' was a true French princess of the blood, and was quickly renamed as such – Marie-Antoinette.

Her new husband, Louis Auguste, heir to the French throne, had only one French grandfather, Louis XV. His other grandparents were Princess Marie Leszczyńska of Poland, King Augustus III of Poland, and Maria Josepha, an Austrian archduchess. He was less French than Marie-Antoinette. To the snobs and gossips, though, this didn't matter. They put it about that the French royal bloodline was being diluted, and the idea stuck in the popular imagination.[2]

There were also many people in Versailles who opposed the marriage for a more practical reason – lack of money. In 1770, Louis XV simply could not afford a lavish wedding for his grandson. After Marie-Antoinette was welcomed at court with a huge party, the King asked his Minister of Finance: 'What did you think of my celebrations at Versailles?' and got a wicked pun in reply: '*Impayables.*' In colloquial French, this means 'extraordinary'. Literally, it means 'unaffordable'. The minister was right – many suppliers of food, fireworks and costumes for the royal festivities in 1770 were not paid. After the Revolution, some of them would present the new government with credit notes.

---

[2] Despite the racist remarks, Marie-Antoinette already spoke excellent French when she arrived in France. This was fairly common amongst European aristocrats, but Marie-Antoinette had been linguistically prepared for her marriage. At first she spoke French with an Austrian accent, and used Germanic sentence constructions, but these soon disappeared and she quickly became a perfectly French princess.

Doubts about the match between Louis Auguste and Marie-Antoinette went even deeper, right into the national subconscious. Both the wedding ceremony and the identity of the bride had superstitious people all over France delving into their almanacs. It was pointed out that the Austrian interloper was born on 2 November 1755, the day after a massive earthquake in Lisbon that had cost tens of thousands of lives. To people who still believed in a direct link between royalty and deity, such a birthday did not augur well. One of Marie-Antoinette's French ladies-in-waiting, Henriette Campan, later remarked in her memoirs that the earthquake was a 'catastrophe that seemed to put a fatal stamp on the time of [Marie-Antoinette's] birth'.

Louis XV's own family had been hit by plenty of tragedy in the years just before the new royal wedding. In 1765, the Dauphin (heir to the throne), Louis XV's only son Louis Ferdinand, had died of a lung infection at the early age of 36. Louis Ferdinand's own eldest son had died aged nine, leaving Louis Auguste, a much less charismatic boy, as heir.

If King Louis XV was hoping to put everyone's mind at rest by announcing the swift arrival of the next royal generation, he must have had second thoughts as soon as he greeted Marie-Antoinette in the forest near Compiègne, just north of Paris, on 14 May 1770. He saw a pubescent girl with disappointing breasts (this was 'the first thing he looked at', he told his ambassador to Vienna). She was about the same age as the prostitutes he cavorted with at Versailles, but had none of Mademoiselle O'Murphy's flirty sensuality. The King pronounced her 'childish'. Louis Auguste, meanwhile, stood by awkwardly, a chubby figure doing little more than stare bemusedly at the girl to whom he had been married in his absence, and whom he was meant to bed in a few days' time.

The following evening Marie-Antoinette made a sexual innuendo that must have delighted and deflated Louis XV at the same time. When informed primly that Madame du Barry's role at court was 'to give pleasure to the King', Marie-Antoinette replied: 'So I shall be her rival, for I also wish to give pleasure to the King.'

Marie-Antoinette wasn't the only one to make a spectacle of her innocence. At dinner on 16 May 1770, after a wedding ceremony in Versailles at which both bride and groom had been present, the highly sexed Louis XV indulged in some macho badinage with his grandson. Or tried to, anyway.

'Don't overload your stomach before tonight,' the King said.

'Why not?' Louis Auguste asked. 'I always sleep better after a big dinner.'

It is all too easy to picture Louis XV being struck by a sudden premonition that the monarchy's days were numbered. With almost comic symbolism, the firework display planned in Versailles for that evening was rained off. The princely squib was doubly damp.

Worse, when the city of Paris held a firework display two weeks later, on 30 May, in the place Louis XV (now place de la Concorde), a misfired rocket set off an explosion, causing a stampede in the packed crowd of spectators. More than 100 Parisians were trampled to death and hundreds were badly injured. The young royal couple donated a full year of their civil list income to the families of the dead and injured, but the damage was done. A black cloud hung over their union from the very start. Félicité de Genlis, a Versailles courtier and tutor to the royal family, referred to the Paris firework disaster as: 'This deplorable event that everyone viewed with the darkest foreboding.'

Hindsight only added to the list of omens. Writing after the Revolution, Madame de Genlis pointed out the coincidence that so many deaths occurred on the very square where both Marie-Antoinette and Louis XVI, as well as more than 1,000 of their supporters, would later be guillotined.

To those in search of eerie coincidences, the date on which the young couple's wedding festivities officially ended seems to have been yet another nail in the royal family's coffin – it was 14 July 1770, exactly 19 years to the day before the Bastille would be stormed by revolutionaries.

With so much misfortune overshadowing the marriage that was meant to ensure the future of the French monarchy, is it surprising that the regime would soon come to a bloody end?

Well, yes, because as we saw in the previous chapter, in 1770 the French people as a whole were not fantasizing about the day when they would be able to erect a scaffold on the place Louis XV and start removing royal heads. When Marie-Antoinette went to Paris for the first time that July, the crowds outside the Tuileries palace demanding to see her were so big that she appeared on a balcony to greet them and was met with rousing cheers. The Duc de Brissac, governor of Paris, told her that: 'They are all in love with you.'

Starstruck French people would also make the trip to Versailles just to catch a glimpse of the Viennese girl. And after Louis XV's death of smallpox in 1774, when the young couple took refuge from infection at La Muette, on the western edge of Paris, Madame Campan noted that: 'The shouts of *"vive le Roi"* started at six in the morning and went on almost without interruption until sundown.' She also wrote about a Parisian jeweller who made a fortune from hastily produced lockets containing a portrait of Marie-Antoinette in mourning for Louis XV. 'Never', Madame Campan said, 'has the start of a reign evoked a bigger show of love and affection.'

The problem for the French royal family was not so much that the stars were set against Louis XVI, or that anti–Austrian factions were determined for the foreign princess to fail. It was that this 'love and affection' did not permeate into the royal bedroom. As Louis XV might have guessed when trying to banter with his grandson about sex, the future monarch simply did not have the *cojones* to lead the monarchy safely into the next century.

II

Surely almost any 15-year-old boy would be more than grateful if his parents (or in this case, grandfather) were so laid-back about sex that they provided the partner and the bed, and said,

'Enjoy yourself, lad.' No furtive fumblings in the nightclub toilets for young Louis Auguste. The pubescent, exiled Marie-Antoinette was probably not quite so keen, but her own duty had been drummed into her by her domineering mother, and despite her extreme youth she was consenting. She knew that she was expected to get pregnant as soon as physically possible.

So all the teenage Prince had to do on the night of 16 May 1770 was climb into bed and lose his virginity.

The fact that he didn't was a source of gossip throughout Versailles the very next morning.

After the second night, courtiers were horrified to find out that he had slept in his own room, leaving his young wife alone. From then on, he would occasionally visit her at bedtime and, as he later confessed to Marie-Antoinette's brother Joseph, 'insert his member, stay there without moving for maybe two minutes, then withdraw without ejaculating, still erect, and wish her good evening'.

At first, the gossips put this down to teenage shyness. Even so, Louis XV was anxious enough to ask his doctors to perform a quick inspection of the Prince's marital equipment. They reported that everything down below looked perfectly normal.

Since sex was a political necessity – an unconsummated marriage could be quickly and legally annulled – the Austrian ambassador to France, a Belgian-born career diplomat called Florimond Claude de Mercy Argenteau (known as Mercy for short), demanded regular updates from the young bride, and kept getting the same reply – Franco-Austrian union had not yet been cemented.

France's Foreign Minister, the Duc de Choiseul, naturally made it his business to ask for updates. The Spanish ambassador also wrote home about the lack of action in Marie-Antoinette's bed, which soon became everyone's favourite subject. Marie-Antoinette's mother, the Austrian empress Maria Theresa, fired off letters to her daughter encouraging her not to despair – the teenage bride should try 'caresses and cajoling, but too much hurry would spoil everything'.

Not that Louis Auguste was hurrying with anything except hunting. To improve relations between them, Marie-Antoinette decided to start spending more time with her husband outside the four-poster. She went along to his hunts, without taking part herself, and even handed out food to the hunters, ignoring criticisms that she was acting too much like a servant. And her technique began to work. By sharing the Prince's hobby, she cajoled him into confiding in her.

It was now July 1770, almost two months after the couple had met for the first time. Louis Auguste confessed to his wife that he was fully aware of his duty, and that he had given himself a deadline to perform it. However, when this deadline passed, he asked for another *'délai de réflexion'* (which would translate in a modern business contract as a 'cooling-off period', the last thing the couple needed).

Ever the dutiful daughter, Marie-Antoinette recorded all the details for her mother in monthly letters, usually scribbling hastily so that her revelations would not lie around on a desk to be read by snoopers. In January 1771 she reported that Louis-Auguste had explained what went wrong on the wedding night: he had resolved to consummate the marriage, but last-minute anxiety had stopped him, and ever since then the fear had grown worse.

It is easy to imagine how embarrassing this must have been for the young Prince and his bride. Being a teenager has never been easy, but belonging to the most famous couple in the country and being a source of national ridicule because you have failed to have sex with your partner must have been unbearable.

Even so, Marie-Antoinette promised her impatient mother that they were growing fonder of each other, and in March of that year, Louis Auguste began spending every night in her bed. On 26 March, they achieved penetration, but again, without ejaculation. We know the details because the Austrian ambassador, the more and more inaccurately named Mercy, described the encounter in his next dispatch to Vienna, presumably after interrogating Marie-Antoinette.

The only compensation for the royal couple in all this sexual humiliation was that the Prince's younger brother, Louis Stanislas, got married in May 1771, and was an even bigger sexual failure. According to different historians, either he was impotent due to the obesity that would eventually kill him, or he simply found his bride unattractive. By all reports, the Savoyard–Spanish Maria Giuseppina was ugly, dull-witted, and never brushed her teeth. By comparison, Louis Auguste and Marie-Antoinette were universally acknowledged to be handsome, graceful and even touchingly innocent.

In any case, the prospect of Louis Stanislas producing a baby, a rival future heir to the throne, seemed unlikely. But this didn't stop Marie-Antoinette's frantic mother hammering away in her letters that Austrian influence in France needed to be sealed with a royal birth.

By the end of October 1772, more than two years after the wedding, Louis XV was finally worried enough to summon the couple to a confessional with Granddad. The ageing King was in his early sixties but still cavorting merrily with Madame du Barry, and must have been completely bemused by his two grandsons' lack of hormonal activity. Louis Auguste revealed that he had 'made attempts to consummate his marriage, but was always stopped by painful sensations'. A few days later, Mercy reported to Vienna that Louis XV had personally examined his grandson's anatomy and found that 'the very small obstacle is an accident that is very common to adolescents and does not require an operation' – though the old King was no expert on male members, having devoted all his research to the female body.

Louis Auguste promised to do his duty at the earliest opportunity, but Marie-Antoinette wrote to her mother that he didn't keep his promise. She was coming to realize that he possessed 'a nonchalant attitude and laziness that leave him only when he hunts'.

In 1774, when Louis XV died and the young couple became the childless heads of one of Europe's most powerful dynasties, political panic began to set in. By now, Versailles was buzzing with theories. Some agreed with Marie-Antoinette that her husband was too lazy to have sex; others suggested that his foreskin was too small, and caused pain when he attempted penetration, or that it was stuck to the glans and would not budge at all; another theory was that the skin of his penis was partially attached to his scrotum; gossips even began to spread rumours that Marie-Antoinette must be a lesbian, or that Louis was gay. A poem called '*Le Godemiché royal*' ('The Royal Dildo'), officially published in 1789, but reflecting much older ideas, depicted Marie-Antoinette, her skirts lifted, masturbating and lamenting that:

> *Le bougre porte ailleurs un encens qui m'est dû;*
> *Son vit est mou pour moi et bande pour un cul.*

(The bugger takes elsewhere an incense that is my right,
His member is soft for me but hardens for an arse.)

In 1774, the newly crowned Louis XVI consulted doctors, agreed to have an operation, pulled out at the last minute (no pun intended), set a new date for the procedure, but changed his mind yet again. Not surprisingly, Marie-Antoinette despaired, her mother even more so. From being the sweet young couple who were too shy to have sex, they became something of a national joke. A popular song of 1776 went:

> *Chacun se demande tout bas:*
> *Le roi peut-il? Ne peut-il pas?*

(Everyone is whispering the question:
Can the King do it? Or can't he?)

It was now June 1777, and the sexless marriage was seven years old with not a sexual itch in sight. Maria Theresa of Austria gave up her correspondence course in sex therapy (though few therapists would think that it might help to insult their patient's attractiveness, seductiveness, intelligence and patriotism like the old Empress had been doing), and sent her eldest son, Joseph (Marie-Antoinette's big brother), for a hands-on investigation – literally.

Joseph was an inspired choice as a go-between. He himself had been traumatized by a first marriage to a depressive wife who had died of smallpox. He had remarried, but the match had been so loveless that he didn't even attend his second wife's funeral when she also succumbed to smallpox. His only daughter had died in 1770. He therefore knew all about the pains of being a royal husband.

Louis XVI seems to have had no complexes about his inadequacy. He confessed to Joseph that he had wet dreams, so he was certain that he could ejaculate, and he described the partial penetrations that he had achieved.

Joseph was pleased by such frankness, but exasperated. He wrote to his younger brother Leopold that 'he [Louis] is happy, and only does it out of duty because he has no taste for it ... Oh, if only I could be present just once! I would sort it out. He needs to be whipped so that he comes, like a donkey.'

Joseph left Versailles at the end of May, exhorting his sister to consider her own responsibility: 'Are you not cold or distracted when he caresses you? Do you never seem bored, or even repelled?'

According to Madame Campan, Marie-Antoinette 'became insulted by the indiscreet sincerity' of her brother, but his frank approach worked miracles, with no need for whipping or an operation. Opinions differ, but there is little proof that Louis XVI's foreskin went under the surgeon's knife – there are no descriptions of the procedure, and no gaps in his diary that would suggest convalescence. And two months after his session with Joseph, Louis XVI was joyfully informing his aunts that: 'I like pleasure a lot, and regret that I did not know it for so long.' On 30 August 1777, Marie-Antoinette was able to tell her mother: 'I am enjoying the most essential happiness ... The marriage was consummated over a week ago. The exploit was repeated yesterday, even more fully than the first time. I don't think I am pregnant yet, but at least I can hope to be so soon.'

Typically, the Austrian ambassador was more matter-of-fact, and reported that on Monday, 18 August 1777: 'The King came to see the Queen when she was getting out of her bath; man and wife stayed together for an hour and a quarter ... The royal surgeon Lassonne confirmed that the marriage had been consummated.'

The farce was finally over. The gossip could stop. Or could it?

III

Louis XVI's lack of sexual appetite could easily be dismissed as an excuse for prurient tittle-tattle, in the same way that people speculate how the teenaged Catherine Howard (Henry VIII's number five) coped with the bulk of her aged husband, or enjoy stories of the frisky young Queen Victoria bolting her bedroom door when she first married Prince Albert.

But Louis XVI's interminable virginity had dire repercussions, and not only because the French royal couple was without a son and heir for several years.

Even though France's kings were no longer forced to put on armour and lead armies into battle, they had to be real *hommes*. Almost all of them had official mistresses, and most produced tribes of illegitimate children. Louis XV had pushed things too far by devoting practically *all* his attention to what went on below the waist, but sexual attractiveness was part of a usual French monarch's mystique. The idea that a king could bed any woman in France, from a pert young servant to the wife of the noblest aristocrat, cemented his status as head *homme*. By being a total failure in the bedroom for several critical years at the start of his reign, Louis XVI betrayed an animal weakness. He was sending out the message that he had no authority, even in his own bed. If he had been a lion, he would have been expelled from the pride.

This question of a ruler's reputation was one that William the Conqueror, Duke of Normandy, had solved with brutal efficiency – the way he solved every problem. His wife Mathilde was only about 4 feet 4 inches (130 cm) tall, but possessed a fiery temper and was not afraid to stand up to her giant warrior of a husband. On one occasion, however, she provoked a public row. William grabbed her by the hair and dragged her through the streets of the Norman town of Caen. Such domestic violence is of course morally unacceptable, but William clearly realized that he had to show everyone that his manliness, and thereby his authority as a leader, should never be in doubt. Fathering ten children and invading Britain also helped.

Louis XVI, on the other hand, was letting his subjects know that it was OK to doubt his prowess. And people began to say that his poor sexual performance was just one symptom of a more general inadequacy.

Almost everyone who knew the young Louis XVI described him as unremarkable, the kind of youth who would have been ignored if he hadn't been wearing a crown. He wasn't exactly ugly, but he was no looker, either. One of his pageboys, a young nobleman called Félix d'Hézecques, wrote in his memoirs that: 'His face was pleasant, but his teeth, unevenly spaced, made his laugh ungracious.' The English politician William Wilberforce saw Louis out hunting and called him 'so strange a being (of the hog kind)'.

In her memoirs, Madame Campan described Louis XVI's graceless walk, messy hair and melancholic demeanour. She even made an accidental innuendo: 'His organ, without being hard, was not at all pleasant.' In fact she was talking about his strident voice.

In a similarly dismissive vein, Marie-Antoinette's brother Joseph wrote home that his new brother-in-law was: 'A bit weak though not stupid. He has opinions and judgement, but he is apathetic in body and mind.' It seems that poor Louis had nothing going for him except the accident of birth that made him heir to the throne.

Even in his own family, as a teenager he was compared unfavourably to his younger brother, Louis Stanislas, an obese but self-confident wit with a cruel tongue, and his cousin, Louis Philippe, who had inherited their grandfather Louis XV's dashing good looks and sexual appetite. Louis Philippe, for example, bedded his 16-year-old wife Louise Marie immediately, and then set about creating a reputation as a serial adulterer – much more like an old-school French monarch (though he would later side with the revolutionaries to save his own head, and even vote in parliament to guillotine Louis XVI).

The most frequent comparisons, however, were with Louis XVI's youngest brother, Charles, who produced a son and a daughter before Louis had even started sleeping with Marie-Antoinette. Charles's obvious willingness to do his royal duty got the satirists dunking their quills in their inkwells. In 1779, an anonymous pamphlet appeared, *Les Amours de Charlot et Toinette* (*The Loves of Charlie and Toinette*). It was a 155-line erotic poem, purportedly 'stolen from V . . .' (that is, Versailles), which describes how the Queen has got fed up with waiting for 'her husband, the bad fucker' (*'mauvais fouteur'*), 'whose matchstick is no bigger than a straw, always soft and always bent'. She therefore turns for consolation to Charles, whose 'member is a poker' and who lays her on a velvet sofa and sets her 'pretty nipples trembling'. It is a vulgar piece of soft porn, and surprisingly forgiving, because the author ends on a philosophical thought:

> *Quand on nous parle de vertu,*
> *C'est souvent par envie;*
> *Car enfin serions-nous en vie,*
> *Si nos pères n'eussent foutu.*

> (When one talks about virtue,
> It's often out of envy,
> Because would we be alive
> If our fathers hadn't fucked?)

Despite this apparent forgiveness, though, the poem shows how, even after Louis XVI and Marie-Antoinette had produced a child together, people were freely joking about the King's lack of sexual appetite.

As a young married man, Louis XVI seems to have other things on his mind. He has gone down in history as what would nowadays be called a nerd. He had his grandfather's gaming room turned into a library (he was an avid reader, especially of books on geography and history), and set up workshops in his apartments where he would carry out all sorts of mechanical experiments. He even had a forge installed in the palace, no doubt provoking comment to the effect that instead of hammering at lumps of metal, he should have been turning his energies to lewder sorts of banging.

During the period when everyone at Versailles was trying to cajole the Prince into having sex, Mercy, the Austrian ambassador, said exactly this, albeit more elegantly. He wrote to Marie-Antoinette's mother in despair that:

> All the influence she [Marie-Antoinette] has over him has not been able to distract this young Prince from his extraordinary taste for everything to do with building work, such as masonry, carpentry and similar things ... He works alongside the labourers, shifting materials, beams, and paving stones, spending hours on this tiresome exercise ... We must try to lure him away from this with the promise of more pleasant, suitable activities.

When he became king, Louis XVI transferred his love of manual work to even more obsessive pursuits, and would spend hours building clocks and combination locks. While still a prince, he studied with the country's best locksmiths and makers of decorative ironwork. The writer Jean-Louis Giraud-Soulavie, a virulent anti-royalist usually known as the Abbé de Soulavie, visited Louis XVI's (abandoned) apartments at Versailles in 1792 and found: 'above the King's private library, a forge, two anvils, a thousand iron tools, various ordinary locks, but delicate and perfectly made, as well as secret locks and others decorated in gilded copper'. These were probably made by Louis XVI himself.

Louis also took lessons from a master clockmaker, Pierre Le Roy (whom he put on a regular salary), learning how to create and assemble the tiny components necessary to build beautiful timepieces. In 1890 a clock was sold at auction in London for £30,000 (a vast sum, equivalent to 50 times the annual living expenses for a well-off middle-class family at the time). It was listed as a wedding present made for the Fitzwilliam family by Louis XVI.

All this points to much more than a hobby. If Louis had been allowed to survive the Revolution, he could have earned a decent living making padlocks, repairing watches or tiling bathrooms.

To be fair, though, this nerdish taste for manual work was a sign of modernity. It was the writer Jean-Jacques Rousseau in his 1762 treatise on education, *Émile,* who suggested that children (boys, anyway) of the privileged classes should learn 'a purely mechanical art in which the hands work more than the head'. Rousseau saw this as a means of bringing about social awareness. Émile is told:

> It is less about learning a craft than overcoming the prejudices against crafts ... You will never have to work to earn a living ... but no matter, don't work out of necessity, work for the glory of it. Lower yourself to the status of a craftsman in order to rise above your own status.

In the later eighteenth century, the whole French royal family was educated along these lines. King Louis-Philippe, the son of Louis XVI's cousin also called Louis Philippe (though without the hyphen), would later write in his memoirs that the education he received from his governess Madame de Genlis 'was very democratic, like the century, and became more so as the Revolution approached'. He complained that 'Madame de

Genlis put the blame on Rousseau and followed his system, meaning that she was obliged to make me plane wood so that, like Émile, I became a carpenter.'

In other words, Louis XVI's talent for building complex machines was the result of his grandfather Louis XV's wish that his male heirs should embrace modern philosophical ideas about some measure of social equality, and therefore needed to learn respect for manual labour.

IV

Despite his modernity, Louis XVI had one obsession that marked him out as an old-school royal. This was hunting. When he wasn't building locks and clocks, he was out in the forest massacring wildlife.

Regular hunting was what set the upper classes apart from everyone else, just as it did at the same time in England. Hunting in France was still governed by tradition – with a few exceptions for government ministers and high-ranking military officers, only people who could prove their nobility going back to 1400 were allowed to join the royal hunt, or even follow along in a carriage.

Louis XVI started riding to hounds when he was 15, mainly in pursuit of wild boar and stags. As a teenager, he was free to hunt whenever he wanted. In October 1772, for example, he went on 14 stag hunts, 2 wild boar hunts and 6 shoots. That came to 22 days out of a possible 31, often a long way from Versailles, in the royal forests of Rambouillet, Fontainebleau and Saint-Germain. Later, as king, he cut this down to about two hunts a week, but they were still the highlights in his calendar.

Hunting was one area in which Louis displayed what were seen at the time as manly, and truly royal, qualities. Félix d'Hézecques, the former pageboy, tells a story about one of the gardeners at Versailles, a Swiss man who owned an immense, heavy musket. Louis XVI heard about the weapon and went to try it out. Félix wrote that: 'Taking the rifle, he [the King] lifted it effortlessly to his shoulder and fired, without being in the slightest overbalanced by the report. Despite his bad eyesight, he was an accurate shot.'

Louis XVI seems to have felt like one of the lads when he was out hunting. His shyness disappeared and he let himself go. When he got back home, his post-hunt suppers would be lively occasions when he would gleefully buttonhole some unfortunate *aristo* and describe the thrill of the chase. Joseph-François-Régis de Séguret, one of Louis XVI's valets, gave a comic description of one such supper in his memoirs:

> The conversation didn't finish until the King had transported the listener to all the places that the stag had taken him, named the villages and farms he had been to, the rivers he crossed and how he crossed them, described all the tricks the animal tried in its attempt to shake off the hounds, recalled the difficulties of the terrain, etc. ...

The boar hunts sometimes ended in the animal being driven into a pen where it would be stabbed to death with lances, either by Louis XVI himself or a lucky hunter nominated by him to do the honours.

After such a physically and emotionally charged day, it is hardly surprising that often, come bedtime, Louis would just flop on to his mattress and pass out.

In short, as far as his own reputation and the dynastic future of the monarchy were concerned, Louis XVI managed to turn even hunting, the most macho and most royal of pastimes, into sexual-avoidance behaviour.

It was also his attitude to hunting that gave written proof to what is often quoted as Louis XVI's most serious character fault – his apparent lack of passion about almost anything except his hobbies.

The most commonly cited evidence for this is an infamous diary entry on 14 July 1789 that is taken as a clear sign of his detachment from everyday life in France. He wrote *'Rien'* – 'Nothing'. The Bastille, the prison where people were held by royal warrant, was stormed, its governor lynched, and armed mobs ruled the streets of Paris, but to the King this counted for 'nothing'. It was a *'rien'* that he would come to regret.

In fact, though, this *'rien'* simply meant that Louis had killed no animals that day. Whatever ceremony he attended, whichever noteworthy person visited him, whoever at court was promoted or died, he would always make a note in his diary of that day's hunting. Details of his kills were recorded with the same meticulous attention he gave to his clockmaking, and at the end of each year he had the dates and numbers copied out by a calligrapher, framed, and hung on the staircase leading up to his library.

His hunting entries are almost enthusiastic – on 6 October 1775, he wrote: 'Shoot on the plain of Créteil, 282 kills.' By contrast, on the day he first met Marie-Antoinette, the young girl sent from Austria to warm up his bed, his only comment in the diary was a blunt: 'Met Madame la Dauphine.' When a long-serving minister of state died, he noted: 'Nothing, death of M. Maurepas at 2.30 in the morning.' On 6 October 1789, when Louis had been taken by force to Paris and was being held captive in the Tuileries palace by armed renegades, he wrote only: *'Rien,* my aunts came to dinner.'

Perhaps he was showing reserve; perhaps he didn't have much spare time for writing (though he always managed to tot up his annual score of hunting kills); maybe he didn't think it necessary to keep a personal record of the major events in his life when a king's every move is chronicled by courtiers and historians. But what the diary seems to suggest most of all is someone who is a passenger in almost all aspects of his life, a passive observer of anything that doesn't involve chasing after animals.

The problem for the French monarchy was that this is not the kind of leader that a regime needs when it is being challenged. Napoleon Bonaparte, who was willing to cross continents and sacrifice whole armies to defend his authority, gave a typically Napoleonic analysis of Louis XVI's character:

At another time, he would have been an excellent king, but he was worthless during a revolution. He lacked resolution and firmness ... In his place, I would have got on my horse, and, making a few concessions on one side, and giving a few cracks of the whip on the other, I would have restored order.

If the revolutionaries had been stags or wild boar, maybe Louis XVI would have brought them to heel. As it was, France now had a king who, when the political terrain became difficult, would let his opponents outrun him.

V

Nevertheless, by all accounts Louis XVI was not the indifferent tyrant that the revolutionaries would later make him out to be. Yes, he was rich, privileged and out of touch, but he was a benevolent human being – sometimes too much so. Félix d'Hézecques describes in his memoirs how one day:

> Louis XVI, returning from the hunt on the road to Saint-Cyr [near Versailles], met a poor deserter who was being taken back to his regiment for punishment. The soldier ... dropped to his knees and, holding out his arms towards the King, begged for clemency. The monarch immediately ordered the officer of his guards to have the letters of pardon sent out. For the rest of the day, the King's cheerfulness showed how satisfied he was to have exercised this royal prerogative.

After this, Félix d'Hézecques says that Louis XVI was kept away from processions of galley slaves being marched to Brest, for fear that he would free them all.

In general, however, this royal compassion was well received. The Maréchal de Richelieu,[3] an old friend of the previous king,

---

[3] Amusingly, Richelieu leaves out these earlier kings' love of women, perhaps because he himself was such a prolific womanizer that Laclos is said to have used him as the model for Valmont in *Dangerous Liaisons*.

said that earlier generations of the royal family had loved 'paint-ings and war … King Louis XVI is different: he loves the people.'

Marie-Antoinette's brother Joseph, a worldly-wise man, told Louis that he should get out amongst his people and show his affection – or at least his respect – for them. Madame Campan reported in her memoirs that Joseph 'said in our presence that he [Louis] should not only know everything there is in Paris, but that he should travel everywhere, and reside a few days in every large city in France'. Sadly, the advice went unheeded.

Today, the British royal family has learnt that shaking a few hands, smiling for the crowds and showing interest in an exhibi-tion of local vegetables does wonders for the popularity of a monarchy. Before the Revolution brought Louis XVI into enforced contact with his people, he wasn't that kind of monarch, and it was to cost him dear.

Chapter 7

MARIE-ANTOINETTE, THE QUEEN OF ROYAL EXCESS

'Il faut bien que je me distraie et je n'en trouve les moyens qu'en multipliant mes amusements.'
'I have to entertain myself, and the only way I have found is by multiplying my amusements.'

Marie-Antoinette (1755–93), in a letter to
her mother, Maria Theresa, Empress of Austria

I

Marie-Antoinette has become such a symbol of royal extravagance and arrogance that it is often forgotten how popular she was for the first few years after her arrival in France.

Stories about her kindness and compassion were common currency amongst ordinary French people in the early 1770s. The most famous concerned a hunting accident in October 1773. Marie-Antoinette was out watching her young husband exhaust himself chasing deer when a stag panicked and gored a peasant who was working in the forest. His wife fainted, and Marie-Antoinette got out of her carriage, revived the woman with smelling salts, and then gave her her purse. While the wounded peasant was being tended to, the wife was carried into Marie-Antoinette's carriage and taken home. Later, royal doctors were sent to check up on the couple, and after this, Marie-Antoinette asked for regular updates until both the peasant and his wife were back on their feet.

Embellished versions of the story were written up, illustrated in cheap engravings and printed on fans, and soon the whole of France knew that it possessed an angelic Austrian princess. People began coming out to the sites of royal hunts to cheer her – and maybe also to throw themselves in the path of a passing stag in the hope of making some money.

The generosity of the young Princess and her husband extended to much larger sums than the few coins in a purse. We saw earlier how Marie-Antoinette and Louis donated money to the Parisian victims of the stampede after their wedding. While Louis XV was on his deathbed, the soon-to-be Louis XVI asked for 200,000 *livres*[1] to be taken from his and his wife's personal funds to be distributed amongst the paupers of Paris as compensation for the national sense of loss. The Austrian ambassador, Mercy, reported to Marie-Antoinette's mother in Vienna that: 'It was done immediately and created the greatest possible sensation amongst the public.'

The young couple went even further. On acceding to the throne, every French monarch was entitled to what was called a 'gift on the happy succession'. This amounted to about 100,000 *livres*. At the same time, his wife was usually granted the less elegantly named *'ceinture de la reine'*, or 'queen's belt', which was in fact a tax levied as an expression of the people's love for the new lady on the throne, whether they loved her or not. Naturally, like most other French taxes at the time, this one didn't apply to the aristocracy or the clergy.

In 1774, both Louis and Marie-Antoinette declined these gifts. One could argue that it was an empty gesture – they didn't exactly need the money – but it was a gesture nevertheless, and was probably sincere. A year earlier, Marie-Antoinette had written to her mother after a visit to Paris, talking about 'the

[1] At the time, a working family needed to earn about 500 *livres* per year to survive in any comfort.

tenderness and enthusiasm of this poor people who, despite the terrible weight of taxes, were transported with joy to see us'. She really does seem to have felt for the ill-clad, underfed residents of Paris's filthy, narrow streets who came out in their masses to greet her – probably the first really poor people she had ever seen (and smelt).

Marie-Antoinette's act of generosity over the 'queen's belt' inspired an aristocrat from the north of France, the Comte de Couturelle, to pen a witty poem:

> *Vous renoncez, charmante souveraine,*
> *Au plus beau de vos revenus;*
> *A quoi vous servirait la ceinture de reine?*
> *Vous avez celle de Vénus.*

> (You decline, charming sovereign,
> The greatest of your revenues;
> But what use would you have for the queen's belt?
> You have that of Venus.)

Admittedly this was a shameless piece of crawling from a man who wouldn't have had to pay his share of the tax anyway, but it was the kind of well-expressed praise that could spread around the country and create a reputation. Refusing the 'belt' was an easily understood news item that told everyone who this new queen really was, in exactly the same way as Princess Diana would later shape public opinion by shaking hands with an Aids patient in the 1980s and walking through a minefield in the 1990s. It was both positive and astute, and established Marie-Antoinette's place in the nation's hearts as an admirable, kindly consort.

Sadly, instead of nurturing this capital of public goodwill, Marie-Antoinette seems to have taken it for granted, and she was soon frittering it all away in a series of public-relations disasters that would turn her from an angel into a figure of hate. Her mother wrote to her, advising that France was living through 'a time when minds are undergoing the strongest fermentation', and that 'everything depends on this happy beginning – which has surpassed all expectations – being preserved, so that it makes you two happy, along with your people.' The hint seems to have fallen on deaf ears.

It wasn't entirely Marie-Antoinette's fault. For a start, as we have seen, the young bride was being more or less ignored by her new husband, and was under huge pressure to turn the sexual situation around, via the non-stop stream of moralizing letters from her mother in Vienna and the constant, hectoring voice in her ear of the Austrian ambassador to Versailles. As well as wanting her to breed, they urged Marie-Antoinette to take on her role as the most senior woman at the French court. She had to impose her presence and shake off the *'Autrichienne'* label.

Largely because of the free time and frustration imposed on her by her husband, and because of this pressure to act like a queen, Marie-Antoinette began her transformation into the snobbish, frivolous, over-spending narcissist who would later inspire the famous (and fake) rumour that she had joked about starving Parisians needing to eat cake.

II

The process started even before Marie-Antoinette became queen, with a war of supremacy against Louis XV's mistress, the lower-class Madame du Barry. Obliged to fit in with the snobs, keen to stress her own royal origins, and no doubt a little envious of another woman's sexual power, Marie-Antoinette turned her back – literally – on the official royal mistress, ignoring her whenever their paths crossed.

In the end, it was only her mother's insistence that it would be diplomatic to please Louis XV that forced Marie-Antoinette to step off her pedestal. In a scene illustrating all the futility of life at Versailles, the teenaged Princess (who had just turned 16) was greeting a crowd of well-wishers on New Year's Day, 1772, when she half turned in Madame du Barry's direction, and said:

'Il y a bien du monde à Versailles aujourd'hui' ('there are a lot of people at Versailles today'). This public concession caused a sensation at court, as if two battling generals had called a truce after a day of slaughter, and Louis XV was delighted that peace had broken out.

A few months later, Marie-Antoinette gave a similar performance, conversing about the weather with courtiers while facing the whole group, including Madame du Barry. Again, Louis XV was ecstatic, and Marie-Antoinette's mother congratulated her on a diplomatic triumph.

But Marie-Antoinette's heart was not in these gestures of reconciliation. She wrote to her mother that she had betrayed her principles. She would have preferred to carry on snubbing the low-class interloper, and winning moral victories that would keep the anti-Barry gossips busy. In short, she was being drawn into the cloying, cliquish atmosphere at court that would eventually bring down the whole regime.

In her defence, it is often pointed out by Marie-Antoinette's admirers that she cut back on the senseless rules of etiquette at Versailles, and encouraged her husband to do likewise. Madame Campan explained this by saying that Marie-Antoinette had been brought up at court in Vienna where 'simplicity was allied to majesty', so that it was 'not surprising that she wanted to free herself from constraints that she thought unnecessary'.

For example, in 1778 one of the palace's most unpleasant traditions was scrapped. In the past, presumably to make sure that princesses and princes really were born of queens, anyone could enter the bedchamber as soon as it was announced that *'la Reine va accoucher'* ('the Queen is about to give birth'). But on 19 December 1778, there were so many courtiers crowded around the bed that Marie-Antoinette felt faint, and Louis XVI had to fling open the windows to let in some (dangerously cold) air, while servants chased out the spectators. From then on, it was decided, queens would deliver in peace – not that any more queens would ever give birth at Versailles after Marie-Antoinette.

The most famous (and apparently true) story about Marie-Antoinette's attitude to royal ritual came when she was left naked in her bedchamber in midwinter because of the absurd protocol as to who should hand her her clothes.

Madame Campan paints the scene vividly in her memoirs. The problem was, she says, that 'dressing [Marie-Antoinette] was a masterpiece of etiquette; everything was regulated'. Each item of clothing had to be given to the woman of highest rank present, who would then put them on Marie-Antoinette. On one occasion, Madame Campan herself was about to clad Marie-Antoinette in her *chemise* (undershirt) when a *dame d'honneur* (a more noble courtier) entered the room. This lady naturally took off her gloves and claimed the *chemise*. However, just then, the Duchess of Orléans arrived, an even higher-ranking courtier. Etiquette demanded that the *chemise* be handed back to Madame Campan, who would then pass it to the Duchess, once she too had removed her gloves. Her hands were barely bare before the Countess of Provence (Marie-Antoinette's sister-in-law) entered – a still more royal personage.

By this time, Madame Campan, says, 'the Queen had folded her arms across her chest and appeared to be cold'. Seeing this, the Countess didn't bother to take off her gloves. She quickly slipped the *chemise* over Marie-Antoinette's head, knocking her hair out of place.

Madame Campan remembered that Marie-Antoinette 'laughed to disguise her impatience, but only after muttering through her teeth: "This is unbearable! What effrontery!"'

No doubt echoing Marie-Antoinette's own sentiments, Madame Campan went on to denounce this senseless protocol, talking about...

> ... etiquette that, in the domestic life of our princes, led them to have themselves treated like idols, and in their public life, made them victims of all these customs ... At the palace of Versailles, Marie-Antoinette identified a whole host of established and revered traditions that seemed unbearable to her.

The *chemise* ceremony was duly scrapped, and Marie-Antoinette carried out an audit of the pointless rituals that had made Louis XIV's Versailles such a nightmare. She complained that if she was thirsty, for example, only a noble lady-in-waiting could give her a drink. If none was present, she had to stay parched until a suitably aristocratic woman was found. This constraint was crossed off the protocol list.

Even more radically, Marie-Antoinette decreed that from now on, she wanted male servants. Until then, only women had been allowed to serve her directly. Men's roles had been limited to specific tasks. For example, it was men who turned over the heavy royal mattresses, and if she wanted dust removing from under her bed, she had to call the *valet de chambre-tapissier* (upholstery valet). That, Marie-Antoinette decreed, would now change, and any of her male or female staff members would be able to perform any task (within reason) for her.

Marie-Antoinette also had her apartments transformed so that she would have a special room in which to receive her personal hairdresser and 'physionomist', a Parisian celebrity called Léonard. This was a scandalous breach of etiquette because normally, anyone providing such a personal service for a king or queen had to work exclusively for their royal client so that they wouldn't give away intimate secrets. But according to Madame Campan, Marie-Antoinette ordered Léonard to keep his finger on the pulse of changing fashions (even though by all rights, Marie-Antoinette was meant to be creating all the latest trends): 'The Queen, fearing that the hairdresser's good taste would be lost if he changed his way of working, wanted him to carry on serving several women at court and in Paris.' This was a very modern view – democratic even – but some people at Versailles thought it all very un-royal.

Marie-Antoinette also hated eating lunch[2] in public. She saw it as an opportunity for curious people to come and stare, as Madame Campan humorously put it:

[2] At Marie-Antoinette's Versailles, lunch was called *'dîner'*, as it had always been called at the French court.

This spectacle thrilled the provincials. At lunchtime, the only people one met on the stairs were good folk who, having seen [Marie-Antoinette] drink her soup, were on their way to see the princes take their broth, and who would then rush breathlessly to watch Mesdames [Louis XV's three spinster daughters] eat their dessert.

III

At first, Louis XVI disapproved of these loosening standards, toeing the official line that 'appearances at court produce more effect than realities'. To uphold these appearances, he was willing to bow to some of Versailles's worst traditions. Staff were allowed to sell off uneaten food and drink, just like in Louis XIV's day. Now they went even further. Every time a member of the royal family left a room, candles were snuffed and replaced with new ones. In Marie-Antoinette's apartments alone, 109 candles were lit on summer evenings, 145 in winter – not counting balls and parties, of course. Soon, the whole of Versailles was lit by these barely used candles that had been sold off at personal profit by servants. Marie-Antoinette's staff even received a daily *droit aux bougies* (right to candles) of 80 *livres* each, to offset days on which few candles were saleable. This was a sizeable sum, about enough to buy two cows.

Maintaining these traditions caused other abuses, too. Palace guards were still paid a bonus for buying straw bedding, whereas their barracks were now fitted with mattresses. Servants received a travel allowance, even though monarchs no longer migrated around the country as they had done in medieval times. The Queen's apothecary was paid 2,000 *livres* a year to buy drugs, whether she was ill or not. Most servants began to request – and receive – tips just to perform their duties. All this etiquette and tradition was coming at an extortionate price.

For at least the first few years of his reign, though, Louis XVI clung on to some of the appearances that 'produced more effect than realities'. According to Félix d'Hézecques, Louis was highly conscious of his ceremonial role, and would lunch in public every Sunday – in Marie-Antoinette's own antechamber, so that she had to join him. Hézecques says that:

> For the Queen, this *dîner* was purely for show. She ate in her apartments later. But the King would eat with, if I may use the expression, all the frankness of his character. His vigorous, healthy temperament, bolstered by continual exercise, gave him an appetite that he satisfied with a good humour that it was a pleasure to see.

An English farmer and writer called Arthur Young[3] went along to one of these meals, and confirmed what Félix d'Hézecques said: 'The ceremony of the King's dining in public is more odd than splendid. The Queen sat by him with a cover before her, but ate nothing; conversing with the duke of Orleans, and the duke of Liancourt, who stood behind her chair.'

Louis XVI was putting on a good show for his audience, but his wife was just pretending – a neat summary of their early attitudes to life at Versailles.

Louis also made sure that Marie-Antoinette took part in one of her most important public duties. Despite her allergy to giving birth in front of a crowd, she did receive the hordes of unsavoury revellers when her first son was born in October 1781. Ordinary people greeted the event with almost tribal delight. Representatives of Parisian trades paraded out to Versailles to put on street shows – chimney sweeps carried a wooden chimney with a boy perched on top, sedan-chair carriers brought out a woman and a baby dressed up as the newborn Dauphin and his nurse, locksmiths hammered on an anvil, shoemakers made a pair of boots for the baby, tailors made him an army uniform, butchers came with a fatted calf. The only tradesmen kept away from the Queen were the gravediggers, who came out to

---

[3] For more of Young's impressions of France, see Chapter 10.

Versailles armed with their spades. The police wisely sent them straight back to Paris.

Louis XVI greeted this spontaneous show of public loyalty from a balcony, while Marie-Antoinette stayed indoors. But she agreed to let fifty or so of the most raucous, and probably malodorous, visitors into her bedroom.

These were the *poissardes*, a name meaning vulgar women, coming from the French word *poisse*, or filth (itself derived from *poix* – pitch – rather than *poisson* – fish). They were loud-mouthed market women, not exactly Marie-Antoinette's kind of people. Once inside the Queen's bedchamber, the chief *poissarde* gave a speech that had been inscribed for Marie-Antoinette on the back of a fan. Much of the speech was addressed to Louis XVI, who came in to meet the women. The woman announced, in her coarse lower-class accent, that: 'This child must be like you. You will teach him, Sire, to be good and just, as you are. We promise to teach others how they should love and respect their king.'

It was a key political moment. These were the woman who, almost exactly eight years later, would march out to Versailles again, this time in their thousands, armed with knives, pikes and even a couple of cannons, to storm the palace and demand bread.

More pleasurable elements of royal spectacle were preserved, largely as a sop to Marie-Antoinette. Grand balls were held at Versailles every Wednesday from the New Year until Lent. During these *soirées*, according to Félix d'Hézecques, 'one still saw the nobility and magnificence worthy of a great king, and the gallantry worthy of France'.

Entrance to the balls was restricted to courtiers who arrived by carriage. Guests were encouraged to dress simply so that they could dance, and maids were on hand to 'repair the disorder that lively dancing might bring to the costumes'. Supper was served at midnight, with the royal couple eating in full view of the guests. Louis XVI would usually leave at one in the morning, partly because he wanted to get up early to hunt, but also because he knew that the partygoers would only relax once he was gone. The dancing would carry on until dawn, but things rarely got out of hand. Hézecques says that these *soirées* reflected Louis XVI's character, his *'simplicité et bonhomie'* – young danced with old, and courtiers were encouraged to join in rather than sneak off to gamble, so that 'never at court did one see such decency reign, or at the same time such open gaiety'.

IV

True to character, though, regarding other aspects of palace life, Louis XVI gradually weakened. He took to moving about the palace as if he were just an ordinary courtier, or even a visitor. Observers were often shocked to see him wandering into a room unannounced. According to Félix d'Hézecques, the King 'should have been set apart, surrounded at a distance, so that his subjects would have time to examine him, take in his image, and engrave it on to their memory' – this was, of course, the tactic that had protected Louis XIV's mystique for so long.

Under Marie-Antoinette's influence, the very nature of life at the palace began to change. Instead of a place where royals and aristocrats gathered to affirm their own superiority and celebrate what Hézecques called 'the magnificence worthy of a great king', Versailles became the headquarters of Marie-Antoinette's young in-crowd. True, the previous monarch Louis XV had allowed sexy and/or talented outsiders into his inner circle, but he was king. And besides, other less beautiful and gifted *aristos* had been welcome at his court. Marie-Antoinette excluded anyone she didn't like.

This exclusion process had begun as soon as Louis XV fell ill with the first symptoms of the smallpox that killed him. Instantly, Madame du Barry was out – a move made easier because a dying king was always obliged to send away his mistress so that he could confess his sins and receive the last rites. And once Marie-Antoinette became queen, the only people she wanted to see at court were a crowd of pretty young things, all of them determined to have fun. Her frequently quoted motto was: 'I don't know why anyone dares to appear at court after the age of thirty.'

To be fair to Marie-Antoinette, she wasn't alone in her disrespect for some aspects of palace etiquette. Her 'undershirt scene' has been immortalized on film, but less well known is Louis XVI's own rebellion against the *cérémonie du coucher*, when selected courtiers were supposed to dress the King in his nightshirt. Louis XV used to submit to the ceremony before nipping away in secret to another bed. But Louis XVI had little patience for the ritual. He would perform it, but whenever a new courtier was given the honour of conducting the nightshirt ceremony, he would duck out of the way, forcing the embarrassed *aristo* to chase him around the bed, laughing all the while at the absurdity of the situation and, according to one observer, 'tormenting people who were sincerely attached to him'.

Louis XVI also became disrespectful to the most esteemed members of the court, and not only in the privacy of his bedchamber. On 2 January 1776, he was due to attend the traditional procession of the Order of the Holy Spirit,[4] France's most prestigious, and most devoutly Catholic, noble order. But the weather was perfect for hunting, so Louis was impatient to get the ceremony over with, and his brother Charles yelled at the knights of the order to hurry up. The old-school aristocrats – coincidentally, to join the order, one had to be older than 30, Marie-Antoinette's cut-off age for fashionable courtiers – were predictably 'scandalized'.

Lack of respect from two young royal men went far beyond impatience with meaningless etiquette, and struck at the heart of the monarchy's role. If the King was no longer the figurehead

---

[4] The members of this order wore blue ribbons and were therefore nicknamed *'les cordons bleus'*. By association, the name became linked with anything of great distinction. The order was disbanded after the Revolution, but the name was revived in 1895 when a journalist, Marthe Distel, founded a cookery magazine, *La Cuisinière cordon bleu – The* [female] *Cordon Bleu Cook* – followed by the first *École du cordon bleu* in 1896.

for France's oldest institutions, if he was just a lout who wanted
to go hunting, what was the point of him? The same went for
Marie-Antoinette – if all she wanted to do was party and put on
plays with her friends, why should the country finance her lifestyle, especially as she was foreign?

Such youthful exuberance might sound like a healthy rejuve-
nation of fusty court life, but more than anything else, it simply
introduced a new level of snobbery. Versailles became divided
between those who tried to maintain traditional court life, and
those who turned up their nose at it. Older courtiers, even
members of the royal family or the noblest dynasties, began to be
ignored or snubbed by the youngsters. They took to staying away
from Versailles, or to travelling there from Paris for specific occasions, such as the grand balls where appearances were upheld
and where they were sure to outnumber the young trendies.

Meanwhile, artists, musicians and even hairdressers had constant access to the Queen's apartments and could sneer at the
unfashionable oldies who were excluded. As the Austrian writer
Stefan Zweig put it in his biography of Marie-Antoinette:
'Gradually the circle of privileged people around Marie-
Antoinette formed an unbreachable barrier. The rest of court
knew that behind this artificial wall lay earthly paradise.' Older
courtiers wondered, says Zweig:

> What is the use of having a modest and honest young king, a
> sovereign who is not the plaything of mistresses, if we are still
> forced to beg from a favourite? ... Are we really going to put up
> with being treated so negligently, with being excluded so insult-
> ingly, by this young *Autrichienne* who surrounds herself with
> foreign rascals and women of dubious repute?

Marie-Antoinette caused a scandal by inviting her old harpsichord teacher, the German composer Christoph Willibald
Gluck, into her boudoir. Not only was he trying to make French
opera lighter, comic even, he was, as Madame Campan put it,
'allowed to attend the Queen while she was being made up, and

all the time he was there, she would speak to him'. Even Marie-Antoinette's closest (and youngest) attendants were shocked by this intimacy with a mere musician – and Madame Campan was only a few years older than her queen.

The Prince de Montbarrey, Louis XVI's Secretary of State for War (who was in his late thirties when Marie-Antoinette arrived at court) summed up the new atmosphere as: 'Familiarity which, confusing everything ... destroyed the respect and veneration with which Louis XIV had deemed it necessary to surround himself, based on his knowledge of the character of his people.'

In short, Louis XVI and Marie-Antoinette were putting the final, shocking, touches to the process that had begun with Louis XV's flagrant immorality. And the royal family's reputation was about to sink to a new and fatal low.

V

One might think that the French monarchy could have survived a shake-up at Versailles. After all, would ordinary people really care if a few powdered old aristocrats were no longer allowed to handle the King and Queen's undershirts? Would they object if the King shortened parades by self-congratulating knights? Or if Marie-Antoinette actually started to use a publicly available hairdresser?[5]

But this shake-up had disastrous consequences: first, by allowing Marie-Antoinette to snub and alienate large sections of the aristocracy, Louis XVI was losing potential political allies. Secondly, Marie-Antoinette's young in-crowd encouraged her worst instincts: soon she was staying out half the night at Parisian parties while her husband waited back in Versailles, and spending fortunes on clothes, jewellery, wigs and similar frivolities.

[5] Amusingly, in 2016, France's President François Hollande caused a scandal in the French press when it was revealed that his own – exclusive – hairdresser was on a retainer of 9,895 euros a month.

She also began doling out vast *pensions* to her friends and allies. In a letter to Vienna in 1776, the Austrian ambassador Mercy listed some of them: Marie-Antoinette's closest confidante, Marie-Thérèse-Louise de Lamballe, was given 150,000 *livres*, while her brother received 40,000 plus a salary of 14,000 as a colonel (when a normal colonel's pay was only 4,000 *livres* a year). Mercy warned that people were criticizing Marie-Antoinette for this, and even blaming her for abuses that weren't her fault, such as the 40,000-*livre* pension given to a certain Chevalier de Luxembourg. The most serious allegation against her, he wrote, concerned the 6,000 *livres* given to Madame d'Andlau, a lady-in-waiting who had been dismissed for lending a *livre infâme* (vile book) to Adélaïde, one of Louis XV's spinster daughters. 'People were revolted that this lady should have been rewarded,' Mercy said. 'The Queen may not have granted this pension, but how can we make people believe it?'

It was a question that would have dire consequences later on.

As early as 1776, then, in the public eye, the young girl who had refused her 'queen's belt' had become a wanton spendthrift who was emptying the royal purse (which was, of course, filled by the people's taxes) into the hands of cronies and purveyors of luxury accessories. It was Louis XV all over again, but this time from an *Autrichienne* interloper, and a woman at that.

Everyone could see the effects of Marie-Antoinette's over-spending on her physical appearance. Until about 1775, hairstyles at court were rather elegant, usually involving lifting hair off the face or curling it down the shoulders – one of these was the *hérisson*, or hedgehog, in which hair was pinned up and curled into a sort of frizzy bonnet. But by 1777, the star *coiffeur* Léonard and his growing band of disciples were encouraging all the women under their spell to adopt increasingly ridiculous, and costly, hairstyles.

Women would wear ribbons, flags, feathers, stuffed birds, fresh flowers, and fruit and vegetables on or in their hair. A courtier, the Baronne d'Oberkirch, remembered fondly wearing 'small flat bottles of water on my head, into which real flowers were dipped so that they stayed fresh ... Springtime amidst the snow of powder created a marvellous effect.'

Hairstyles were so complicated that women needed a sort of metal scaffolding – called a *pouf* – to hold their locks aloft. The most notorious of these creations was the *Coiffure à la Belle Poule*, launched in 1778 to commemorate the ship of the same name, whose captain, Jean de la Clochetière, died fighting an English fleet during a sea battle in the Channel on 17 June 1778. Led by Marie-Antoinette, fashionable women had their hair modelled in the shape of a three- or four-masted frigate in full sail, complete with jewelled portholes and tasselled rigging. In truth, these creations were a cross between hats and hairstyles, with boats apparently floating on waves of hair that had been mounted on a *pouf* and supplemented with hairpieces.

Madame Campan admitted in her memoirs that the fortunes spent by women on their hair often caused 'angry family scenes' that were blamed on Marie-Antoinette: 'The general opinion was that the Queen would bankrupt every woman in France.' Though of course not all Frenchwomen could afford hairpins, let alone model frigates.

As well as provoking neckache and scornful glances from poor Parisians and older aristocrats, these absurd hairdos meant that young *élégantes* had to face the humiliation of manoeuvring themselves into carriages rather like giraffes entering a dog kennel. They often had to kneel on the floor for the long journey from Paris to Versailles and vice versa. A soldier and courtier, the Comte de Vaublanc, remembered that he once 'saw a woman who was not only kneeling in her carriage, she also held her head out of the door'.

Some enterprising hairdressers devised collapsible frames that could be let down at a moment's notice when entering a carriage or to hide their follies from disapproving oldsters. But the general opinion was that buildings would soon have to adapt – ceilings and doorways would need to be heightened, and theatres rebuilt with higher ceilings for their boxes.

There were even greater dangers attached to the monstrous hairdos. The Comte de Vaublanc recalled that: 'When a woman with such a topping danced at a ball, she had to be especially careful to duck if she passed under a chandelier.' The *coiffures* were serious fire hazards because the hair was liberally doused in grease to make it stay in place. A magazine called *Correspondance littéraire, philosophique et critique* asked a question in the scientific spirit of the age, with tongue firmly in cheek: 'All this ironwork – on stormy days, won't it attract lightning?'

Typically, Louis XVI, the King of Moderation, disapproved of this fashion, but did little to discourage it. Fortunately for him – although sadly for Marie-Antoinette – in 1781, during her second pregnancy, she began to suffer from hair loss, and her *coiffures* became much more restrained, often involving just a small bun on top of her head. She tried to encouraged fashionable Versailles and Paris to follow suit, but with mixed success. In 1784, the Baronne d'Oberkirch was still boasting of wearing her hair 'as high as possible, according to the fashion, with my diamonds and a bouquet of feathers'. As revolution loomed, a whole class of rich women still thought of nothing but decorating themselves.

Aside from the enforced moderation of Marie-Antoinette's hairstyles, excess coloured every aspect of her life. As she explained to her mother in a letter: 'I have to entertain myself, and the only way I have found is by multiplying my amusements.' The problem was that the public knew all about these 'amusements', and embellished them in an ever-increasing number of rumours.

There was plenty of gossip about what went on at the many *bals masqués* she attended in Paris. These had always been notorious pick-up parties – Louis XV first got together with Madame de Pompadour while he was disguised as a yew tree. Marie-Antoinette usually attended dances in more conventional dress, but with elaborate masks that supposedly hid the wearer's identity. Inevitably, though, she was often recognized,[6] and tongues wagged.

The most notorious of these Paris balls were *soirées* at the Opéra during the carnival season around New Year. Revellers would stream into the city from Versailles and every château in the region, and dancing would begin at around midnight, going on till dawn. Louis XVI rarely, if ever, attended these balls – he came a few times when they were first married, but got bored. After that, he often decided to sleep alone when Marie-Antoinette went out late, so as not to be woken when she came home in the small hours. Predictably, this only added fuel to the fire of gossip about the Queen's secret private life.

Surrounded by handsome young 'rascals', it was inevitable that salacious rumours sprang up. Marie-Antoinette's defenders are adamant that nothing untoward ever happened. Félix d'Hézecques assured his readers that: 'She knew how to conserve the affection of her husband, a favour that an unfaithful wife loses very fast,' and wrote that he refused to repeat the 'scandalous anecdotes ... about this unfortunate princess', which were 'too much the fruit of the vilest bad intent to sully my memoirs with them'.

Madame Campan, meanwhile, stressed that despite all the rumours about wantonness, Marie-Antoinette was so decent that she took baths wearing an undershirt buttoned to the neck, and when she got out, she always asked for a towel to be held up so no one else could see her. But this didn't stop the Abbé de Soulavie claiming that Marie-Antoinette bathed in the nude and had even received a clergyman while in the bath.[7]

A clergyman's fantasies might not be the most reliable source of information, but it was partly to check up on similar gossip

[6] For one thing, apparently Marie-Antoinette couldn't dance in time, though – as witty courtiers said – it was the music's fault, not hers.

[7] Madame Campan called Soulavie's book *'un recueil infâme'* – 'a vile collection' – and her nineteenth-century publisher added that 'what he allowed himself, any self-respecting author would forbid themselves'.

that Marie-Antoinette's brother Joseph was sent to Versailles in 1776. As well as giving sex-therapy sessions to Louis XVI, he attended Marie-Antoinette's parties, and came away decidedly anxious. She was, he said, an 'airhead' (*'tête de vent'*) who only listened to 'those who procure her the greatest pleasures'. His consolation was that, 'for the present, at least', she had not given in to the temptation to stray.

Some say that she didn't hold out forever. It was at one of the Paris balls that Marie-Antoinette met Axel von Fersen, the handsome Swedish count who, according to popular legend and Sofia Coppola's film, was to become her lover. He first spoke to her when she was 'incognito' at the bal de l'Opéra on 30 January 1774. Both of them were 19. He was away on his grand tour of Europe, while she was deeply frustrated by her sexless marriage – so they were the perfect match. Four years later, when Fersen was received at Versailles, she recognized him from their one encounter and exclaimed: 'An old acquaintance!' They became inseparable, and, it is often alleged, more than just good friends. It was Fersen who later organized the royal family's (disastrous) escape attempt in 1791 (of which more later), and who, in January 1792, received a letter from Marie-Antoinette saying that: 'I love you madly and never, never can I spend a moment without adoring you.'

It is not clear, though, that such declarations of love implied a sexual relationship. At the time, letter writers very often 'loved' each other, in much the same way as text message-writers now 'laugh out loud' at every joke and Facebookers assail their friends with hearts. Also, while at Versailles in Marie-Antoinette's circle of friends, Fersen was bedding any French lady who would have him. Would a queen have put up with being just another notch on his bedpost? Perhaps, if she felt so unloved that the occasional encounter with a Swedish Apollo eased her frustrations.

But whether or not Marie-Antoinette actually engaged in illicit Austro-Swedish relations is unimportant. What counted was that people believed it. A king could sleep around (and in some minds was under obligation to do so); a queen had to stay pure, ensuring that any babies she produced were of true royal blood. Rumours of female infidelity in the royal family undermined the monarchy itself.

In fact, there were few if any accusations about Fersen at the time. Most of these arose later, when revolutionaries began to dig for dirt about the man who had tried to help the King escape from France. On the other hand, as we saw earlier, there were plenty of rumours that she had slept with Louis XVI's youngest brother, Charles.

Strangely, in the openly adulterous climate of eighteenth-century France, most sexual tittle-tattle about Marie-Antoinette centred on the idea that she had lesbian lovers. Perhaps some part of the public consciousness found it hard to conceive the notion that a queen might sleep with any man less royal than a prince. Conveniently for Marie-Antoinette's enemies, at the time lesbianism was nicknamed 'the German vice', and was therefore a logical occupation for a Viennese woman. Male homosexuality was known as 'the Italian vice', because neither of these sexual 'deviations' was French, *bien sûr*.

Semi-pornographic engravings were sold depicting Marie-Antoinette and her beautiful confidante Yolande de Polignac in a passionate embrace. There was also a 16-page play called *L'Autrichienne en goguettes, ou L'Orgie royale* (*The Carousing Austrian Woman, or The Royal Orgy*) in which Marie-Antoinette enjoys the favours of both the above-mentioned Charles and Yolande de Polignac. In one of the first scenes, the three partici-pants in the orgy are just getting ready for action when Louis XVI wanders in, apparently under the impression that this is an ordinary social get-together. He apologizes for being late – 'I was busy finishing a lock, which I'm very happy with' – then drinks some champagne and falls asleep, at which point Charles immediately shoves his hand up Marie-Antoinette's dress. It's a double insult – not only is the King's wife having extra-marital romps with lovers of both sexes, she is doing it while he snores in the same room. Wittily, the anonymous author claims that 'musical accompaniment' to the soirée is provided by the Queen. Indeed, the whole play is so professionally written that it has been suggested that it was the work of Beaumarchais, the spurned courtier out for revenge on the royal family.

Marie-Antoinette's best friend when she first arrived at Versailles, Madame de Lamballe, was also the subject of lesbian rumours. A compendium called *Les Pamphlets libertins contre Marie-Antoinette* (*Sexual Pamphlets against Marie-Antoinette*), published in Paris in 1908, devotes a whole chapter to her, coyly headed 'Madame de Lamballe, or Embarking for Lesbos'. The revolutionaries nicknamed Lamballe the 'Sapho de Trianon' (after Marie-Antoinette's private house in the gardens of Versailles), and she was under interrogation about her supposed affair with Marie-Antoinette when she was stripped naked and decapitated by a mob in September 1792.

Marie-Antoinette's mother was worried enough about all these sex-related rumours to insult her daughter in a letter. Receiving a portrait of Marie-Antoinette in her Versailles finery, Maria Teresa wrote: 'I didn't see the image of a Queen of France. I saw an actress' (a thinly disguised, or completely undisguised, euphemism for a prostitute).

An increasing number of French people would have agreed. In their eyes, the Queen had fallen from the pinnacle of French society, virtual sainthood even, to the gutter. And by 1789, any remaining reverence for Marie-Antoinette would be gone.

VI

Louis XVI does not seem to have taken the rumours about his wife's infidelities seriously. Or maybe he was just too passionless to care. The proof of this is that he actually provided the venue for her most intimate parties – le Petit Trianon.

As we saw earlier, this 'small' château, a kilometre or so away from the main palace of Versailles, had been built by Louis XV for one of his official mistresses, so when Louis XVI gifted it to his wife in 1775, he was actually giving it a stamp of respectability. He graciously told Marie-Antoinette: 'This beautiful place has always been the refuge of the King's favourites. It must therefore be yours.' And for a French king to call his wife his 'favourite' was a very rare compliment.

When Louis referred to le Petit Trianon as a 'refuge', he used the French word *'séjour'*, meaning a temporary place to stay (nowadays it also means living room). He was overtly offering Marie-Antoinette the chance to escape the stifling etiquette at court, as well as the critical gaze of the courtiers who were constantly scanning her for proof that she had managed to tempt her husband into bed. It was a noble gesture, but one that quickly went awry.

When he made the gift, a year after he had come to the throne, Marie-Antoinette was already on the slippery slope downhill from respectability. So it delighted the gossips when she blacked out some of the windows at le Petit Trianon to shield herself and her in-crowd from prying eyes. And when she spent a fortune redesigning its gardens, shaping them into the fake 'English' hamlet that visitors can still see today.

Jardins anglais were all the rage in France at the time. This did not imply decking over the lawn and dotting gnomes around an electric fountain, as it might today. It meant a less formal space than the classical French garden with its gravelled walkways and rigidly shaped flowerbeds. Landscaping a garden as an idealized version of the English countryside, a perfect place for genteel strolling and picnics, was a habit of the British nobility, but it was also very much in the French 'back to nature' ideal inspired by Jean-Jacques Rousseau, even though a French *jardin anglais* was every bit as artificial – and costly – as geometric lawns or flowerbeds shaped like fleurs-de-lys.

Marie-Antoinette hired a French painter, Hubert Robert, who specialized in picturesque ruins, to design her romantic garden. Along with an architect, he was made to produce 14 plans before the Queen was satisfied. In the end, her 'refuge' in the grounds of Versailles included a rural hamlet (with cracks painted into the plaster to make it look old), a fake ruin, a romantic grotto, a bell tower on a hillock, an alpine garden to remind her of her homeland and a 'love temple' in front of her bedroom windows – not to forget the famous 'sheep park' where she kept her small collection of neatly groomed sheep, cows and chickens. It also had 'lakes' and a meandering 'river', the only water features in the whole vast grounds of Versailles that weren't either angular or part of a perfect circle.

It was a unique, truly idyllic setting where Marie-Antoinette could combine living on the real-life set of a Romantic painting with the Rousseauian fantasy of a peasant life free of crop disease and back-breaking labour. And all at a cost of some 300,000 *livres*, or about 3,000 years' rent on a real farm of similar size.

Marie-Antoinette later admitted while under arrest that she had 'spent more than I would have wished' on the Petit Trianon.[8] Her extravagance, as well as the almost insulting gesture of pretending to be a peasant when real farmers had to eke out a living under the yoke of frequent famine and crippling taxation, was so deeply etched on the French national consciousness that even today everyone pictures Marie-Antoinette in her meadow playing the shepherdess. Public distaste for her fantasy world was so strong at the time that it has lasted down the centuries.

However, this, like her supposed 'let them eat cake' remark, is a piece of eighteenth-century fake news. Marie-Antoinette didn't actually pretend to be a shepherdess, cowherd or chicken farmer. Or rather, she didn't act out the role in her hamlet – what she did was play the part in the theatre she had built near the Petit Trianon, at a further cost of 200,000 *livres*, at the end of the 1770s. Here, she and her friends could put on amateur dramatics – and Marie-Antoinette herself would usually play peasant girls or servants, roles that must have tested her acting skills to the full.

---

[8] Incidentally, the nearby Grand Trianon, a much larger palace, is now a presidential residence where politicians and visiting dignitaries can enjoy some isolation from *le peuple* – proof that where luxury living is concerned, the Revolution didn't really change things that much.

Louis XVI was delighted, not only by her performances (for which she took acting and singing lessons), but because the dramatics distracted her from all-night Paris *soirées* and gambling. She was a notoriously bad card player and had once been forced to beg Mercy, the Austrian ambassador, to pay off gambling debts of 487,000 *livres*. Nevertheless, Marie-Antoinette's more innocent activities on the stage in no way compensated for the bad publicity surrounding the cost of the Petit Trianon, or the rumours about what else she was getting up to in her splendid isolation.

In 1779 Marie-Antoinette suffered a bout of measles and went to stay at le Petit Trianon for three weeks, accompanied by friends who had had the disease before, including four of her young 'rascals' (two dukes, a count and a baron). Gossips asked whether Louis XVI would go into quarantine with four buxom wenches if he fell ill – the obvious answer being no, he would take a locksmith, a clockmaker and a couple of hunting buddies so that he could shoot birds from his windows.

The rumours weren't quashed when Louis visited his ailing wife during her quarantine and had a long and 'tender' conversation with her while he stood in the garden and she leant out of an upstairs window.

It was also rumoured that the grotto in her garden led to a secret passage, allowing her male guests to exit in secret before the arrival of a visitor – her husband, for example, who was only allowed into the Petit Trianon if invited, and never once slept there.

Madame Campan deals very frankly with Marie-Antoinette's unwise attempts to shut herself away from the world. At one point, she says that: 'I don't mean to defend the type of entertainment that the Queen enjoyed ... The consequences were so dire that the fault must have been serious.' She gives a long description of a *soirée* in the English garden, lit with torches in 'earthenware pots hidden behind green-painted boards'. Meanwhile, 'several hundred bundles of firewood, burning in a ditch behind the temple of love, gave off a great light that made it the most brilliant part of the garden.' So far so tasteful, but Madame Campan goes on:

> It was talked about a lot. The venue made it impossible to invite a large proportion of the court; those who were not invited were unhappy, and the people, who only forgive parties to which they are invited, also contributed a great deal to the malevolent exaggeration of the cost of this small party, quoting such a ridiculous price that it was as if a whole forest had been cut down for the bundles of firewood.

When it came to Marie-Antoinette's parties, people would believe anything.

And it wasn't only her parties that attracted gossip.

The winter of 1776 was very harsh, with snow lying on ground for six weeks. Marie-Antoinette and her friends had carriages turned into ornamental horse-drawn sleighs, so that they could glide around the grounds of Versailles. Some courtiers used these to ride into Paris, and they were seen sledging along the Champs-Elysées wrapped in furs. Rumours sprang up that Marie-Antoinette was among them, frolicking in the snow while the rest of Paris suffered from the icy cold – some families lacking firewood because the Queen had been burning so much during her garden parties. The public outrage was so vehement that Marie-Antoinette stopped sledging and never did it again, even during snowy winters. Meanwhile, Louis had firewood delivered to the poor of Versailles – one day he showed these wood deliveries to courtiers and told them: '*Messieurs*, these are my sleighs.' But the damage limitation does not seem to have worked.

The scandal sheets, known as *libelles* – a word originally meaning a small booklet, but which came to mean a satirical, libellous pamphlet – did not even spare Marie-Antoinette when she was pregnant. While she was carrying her first baby – nominally a cause for national celebration – there were rumours of orgies in the gardens of Versailles. In the hot summer of 1778, she spent most days shut away in her apartments, and would only go outdoors after dark, when she liked to stroll on the terrace outside her apartment, the raised area with two octagonal ponds above the garden that, in the daytime, overlooks the Grand Canal. Here she would chat with just a few members of her family – minus her husband, who liked to go to bed early.

During these nocturnal outings, a small group of string players would play on a small, specially constructed stage set up in the grounds. Madame Campan assures her readers that:

> There was nothing more innocent than these evenings, but soon the whole of Paris, France, even Europe was using them to talk in the most offensive terms about Marie-Antoinette's character. It is true that everyone in Versailles wanted to attend these serenades, and soon there were crowds from eleven in the evening until two or three in the morning ... I don't know if some unwise women dared to go out into the depths of the park; perhaps, but the Queen, Madame and the Countess d'Artois [Marie-Antoinette's two sisters-in-law] were arm in arm and never left the terrace.

They weren't on their own, of course. This was the problem with Versailles – even a sisterly chat on a terrace would attract a small horde of courtiers, including gatecrashers who could wander up the steps from the immense park beyond. On two occasions, when men approached the Queen to talk to her, there were innocent conversations, but Madame Campan complains that: 'The most scandalous stories were invented and printed in the *libelles*.' When the family tried to keep out strangers by issuing handwritten invitations to the night performances, 'the most revolting lies were circulated about this private concert'.

One must not forget that Madame Campan was a friend and lady-in-waiting of Marie-Antoinette, so she was bound to defend the Queen. Even so, it is hard to imagine Marie-Antoinette, uncomfortably pregnant with her first child, enjoying semi-public assignations with lovers just outside the galerie des Glaces at the palace of Versailles while a thousand curious courtiers and jealous townies milled about.

Nevertheless, Madame Campan says that the malicious rumours 'were avidly received by the public'. One night, an anonymous messenger left a 'whole volume of songs about her and other women who were known because of their rank or their position' in the royal apartments. Louis was horrified. The verses he saw raked muck over Marie-Antoinette and a whole collection of noble ladies, and he commented wryly that 'such songs would damage the union of twenty couples at court or in the town'. But it must have worried Louis that even while pregnant Marie-Antoinette could not attract favourable publicity.

VII

The time was ripe for one, huge scandal, namely *'l'affaire du collier'*, or 'necklace affair', a massive fraud scandal involving Marie-Antoinette that rocked the throne in 1785. And probably the worst thing about it was that for once it was true.

Marie-Antoinette was an innocent party, but the sad irony was that the scam only worked because of her bad reputation. The chief trickster was a young woman called the Comtesse de la Motte, an illegitimate descendant of King Henri II via one of his mistresses, who had used a favourable marriage to raise herself from the rank of impoverished minor aristocrat to that of impoverished countess.

In about 1783, la Motte (whose name meant clod of earth) became the lover of the Bishop of Strasbourg, a man called Louis-René de Rohan, a member of one of France's most ancient noble families. Rohan was in disgrace at the time. Ten years earlier, he had been ambassador to Vienna, but his irreligious sexual mores and excessive spending had caused Marie-Antoinette's mother, the Empress of Austria, to demand his repatriation to France. Rohan had then written an insulting letter about the Empress that had been read out at court by

Louis XV's lover, Madame du Barry, humiliating Marie-Antoinette and causing her to bear a deep grudge against Rohan. Several years on, with Marie-Antoinette now Queen of France, he was serving at Versailles, and was desperate to get into her good books. This, unfortunately for him, was where his new lover, the beguiling Comtesse de la Motte, came in.

La Motte knew that one of Paris's most exclusive jewellers, Auguste Böhmer, was struggling to offload a fabulously expensive diamond necklace. It was an enormous piece, consisting of long, woven strands of diamonds, two gigantic pendants and four tassels of smaller stones. It had originally been commissioned by Louis XV for Madame du Barry, but the old King had fallen ill with smallpox before the deal could be completed. Böhmer had tried to sell it to the new man on the throne, and Louis XVI had been willing to buy, but Marie-Antoinette had refused the gift, saying (depending on which version one believes) either that the money would be better spent on a new ship for the navy, or that she didn't want any of Madame du Barry's hand-me-downs. In any case, Böhmer was stuck with his unsaleable treasure.

This situation gave the devious la Motte her idea. She began by persuading Rohan that she was an intimate friend of Marie-Antoinette, and then gave him a letter, purportedly from Marie-Antoinette, saying that he could redeem himself if he gave her dear friend la Motte 60,000 *livres*. Later, it would be proved that the letter was a forgery because it was signed 'Marie-Antoinette de France', a signature that the Queen never used. But it certainly fooled Rohan, who handed over the cash.

La Motte then made the most of Marie-Antoinette's bad reputation by setting up a private meeting between Rohan and the Queen at 11 p.m. in the gardens of Versailles. Sadly for Marie-Antoinette, it was perfectly credible to an experienced nobleman and diplomat like Rohan that she would meet a man, alone, late at night and in secret.

Rohan turned up and was greeted by a lightly veiled figure who handed him a rose and murmured: 'You know what this means.

You can rest assured that the past will be forgotten.' A servant in Marie-Antoinette's livery then arrived and told them that someone was coming – the Queen had to leave immediately.

Rohan was in raptures that his disgrace was over, blissfully ignorant that the 'Queen' he had just met was a prostitute in disguise, and the 'servant' la Motte's lover, a forger of letters.

A few months later, la Motte upped the stakes and produced another letter asking Rohan to advance 1.6 million *livres* (an immense fortune) to buy a jewel on Marie-Antoinette's behalf. To convince him that this breathtaking request was genuine, la Motte paid a fashionable healer and spiritualist, an Italian crook called Balsamo, to conjure up a spirit who predicted that Rohan would very soon be made Chief Minister by Marie-Antoinette out of gratitude for this personal favour.

Again, Marie-Antoinette's bad reputation was exploited to her cost. Everyone knew her history of extravagant spending. During her reign, she ordered an average of some 150 dresses per year at an annual cost of 200,000 *livres*. In the space of a few months in 1775 she had bought earrings for 300,000 *livres*, diamond-encrusted candlesticks for 200,000 and bracelets for 250,000. On one occasion she had bought some earrings for 450,000 *livres*, and been obliged to ask Louis to cover the debt. All this spending had earned Marie-Antoinette a broadside in a letter from her mother: 'The news from Paris is that you … have misspent your budget and are loaded down with debt. People assume that you are dragging the King into useless extravagances, which are on the increase and are plunging the State into poverty.' Ever the insightful critic, Marie-Antoinette's mother concluded that: 'Such anecdotes break my heart, especially with regard to the future.'

So, a necklace worth 1.6 million? Everyone knew that it would tempt Marie-Antoinette, but it was such an immense sum that she might well have to act in secret. The scheme was all too credible.

On 1 February 1785, at la Belle Image, a notorious Versailles inn and tricksters' hangout, Rohan signed the credit notes, and received the necklace from Böhmer. A messenger, supposedly from the Queen, arrived and took possession of the jewels. A few days later, the necklace was in pieces and the 540 diamonds were being sold in Brussels and London. Most of the jewellers involved were highly suspicious that diamonds of such quality were being hawked by French sellers at relatively low prices, but when they made enquiries in Paris, no jewel thefts had been reported, so they paid up in good faith.

Meanwhile, Rohan held his breath for news of his redemption, and Böhmer waited for his money. As we saw in an earlier chapter, aristocrats were notoriously slow at settling their bills, but this was such an enormous sum that the jeweller finally lost patience, and went to Versailles to present his invoice to Madame Campan. She knew nothing of the deal, and asked Marie-Antoinette, who rushed to her husband and demanded that Rohan, her old arch-enemy, be arrested for extortion.

By now it was 15 August, the Feast of the Assumption, and Rohan was in his bishop's robes, about to celebrate mass in the palace chapel at Versailles when guards marched in and escorted him away. At Marie-Antoinette's insistence, Rohan was locked up in the Bastille and then sent to trial before the judges of the Paris parliament – who found him innocent.

This was a terrible slap in the face for Marie-Antoinette. As well as fraud, Rohan had been accused of *lèse-majesté* – lack of respect for the Crown – on the grounds that he had believed that the Queen would actually agree to meet him alone in the gardens of Versailles at night, and that she would buy immensely expensive jewellery behind her husband's back. When Rohan was acquitted of this charge, it meant that in the eyes of the Paris parliament and the French state, he was entirely justified in believing Marie-Antoinette capable of such scandalous, unregal behaviour.

La Motte, Balsamo the spiritualist and the prostitute who had pretended to be Marie-Antoinette were arrested, and all found guilty. La Motte was sentenced to life imprisonment, and to be branded as a thief. Two letter Vs were to be burned into the skin of her shoulder blades, but she struggled so much that the second red-hot iron was brutally thrust against her breast. Balsamo was briefly imprisoned before being deported. The prostitute, now nursing a baby, was released. La Motte's forger lover managed to flee to London.

In the public's eyes, the other guilty party who escaped punishment was of course Marie-Antoinette. Her crime: being so disreputable that massive fraud in her name had become feasible.

Incredibly, even worse was to come. La Motte escaped from prison, fled to London and published her story in a book called *Les Mémoires justificatifs de la comtesse de Valois de la Motte*. There she alleged that she had had an affair with Marie-Antoinette (whose lesbian tendencies were 'common knowledge', as we have seen), and that the Queen had even helped her to escape from prison. La Motte insisted that, in the bid to buy the necklace for Marie-Antoinette and cover up the subsequent scandal, she was merely the 'accomplice of people who were too powerful for my weakness' (namely Marie-Antoinette and Rohan). She had been seduced by them both, she claimed, and described midnight trysts with Marie-Antoinette at le Petit Trianon – 'moments of rapture that I hardly dare recall' – while alleging that she was just 'a feeble bird in the hands of a cruel child who, after amusing herself for a few moments, plucks its feathers one by one and then throws it to the cats'.

La Motte accepted that her story sounded incredible, but concluded: 'If the Queen of France was what she was meant to be, or rather was not what she is, these memoirs would not exist.' And this, to the French public, was the clincher. Everyone 'knew' that Marie-Antoinette was an extravagant spender, a wife with a hideaway where her husband never went, and both a lesbian and the type of woman who met up with strange men after dark. The necklace story simply confirmed all the rumours at once.

Yet again, though, Louis XVI was partly at fault. He made the key error that turned the affair from a Versailles con trick into a full-blown national scandal. It was Louis who offered Rohan the choice between a private hearing in camera, judged by Louis himself, or a public trial. Rohan, furious that he had been wrongly accused, and no doubt desperate to have his 1.6 million *livres'* debt cleared, chose the trial.

Louis XVI should have known that the Parisian judges would side with Rohan. These were the men whom his predecessor Louis XV had stripped of their generous salaries, their private income from corruption, and the right to pass on their noble titles to their sons, when he had abolished the regional parliaments. They had been reinstated by Louis XVI almost as soon as he came to the throne, hoping to heal the rift between the *noblesse de robe* (the appointed judges) and the monarchy. But this attempt at reconciliation had been a double failure. Not only had it sent out a message to ordinary people that the justice system was going to remain biased in favour of the aristocrats, it also did nothing to make the judges loyal to the Crown, because they saw that the new King was so weak that he didn't dare uphold his grandfather's policy.

The Rohan trial was the perfect opportunity for these nobles to make a show of their disrespect for the monarchy. Rohan was clearly innocent of fraud, even if he was absurdly foolish, so acquitting him was a foregone conclusion. But by clearing him of *lèse-majesté*, the noble judges had flexed their muscles, and Louis XVI could do nothing about it, even though it humiliated his wife, and therefore the Crown.

In short, when that double non-guilty verdict was announced, it lit the fuse that four years later would explode into revolution.

Chapter 8

LOUIS XVI TRIES HIS HAND
AT POLITICS

'Qui veut le roy, si veut la loy.'
'What the King wants, the law wants.'
The first law in the pre-Revolution French legal system,
drawn up by Antoine Loysel (1536–1617)

I

As France toppled slowly but surely towards revolution, its
political and social structure still bore the scars of its feudal
past.

Its people were divided into three classes, or *'états'*, which can
be translated as 'states', a name suggesting that the difference
between them was as radical as that between solids, liquids and
gases.

In feudal language, the *états* are known in English as 'estates'.
In early medieval England, this signified the division of society
into three main functions: working, praying and fighting. In
other words the three classes consisted of those who had to toil
for a living (including servants, labourers, farmers, craftsmen,
merchants and lawyers); the clergy; and knights, including the
King. But by the early 1400s in England, the divisions had
become very blurred. The success of common archers at battles

like Crécy (1346) and Agincourt (1415) had devalued the status of knights in armour, while some rich merchants were the social equals of almost anyone in the country. In addition, the devastation of the Black Death in 1348–9 had restructured the English labour market, with the surviving commoners and former serfs driving a hard bargain for their labour. By the eighteenth century, social divisions still existed in Britain, of course, but they were more to do with money and connections than birth, and social mobility was possible. And most importantly, the commoners in parliament held political sway over the monarch.

In eighteenth-century France, on the other hand, the weight of the medieval estates could still be felt, and they were enshrined in law. The three functions of the *états* had changed from 'work, pray, fight' to something like 'work, earn, lounge'. Or more precisely: work and pay rents and taxes; pray while earning huge salaries and collecting rents and taxes; and lounge about while collecting rents and taxes. Praying and fighting still got done, but they had become secondary functions.

And, most importantly, the three estates in France had really become two. The clergy and the aristocracy were more or less combined (with top jobs in the Church and the armed forces all going to *aristos*), while the other 95 per cent of the population were lumped together as the *'tiers état'*, or 'Third (E)state',[1] a label clearly designed to put them in their place. But by the time Louis XVI came to the throne, the *tiers état* was an increasingly absurd grouping, as it contained everyone from the plumpest millionaire grain merchant to the poorest labourer with no money for bread, and merely signified that the person was a commoner with little or no political power.

[1] This French label is also the origin of the term 'Third World'. The concept was invented in 1952 by a French demographer, Alfred Sauvy, who gave the name *'tiers-monde'* to the underdeveloped parts of the planet as a reference to the *'tiers état'* that had previously grouped together the underprivileged sections of French society.

Ever since the fourteenth century, French kings had periodically made a democratic gesture by convening assemblies known as the 'États généraux', at which delegates from the three groups were consulted on some national problem or other.

However, this consultation did not mean fair representation. For a start, the États généraux were only convened when a king felt like using them. And secondly, voting was by block. The aristocracy had one vote, the clergy one vote, the *tiers état* one vote. The number of delegates varied from one assembly to another: in 1355 there were 800, in 1614 only about 500. But although the *tiers état*, the commoners, represented the vast majority of the population, they had only the same number of delegates as the other two groups. Consequently, the vote of a single duke or bishop carried as much weight as a whole town's worth of commoners. And as voting was by estate, if the (noble) clergy got together with the aristocracy, their block votes would always beat the *tiers état* by two to one.

In any case, regular political decisions were taken not by the États généraux but by the King and the noble parliamentarians. A democracy it was not.

In 1789, France's *tiers état* represented the biggest group of commoners in the whole of Europe. France was the continent's most populous country, with a population of about 28 million – more than Britain's 16 million, Spain's 10 million and Russia's 25 million.

Approximately 650,000 of Louis XVI's subjects lived in Paris (a number that would plummet during the chaos of the Revolution, and would not recover until after Napoleon's empire fell in 1815). The other big French cities, Lyon, Marseille and Bordeaux were all home to between 100,000 and 150,000 people. However, all these French cities combined had a population no bigger than London with its million inhabitants.

The vast majority – 85 per cent – of the French population lived out in the country, two-thirds of them working the land.

Less than half of these *paysans* were tilling their own fields, though – in 1789, about 40 per cent of French farmland was owned by the social class known as *laboureurs* or ploughmen, people who had a plough and used it on their own land. Of the rest, roughly 20 per cent of farmland was owned by aristocrats and royalty, 6 per cent by the Church and 30 per cent by commoner landlords, who might be absentees or richer villagers.

In more profitable agricultural areas, especially around large towns, these statistics changed, of course. Small peasant landowners could not be permitted to hang on to their fields if big money was to be made selling food to urban markets. In the Île de France, the bowl of excellent farmland around Paris, the Church owned about 30 per cent and the nobles 40 per cent. It was a similar story around Versailles, where food prices were at their highest, and *aristos* owned some 70 per cent of the land. Meanwhile, in the far-flung rural corners of Brittany and the deep south of France, the nobles and the Church owned very little.

A growing number of landowners were bourgeois. Literally, all this means in French is 'townie' – someone who lives in a *bourg*, which originally meant a castle or fortified village, but later came to signify a market town. The term 'bourgeois' only took on a negative connotation in France when the peasants saw the rich townies encroaching on their domain, and the nobility started to feel threatened by these common upstarts. In the 1780s, the bourgeois acquiring land were often lawyers, bankers or merchants, buying from aristocrats who needed money to finance their lavish lifestyles, or from small farmers who couldn't make their land pay.

Many of these town dwellers were putting together big farms of 100 hectares or more, and trying to modernize ancient farming methods. They formed a burgeoning non-aristocratic class of landowner that was hungry both for profit and for political representation. That might make them sound like a force for democratic change, but when the rich bourgeois bought up land, they inflated prices and made it impossible for the poor peasants in their region to dream of social advancement. In this way, a doubly disgruntled rural population was being engineered – the rich bourgeois commoners without fair political representation were as frustrated as the dispossessed poor, who had neither land nor representation.

In 1789, being a landowner did not guarantee a decent standard of living. As the post-revolutionary politician Joseph de Verneilh Puiraseau wrote in 1807, in a study of the French population:

> This title [of landowner] includes the owner of the tiniest stretch of earth, and the most fragile cabin ... No one is as poor as these rustic households, reduced to living off the mean product of some snippet of land constantly dug at by the spade, and often in vain.

Small landowners were only their own masters in the sense that their tiny plot was in their name – they couldn't live there free of charge, because they had to pay cripplingly high taxes to the King, the Church and the nearest noble château owner, which were, in effect, land rents.

In any case, the land in small villages was often treated as communal – a whole community would sow the same cereals at the same time, and then everyone's animals would graze all the fields after the harvest. A small landowner would find it almost impossible to specialize in, say, flowers to sell in Versailles. In most French villages, it was a case of 'Allez, Marcel, why don't you sow wheat and oats again, as we've always done, and probably always will do? If you plant lilies in that field of yours, everyone's pigs will eat them, and our bacon will be perfumed.'

Around half of these small landowners could grow enough to subsist without seeking extra work, and could also employ labourers, who often lived much like serfs, in that they depended for work, food and accommodation on the farmers. These were often day labourers, who were paid a pittance – at the time,

French rural wages were about 75 per cent lower than those in England, while food prices were the same.

Not only were the rural poor at the mercy of economic and climatic changes, some of them were still bound by the ancient *mainmorte* (dead hand) law, which stipulated that their belongings went to the Church or the landowner when they died. This might involve little more than a pig, a scythe and a tattered pair of breeches, but it was the principle that counted – the dead labourer's children were doomed to stay as poor as ever. And even small farmers who inherited were almost bound to be worse off than their parents, because of France's law that property should be equally divided amongst the children (at that time, males only, of course). On the death of a father, an already small farm, barely able to support a family, might be divided up amongst two, three or four sons, into totally unproductive units.

These unfavourable conditions were driving waves of poor farm labourers away from the countryside. The lucky ones found unskilled manual work as servants, builders, gardeners, or tending small vegetable plots on the edge of town. Many others had to resort to begging.[2] At the time of the Revolution, these rural migrants made up about a fifth of the urban population – a sizeable chunk. When work was scarce or food prices rose, they couldn't strike – all they could do was riot. And as of 1788, they began to do so with increasing frequency and violence.

Of the four million or so town dwellers, about half worked for an employer. These were, for example, the staff of the countless *boutiques* – eighteenth-century urban France was very happy to be a nation of shopkeepers (only Napoleon's forced conscription later on would turn it into a country of fighters, largely against its will). Under Louis XVI, many of the salaried employees in French towns had prospects, especially if they were

[2] However, according to Puiraseau's population study of 1807, the number of beggars in France rose after 1789, showing that employment prospects went *down* after the Revolution.

apprentices in skilled crafts like furniture-making, carriage-building, metalwork, stone-carving, the food industries, and the huge variety of garment trades. There was a chance that one day they might be able to start their own business. The last thing they wanted was social disruption. They longed for reduced taxation, definitely, but anarchy, not at all.

And contrary to what one might think, another large section of the urban poor was much less prone to resentment, rioting and revolution. About 10 per cent or so of town dwellers were in domestic service. These were mainly women whose well-being depended on that of their masters and mistresses. If the rich stayed rich, they kept their jobs and their homes and never lacked for food. Some of them even enjoyed a certain social status. They would have liked higher wages and shorter hours, of course, but overall they were pretty much in favour of the status quo. For the moment, anyway – once social resentment took hold, it would turn brutally violent.

The croutons floating on top of the onion soup that was French urban society under Louis XVI were the bourgeois. After the disastrous speculations under Louis XV, trade was on the up again, property values were rising, and the industrial revolution was beginning to make its mark in some areas of the country. All this favoured the non-aristocratic, business-owning middle class. As well as merchants in high-value goods like sugar, alcohol and jewellery, some of the biggest fortunes were being made in textiles, an industry that grew by 80 per cent from 1700 to 1789; in iron smelting, up by 200 per cent in the same period; and in coal mining, which rose by 700 per cent, showing that France might well have begun to compete with British industries if its growth had not been rudely interrupted by the Revolution.

The bourgeois weren't totally satisfied with their increasing wealth, however. In his memoirs, the royalist general François Claude Amour de Bouillé (a nobleman) wrote that at the time of the Revolution: 'In Paris and in the large towns, the bourgeoisie was superior to the aristocracy in wealth, talent and personal merit. In provincial towns, it had the same superiority over the rural aristocracy. It felt this superiority, and yet everywhere it suffered humiliation.'

The problem for these bourgeois was that they weren't aristocrats. They were enjoying an aristocratic lifestyle, earning income from rents and splashing out on carriages, clothes and jewels that were every bit as ostentatious as those of their local *marquis*. But there was a glass ceiling to their social pretensions. Some bourgeois managed to buy a noble name by obtaining a government office (at vast expense), but failing that, they were stuck on a lower rung of the social ladder, staring up at the *aristos'* trouser seats.

Commoners could not rise to the top of the clergy; they could not be army or navy officers; they had no access to the best-paying government jobs; and – most importantly of all – under the French system of government, they had almost no political voice. As we have seen, real political clout was in the hands of the noble parliamentarians and the Crown's top administrative officers, all of whom were aristocrats and could pass on their job titles on from father to son.

The well-educated, wealthy bourgeoisie, who had a growing stake in their nation's prosperity, had practically no influence on its policies. They were therefore torn between the need for stability as a base for developing their businesses (and increasing the rents on their properties) and the desire to grab political power away from the idle aristocrats.

Louis XVI recognized this, and knew that it was vital to reform government so that the bourgeoisie had more of a voice. The trouble was that his aristocratic parliament felt quite the opposite.

Also present at the pinnacle of urban society were certain members of the clergy. There were about 120,000 men and 38,000 women earning a living from the French Catholic Church, some of them amongst the richest aristocrats in France.

Until 1789, joining the clergy was a real career choice for members of the French aristocracy. The bishop of a rich diocese could command a salary well over 100,000 *livres* per year, so it was only natural that the jobs were grabbed by the country's top families. At the start of 1789, not one of France's 130 bishops was a commoner.[3] They were men like Charles-Maurice de Talleyrand, who would go on to be one of Napoleon's closest advisors (and whose backstabbing would spur the Emperor to call him 'a turd in silk stockings'), and who only went into the Church because a club foot made him ineligible for the army. Talleyrand was made Louis XVI's *agent général du clergé* at 26 and a bishop at 35. Louis-René de Rohan, the aristocrat implicated in Marie-Antoinette's necklace affair, became Bishop of Strasbourg at only 26.

The highest patriarchs of the Church weren't the only clerics to earn a more than comfortable living. About 95,000 clergymen and -women were allowed to receive a personal share of what was called the 'revenue from the property devoted to God' – that is, rents and taxes on Church land and buildings. An abbot or abbess might be paid a salary as well as getting their hands on a personal slice of the abbey or convent's income, both in cash and in food. Some of this wealth might be distributed to the poor, but a lot would end up inside a habit.

The French historian François Bluche has written about a certain François-Yves Besnard, a 28-year-old farmer's son who was appointed the *curé* (priest) of the village of Nouans, near Le Mans, a community of just 480 people. Overnight he acquired a large presbytery with a kitchen garden, fishponds, a farm and 3,000 *livres* in tax and other income. In his memoirs, published when he was 90, Father François-Yves admitted spending two or three hours a day reading – not the Bible but *'la littérature grecque, latine, italienne et française'*. He also took over active

---

[3] Where the Church was concerned, Louis XVI was even more snobbish than his predecessors. The most absolute of France's monarchs, Louis XIV, had elected 19 commoner bishops, his successor Louis XV ten.

management of his farm, without getting his hands dirty, and was never short of loaves and fishes. Naturally he took time out from farming to perform mass and see to his human flock, but the home visits he wrote about were more often to upper-class parishioners than starving peasants in need of spiritual succour. All in all, an easy life, and one that wasn't necessarily without its sexual comforts, too. Even today, it is (allegedly) common in France for supposedly celibate priests to be more than just employers to their housekeepers, who are traditionally ladies of the *âge canonique* – that is, in practical terms, post-menopausal, to avoid the embarrassment of non-immaculate conception.

To increase their income, French clergymen could become ungodly in other ways, too. In 1780, the bishops of the Tours region reduced the number of religious holidays so that their tenants would be more productive and pay more tax.

Not all churchmen were rich, of course. The average priest was a commoner and barely better off than his parishioners, and was just as jealous of his aristocratic superiors' wealth. His salary was paid by higher-ranking clergymen, who distributed what was left of the Church's tax income after they had creamed off their share. The residue handed on to the parish priest was known as the *portion congrue* (resulting portion), and was usually so tiny that the term passed into ordinary French to mean the smallest share of something.[4]

Country priests would have to supplement their meagre salaries by charging pennies for baptisms, weddings and funerals, and as Louis XVI's reign went on, they would begin to grumble about inequality as loudly as the peasants. In 1789 a group of priests from the Dauphiné region of eastern France published a pamphlet warning other low-paid clergymen that: 'Our bishops do not consider us to be their colleagues, and you [other priests] will only obtain your full rights when the people obtain theirs.'

[4] In his *Illusions perdues*, Balzac wrote about some aristocrats eating bad food in a provincial inn – 'meanly served meals that smacked of the *portion congrue*'.

It's easy to imagine the kind of sermons that were being preached in small churches all over France in 1789.

Louis XVI did little to help these poor clergymen. His only real contribution to church matters was to make the upper clergy feel threatened. In 1787, Louis passed an *édit de tolérance*, giving Protestants and Jews the right to worship freely, which had been denied since 1685. Presenting it to parliamentarians, he said that he respected the Catholic faith above all others, but 'this faith orders me not to deprive a part of my people its natural rights'. The aristocratic parliament of Metz in eastern France continued to deny Jews their religious freedom, but elsewhere non-Catholics began to enjoy full citizenship rights, including marriage, without having to convert to Catholicism.

Sadly for Louis XVI, like every other democratic move on his part, this would only serve to turn the establishment against him.

Finally, at the peak of French society, both urban and rural, sat the aristocrats. There was not really enough cream for them to be called the *crème de la crème*. To return to the earlier onion soup analogy, they were more like the *fromage de la soupe* – the cheese baked on top of the bowl, weighing down both the croutons and the onion bits floating below.

Despite being the most powerful section of the population, the French aristocracy numbered only about 400,000 people. These were elite members of the ancient *noblesse d'ancienne extraction*, the only slightly less ancient knight class, the *noblesse d'épée*, as well as the more recently appointed public servants, the *noblesse de robe*.

One of the tenets of the French aristocracy that dated back to its armour-wearing days was: 'Thou shalt be, everywhere and always, the champion of the just and the good against injustice and evil.' The problem for France, and especially for Louis XVI, was that many of them were living according to a more modern rulebook based on the motto: 'Thou shalt hold on to what thou hast with both of thy hands.' The caricature of the foppish, money-grabbing landlord squeezing every possible penny out of his starving tenants was an everyday reality in pre-revolutionary France, and was one of the stereotypes that Louis XVI wanted to do away with (while, of course, hanging on to the most pleasant aspects of his own foppish lifestyle).

There were a few French aristocrats who wanted to move with the times – the Solages family in Albi, for example, who were developing their coal mines and iron foundry. There were also some highly efficient aristocratic public servants – Louis XVI would appoint two of the most democratically minded of these, Turgot and Calonne, as his Finance Ministers (see section IV below). But too many of the *privilégiés* were content to live in selfish idleness.

As early as the seventeenth century, the writer Paul Hay du Chastelet (*fils*), who was imprisoned by Louis XIV for protesting against the persecution of Protestants, ironized that: 'Nobility is a quality which makes those who possess it generous, and which opens the soul to a life of decency.'

As of 1789, it was a general lack of both generosity and decency in the aristocrats that would cost many of them their social position, their land, and often their head.

II

Because of Louis XV's failure to impose his will on the parliament in the early 1770s, taxes during Louis XVI's reign were still monstrously unfair. Nobles were exempt, and the land-owning clergy paid a voluntary *don gratuit* (gratuitous donation) according to its conscience, which didn't always trouble it very deeply. Under Louis XVI, the *don gratuit* was only about 2 per cent of the Church's revenue from taxes, while its earnings from rents went largely untaxed.

The poor, meanwhile, and especially the rural poor, shouldered almost all the burden of a jumble of ancient taxes that could be increased at will by the local *aristos*. A rural labourer or small landowner might see half their income taken away in taxes of one sort or another.

These taxes varied from region to region, sometimes between châteaux or dioceses, but the main ones were:

– The *taille*. Depending on the region, this was either a land tax based directly on property, or an almost random sum decided by the landlord according to how rich his tenants seemed to be. Nobles, clergymen and richer urban bourgeois were exempt from *la taille*.

– The *gabelle*, the tax on salt that, again, was almost randomly applied according to how much money the local *aristo* or the King needed to squeeze out of the population at any given time.

– The *capitation*, a poll tax occasionally imposed to pay for a war or to cover a national debt. It was meant to be universal, but in 1789 it represented about 10 per cent of the income of a poorer taxpayer, and only about 1.5 per cent for a member of the privileged classes.

– The *corvée*, which was free labour given either to the local landlord or, in the case of the *corvée royale*, to the King. His administrators usually got the *corvéables* to repair roads, bridges, drainage ditches and other public utilities. On average this represented about six days' labour per year, but could rise to 30 in some regions. The *corvée royale* was often useful work – at the time, many French roads were just muddy, pot-holed tracks, a hindrance to any modernization of the countryside. The landlord's *corvée* was much more about personal gain – in his novel *La Terre*, Emile Zola says that the peasant tenant 'gave his body and his time, [and was forced to] plough, harvest, scythe, cut vines, and clean out the château's ditches'. Naturally, no one ever saw men in wigs or mitres digging mud out of a drainage ditch – aristocrats were exempt from the *corvée*, as were clergymen and their servants, all teachers, and most town dwellers. It was usually farm labourers who ended up giving their time, making their lives even harsher than usual.

– The *dîme*, short for *dixième* or tenth,[5] as if saying it quickly made it less painful to pay. This was a tax paid by the tenants of all land and buildings owned by the Church. It was the biggest single landowner in France, and collectively would have found it very difficult to pass through the eye of a needle. It saw no reason to change this situation – Charles-Maurice de Talleyrand, Louis XVI's *agent général du clergé*, confessed that: 'In its management of everyday affairs, the clergy of the eighteenth century made absolutely no concession to the spirit of the times.'

– The *cens*, a feudal cash tax paid by smaller landowners to their *seigneur*, or lord, supposedly in return for protection from bandits and invaders, though *aristos* in their châteaux or at court in Versailles did not give much protection to eighteenth-century farmers.

– Tenant farmers also paid a *champart* (field share), usually between 6 and 10 per cent of their harvest, though this sometimes rose to a fifth, and was especially burdensome in lean years, when there was already not enough to go round.

In addition to these taxes, small farmers would be subjected to feudal-like obligations: they were forced to use the local *châtelain*'s windmill, bread ovens and grape or olive press – at his prices, of course. This same *seigneur* could also decide on the date of the grape or grain harvest on his land, and could dictate when small farmers could start selling their new wine. This privilege was called the *banvin*, and allowed the big landlord to sell his wine before anyone else, thereby limiting the supply for a period, and earning him the best price. Only once he was satisfied with his sales did his peasants get the right to sell theirs.

As if things weren't bad enough, in some regions, so-called *'feudistes'* ('feudalists') were doing the rounds, making sure that the *seigneurs* imposed all the taxes they were entitled to, and

[5] The origin of the English word 'tithe' is the same, being derived from *teogoþa*, the Anglo-Saxon word for tenth.

looking into the possibility of reviving old, forgotten taxes. Some were even claiming that communal land should revert to the ownership of the local *châtelain*. While eighteenth-century French intellectuals looked to the future with their philosophy and their scientific discoveries, many country dwellers were heading back to the Middle Ages.

The folk memory of all this unfair taxation lives on in the French language today. Anyone who feels exploited by their boss – even if it is just having their cigarette breaks cut down to ten minutes every half an hour – will moan that they are *'corvéable à merci'* – *'merci'* here meaning not 'thank you' but at the mercy of the ruling class.

Largely thanks to all this harsh taxation of the poor, the average life expectancy in France in 1789 was only about 30 years. This average was artificially low because of infant mortality and the dangers of childbirth, but it still reflected the gruelling hardship of everyday life for the underprivileged sections of the French population.

It becomes all the more shocking when you read the biographies of prominent French aristocrats of the time, who very often lived comfortably into their sixties and seventies, or even beyond.

This imbalance in life expectancy for the rich and poor would be starkly reflected in the ages of people guillotined during the Revolution. In Paris, for example, of the 2,918 officially documented victims, about 2,000 of them were over 30, and 846 of these were over 50. In revolutionary Paris, the social class that was destined to die young seems to have used the guillotine to get revenge on the unfairly old.

However, probably the most telling demographic statistic that Louis XVI had to face as he got to grips with French politics was this one: he had inherited a country where political and economic power still lay in the pampered hands of a mere 2 per cent of the population – 560,000 or so aristocrats and clergymen. And even though he was about to suggest reforms that would benefit the other 27 million of his citizens, his campaign for political change was going to feel like 560,000 against one.

III

The astonishing thing is that despite the taxation, the poverty and the low life expectancy, even despite Marie-Antoinette's necklace affair, most ordinary people did not hate Louis XVI. Some of the most outspoken satirists were relatively kind to him.

In the pornographic play *L'Autrichienne en goguettes, ou L'Orgie royale*, Marie-Antoinette calls Parisians *'les grenouilles de la Seine'* ('Seine frogs'), and, as she frolics with her male and female lovers, merrily sings:

Dissipons tous les biens
Des bons Parisiens.

(Let's fritter away all the money
Of the good Parisians.)

Poor Louis XVI, meanwhile, is having a snooze. He is presented as the (admittedly foolish, inattentive) victim of the immoral goings-on at Versailles.

A six-page poem called *'Ode à la Reine'*, published in 1789, heaps all the blame for the Revolution on Marie-Antoinette, calling her the 'monster that escaped from Germany' and accusing her of wanting to 'send France's treasure to Germany' – the money she hadn't already spent, that is, because the poet harangues her directly: 'Your lust procures disgusting, shameful pleasure for itself with the state's gold.' The poet even tells Marie-Antoinette that: 'You were the mother of three children, three times an adulterous flame carried the seed to your breast' – a bizarre mixed metaphor, but one which shows that the anonymous writer was not exactly a royalist, because calling the legitimacy of Louis XVI's offspring into doubt was an anti-monarchist gesture.

Even so, the poet clearly retains some affection for Louis XVI. The ode calls Marie-Antoinette 'an impious woman [who] blackens the object of our love', obviously meaning Louis XVI. It also reminds its readers that before the Revolution:

Joy and hope were coming to replace our tears,
And Louis XVI of France was already reversing our misfortunes.

This seems to reflect the opinion amongst many of Louis XVI's subjects that, in between hunting sessions and catering to Marie-Antoinette's whims, he was actually trying to improve the lot of his people – or at least, choosing the right kind of politician to do so while he was out in the forest.

And the men he selected were enjoying some success. As we shall see, it would only be a combination of factors – most importantly, sabotage by the aristocracy, and then bad luck with the climate – that would scupper their (and Louis XVI's) plans for a more stable, more modern, better educated and more democratic France.

Critics of the monarchy maintain that Louis XVI was a sovereign king imposing his 'divine right' on everyone else in France, whereas in fact he was no more a lone ruler than a modern French president. For most of his reign, Louis XVI had a chief advisor called the *Ministre principal de l'État*, a kind of prime minister. The *Ministre principal* wasn't elected, of course – all the ministers were chosen by the King. But even today, French ministers aren't chosen by the people. They are appointed by the President, and don't need to be elected officials – modern French ministers can be bureaucrats who have been promoted into the job, or simply political allies whom the President wants by his side. This was the case when President François Hollande selected the unknown former bank employee Emmanuel Macron to be his Minister of the Economy in 2014. A degree of absolutism at the head of the French state is by no means finished.

Louis XVI's *Ministre principal* was the nominal leader of a team of ministers whose job titles varied but whose main responsibilities were usually divided into: Finance, Foreign Affairs, Justice, War, Navy and (this being an absolute monarchy) the Royal Household. All of these ministers lobbied for their own policies and budgets, but ultimately of course it was the King who took the decisions. And this was the problem – Louis XVI was not the decisive type. He was more like the pendulum on one of the clocks he enjoyed building.

One of his Finance Ministers, Henri-François d'Ormesson, wrote in his diary that Louis XVI 'desires justice ... and relief for his people', but that he 'absolutely lacks the character of a king'. And obviously, the most desirable characteristic of an absolute ruler would have been the ability to rule.

Louis was supposed to chair the meetings of different *'Conseils'* ('Councils') of ministers – the French word *'conseil'* also means 'advice'. His advisors were meant to meet and counsel him at one general meeting on Mondays, involving about 25 people, as well as twice-weekly gatherings of the Conseil d'État (for Foreign Affairs), Conseil des dépêches (the Interior), Conseil royal des finances, and the Conseil royal du commerce. But right from the start of his reign, Louis hated the Monday meetings and would often sit in silence as ministers pontificated about the general state of the realm. Meanwhile, the individual Conseils dwindled away, so that by the end of his reign, the all-important Conseil royal des finances was meeting only twice a month.

In any case, Louis was often exhausted after hunting, so sometimes he would simply look at a minister's proposal before scribbling *'bon'* on the cover page. Alternatively, according to Ormesson, after a show of apparent indifference, Louis would take 'snap decisions that his ministers did not dare contradict'. (Though this suggests that it was the ministers who were weak, not Louis XVI.)

Another minister, Charles-Gravier de Vergennes, who was Foreign Secretary from 1774 to 1781 and Finance Minister from 1781 to his death in 1787, said that on the contrary, Louis XVI was easy to influence – all a minister had to do was make

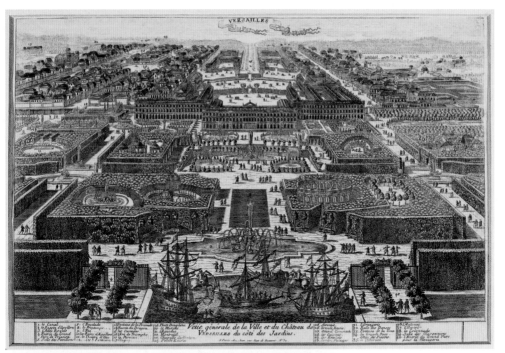

VERSAILLES

Veüe générale de la Ville et du Château de Versailles du côté des Jardins.

Above: Versailles under Louis XIV. His gardens were as big as the town beyond the palace. Note the miniature galleons on his 'Grand Canal', some of which were rowed by real galley slaves – a clear threat to potentially rebellious aristocrats.

Left: An astonishingly un-heroic portrait of the 'Sun King' Louis XIV in old age, circa 1705, created by Antoine Benoist, and commissioned by Louis himself. By this time, Louis had lost almost all his teeth, and a botched operation had left him with a permanently suppurating palate. His personal decay was cruelly symbolic of the declining reputation of the French monarchy.

Right: Maurice Quentin de la Tour's portrait of Louis XV in early middle age. Louis XV is remembered as an archetypal royal hedonist, more concerned with what went on in his bedchamber than the fate of the country at large. This was a largely accurate view, but he still found time to stand up to the all-powerful aristocrats, and even tried to make government (slightly) more democratic.

Below: Madame de Pompadour, original name Jeanne-Antoinette Poisson ('fish'), Louis XV's mistress turned procurer. When her own charms waned, she encouraged Louis to take very young – but unambitious – sexual partners.

Left: The Marquis de Sade, rapist, kidnapper, (probable) murderer and self-styled 'philosopher'. Fans of his writings ignore the fact that he was the epitome of an abusive 18th-century French aristocrat who thought himself above the law.

Above: A satirical cartoon from 1789. Poor men wearing rustic clogs try desperately to save themselves from the many-headed tax monster.

Right: Louis XVI. His empty, complacent gaze seems to confirm his reputation as a monarch who was disconnected from real life. On 14 July 1789, his diary entry was simply the word 'Nothing'. In fact, however, since the start of his reign in 1774, Louis XVI had been struggling to reduce aristocratic privilege. Even in 1789, on a personal level, he was still popular with most French people.

Right: Jacques Necker, one of Louis XVI's finance ministers, a hero to most of the population in 1789 thanks to his attempts to end abusive taxation and improve the lot of the poor. Note the '*Taxe*' lying at his feet, a metaphor for his radical proposals that were thwarted by the aristocrats.

Left: Louis XVI's wife, Marie-Antoinette, portrayed as a devoted mother in 1787, no doubt to combat the true stories about her over-spending, as well as the vicious slanders about her infidelities with both men and women. Her enemies had long since dubbed her '*L'Autrichienne*' (The Austrian woman), a literally accurate description of her origins, but which also contained the word '*chienne*' – French for 'bitch'.

Right: The height of French pre-revolutionary madness. Rich women's hairstyles became so absurd in the late 18th century that they had to kneel in carriages. Here, the '*Belle Poule*', inspired by a British attack on the French warship of the same name in 1778.

Right: One of the 40,000 or so *'cahiers de doléances'* (complaints books) commissioned by Louis XVI in 1789, allowing ordinary people to express their grievances. This one called for an end to aristocratic privilege, which it refers to as: 'this tax so odious by nature, that causes so much hardship.'

Below: The opening of the *États généraux* in Versailles on 5 May 1789. The three 'estates' (classes) of society – clergy, commoners and aristocrats – were separated. The women present were mere observers. Within days, the under-represented commoners rebelled and founded the *Assemblée nationale.*

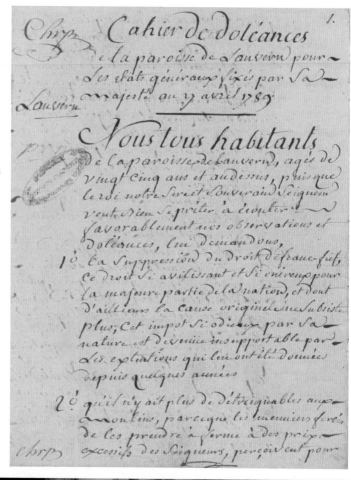

Left: Jean Sylvain Bailly, the first president of the *Assemblée nationale*, and first mayor of Paris. Too principled to survive once the Revolution mutated from a fight for democracy to political warfare, he was sentenced to be guillotined by a revolutionary tribunal in 1793.

Below: 13 July, 1789. Rioters attack the convent of Saint-Lazare in Paris, demanding money, destroying the library, and stealing food stored there for the nearby hospital. Predictably, this is one of the events of 1789 that are not commemorated these days.

Above: 20 June, 1789. Three weeks before the storming of the Bastille, the new, democratic *Assemblée nationale* peacefully takes power. Here, Jean Sylvain Bailly reads an oath swearing that the new parliament would meet 'until the kingdom's [sic] new Constitution is established'.

Below: 17 July 1789, three days after the Bastille, Louis XVI is welcomed by the Paris city council and re-affirmed as King. A constitutional monarchy had begun to function. The Paris riots were seen by most democrats as a regrettable sideshow.

the King believe that he had come up with an idea. Vergennes would outline a problem without giving a conclusion; he would then ask an obvious question, allowing Louis to provide the answer that Vergennes wanted.

One thing was for sure, Louis XVI was not a man who found it easy to stick to his political guns. Madame Campan gave a kindly explanation for this: 'His heart inclined him towards ideas of reform, but his principles, prejudices and fears, as well as the voices of the pious and privileged [the clergy and the aristocrats], intimidated him and caused him to abandon plans that his love for the people made him adopt.' Put more bluntly, Louis would try to take a stand, then get cold feet. Before taking yet another stand. And then getting cold feet again.

The result of Louis XVI's wavering was that he changed ministers almost as often as he switched hunting horses. From 1774 when he inherited the throne, to the end of summer 1789, when the Revolution really began to take hold, Louis XVI had 16 Ministers of Finance, including three in July 1789 alone. Most of them lasted a few months, while some, especially as the 1780s wore on, kept their job for just weeks.

This might be no bad thing, you would think. In France today, it is almost impossible to oust an inefficient minister from his or her job, outside of regular reshuffles. Firing a top official is seen as a sign of weakness, an admission of defeat. At least Louis XVI was capable of telling a minister that his plan hadn't worked and that it was time for a successor to have a try. But the truth was that, even though it wasn't entirely Louis XVI's fault that he changed ministers so often (as we shall see), promising strategies were rarely or never pushed through to a conclusion, and the sheer frequency of the changes began to convince his opponents that he was panicking, and give them renewed strength.

Louis XVI might have been an absolute monarch in theory, but it was his political opponents – who were just as unelected as he was – who held the real power. Pierre-Victor Malouet, a politician who served under both Louis XVI and the revolutionary government, described the situation in his memoirs:

'The nobility thought it very good that the King should be the absolute master over everything – except their class.'

As Louis XVI embarked on his stop-start campaign of reforms, the aristocrats who had bought or inherited their seats in the regional parliaments and the rich, tax-evading, tax-collecting landowners, including the Church, were determined to protect the status quo and oppose any democratization of politics and finance in France. By comparison with them, Louis XVI was going to prove himself a real revolutionary.

IV

Louis XVI's first political appointment showed the kind of man he was – or at least, the man he wanted to be. The day after his grandfather's death, the new King wrote a letter to a 72-year-old former Minister of the Navy who had served under Louis XV and lost his job 24 years earlier, after crossing swords with the royal mistress of the time, Madame de Pompadour.

This was Jean-Frédéric Phélypeaux, also known as the Comte de Maurepas. Louis XVI wrote to him:

> I am King. This word embodies many responsibilities, but I am only twenty years old. I do not think that I have acquired the necessary knowledge ... I have heard much about your probity and the reputation that your profound knowledge of affairs has justly earned you. This is why I have decided to ask you to help me with your advice and ideas.

The word Louis XVI used was not *'idées'* but *'lumières'* – literally this means 'lights', but, as we have seen, it was also the nickname given to France's freethinking philosophers. The young King was showing that he was a man of the times, in favour of change.

Nine days later, Louis XVI chaired the first meeting of his new cabinet of ministers, headed by Maurepas, and told them: 'My sole wish is to ensure the glory of the realm and the happiness of my people, so it is only by following these principles that you will earn my approval.'

Even if Louis XVI's first crop of ministers were all unelected aristocrats, chosen by an absolute monarch, they were amongst the most competent people in France. Louis displayed none of his wife's allergy to wrinkles, and appointed men[6] of sound practical experience. Charles Gravier de Vergennes, Louis XVI's first Minister of Foreign Affairs, was a former ambassador to Lisbon, Constantinople, Hanover and Stockholm. The Minister of War was Louis Nicolas Victor de Félix d'Ollières, a general who had seen action at the Battle of Fontenoy in 1745, one of France's few victories over the British. And the key post of Minister of Finance went to Anne Robert Jacques Turgot, who despite the first name was a male, a former regional administrator who, during a famine in 1770, had obliged landowners to help their tenants, and who believed in an *impôt unique*, a universal tax on the product of the land. He was an aristocrat with democratic tendencies.

On paper, it was probably as good a team as any French government since.

Below these ministers, there was a whole tranche of individual *bureaux* implementing policies. The different regions of France were run by 32 *intendants de police, justice et finances*, administrators whose duties included deciding how to spend royal funding on public works, agriculture and industry. They were all aristocrats appointed by the King, but this didn't mean that they were all in it for the personal profit to be obtained from suppliers. The above-mentioned Turgot, for example, had been

---

[6] At the time, no woman had a chance of being appointed a minister. Under previous kings, official mistresses had wielded considerable political power, both as advisors and intriguers, often getting ministers selected or fired. But Louis XVI wasn't the type to have a mistress and, as his reign went on, would mostly do his best to resist Marie-Antoinette's intrigues, especially after she proved to be so bad at money management. His would be a government by males.

intendant of the Limousin in central France, and during his 13 years in the job, he sponsored potato production, promoted manufacturing and improved the region's roads – which had been little more than a collection of potholes, making it impossible to transport goods anywhere. He also carried out a study of the area's agricultural productivity, and negotiated a reduction in regional taxes as a result.

Another noteworthy *intendant* was Claude-François Bertrand de Boucheporn, a magistrate from Metz in northeastern France who was parachuted into the troublesome island of Corsica in 1775 and managed to introduce an overall 5 per cent tax on agricultural production to replace the island's complex tax system, without provoking opposition from the local landowners, including the Bonaparte family. He also spent royal tax income on improving all of Corsica's ancient bridges, vastly improving the lot of every local who had to transport goods, people or animals.

So these aristocratic administrators were not all the lazy, corrupt tyrants they were later painted as by the revolutionaries. Indeed, they were more or less the equivalent of modern French regional *préfets*, who are not elected, either – they are appointed by the President. Another example of the monarchistic systems still in place in present-day France, simply because they were relatively efficient.

V

The most urgent matter that Louis XVI had to deal with was the country's disastrous finances. After Louis XIV's expensive warmongering and Louis XV's failure to tax the nobility, the poor were being squeezed as tightly as ever. Even if no one was talking seriously about revolution as yet, localized uprisings and riots were just a bread shortage or a tax increase away.

Louis XVI showed his intentions by making cuts in his own budget. He even made savings on his beloved hunting. He reduced his boar and deer hunts, and over the course of his reign, he was to halve the number of horses in the stables for his personal use and that of his immediate entourage, from 2,400 in 1774 to 'only' 1,125 in 1787, thereby saving about 3.4 million *livres*.

The palace staff had to walk more often, too – the equine population of the inaccurately named Petite Écurie (Small Stable) at Versailles, which housed the horses for workaday wagons as well as pleasure vehicles, was cut from about 6,000 to 1,800.

Louis also decided not to use the royal palace of Saint-Germain-en-Laye, west of Paris. When Félix d'Hézecques went there, he said: 'It hurt to see so many huge rooms abandoned to the rats and spiders, with neither furniture nor decorations.' It's true that Louis XVI didn't donate the château to the poor – according to Hézecques it was inhabited by a few impoverished aristocrats who, 'thanks to wise saving and cheap food, restored their wealth' – but leaving it was a symbolic gesture. The Sun King Louis XIV had been born at Saint-Germain-en-Laye, and had spent a fortune refurbishing it. In 1776, Louis XVI sold off the château and some of the grounds to his brother Charles.

Louis XVI even decided that his personal pleasure department had to suffer cuts. For his grandfather, this might have meant less fluffy pillows for visiting prostitutes. But for Louis XVI, it involved reducing the staff at the Menus-Plaisirs (Small Pleasures), a modest name for the barrack-like building in Versailles that housed the musical instruments, theatre sets, costumes, party accessories and sporting equipment necessary to provide entertainment at the palace.[7] Again, given his wife's notorious taste for amusements of all kinds, this was an important gesture.

Of course, Louis XVI's version of austerity did not mean that he was on a diet of bread and water. As we have seen, he still organized balls and theatrical performances, and Marie-Antoinette was allowed to spend ruinous sums on clothes and

[7] Appropriately, this is now the town's Centre de musique baroque.

jewellery. Louis also preserved some absurd relics of the past on his payroll – he still paid three organ-makers; one man to wind his watch every morning; one man whose only job was to ask the King at what time he would be attending mass; two commode carriers, even though he used his own modern water closet, in private;[8] and a royal mule driver, despite the fact that the palace had no more mules.

But we know that Louis XVI's cuts hit where it hurt because his brother Charles wittily accused him of stinginess, dubbing him *'Roi de France et avare'* (King of France and a miser), a pun on the monarch's official title of *'Roi de France et Navarre'* (after the province in northern Spain that had been French since 1589).

The editor of Madame Campan's memoirs, François Barrière, tells a story in his notes to the 1823 edition of the book about a bishop who was asked by a member of Turgot's family whether it was possible to celebrate Easter and the Pope's jubilee year at the same time. The bishop replied ironically: 'We are living in a time of economies. I think we can make that one, too.'

If such high-ranking members of the royal family and the clergy were unhappy about the budget cuts, we can be sure they were good for France.

Turgot, Louis XVI's first Finance Minister, also embarked on a radical programme of change. He had been chosen largely because he believed in progress: 'The total mass of humanity,' he once wrote, 'in alternate waves of calm and agitation, good and evil, marches slowly but constantly onward towards greater perfection.' If this sounds more revolutionary than royal, it is not a coincidence – the reforms that Turgot proposed were

[8] Louis might have missed the old days of having servants to do everything, because one day, he went to sit on his water closet, not noticing that a cat had curled up in the toilet bowl. Louis began to go about his business, at which point the cat woke up and expressed its objections with tooth and claw. Louis leapt off the toilet clutching his trousers and yelling for his servants.

almost as daring as anything suggested after 1789 (except, of course, in matters related to mass decapitation).

A list of Turgot's policies reads almost like a call for modern democracy, and did not endear him to France's privileged classes.

He proposed to end the dishing-out of jobs for life and undeserved pensions to aristocrats, and to review the 'Ferme générale' ('general farm'), the collective name for the aristocrats who organized the collection of all the country's taxes – and who helped themselves to a generous commission. This naturally caused perfumed tantrums of protest in châteaux all over the country.

Turgot also tried to cure France's perpetual bread shortage – the most frequent cause of social unrest – by abolishing the so-called *'droit de hallage'*, a market tax on sales of grain, and by allowing toll-free movement of grain around the country, as well as imports from abroad.

This infuriated not only the tax collectors but also members of the royal family who made money speculating on cereal prices. Their opposition was so ferocious that Turgot rewrote his bill on the subject in clear, everyday language, to make sure that everyone in the country could understand the issues involved. In a long treatise on the need to protect ordinary people from food shortages, he explained that free trade was 'the only way of preventing excessive inequalities in prices, and ensuring that nothing may alter the fair and natural price' of grain. The freedom to store grain in years of abundance, and to transport it into areas that had suffered bad harvests – without paying taxes on these operations – would help to prevent famine, he said, and 'if during the course of his reign, the provinces should be afflicted by shortage, His Majesty promises to do everything in his power to procure efficient help for that portion of his subjects which is suffering the most from public calamity'. A little wordy, perhaps, but it was a clear message to the non-privileged that the new King had their interests at heart.

Turgot assured people that Louis XVI had approved all these radical measures *'avec grande satisfaction'*. It was unfortunate that the wheat harvest of 1774 was less than satisfying, so that Turgot's law had entirely the wrong effect. Traders were free to sell grain at high panic prices where it was most keenly needed, so that areas with decent wheat harvests were perversely affected by shortages.

In short, Turgot had shown too much faith in the free market, and the result was a so-called 'flour war',[9] a series of minor uprisings in the spring of 1775 that are often seen as rehearsals for the main event of 1789. In the Paris region and the northern half of France, grain warehouses were pillaged, bakeries and flour mills were attacked, and boats and wagons carrying grain were hijacked. Louis XVI resorted to force, and 25,000 soldiers were sent out to restore the peace. Hundreds of rioters were arrested, and two men were hanged.

Not for the first time, though, a serious upset did not turn people against Louis XVI. On the contrary, there were calls to return to the old system whereby the King would step in and pay for grain during a famine. People still wanted a 'father of the realm'.

In fact, that was the role that Louis XVI – or his agents, anyway – had been trying to play. Some of the warehouses attacked during the flour war were stockpiles of what was known as 'the King's wheat'. This was grain bought up by the Crown in order to limit the effect of the free market. Turgot's idea was to lower prices by offering this large supply of stored grain for sale during a shortage. Even if Louis XVI wasn't giving out as much free food aid as before, he was still doing what he could to protect people from 'public calamity'.

---

[9] In some cases, outbreaks of the flour war were provoked by ill-informed (or ill-intentioned) gossips spreading the rumour that Louis XVI was hoarding flour and speculating on the free market for personal gain during the grain shortage. Political fake news *par excellence*.

Despite having caused a minor revolution with his agricultural policy, Turgot held on to his job, and in 1776 he proposed something similar for industry.

He suggested abolishing the *corvée royale*, or royal chore, the tax by which people had to give a variable number of days' labour per year, which they often spent repairing roads. Turgot had already abolished the *corvée* in his region when he was *intendant* of the Limousin. Now he wanted to end it throughout the nation, and to replace the labour with a cash tax that would also be levied from landowners. Labourers would then be paid a fair wage to build the roads, a measure that would provide employment during bad harvests.

This was very much a cause that Louis XVI supported. In his introduction to Turgot's proposals, Louis described the *corvée* in terms that would astonish anyone who thinks he was a heartless exploiter of his subjects:

> Those who have most to gain [from the *corvée*] are the landowners, almost all of them privileged, whose property rises in value thanks to the building of roads. By forcing the poor man to repair them, by obliging him to give his time and his work without pay, one is taking away the only resource he has against poverty and hunger, and making him work so that the rich will profit.

No left-leaning philosopher could have expressed it better.

Naturally, the aristocrats were furious. In a shameless defence of noble privileges, the Paris parliament condemned the idea of a cash tax on all landowners as 'an inadmissible system of equality'. (Well, at least they were honest.)

But Turgot went further, and called for the abolition of France's *corporations* and *jurandes*, the guilds that regulated employment in every trade from water-carrying to hat-making, and from wine-selling to goldsmithing.

Writing in the preface to his bill, Turgot complained that 'in almost every town in our kingdom, the exercise of different crafts and trades is concentrated in the hands of a small number of masters ... who have the exclusive right to make or sell objects,' and that 'citizens of all classes are deprived of the right to choose the tradesmen they wish to employ'. Furthermore, anyone seeking to become a skilled worker had to pay the *corporation* or *jurande* for a long apprenticeship, 'wasting some of the money that they would have used to set up their own shop or workshop, or even to live'.

This sounds to modern ears – especially French ones – like an attempt to break unions and cut wages by allowing bosses to employ underskilled workers. In part it was, but Turgot's main goal was to end the monopoly of the organizations that paid the King for the lucrative privilege of regulating the whole employment market. Turgot was trying to reduce the cost of becoming a skilled worker or a trader.

Once again, however, there were so many vested interests at stake, not only amongst aristocrats but also in the growing middle class, that the aristocratic judges in the Paris parliament refused to ratify the law, proving that their true *raison d'être* was to oppose democracy.

By May 1776, the scope of Turgot's desires for reform, and the sheer volume of his opponents' protests, was making Louis XVI nervous. In less than two years, there had been famine, riots, a parliamentary revolt, as well as constant complaints from Marie-Antoinette that she wasn't allowed to dish out as many pensions to her friends. So when Turgot went yet further, and proposed to end the tyranny of the regional parliaments by depriving them of their law-making power, and to introduce a single tax based on property values – another measure that was sure to make the aristocrats squeal – Louis caved in and sacked him.

In Turgot's place, Louis selected another experienced former *intendant*. This was Jean Étienne Bernard Ogier de Clugny, Baron de Nuits (just one person despite the list of names), who had presided over four regions, including Saint-Domingue (present-day Haiti), which was of course a slave island. Even so, he wasn't against Turgot's attempts to lighten the workload of the rural poor in mainland France, and oversaw a law that made it possible for regions to hire paid workers to build its roads, instead of using the forced labour of the *corvée royale*.

However, the many-titled Jean Étienne had little time to make a name for himself because he dropped dead after only five months in his new job, at the premature age of 46. Gossips alleged that his demise was hastened by a dissolute lifestyle. He was said to have been living in sin with three sisters, one of whom, a married woman called Françoise-Augustine Sentuary, had also been the lover of America's famous admiral John Paul Jones, and had inspired an erotic ode by a poet called Évariste de Parny that began:

> *Aimer à treize ans, dites-vous,*
> *C'est trop tôt: eh, qu'importe l'âge?*
> *Avez-vous besoin d'être sage*
> *Pour goûter le plaisir des fous?*

> (To love at the age of thirteen, you say,
> Is too early; but what does age matter?
> Do you need to be well behaved
> To taste the pleasure of the insane?)

Apparently the experienced Françoise-Augustine proved too much for the new Finance Minister, and Louis XVI was forced to admit: 'I think we made another mistake.' Yet again, his attempts to reform French politics and save the nation from bankruptcy had come to nothing. It seemed to be only a matter of time before one of the flour wars erupted into a full-blown popular uprising.

To his credit, Louis reacted by making his most daring appointment yet.

Chapter 9

LOUIS XVI'S REVOLUTIONARY REFORMERS

'Some master hand, of very superior talents, and inflexible courage ...
at the helm to guide events, instead of being driven by them.'
Arthur Young (1741–1820), British agriculturalist
and writer, describing what France needed in the 1780s
if it was to avert Revolution

I

On the face of it, Louis XVI's next Finance Minister was a safe pair of hands, a 58-year-old former *intendant* called Louis Gabriel Taboureau des Réaux. Publicly, he received the message: 'Leave things as they are ... until we can make some reasonable improvements.'

It might have sounded as though the radical reforms were over, but in fact Réaux was just a figurehead for the de facto Finance Minister, who could not be given the title because he was a Protestant – despite Louis XVI's law on religious freedom, only Catholics were allowed to serve in the King's Council.

This was Jacques Necker, a Swiss financier who had shown such skill at money-management that he was made partner of a Parisian bank before he was 30 and retired, a multi-millionaire, at the age of 40 – all this after starting his career as a humble bank clerk.

Behind the reassuring smokescreen of the mature Réaux, Louis XVI hoped that Necker could inject some dynamism into France's finances, and appointed him Director General of the Royal Treasury.

Necker set out to show that he was just as radical a reformer as Turgot, but a man who was not going to put all his trust in the free market. He wrote an essay for Louis XVI, the *Note to the King on the Establishment of Provincial Administrations*, setting out his aims, all of which sounded perfectly laudable.

He promised Louis that he would 'use only slow, gentle and wise means', and that he would 'offer multiple guarantees of the happiness of the people, without disturbing public order'. If his measures were accepted, Necker said, 'we would no longer see the people weighed down beneath taxes and legal fees ...' – a direct jibe at the parliaments – '... we would free the inhabitants of the countryside painlessly from the yoke beneath which they are living'.

Necker recognized that taxes were necessary: 'It is the power to tax that constitutes the essence of sovereignty.' But, he warned, the people who collect these taxes and have the power to spend them must be well chosen: 'In whichever hands the monarch places this trust, only those of his subjects who use it well will remind the people that a good king is watching over them.'

Necker concluded his essay by reminding Louis XVI that times were changing. In the past, kings had been remembered for winning wars or for their 'magnificence'. But 'today, concentrating on the people's happiness, and establishing the laws that can guarantee it, seem to offer the only new, and the most noble, ambition.' Necker told Louis that 'the eyes of the nation are on Your Majesty, and they seem to see a harmony between its needs and its sovereign's character.'

Whether Louis XVI actually read this dense, 25-page document is debatable. After a day's hunting, he might well have fallen asleep during the central chapter where Necker outlined all the practical details of his reforms. But a canny operator like Necker probably read out the key, flattering sections, and Maurepas, the Chief Minister, would have reassured Louis that the Swiss banker had his head and heart in the right place.

Necker's plan was daring. At a stroke, he proposed to replace a whole tranche of job-for-life, commission-raking tax collectors with administrators who were on a fixed salary. He also wanted to strip the noble parliaments of their powers, appointing the 'provincial assemblies' proposed in his essay on reforming administrations. The parliamentarians were so furious at this that they instantly started a resistance campaign, and managed to stop all but two of the assemblies taking over in the provinces.

But Necker was like a wheel of Gruyère cheese bouncing down a Swiss mountainside – on a roll. With Louis XVI's blessing, he worked on immediate, short-term savings while planning a complete overhaul of France's finances. And if he had been able to push through all his reforms, the Revolution might never have happened.

II

It is fascinating to read Necker's progress report, published in 1781. Simply entitled *Compte rendu au Roi* – a report to the King – it is a lucid, easily readable 100-page essay on the state of France's financial health after four years of Necker's reforms.

The bottom line is promising for a country that had been on the verge of bankruptcy – a profit of ten million. But ten million was a dangerously low amount to be in the black. That was less than a third of the amount spent on the royal households in a year. It certainly wasn't enough to protect France against a famine or an epidemic. But, as we shall see, Necker gave some very precise excuses for not producing a much better result. And he offered radical suggestions to cure the chronic French tendency to overspend – most of them just as democratic as anything proposed after the Revolution.

The report opens with Necker reminding Louis XVI how wise he was to commission the audit. In Britain, he says, 'every year the [financial] situation is presented to parliament and then published. In France, we have constantly made a mystery of our accounts.' Necker is in favour of 'shedding a light upon the financial situation' (that ultra-modern word *lumière* again). He recommends passing a law obliging the Minister of Finance to publish the state's accounts at any time the King wishes. This, he says, is how Britain manages to negotiate cheap loans for itself. Lenders will only offer low interest rates if they trust the borrower.

Necker then hits Louis with the first punch: when Necker took over the accounts, 'everything was a model of pointless and complicated spending. A multitude of officers were acting as suppliers, cooks and dinner guests.' This kitchen metaphor was a none-too-subtle hint that job-for-life aristocrats were still exploiting the system to cheat Louis and the country as a whole. And Necker followed it up with a clear threat to the complacent hangers-on at Versailles and all over France. Praising Louis for 'Your Majesty's particular taste for order', he says that the required savings can be achieved 'by ending a lot of privileges and useless occupations'.

For example, Necker pinpoints the massive 28 million *livres* dished out in *pensions* awarded to favoured aristocrats. He notes that Louis himself was surprised to learn that the sum was so enormous – thereby defending the King against frequent charges that the pensions were being given to his cronies.[1]

Necker goes further, suggesting several revolutionary ways of helping the poor, 'this class of your subjects towards which the benevolent hand of Your Majesty must constantly stretch out'. Necker intends, he says, to lessen the sufferings of the poor beneath 'the imperious yoke of property and wealth'.

---

[1] Necker underlines his own squeaky-clean financial morals by writing explicitly that 'if anyone has received a pension, a rank or job thanks to my favouritism, let them be named.'

Necker wants to alleviate their tax bill, first of all by reforming the *taille*, the tax paid by non-aristocratic landowners, mostly peasant farmers trying to eke out a living. This, Necker points out, is the only tax that has risen steadily, and the only one 'that can be increased in secret, often without the sovereign knowing'. Capping the *taille* would therefore help a large section of the low-earning French population.

What's more, Necker says, income from the *taille* often doesn't reach the King's purse. Aristocratic tax collectors are creaming it off. From now on, Necker proposes a fixed tax based strictly on the size of a landowner's property, with the possibility to challenge any unwarranted increases in the rate.

Necker repeats his call to end the *corvée*, the workdays served mainly by the rural poor, and praises Louis for releasing his own bonded labourers – other landowners must do the same, Necker says, and put an end to the exploitation of feudal serfs by aristocratic landowners.

He also turned his attention to the sensitive issue of grain shortages. Grain, Necker says, is 'the only product for which changing prices influence the people's ability to subsist, and public tranquillity'. According to him, the only way to protect the people from famine and the regime from riots is to ban exports of grain during times of shortage.

Necker naturally tries to reassure Louis that democratization of the tax system won't bankrupt France, and suggests that the country holds its salvation in its own hands. Already, he says, innovative, well-made French products attract visitors who spend 30 million *livres* per year, but the manufacturing sector needs to be encouraged and expanded,[2] which is exactly what Louis was

---

[2] Concentrating on high-quality, hand-made products was the model that France adopted to regenerate its economy after the disastrous Napoleonic Wars. Unable to compete with Britain's Industrial Revolution, it concentrated on 'typically French' luxury products, and built the reputation it enjoys today for the handbags, *haute couture* and perfume that inspire pillaging raids on Paris by tourists from all over the world. Again, Necker seems to have been a visionary.

doing by creating an 'annual award for the invention most useful to trade and industry'. Necker likes the idea of this award because, he says, 'any type of glory is the best motivation for the French'.

It all sounds *formidable* – Louis XVI, modern monarch, benevolent mentor of France's most democratic Finance Minister, tackling the country's problems head on, with an audit that is ten times more transparent than most modern governments would dare to be. It is hardly surprising that the *Compte rendu au Roi* was a huge hit, and sold 100,000 copies, earning a tidy sum for the public purse. It is difficult to imagine a modern politician's budget speech topping the book charts.

But openness can come at a price, and Necker's report was peppered with embarrassing revelations about excessive spending by Louis XVI and his family. It was as though one of Marie-Antoinette's necklaces had broken during one of her husband's speeches promising budget costs, scattering diamonds at the feet of the scandal-hungry pamphlet-writers.

Necker's essay revealed to a hungry public that the running cost of the King's household and those of Marie-Antoinette and Louis XVI's three sisters had come to 25.7 million *livres* for the previous year. And this did not include the 8.04 million lavished on his three brothers. To ordinary French people, these were unimaginably high sums, the equivalent of billions today – just to keep the royal family in curtains, servants, food, drink and horses. Not forgetting the unforgivable 28 million in pensions to royal cronies.

These revelations were all the more damaging to Louis XVI's reputation because Necker's simplified list of outgoings was concentrated into two crystal-clear pages. Anyone vaguely literate could compare this extravagant royal spending with, say, the mere five million allotted to roads and bridges in the whole of France.

This seems to explain Necker's almost apologetic note to Louis at the end of his report: 'I don't know if people will think that I have followed the right route, but I have sought it.'

Sorry, Your Majesty, Necker seems to be saying, but you *did* ask...

III

As well as embarrassing the royal family, Necker terrified the privileged classes, and certainly made a lot of them poorer. And he didn't stop at financial reform. He began hijacking other ministers' responsibilities if he thought they weren't being radical enough. In the early 1780s, France's poorest citizens could be grateful to Necker for alleviating their sufferings, exactly as he had promised.

In 1780, Louis XVI visited the Hôtel-Dieu, the hospital in central Paris, leaving in tears after seeing three or four patients to a bed, with the dying nudged on to the floor as soon as they were too weak to resist. He commissioned Necker to reform French hospitals, and the Swiss minister immediately sprang into action.

In order to set up the Hôpital Necker,[3] he had to haggle fiercely with the Bishop of Paris, who was insisting that the building he wanted belonged to the Church and should be used to house nuns. Necker responded by forcing the bishop to grant him a lease at a reduced price. No noble-born clergyman was going to stand in the way of humanitarian reforms.

The new hospital's manifesto, *Rules and Customs of this House*, smacks very much of Necker's writing style, though it may well have been written by his wife. It begins:

Imperceptibly, time introduces and establishes abuses in the best institutions. Even hospitals have not been immune to this general law, and these monuments to humanity have sometimes become monuments to indifference and even barbarity. Is it not necessary, or at least useful, to work on reform and to seek to establish more order and economy in these charitable institutions?

[3] The hospital still exists, and bears the name of Necker's wife, Suzanne, who was its first director. She was a Parisian pastor's daughter who is said to have done much to shape Necker's ideas for social reform.

The express aim of this new hospital was to serve as a model:

> We have tried by order of His Majesty to test a small hospital of
> 120 patients, one to a bed, cared for in the greatest cleanliness,
> and with all the necessary attention to ensure their cure; they
> will be housed in well-ventilated rooms, free of noise, and cared
> for by sisters of charity, as well as a doctor and surgeon who will
> live on the premises and devote themselves entirely to this job.
> They [the patients] will be given the healthiest food and the
> most carefully selected drugs.

Necker also convinced Louis XVI that French prisons needed
urgent modernizing. This idea was inspired by an Englishman,
John Howard, who had published a report, *The State of the
Prisons*, in 1777. Again, a sign that Necker and Louis XVI were
men of the times.

Necker visited some of Paris's worst jails, and noted that not
only were conditions dirty and cruel (unless you were rich
enough to pay off the warders), but the most violent criminals
were locked up with harmless debtors and even actors who had
disappointed their noble audience and provoked a *lettre de cachet*
(the royal decree whereby an aristocrat could have any commoner imprisoned on a whim).

In August 1780, Necker published a *Declaration on the
Establishment of New Prisons*. In it, he informed the people that
Louis XVI wanted to 'give a helping hand to those who owe
their misfortune to their transgressions', and that 'we have been
moved for a long time by the state of the prisons in our
kingdom'.[4] Prisons, Necker said, needed to be cleaner, better
managed and less crowded, and it was necessary to 'destroy the
underground dungeons, so that men who have been unjustly

---

[4] By now, four years after being appointed, Necker is no longer just describing Louis XVI's wishes. He is writing almost as though they were equals – a
sign that the Swiss reformer was getting too big for his Versailles boots.

accused or suspected, and then found not guilty by the courts, should not suffer a rigorous punishment just by being held in these dark, unhealthy places'.

As promised in his declaration, Necker got Louis to buy and demolish a sixteenth-century building in central Paris, and build two model prisons in its place: the Grande Force for men, and the more ladylike-sounding Petite Force for women. By 1782, they were ready, and inmates were transferred from crowded, insalubrious cells elsewhere in Paris into a prison that had an infirmary, dormitories with real beds, fireplaces and an exercise yard, as well as a chapel where the inmates were obliged to pray for forgiveness.

John Howard visited the Force prisons in 1783 and was impressed. He wrote: 'The King's Declaration for this alteration, dated the 30th of August 1780, contains some of the most humane and enlightened sentiments respecting the conduct of prisons.' Howard also praised the new system of *commissaires*, noblemen who were appointed to oversee each prison, saying that: 'These officers are very humane towards the distressed. They can oblige creditors to accept one third part of debts.' This at a time when London's Newgate Prison was full of languishing eternal debtors.[5]

What impressed Howard most, though, was the cleanliness. The French prison courtyards were washed down once or twice a day, killing the noxious odours that he had smelt in English prisons: 'I sometimes thought these courts were the cleanest places in Paris.'

Of course, Louis XVI's prisons weren't all transformed into models of modern leniency at a stroke. Plenty of putrid dungeons with cruel, corrupt warders survived. Galley slaves awaiting transfer to the sea ports were still chained up in the château

[5] In 1777 Necker had overseen the creation of the Mont de Piété, a sort of nationalized pawnshop that gave out cheap loans. The idea was to reduce the number of people in prison for debt to usurers. It still exists today, as the Crédit municipal.

de la Tournelle, on the banks of the Seine – where the luxury restaurant the Tour d'Argent (Silver Tower) now stands. And some punishments were as barbaric as ever: women who killed their husbands might be burned alive. Men killing their wives would be broken on the wheel (the system whereby the victim was roped to a wheel, then spun round as an executioner smashed his limbs with an iron bar, before leaving him to die). Commoners could be broken on the wheel just for robbery or arson, while noble murderers might be beheaded, or, if very lucky, declared insane and spared.

However, throughout Louis XVI's reign, the use of the death penalty was being reduced – at Douai in the north of France, between 1721 and 1730, out of 260 defendants accused of a capital crime, 39 were condemned to death (about 15 per cent); in the same town between 1781 and 1790, only 26 out of 500 were executed – 5 per cent. By contrast, after 1792, revolutionary France would be plunged into an era of mass executions and lynchings.

Necker also put an end to torture in prisons. Until 1780 the euphemistically named *'question préparatoire'* was still being used to make sure that people accused of capital crimes confessed that they were really guilty. Methods of torture included the wooden horse (a prisoner would sit on the sharp edge of a V-shaped table with their legs weighted down), *osselets* (bones jammed between the prisoner's fingers), *estrapade* (for which the prisoner had his or her hands tied behind their back and was then winched up by the rope until the shoulders dislocated), and – a Parisian speciality – *brodequins* or boots, in which the victim's legs were crushed between wooden splints. Thanks to Necker, Louis XVI put a stop to confessions obtained in this way.

Reading Necker and Louis XVI's intentions, and John Howard's dispassionate report, it seems that in the 1780s, France's penal system was heading in the right direction. It is slightly ironic that the coming Revolution would take as its most powerful symbol the supposedly inhumane conditions in a royal prison – the Bastille. John Howard tried to visit the Bastille in 1783:

> I ... knocked hard at the outer gate, and immediately went forward through the guard to the drawbridge before the entrance of the castle. But while I was contemplating this gloomy mansion, an officer came out much surprised; and I was forced to retreat ... and thus regained that freedom which for one locked up within those walls is almost impossible to obtain.

But then, as we shall see, there were only seven prisoners locked up there in July 1789, and the Bastille was stormed for its supply of gunpowder rather than to alleviate the sufferings of its inmates – all of whom were reimprisoned after the Revolution, anyway.

IV

All in all, Jacques Necker sounds like the kind of political figure that modern French voters can only dream about – a democratic reformer with his heart in the right place, an efficient administrator who is not scared of shaking up the establishment, and a politician who actually delivers on his promises. Too good to be true, surely.

Well, yes.

The problem with Necker's *Compte rendu au Roi* was that it was written in self-defence and to increase public trust in France's economic prospects. As such, it had two main flaws. First, some of the income he listed had not actually been received yet. And most importantly, he conveniently 'forgot' to include 200 million *livres* of debt.

But this, he would have explained, wasn't his fault: most of the debt had been run up because of circumstances outside his control. He had hinted at these in the first line of his outgoings for 1780: 'Extraordinary war spending ... 65,200,000.'

The circumstances in question were that, in early 1778, at a time when Louis XVI was meant to be cutting expenditure, he

had embarked on a war. He had been seduced, in purely pla-
tonic terms, by the roving American politician and scientist
Benjamin Franklin, who had come to Paris in 1776 to drum up
support for his country's independence.

To Louis XVI's Minister for Foreign Affairs, Charles Gravier
de Vergennes, the arguments in favour of helping Franklin and
his revolutionary friends were obvious: getting Britain –
France's favourite enemy – entangled in a long, difficult war
was sure to weaken its economy. Furthermore, if the British
were busy fighting to stay in North America, they might stop
trying to annex French sugar islands in the Caribbean. And
siding with a major new independent ally would open up a whole
new continent to French trade.

Vergennes was also keen to regain some of the territory in
Canada that had been lost to Britain in the disastrous (to France,
anyway) French and Indian War of 1754–63. He was virulently
anti-British, and saw the American bid for independence as
divine intervention: 'Providence has chosen this as the time for
the humiliation of England.'

As a fan of the sciences, Louis XVI knew that Franklin was
famous for attracting lightning, so he didn't want to provoke the
British, and initially insisted that any French help should be
kept secret. He therefore recruited Pierre-Augustin Caron de
Beaumarchais (the watchmaker, author and fixer who had
schemed for Louis XV)[6] to run guns to America in exchange for
tobacco. Beaumarchais set up a company with a Spanish name
to disguise its French origins – Roderigue Hortalez et
Compagnie – and shipped 30,000 muskets and 2,000 barrels of
gunpowder, as well as cannons, uniforms and other equipment
across the Atlantic.

This did not cost France a penny, because it was trade rather
than aid, but by 1778, Britain had got wind of France's involvement – partly thanks to the young Marquis de La Fayette, a

---

[6] Beaumarchais had not yet written his pornographic pamphlet against
Marie-Antoinette. See Chapter 5.

military adventurer out to avenge his father who had been cut down by a cannonball during the Seven Years War. Not a modest man by nature, La Fayette made a huge public show of going to join the good fight.

So in 1778, with Necker desperately trying to save money, Louis XVI began to commit hardware, men and cash to the American war. Seven French warships were sent, along with 6,000 troops headed by a trusted general, Jean-Baptiste de Rochambeau – whose first battle during the American campaign was to stop his men trying to seduce Puritan women.

And overall, the expedition was a military success for France, which won glory for itself by sealing victory at the Battle of Yorktown in 1781, when the French fleet cut off British reinforcements and forced the garrison to surrender.

With the British distracted, France attacked Malta and Gibraltar, grabbed the islands of Minorca and St Kitts, and regained trading posts in India. The French even felt emboldened to threaten an invasion of Britain, with 60,000 troops massing in Brittany and French ships sailing threateningly up the Channel – though they never actually got close to England, because they had been loaded with barrels of dirty drinking water, and the sailors started dropping dead.

Of course, all this military action came at a price. Necker had to find the running costs for a fleet of warships and thousands of men stationed in the Americas for more than two years, as well as funding for the aborted invasion of England. On top of this, Louis XVI donated 12 million *livres* in cash to the American cause, and granted another 12 million in loans.

In his *Compte rendu au Roi*, Necker was explicit about his struggle 'to find the resources necessary in the middle of a war to defend the state, and the power of the sovereign', without 'neglecting the happiness of the people'.

His solution was to borrow. He raised over 380 million *livres* by offering subscription bonds to the French public – a regular income for life in exchange for a cash loan to the government.

However, this was made more difficult than necessary. France's previous secrecy about its accounts meant that Necker was forced to offer high interest rates in order to gain people's trust. The scheme also backfired because investors began selling off the contracts to the parents of young children, in the children's names, so that these young subscribers would have an income for the whole of their (hopefully long) life.

French critics of the idea of state borrowing are brutal in their demolition of Necker's economics. In the 1970s, even the supposedly neutral *Larousse* encyclopedia contained an entry for 'Necker (Jacques)' which stated bluntly that 'borrowing precipitated financial disaster', and quoted an eighteenth-century economist called Gabriel Sénac de Meilhan, who had declared that Necker had 'neither goal, doctrine or system' – without mentioning that Meilhan was one of Necker's bitterest enemies, having coveted the job of Minister of Finance for himself.

Borrowing was a highly risky strategy, but Necker achieved one miracle – he financed a war without raising taxes. And if the country had defaulted on his loans, it was the bourgeois and aristocratic speculators who would have lost out. In a way, it really was taking from the rich to protect the poor.

Ordinary French people therefore adored Necker, but his social policies and his attempts to end privilege made him dangerous enemies. In May 1781, an anonymous pamphlet appeared, the *Lettre de M. le marquis de Caraccioli à M. d'Alembert*. It was a common format, supposedly a letter from a naive foreigner expressing astonishment at the goings-on in France. This one rubbished Necker's policies. It lambasted him as 'a banker suddenly elevated to functions that he knows nothing about, a foreigner preferred to every subject of the King to occupy a place of trust alongside him; a Protestant given the most important ministry in a kingdom where Protestants are excluded from the lowest office'. Necker's appointment was, the writer said *'une grande bizarrerie'*.

The pamphlet accused Necker of being disrespectful to Louis XVI, and its author expressed his surprise at 'the dogmatic, cutting tone he uses to address the King of France' in the *Compte rendu au Roi*. The author even hints at treason, accusing Necker of threatening to announce his resignation purely to plunge the country's finances into crisis and make himself look indispensable.

The only accurate parts of the pamphlet are the accusations that Necker was 'crushing a whole class of citizens' and 'attacking property rights', and that in his paper proposing provincial assemblies, 'parliaments are violently attacked' and 'the clergy and the nobility mistreated'. Necker really was trying to topple the privileged elite.

As a result, the knives of the establishment were out for Necker, wielded in secret by Louis XVI's brothers who had been criticized in the *Compte rendu au Roi*, and much more openly by the noble parliamentarians.

In response, Necker seems to have decided to brandish his own sword, offering to fall on it if necessary. In mid-May of 1781, he made one final request to Louis XVI to force through the law taking political power away from the parliaments. But Louis had been stung by the public outcry at his excessive spending on the royal households, and no doubt swayed by the furious complaints of his family. We can gauge the tone of conversations in the royal household from the former attendant, Félix d'Hézecques (a nobleman), whose normally genial tone turns much more toxic when he looks back at Necker in his memoirs: 'This Genevan, lifted from his obscure tasks at the bank, concealed, beneath a simple exterior, an immense pride, an overriding stubbornness and an astonishing vanity inspired by constant flattery from the economists.' Louis XVI's brothers' comments would probably have been far less printable.

So at the key moment in his and France's history, Louis XVI showed his true character and weakened. He refused to back Necker.

The Swiss banker promptly resigned, hid himself away in the country north of Paris and wrote a three-volume book, *De l'administration des finances de la France*, explaining what he had done, and suggesting how to make the country richer, fairer and (on average) happier.

His ideas must have hit a chord, because it sold a massive 80,000 copies in France, underlining the sad fact that Louis XVI had just axed the man who might have saved him from the guillotine a few years later.

V

In Necker's place, Louis XVI appointed a man who was in some ways the Swiss banker's opposite. Jean-François Joly de Fleury was in his early sixties and an old-school politician who was said to be vehemently opposed to the modern trend for philosophy. He was generally perceived as a conservative who might be able to mollify the distrustful parliamentarians' opposition to reform. As such, Fleury declared that he was going to scrap Necker's plans to install provincial assemblies, and that he supported the system of selling privileged jobs for life. However, when he tried to cut government spending, Fleury met with such ferocious opposition from ministers that he resigned after just under two years in office.

Undeterred, Louis XVI opted for radical change yet again, appointing a 32-year-old former *intendant des finances* (regional financial officer) called Henri Lefèvre d'Ormesson. When Henri objected that he was too immature for the job, Louis XVI is said to have answered 'I'm younger than you, and I occupy an altogether more important position.' The King was still only 29.

Sadly, though, Louis was showing his own inexperience, because d'Ormesson was a short-lived disaster. All he achieved in his seven months in office was to raise a few million in lotteries (Louis XIV's antiquated method of harvesting cash from the nation) and cause panic in France's financial markets by trying to borrow money in secret. He was fired, and later re-emerged during the Revolution as Mayor of Paris – a post he quit after a week because he was terrified of the mob. A man, in short, who made even Louis XVI look decisive.

The next in line to try and save France's economy was a dashing, witty aristocrat called Charles-Alexandre de Calonne, a friend of Marie-Antoinette's confidante, Gabrielle de Polignac.

Calonne had been an *intendant* in Metz, was the son of a parliamentarian, and was married to a woman whose family included several tax collectors and a supplier of food to the army. On the surface, he was a wholehearted member of the royal-job-for-life, bribe-taking, privilege-protecting aristocracy – the diametric opposite of Necker. It was also widely assumed that Calonne had written the anti-Necker *Lettre de M. le marquis de Caraccioli à M. d'Alembert.*

On being nominated in November 1783, Calonne gave a speech to his treasury officials saying that he had 'an improvement plan which, founded on the very structure of the monarchy, embraces all its parts, without undermining any'. It sounded very much like a coded message to the landowning, tax-grabbing classes that they were safe in his hands.

Calonne proceeded to restore powers to the private tax collectors whom Necker had tried to replace. He paid off 37 million *livres* of debts owed by Louis XVI's brothers Charles and Louis Stanislas. He even rubber-stamped the scandalous policy of giving pensions to royal cronies, after Necker had abolished them. And it was while Calonne was in office that Marie-Antoinette got embroiled in the infamous 'necklace affair' that brought royal extravagance to the forefront of public opinion (see Chapter 7).

If Louis XVI was determined to provoke a revolution, this looked like the perfect way to do it.

Or so one might have thought. But in fact, there was much more to Calonne than his friends and family at court supposed. As a young man, he had helped Louis XV to write the speech he gave to the Paris parliament, warning them not to stand in the way of the democratization of the legal system. Calonne had mainly opposed Necker because he suspected him of dishonesty and self-publicity. And now, Calonne was only trying to keep the trouble-making establishment happy while he implemented his own radical plan to salvage France's economy. Louis XVI's choice of minister was much more astute than it seemed.

Using Necker's idea that a country had to look rich if it was going to attract funding, Calonne embarked on an almost social-ist programme of public spending. He built roads and canals, renovated the city centres of Marseille, Lyon and Bordeaux, and developed the ports of Le Havre, Dunkirk, La Rochelle, and especially Cherbourg, where a vast (and strategically vital) harbour wall was begun. It was so impressive that in 1786 it inspired Louis XVI's only trip[7] to his provinces, to admire the building site.

Calonne defended himself against charges of over-spending with a biblical metaphor that everyone in France would have understood: 'It is not the case that one must *sow* to *reap*?' (His italics.)

Unfortunately, though, he also reaped a fair bit of unrest in Paris. One of his great public works was a 3-metre-tall, 24-kilo-metre-long stone wall to be built around the capital. This was not conceived to give tourists a better view into the medieval streets of the city, or to protect Parisians from uncouth provin-cials coming in for the nightlife. Called the 'Mur des Fermiers généraux' (which could be loosely translated as 'Tax-collectors' wall'), it was to provide 50 checkpoints where taxes could be levied on products arriving in the city.

To give an idea of the scope of the wall, it followed approxi-mately the same route as the present-day loop of Métro lines 2 and 6. And even though it provided two years of work to an army of labourers, many Parisians saw it as a symbol of oppres-sion, especially because the taxing stations were grandiose

---

[7] That is, until his attempt to flee France in 1791, when he got as far as Varennes, near the Belgian border.

mini-châteaux that inspired Louis-Sébastien Mercier, one of the Lumières writers, to say that 'the lairs of the tax collectors have been turned into colonnaded palaces.'

The writer and agitator Beaumarchais also chipped in with a punning line that has since become famous: *'Le mur murant Paris rend Paris murmurant.'*

The alliteration is untranslatable, but what it means is that the wall walling Paris makes Paris wail. It did even more than that, because on 12 and 13 July 1789, mobs would attack the wall and destroy several of the toll stations, getting in some practice before they turned on the Bastille.

Despite this political faux pas in Paris, for a while things in France felt decidedly rosy under Calonne's management. Manual labour was plentiful; there were good grain harvests in 1783, 1784, 1785 and 1787, and an excellent year for wine in 1785; and taxes had not been raised. All this and the *aristos* were happy, too.

However, some of Louis XVI's advisors felt that the rosiness was fragile. His Minister of the Navy, a friend of Necker's called Charles Eugène Gabriel de La Croix de Castries, wrote a paper for the King about the 'public mood', saying that 'irregularity shocks the people.' Some people were saying that the whole country except the permanently disgruntled Parisians was loyal to the throne, but Castries warned that 'one spark could ignite the nation and consume it in flames.'

The problem with Calonne's attempt to end France's financial 'irregularity' was that his public works programme did not generate much income, and he had borrowed heavily to finance it – around 600 million, even more than Necker.

Also, contrary to expectations, Britain had quickly recovered from its war with America. It was now beginning to pump out cheap, mass-produced goods and selling them all over the world – including to America, which seemed to have forgotten its debt to France, and had begun trading with its former landlord. Calonne struck a deal with the British to sell them French food, wine and luxury products, but exports were outweighed by the sudden influx of cheap British industrial goods. Confidence in the French economy slumped, and loans and investments dried up.

In April 1787, Necker weighed into the economic debate by writing an open letter objecting to Calonne's assertion that he had covered up a deficit. The two embarked on a public bout of polite-but-vicious mud-slinging, until finally Necker wrote to Louis XVI complaining of Calonne's 'spectacular injustice', and defending every one of his policies in endless pages of detail that Louis almost certainly never read. Instead the King issued a *lettre de cachet* ordering Necker to leave Paris, and not to come within 20 leagues of the city without his permission (and that included approaching Versailles, too).

In his own defence, Calonne published his *Reply from Monsieur de Calonne to Monsieur Necker, Containing the Accounts of the Financial Situation for 1774, 1776, 1781, 1783 & 1787.* This was, as its title suggests, an almost absurdly detailed, 500-odd page explanation of how he had ended up with a deficit of 126 million *livres*, blaming most of it on debts from the American War, and more particularly on Necker's borrowing to cover them – all 439,759,464 *livres* of it, itemized down to the last *livre*, with a cruel footnote to the effect that 'we have only included in this account genuine, known loans. We did not enter ... secret extensions that we have not been able to calculate.'

Admirable though all this transparency was, it was also an obsessive exercise in 'I'm right, you're wrong', and was exactly the sort of document that sent Louis XVI dashing out of a cabinet meeting to find his hunting breeches. Worse still, even if its main aim was to destroy Necker, whose revelations about spending had done such harm to the royal family's reputation, Calonne's accounts were just as embarrassing for Louis XVI.

In the section on the *'Maison du Roi'*, Calonne declared spending for the previous year of 21,869,000 *livres* on the King's household. This was down on the 25.7 million per year under Necker, but it didn't include the cost of Marie-Antoinette's household – 4.25 million. And spending on the rest of the royal family had gone up since Necker, from 8.04 million to 9.8 million *livres*.

Worse still for Louis, unlike Necker (who had only itemized 89,000 *livres* spent on the royal library, a relatively noble spend), Calonne listed embarrassing individual items like 'Silverware and menus 2,000,000', 'Furniture 1,900,000', 'King's wardrobe 77,000' (less than a pair of Marie-Antoinette's earrings, but still a lot of money) and, predictably, 'Hunting 1,031,000' – the approximate equivalent of ten million loaves of bread, frittered away just on galloping around the royal forests in pursuit of wildlife.

Louis XVI's increased weakness in the face of his wife's frivolities and his brothers' indifference to public opinion was there in black and white for everyone to see.

We know from other sources, too, that Louis had been letting Versailles get out of control. Palace accounts revealed that spending on wine increased from 6,567 *livres* in 1785 to 60,899 *livres* in 1789. This wasn't caused by Louis drowning his sorrows after listening to accountants, because he didn't drink very much at all. Félix d'Hézecques, the former page, wrote that: 'He only drank undiluted wine with his dessert. Often it was a large glass of Malaga with a slice of toasted bread. But the quantity was in proportion to the food he ate.' In wine, as in everything except hunting, Louis XVI was boringly restrained. Much of the increased spending was notched up by Marie-Antoinette's party crowd, and because the palace still overpaid suppliers who in turn gave bribes to the royal buyers – everyone working in and around the palace was creaming off an increasing percentage of the vast spending. It was as if they knew it was all about to end.

Calonne promised his readers that Louis was conscious of the need to economize, and assured them of 'the love of the King for his subjects, and the keen desire, that has never left his heart, to lighten by every means possible the load upon them'. But the figures seemed to disagree. Spending on the royals and their entourage came to 6 per cent of the national budget, compared to only 2 per cent on education and aid for the poor.

Calonne ended his *Reply to Monsieur Necker* with a call to convene an 'Assemblée des notables' – in theory a meeting of the country's wisest, most influential and best-informed men (women were still a long way from being considered *notable*). This assembly, Calonne said, should be appointed and headed by Louis XVI himself, and would oversee 'reform plans and changes that would introduce a new order', and would 'make justice shine even brighter than the crown, give the nation new life, and patriotism a new boost', bringing about 'an unforgettable era in the history of the monarchy'.

He wasn't wrong about the unforgettable era that was just about to begin.

When Louis XVI saw Calonne's new reforms, he told him: 'This is pure Necker that you're giving me,' but he agreed to present an updated finance plan to an Assemblée des notables. Though he must have guessed that it was going to be a very hard sell.

Calonne's central idea was similar to Necker's, and just as naively optimistic. In order to clean up France's finances and calm the social climate, Calonne suggested that:

> France must not be afraid to show itself as it is. By confessing abuses, it also shows its resources ... By revealing what has been undermining its strengths, we show that we are on the right track to revive them. By instructing the nation about its ingrained wrongs, we will enable it to find a remedy for itself and to understand that it must be efficient.

Everything would be fine as soon as the country made a clean breast of its former failings.

But clean breasts weren't enough to pacify the privileged classes, especially when accompanied by Calonne's assertion that: 'One cannot walk a single step in this kingdom without finding different laws, contradictory customs, privileges and exceptions … This wholesale dissonance … increases disorder.'

Calonne's remedy for the privileges and exceptions would be to tax the clergy, cut the *taille* that discriminated against the poor, and introduce a 'territorial subsidy', in other words a standard tax on all income from land and property, however big the landowner. He even suggested that it was necessary to sell certain royal properties over the next 25 years to pay off the national debt.

But like Necker, by proposing economic reforms that might have saved the monarchy, Calonne had gone a painful truth too far.

When the Assemblée des notables was convened[8] in February 1787, it voted against Calonne's plans. This was hardly a shock given that the assembly's 147 *notables* included all of Louis XVI's brothers and male cousins, 12 dukes, 33 noble *parlementaires*, 12 bishops and archbishops (all noble), 8 marshals (all noble) and 25 unelected city representatives – all of them landlords. In short, it was a gathering of the men who had the most to lose if they voted for economic reform.

To be fair, Louis XVI gave his full support to Calonne during the opening days of the Assemblée's debates, standing up to his critics and urging him not to weaken. But either Louis recognized that it was a hopeless cause or, as some say, he was finally swayed by Marie-Antoinette's opposition to the reforms, because in April 1787 he suddenly fired Calonne and exiled him to his country home in the eastern province of Lorraine.

Calonne didn't think this was far enough away to escape his enemies, who had waged a scandal-sheet campaign against him and got the public calling him 'Monsieur Déficit'. There were also calls to have him convicted of embezzlement, so he fled to London.

---

[8] Rather ironically, the assembly gathered at the Menus–Plaisirs in Versailles, the accessory warehouse for Louis XVI's entertainments. A sign that times were changing and the pleasures were almost over.

The Assemblée des notables disbanded in May 1787, no doubt highly pleased with the efficiency of its stonewall tactics. But in political terms, it was as if each member, including Louis XVI, had calmly pulled out a duelling pistol, cocked it, and shot themselves in their silk-stockinged foot.

<h1 style="text-align:center">VI</h1>

Panic was starting to set in. Public opinion was being stirred up by pamphleteers on all sides, both those who wanted change and those who were determined to destroy the reputation of any reformer who raised his head above the parapet.

Perhaps taking a hint from Necker about the need to increase productivity, printers were pumping out an ever-growing torrent of gossip, slander, jokes and songs about Marie-Antoinette, Louis XVI's brothers and his ministers and, to a lesser extent, Louis XVI himself.

As soon as the Assemblée des notables was over, Louis appointed its president as his Principal Minister of State. This was Etienne-Charles de Loménie de Brienne, the 59-year-old Archbishop of Toulouse, a great favourite of Marie-Antoi-nette.

It looked as though Louis had finally given in to the anti-reformers. An aged clergyman, the mouthpiece of the body that had just sabotaged Calonne's rescue plan, a man who enjoyed the full support of the free-spending Queen, was being put in charge of France's politics and finances. Worse still, Brienne had suffered personal humiliation at Louis XVI's hands a few years earlier, when the King had refused him the post of Archbishop of Paris, which was not only prestigious but also paid a salary of 200,000 *livres* per year. It seemed unlikely that Brienne would be a loyal counsel to the monarch.

In fact though, Brienne was yet another shrewd appointment. He was not what we would call today a classic archbishop. Like all high-ranking French clergymen of the time, he was simply an aristocrat who had chosen a religious career path. As a reason for turning him down for promotion, Louis XVI had said: 'At the very least the Archbishop of Paris should believe in God.'

As Archbishop of Toulouse in the 1760s, Brienne had used his power and money to improve the city, and had shut down its inquisition. He was a friend of Louis XVI's former minister Turgot (a reformer) and even of the atheist troublemaker Voltaire. In his inauguration speech as a member of the Académie française in 1770, Brienne had said that the people longed for a king who shows 'goodness, charity and justice', and instead of the blinding light of Louis XIV's splendour, France needed a moderate monarch, 'a soft, temperate warmth to feed and vivify it'. The King as a homely log fire rather than a distant star.

In fact, Louis XVI knew that he would have to stand up to the landowning conservatives, who seemed to think that they could carry on filling their pockets while France itself slid into bankruptcy and food shortages. He had appointed Brienne because he was a man of the changing times, definitely *not* the kind of old-school French clergyman who believed that what the poor needed most was prayer, taxation and the occasional burning at the stake to keep them on the path to salvation.

One of Brienne's first moves was to stop work on Paris's Mur des Fermiers généraux, saying that it was such a waste of money that it ought to be dismantled, and the stone sold off to raise public revenue. This didn't actually happen until 1860, but it was a symbol of where his sympathies lay.

As president of the Assemblée des notables, Brienne had studied all the files and heard all the arguments. Before the Assemblée disbanded at the end of May 1787, he presented the members with a compromise package that he hoped would convince the hard-line anti-reformers.

Tax reform in favour of the poor was still on the table, as were Necker's *assemblées provinciales*, but Brienne offered the privileged classes an olive branch in the shape of a law allowing total free trade of grain – a dangerous move in that it made France more vulnerable when harvests were bad, because speculators could raise prices at will. But Brienne expressed the hope that this would 'prevent shortages and excessive prices and encourage agriculture'.

Docking charges in France's ports were to be scrapped, making it cheaper for French traders to export (and, of course, for foreigners to import). This was another move that would please the rich.

The *notables* were in no mood for compromise, though, and voted down Brienne's proposals, which is why they were disbanded.

To their credit, Louis XVI and Brienne did not give up. Once the Assemblée was over, Louis put more or less the same proposal to the Paris parliament. But they were magistrates, experts in prevaricating, and postponed any decision by saying that it was impossible to vote for a change in the tax laws unless they had all the latest figures on spending and income. Louis replied that they had it – Calonne's embarrassingly detailed 500-page audit published just a few months earlier. Sorry – not recent enough, came the reply, and they refused to pass the bill.

Three days later, Louis issued a *'Déclaration du Roi'* outlining what he intended to make law, with the parliament's approval or without it. It was as radical as anything put forward by Necker or Calonne.

The *corvée* (the tax in the form of labour) would be turned into a 'fairer payment in cash, which will not cause the abuses that the old system made it impossible to avoid' (namely that in the past only the poorest labourers actually performed the work). Meanwhile the *taille*, 'a tax that was a burden for the less well-off classes of our people' would be reduced thanks to the sale of six million *livres* of bonds.

Louis XVI's new declaration also contained Calonne's plan for a 'territorial subsidy', a property tax to be paid by everyone, including the clergy and the aristocracy. Brienne and Louis were still insisting that this new, fairer system should be overseen by *assemblées provinciales*, and Brienne had added even more democracy to the concept, proposing that, although they would not be elected, these assemblies should be composed equally of members of the nobility, the clergy and commoners.

In a separate paper with the catchy title *Simplification and Generalization of Finances, and Suppression of Unfairness in Taxation* Brienne wrote that: 'These *assemblées provinciales* will always be seen by the nation as a gift from the King and as the reflection of a mild, moderate government. What greater gift than to let one's subjects decide how taxation should be imposed? What better way to ensure that they are attributed fairly?'

Fairness was the last thing on the Paris parliament's mind, though, and they simply declared the whole process illegal, so Louis banished them all to Troyes, 160 kilometres away to the southeast, a pleasant medieval town that seems to have been considered a boring backwater in 1787, a place where you sent badly behaved judges to cool off.

Three months later, Louis XVI reconvened the parliamentarians in Paris, hoping that they would have learnt their lesson. To make doubly sure, the November session of parliament opened with a statement by his Keeper of the Seals (de facto Minister of Justice), Chrétien François de Lamoignon, who affirmed that:

The principle, universally acknowledged by the whole kingdom, is that the King alone must possess sovereign power in his kingdom ... He is answerable only to God in the exercise of his power ... The King is the sovereign of the Nation, and everything he does is with its interests in mind, and ... legislative power resides in the person of the King independent of all other powers. These, gentlemen, are the inviolable powers of the monarchy of France

Crucially, though, despite this apparent show of force, Louis XVI had weakened. The bill he was ordering the parliamentarians to accept was watered down. The universal 'territorial subsidy' that would have forced the privileged classes to agree to democratic taxation had gone. In its place was a plan to borrow 420 million *livres* over five years, which was simply postponing the crisis.

The parliamentarians must have felt emboldened, especially when the King's own cousin, the ambitious Louis Philippe d'Orléans (father of the future King Louis-Philippe), objected to the royal show of force, declaring that 'this is illegal.'

Louis replied: 'No, it's legal, because I want it,' which was in fact simply a statement of French monarchic law. As punishment for this treasonable outburst, Louis banned his cousin from sitting in parliament – for two whole days.

In May 1788, after months of back and forth between Paris and Versailles, with no decisions taken, things finally came to a head.

One of the most vociferous members of the Paris parliament was a magistrate called Jean-Jacques Duval-d'Esprémesnil. The model of a disreputable *aristo*, he was involved in a very modern-sounding scheme to demolish a hospital in central Paris and sell the valuable plot of land to property speculators.

Always keen to protect his own interests, Duval-d'Esprémesnil stole some documents detailing Brienne's and Louis XVI's plans to reduce the political power of the parliaments, and revealed their contents to his colleagues. When a warrant was issued for his arrest, he took refuge in parliament, along with an accomplice, Anne-Louis-Marie Goislard de Monsabert (yet another French male with a female first name). Around 900 armed soldiers were sent in to fetch them, but they had no idea what the fugitives looked like. When the captain asked the parliamentarians to identify Duval and Goislard, all of them stepped forward, saying either *'je suis Duval'* or *'je suis Goislard'*.[9] The guards went away frustrated.

Duval and Goislard eventually gave themselves up, and Duval was sent to cool his heels for four months on the island of

---

[9] A precursor to the events of 2015 when, in solidarity with the assassinated members of the staff of the satirical magazine *Charlie Hebdo*, French people began tweeting *'je suis Charlie'*.

Sainte-Marguerite, just off the Mediterranean coast from Cannes. This sounds idyllic, but it was in fact the prison where, a century earlier, the Man in the Iron Mask had rotted for 11 years before being transferred to the Bastille.

Meanwhile back in Versailles, Louis XVI and Brienne made one final attempt to impose their will on the men who wanted to defend the unworkable status quo. Louis summoned the Paris parliamentarians to Versailles and tried to force them to accept a ruling that their power, and that of every parliament in the regions, should be replaced by a 'plenary court' under the authority of the King. This court was not going to be a democratically elected body, of course – it would be composed of princes, nobles, marshals and clergymen, along with some noble magistrates. But the Parisian parliamentarians, who were being held semi-hostage in Versailles, declared that it would be illegal for them to disregard the 'ancient and lawful institution of parliament'.

Their colleagues in Rennes, in Brittany, went further: they said that anyone attending a plenary court would be *'infâme'* ('foul and dishonourable'), so Louis had 12 of them arrested, provoking rioting in the streets. More or less the same thing happened in Grenoble, where the parliament threatened to declare independence for the Dauphiné region, and troops had to be sent in to maintain order.

Brienne had failed, and was given a cardinal's hat and allowed to disappear to Italy. Louis XVI was left in Versailles with the realization that the magistrates had in effect started a revolution – in favour of aristocratic privilege, and against the democratic change that he, the apparently powerless absolute monarch, wanted.

VII

Hypocritically, the Parisian parliamentarians now affirmed their loyalty to Louis XVI – rather as if they were holding a pistol to his head and promising that everything would be OK as long as he didn't do anything stupid.

In a declaration on 3 May 1788, they recognized 'that France is a monarchy governed by the King, according to its laws, and that these laws ... include the right of the reigning royal family, from male to male, in order of birth, excluding all girls and their descendants'. It was the status quo in its purest form.

However, the declaration went on to affirm the parliamentarians' own rights, and those of the ruling class in general, insisting on 'the unmovability of magistrates; the right of courts to examine the King's wishes in each province, and to order their application only when they conform to the laws of that province, and the fundamental laws of the state'.

What they were saying in effect was that the absolute monarchy was over. France's ancient law, *Qui veut le roy, si veut la loy* (if the King wants it, the law wants it), no longer applied. When Antoine Loysel published his list of French laws and customs in 1607, this was the first line in the first chapter of the first volume. Now it counted for nothing.

This was more than a year before most history books deem that the French Revolution began. No one had tried to storm the Bastille; no one was calling for the King's head; most ordinary French people were going about their daily business, hoping that Louis XVI's call for fairer taxes would be implemented.

But it was revolution. Not by the people calling for *Liberté, Égalité* and *Fraternité* – that was what Louis XVI and his successive finance ministers had been trying to give them, albeit in a smaller dose than many would have liked. This was revolution by the rich, calling for their own liberty to carry on preventing any equality.

The former royal attendant Félix d'Hézecques described the irony of the situation succinctly in his memoirs: 'The magistrates, those natural defenders of the monarchy, and the princes themselves, born supporters of the throne, got together to destroy the monarchy and the throne.'

If there had been a referendum of the whole nation in May 1788, Louis XVI's manifesto would almost certainly have been a promise to put all of Necker's ideas into practice. And if, during the referendum campaign, Louis had been able to prevent provincial parliaments broadcasting fake news to the effect that all he wanted was to carry on buying necklaces for Marie-Antoinette, the people would almost certainly have voted in favour of their monarch's policies.

But as of May 1788, Louis had no real power. Despite being an indecisive man by nature, with a reputation for wanting to spend every day hunting instead of managing the country's affairs, for a few years he had appointed a series of highly motivated ministers, and encouraged them to stand toe to toe with the most objectionable, self-serving members of France's aristocracy. Occasionally, he had even missed out on a day's hunting to defend democracy in person. He had also put up with public humiliation while Turgot, Necker, Calonne and Brienne battled to put the country on a stabler, fairer footing. Admittedly, despite the cuts to his personal budget, Louis XVI and his family were still living a life of unimaginable luxury compared to most of his subjects, but he had genuinely tried to ease the burden on them.

In May 1788, however, these attempts at peaceful, relatively democratic, reform were over. The anarchy and violence of July 1789 and beyond were now inevitable.

PART II

The Revolt Sets In

Chapter 10

WAS EVERYDAY LIFE REALLY THAT BAD IN 1789?

'Les Français étaient las d'un bonheur qui les ennuyait parce qu'il était tranquille.'
'The French were tired of a contentedness that bored them because it was so peaceful.'
　　　　Alexandre de Tilly (1761–1816), French count, in his memoirs

I

In 1789, for a large proportion of people in France – and not just the money-grabbing aristocrats and their bourgeois imitators – life was getting better. Very slowly, in many cases, it was true, because of the crushing weight of taxes on the poor. But overall, there did seem to be a sense that the *lumière* of progress and prosperity would soon shine on most classes of society, if not today then one day soon, and without the need for violent revolution.

The image of Louis XVI as a man who did little but hunt, make watches and locks and allow his wife to spend France's tax income has been carefully constructed over the two centuries or so since his head was cut off. Today, it is much easier to explain away the violence of the Revolution if it looks as though it was all worthwhile.

It's true that hunting was probably Louis XVI's one true passion, but, as we have seen, this didn't stop him trying to improve the lot of his subjects. And his desire to develop a more democratic (within reason) and more modern France extended far beyond reforming the tax system and improving prisons, hospitals and harbours. Like Necker, who loved the word *lumière* so much, and even Archbishop Brienne, the friend of Voltaire, Louis XVI was a man who wanted to nurture an innovative, dynamic France that would become a key player on the world stage, as a competitor to the economic might of Britain and the newly emerging independent America. The key to this, he thought, was education.

Without standardized reading tests, the measure of literacy used by historians is usually whether people were able to sign their names in the register of marriages. In 1688, 29 per cent of men and 14 per cent of women in France were capable of doing so. This didn't mean that they could write a coherent letter or read one of Racine's tragedies, but they had at least been to school. The others just scratched an 'X', and could probably not read the names of all the taxes they had to pay.

By 1788, over half of all French children were going to school, and the numbers of grooms and brides signing their names had risen to 47 per cent and 27 per cent respectively. In comparison, at the same time in England, around 66 per cent of men could sign their names, and 34 per cent of women. France still had some catching-up to do, but under Louis XVI, literacy rates were growing healthily, and were especially high amongst crafts-men and merchants, three-quarters of whom could read and write. (To put this into perspective, that is only about 10 per cent lower than the literacy rate in the modern-day USA.)

Almost every child in France had an elementary school near their home, ever since Louis XIV had laid the burden of educa-tion on the Church in 1698, with an edict ordering bishops to open a school in every parish and educate children up to the age of 14. Admittedly this meant that the King was denying any direct responsibility for educating his people, but Louis XIV clearly felt that the Church was rich enough to obey the edict, and so *petites écoles*, often for boys only, were set up throughout France, dedicated to 'the arts of reading, writing and counting, and the catechism'. Naturally, the bishops were keen to improve souls as well as brains.

In towns, the standard of teaching was usually acceptable, but in the country, with parishes covering large areas, and children needed for farm work, the literacy and numeracy rates were much lower. Rural teachers, either lay people or priests or nuns, would visit farmhouses or go out into the fields to give lessons to the children working there. On the last Sunday of each month, each family would pay their school fees of five *sous* (about the price of a half-kilo of beef) directly to the teacher, who often received no other salary.

Unless these rural teachers were priests or nuns, they might not be much better at the basic skills than their young pupils. A report in 1793 noted that one teacher was 53 years old, had been teaching for 35 years, but 'though he writes quite well, he cannot spell. A good arithmetician, he knows a little about measuring land.' The reference to spelling probably meant that the man could not write French – lessons would often be given in the local *patois*, and children might be taught their alphabet using religious books in Latin. There was no such thing as a national French curriculum.

But at least the Church was fulfilling its duty to get the poor reading and writing – and in this, it was actually more enlightening than the so-called 'enlightenment' philosophers. Jean-Jacques Rousseau, for example, the champion of the 'noble savage', thought that 'the poor do not need education.' Their innate ability to interact with nature was sacred (as, presumably, was their natural tendency to die when they didn't have enough to eat).

Similarly, in 1763, Voltaire wrote to the attorney general of the Brittany parliament, who had published an essay advocating scientific studies instead of religious education, congratulating him for saying that poor children should be excluded from this modernization of the education system. 'I thank you for forbidding the ploughing classes from studying,' Voltaire wrote. 'I, who cultivate land [Voltaire was an absentee landlord], would like to put in a request for more workers, not more monks.' Admittedly Voltaire was playing his anti-religious card, but he was also indulging in the snobbery that was a mark of the times amongst the upper classes, including the supposedly freethinking intellectuals.

Secondary education was almost entirely a privilege of the rich. The larger towns had *collèges* and *lycées*, most of them run by religious orders, and all of them for bourgeois and noble pupils. During Louis XVI's reign, many of these secondary schools encouraged children to speak Latin amongst themselves, even during breaks, but the sciences were beginning to gain a foothold alongside the classic disciplines. Schools were moving with the times. Sadly, their intake wasn't. For a start these secondary schools were almost all for boys only, and in 1789, they took in only about 13,000 new pupils – a tiny proportion when one considers that almost 10 per cent of the population, 2.7 million, were teenagers.

A young woman's only hope of getting a decent education was at a convent. Even this was mostly restricted to the daughters of the well-off, who were sent away to be turned into respectable young ladies. Each convent girl had a tutrix, a nun whom she was encouraged to call *tante* (aunt), and who saw to her moral and intellectual upbringing – with the emphasis on the former.

The principles of girls' education at the time are outlined by the Abbé Joseph Reyre (naturally this was a man's job) in his novel *L'École des jeunes demoiselles*, published in 1786. In the story, a nun called Sister Rosalie speaks out against the influence of modern philosophers on young girls: 'In the past they were taught nothing; now we are meant to teach them everything.'

Sister Rosalie is all in favour of female education, but she is horrified that the philosophers want to teach girls about science:

'There is nothing more pointless than introducing [girls] to the secrets of chemistry and the mysteries of physics.' Sister Rosalie recommends 'a smattering of history and literature, with just enough mathematics to be able to keep household accounts'. Sewing and knitting were not to be neglected, of course, and girls should also learn to dance, Rosalie says, but only *'danses décentes'* that will improve their posture, and definitely not the new steps that are practised at 'dangerous balls that one cannot frequent without offending God'. In short, the last thing the convents wanted was to turn out a generation of Marie-Antoinettes.

There were calls for equal rights to education for girls. A century earlier, François Fénelon, the private tutor to Louis XV, had published a *Treatise on the Education of Girls* in which he asserted that 'nothing is more neglected than the education of girls' and 'the weaker they are, the more they need to be strengthened'. He was not calling for total equality, but recommended that girls should learn literature, history, Latin, music, art, grammar, arithmetic and 'the main rules of justice'.

This was the programme that was adopted for the Maison royale, a girls' school (for upper-class *demoiselles*, of course) opened in 1684, and eventually closed under Louis XV, apparently because its students were too intelligent. The Marquis d'Argenson, Louis XV's Foreign Secretary, declared in 1750 that the girls coming out of the Maison royale were 'demanding' and 'drive their husbands to madness'. It was duly turned into a convent, and reverted to traditional teaching. Under Louis XVI, despite the rise of the Lumières philosophers, no one thought to revive its more challenging curriculum.

One of the early eighteenth century's most famous female intellectuals, the Marquise de Lambert, adopted Fénelon's principles in 1728 for a text entitled *A Mother's Advice to Her Daughter*, in which she encouraged girls to concentrate on Latin because it 'opens the way to the sciences'. But she didn't intend her treatise for publication, and even forbade political discussions at her Tuesday *salons*, which attracted some of the greatest minds of the day (including Fénelon), so she clearly didn't think that female education was anything more than a private affair.

During Louis XVI's reign, the strongest call for equality in education came from a surprising source – Choderlos de Laclos, author of the erotic novel *Dangerous Liaisons*. In 1783, he wrote an 80-page text *On the Education of Women* in which he stated that 'Wherever there is slavery, there can be no education; in all societies, women are slaves.' Predictably, Laclos pontificates about their natural seductiveness, their beautiful hair and their puberty, but he also states bluntly that, without society's influence, women are naturally the equals of men – 'free and powerful' – and that men have 'corrupted everything'.

This interest in politics expressed by an eroticist is perhaps explained by the fact that Laclos was also secretary to the King's cousin, Louis Philippe d'Orléans, who was espousing liberal causes in an attempt to undermine Louis XVI, and position himself as a potential successor if the regime fell. It may be that women's education was one of the causes that Louis Philippe was toying with. If this was the case, he clearly didn't consider it worth pursuing, because, like the Marquise de Lambert's *Advice to Her Daughter*, Laclos's text remained unpublished at the time – it didn't appear until 1903.

It seems that in spite of the philosophers' claim to call established thinking into question, and despite the attempts of Louis XVI's ministers to introduce a degree of democracy into French society, even despite the influence of women like Madame Necker, no one gave much real thought to the need for women to get a decent education.

But if developments in girls' education were more or less at a standstill, these were exciting times for the sons of wealthy families who managed to graduate from secondary education. Opportunities for rich young men, both common and noble, were becoming much more varied. The universities were still pretty medieval, offering traditional courses in law, letters and antiquated versions of medicine, mathematics and science, but Louis XVI launched a plan to create a range of new schools that would specialize in modern knowledge.

It was around this time that many of France's famous *grandes écoles* were either founded or adapted from existing schools. Most of them still exist today, and though the intake might have become more democratic since Louis XVI's day, the output still forms France's technocratic elite.

The École nationale des ponts et chaussées (literally 'of bridges and road surfaces') had been set up in 1747, but was considerably updated in 1775, to train the engineers who were needed to improve France's transport network – getting unskilled labourers to fill potholes and bolster old bridges was no longer going to be enough. And it wasn't all about stone and gravel, either – students spent between four and 12 years at Ponts et chaussées, and had to master geometry, mechanics and hydraulics, as well as helping surveyors to update maps of France. After the Revolution, when roads were left unrepaired for a decade, it was graduates of this school who got them back into shape (mainly so that Napoleon's armies could march off to war).

In 1783, Louis XVI founded the École royale des mines in Paris, with the aim of creating 'intelligent directors' for France's mines, which were starting to rival those of England. The students were all from the moneyed (and mostly noble) elite, of course, and only they had access to the laboratories. But in a spirit of openness, members of the public were allowed to attend lectures, the idea being to instruct everyone in France about modern technology (well, anyone who had the time and leisure to attend, and who could follow lectures about 'underground geometry'). The school was shut down during the Revolution, but reopened in 1794, without the 'royal' in its name. It is still very prestigious today, and has branched out from mining into all types of energy sources.

These great seats of modern learning were not confined to Paris. Louis XVI created the Ecole royale du génie[1] at Mézières, on the Belgian border. This was mainly for aristocrats, and combined general engineering with military specialities like fortress-building and siege tactics, and after two years, students could become military engineers. The head of this school was Gaspard Monge, a brilliant mathematician who, while there, invented descriptive geometry, the technique for accurately depicting three-dimensional shapes in two-dimensional drawings – a fundamental skill for architects and engineers.

Another great invention at Mézières was the very French system of organizing an entrance exam so difficult and competitive that all but the most brilliant and hard-working students simply don't bother to apply. In Monge's day, one out of six applicants were accepted – today, some French *grandes écoles* take fewer than one in ten of their candidates, most of whom have already done two years of *classes préparatoires* just to be able to understand the questions in the entrance exam. It is a brutal but efficient system which ensures that, just like the aristocratic students of Louis XVI's day, these modern graduates are all too aware that they are superior to common mortals.

Overall, then, access to knowledge under Louis XVI was not becoming less elitist, but by 1789, France's education system was starting to produce some of the best-trained scientists and technocrats on the planet.

II

Louis XVI's avowed intention was that all this science should be used for the common good. As early as 1776 he created the Société royale de médecine, its mission statement: 'To maintain a constant correspondence with all the most skilled doctors in the Kingdom, and even abroad, on the subject of practical

---

[1] '*Génie*' means both 'genius' and 'engineering', the two closely linked in French minds.

medicine, and to provide help during epidemics'. More than 100 doctors and scientists met twice a week at the Louvre, on Tuesdays and Fridays, to share ideas and discoveries.

In 1778, the Société sent out health questionnaires to doctors all over France. They did not content themselves with asking who was suffering or dying of what – they wanted information about the water supply, the soil, the climate, health differences between town and country, common remedies used in the region, and how the sick were being cared for. If they had been operating in the twenty-first century, they would have been called holistic.

Inevitably, the doctors received plenty of depressing replies about epidemics and a whole profusion of fevers (dirty drinking water and mosquitoes still plagued large areas of France), but they also made some real breakthroughs thanks to this consultation process. One of the most interesting came from a doctor in Poitou, in western France, who wrote back explaining why he no longer bled patients who were already weakened by disease or fever. Sadly, his suggestion was not immediately adopted as general practice, in France or anywhere else, and in 1824, Lord Byron would be bled to death, complaining wittily and poetically to his doctor as he faded away that 'less slaughter is done by the lance than the lancet'.

The study lasted until the Revolution, and it may not have stopped the practice of bleeding patients, but it did produce results that are of enormous importance to modern France. The Société was asked to look into 'remedies for which permits and patents are requested', and 'the administration of mineral and medicinal waters'. If France is today home to a massive pharmaceutical industry and the producer of some of the world's most famous mineral waters, it is partly due to Louis XVI's patronage in the 1770s.

The members of the Académie des sciences were also given practical work to do. We saw in an earlier chapter how Louis got his Swiss minister Necker to improve conditions in hospitals (see Chapter 9). Not content with this, in 1785 the King asked the Académie to study the effects of his improvements. In 1787, he also commissioned them to report on how best to manage Paris's abattoirs, after complaints from residents of the city centre that the blood from the killing grounds at Saint-Jacques in the Latin Quarter were turning the streets into smelly, fly-infested mudbaths. Under Louis XVI, the Académie could no longer content itself with theorizing about the universe – it was being brought down to earth.

The Académie des sciences had originally been set up in 1666, but before Louis XVI's time it was not very scientific in appointing new members. In 1731, the Duc de Richelieu had been elected despite the fact that he was almost totally illiterate. During Louis XVI's reign, however, the academy was given a complete overhaul so that its remit included agriculture, physics, mineralogy, metallurgy and mechanics, one of Louis XVI's personal interests. The intake of members was increased to 2,500, and rejuvenated so that its average age was only about thirty – a startling statistic compared to today when most areas of French life are ruled by an ageing, unbudgeable elite.

Outside the official scientific bodies, research was also being put to functional use. In 1777 Louis XVI's brother Charles set up a factory for salts and minerals by the Seine, at Javel on the south-western edge of Paris. In 1788, the *Journal de Paris* raved about one of the new products invented there, which had 'the property of whitening canvas, thread and cotton, and threads on bobbins, in 24 to 30 hours'. The *Journal* explained that this miracle product had been dubbed '*eau de Javel*', or 'Javel water', 'to distract from the idea that there is acid in its composition, which does not act as such when it is used for whitening'. A clever piece of modern marketing that still works today, given that *eau de Javel* is the modern French name for bleach.

The factory also made high-quality, cheap sulphuric acid (useful for cleaning metals), white lead (a component in white paint) and the green pigment verdigris. All these quickly became excellent export products, and even began invading the British market.

But apart from *eau de Javel*, the factory's biggest claim to fame was that, by pouring sulphuric acid over iron filings, it created hydrogen gas, which would be used in one of France's greatest contributions to eighteenth-century technology – the balloon.

III

In the summer of 1783, France was the arena for a frantic race to send the first men up into the clouds. Aware of the experiments going on at the time, Louis XVI had launched a competition for *'l'invention des machines aérostatiques'*.

On 4 June, Joseph-Michel and Jacques-Etienne Montgolfier, two paper manufacturers, conducted the first public experiment, sending up an unmanned balloon in Annonay, in southeastern France, where they had their paper mill. For this flight, they used heated air. Believing that it was the smoke rather than the air itself that caused elevation, they experimented with different ways of making the smoke thicker, burning a variety of substances like sheep droppings, wet wool and meat. On a wave of malodorous fumes, their first balloon rose 30 metres.

They knew that the race for the clouds was a close one. The French physicist Jacques Charles, the first man to formulate a law about gases expanding when heated, had been working on a similar idea in Paris with another two brothers, Anne-Jean and Nicolas-Louis Robert. On 27 August of that same year, they launched a 35-cubic-metre silk balloon filled with hydrogen gas. It flew for 21 kilometres before landing in a field and being pitchforked to rags by terrified peasants.

Meanwhile, Jacques-Etienne Montgolfier had been at work in the wallpaper factory of a friend, Jean-Baptiste Réveillon,[2] in

---

[2] In 1789, shortly before the storming of the Bastille, Réveillon would only just escape with his life when a mob attacked his factory after misunderstanding a speech he had made about the need to cut bread prices. See Chapter 11.

the east of Paris near the Bastille. There, they hand-sewed a 24-metre-tall balloon out of cotton canvas covered with paper. It got rained on during tests, and split, so in only five days they manufactured a new, 19-metre balloon.

On 19 September, they were ready to go to Versailles and give a demonstration before Louis XVI and Marie-Antoinette and a crowd of some 130,000 people. Not daring to commit aerial manslaughter or suicide in front of the King, they sent up a sheep, a duck and a chicken. This miniature menagerie rose to 480 metres and travelled 3.5 kilometres before descending safely. In recognition of its services to science and the nation, the sheep was sent into happy retirement at the *ménagerie royale*, and may well have become one of the stars of Marie-Antoinette's fake farm at the Petit Trianon.

Encouraged by this success, Réveillon and the Montgolfiers built a larger, heavier balloon – 21 metres tall and weighing 850 kilos – decorated in royal blue with fleurs-de-lys and two interlaced golden Ls in Louis XVI's honour. It was finished in under three weeks (let no one say that workers in Louis XVI's France were inefficient), and the world's first manned flight took place in private at the Réveillon factory on 19 October, though in fact it was only an ascension to 81 metres, with the balloon held in check by ropes. The test pilot was a courageous 29-year-old called Jean-François Pilâtre de Rozier, a scientist who had recently created one of the world's first science museums in Paris.

On 21 November 1783, Rozier, now joined by a slightly mad *marquis* called François Laurent d'Arlande (who had almost killed himself a year earlier testing a parachute in Montmartre), went to the royal château at La Muette, in the west of Paris, hoping to pilot the first manned free flight in a balloon. Until the last minute, Rozier and Arlande were afraid that they would be replaced by two condemned prisoners, because Louis XVI did not want innocent lives to be wasted. Finally, though, helped by Marie-Antoinette, they managed to persuade Louis that no one was going to die, and Rozier and Arlande went aloft, rising to around 1,000 metres above the Tuileries gardens before coming down 25 minutes later on the hilltop of the Butte aux Cailles in the south of Paris.

The American scientist and politician Benjamin Franklin was in the crowd at La Muette, and wrote an eyewitness account of the flight in badly spelt French, in which he said that: 'We observed it lift off in the most majestic manner. When it reached around 250 feet in altitude, the intrepid voyagers lowered their hats to salute the spectators. We could not help feeling a certain mixture of awe and admiration.'

French inventiveness didn't stop there. The danger with the hot-air balloons was that they needed a fire to keep the air heated and the heavy structure aloft. In the years to come, several accidents would be caused by paper balloons catching fire. An alternative light gas was required, and this was where Javel's hydrogen came in.

On 1 December of that same year of frenetic experimentation, 1783, Nicolas-Louis Robert and the physicist Jacques Charles took to the air from the Tuileries gardens in the first ever hydrogen-filled balloon. They flew northwest for two hours, hotly pursued on horseback by Louis XVI's cousin, Louis Philippe, and the 71-year-old Charles de Fitz-James, a grandson of the exiled King James II of England.

The two royal patrons saw the hydrogen balloon come down, and signed a document confirming what they had witnessed. Jacques Charles then took off for a second flight, rising to over 3,300 metres before the extreme cold and popping ears forced him to release some of the gas and come down again. We know the exact altitude he reached, because amongst other things, he had invented the altimeter (as well, incidentally, as the method of using sandbags for ballast). Charles also took up a thermometer and barometer with him, thereby conducting the first-ever experiment to measure atmospheric conditions above the earth's surface.

As a reward for their exploits, Louis XVI gave pensions of 2,000 *livres* to Jacques Charles and 1,000 *livres* to Nicolas-Louis Robert. But it was the Montgolfier family who won first prize for innovation, and received an honour even greater than the one accorded to their flying sheep a few weeks earlier. The father, Pierre Montgolfier, was ennobled by Louis XVI, and his paper factory was given the label *'manufacture royale'*. The sons automatically became knights, as well as being elected to the Académie des sciences.

The motto chosen for the Montgolfier family by Louis XVI was a quotation from Virgil, *'sic itur ad astra'*, which could be translated as 'this is the way to the stars'. It is unlikely that Louis was already thinking about space flight. But then again, in France at that time, the sky was no limit.

All of these French air pioneers continued their experiments, and the first-ever cross-Channel flight by a hydrogen balloon was successfully completed on 7 January 1785. Sadly, Jean-François Pilâtre de Rozier was to die that same month, while attempting to make the second crossing, thereby inadvertently establishing another scientific record for France – the first-ever death in a flying accident.

Of course, the Montgolfiers had no way of knowing that it was an awkward time to be made noble. Just a few years later, their new status, even if it had been acquired for truly noble reasons, would make them suspect. Fortunately, they were social reformers and survived the Revolution, though successive new governments were not interested in funding their research, and their experiments in manned flight came to a premature end.

Many aristocratic scientists followed the Montgolfiers' example and stayed in France after the Revolution – as inventors and teachers they were less dangerous, and more valuable, to the new regime than the many *aristos* whose only economic activity was to own property. Most of these scientists carried on their work freely, but some were less lucky – Antoine-Laurent de Lavoisier, for example, one of the creators of modern scientific experimentation methods, who is remembered today as the 'father of modern chemistry', was guillotined in 1794 on a trumped-up charge of trafficking tobacco. When he asked for a reprieve so that he could finish conducting an experiment, the revolutionary judge refused, telling him: 'The Republic needs neither scientists nor chemists.'

Exactly the opposite of Louis XVI's view.

IV

In an age when the great military powers of Europe were still trying to colonize the rest of the planet, a lot of French brain-power was directed towards improving military technology. This was why Louis XVI founded some of Europe's most modern military academies: in 1776, 13 of them were created, including Brienne, where the nine-year-old Napoleon Bonaparte would arrive as a cadet in 1779.

The idea was to recruit young men – virtually all of them of aristocratic birth – and turn them into modern military geni-uses. Applicants to the new academies had to be 'well instructed in the Latin, German and French languages, in history, geography, mathematics, drawing, and music, and be trained in arms and dancing.' Clearly, it was thought that French officers should be able to conquer ladies as well as colonies.

By restricting most of this new knowledge to the nobility, Louis XVI was probably sending out a signal that, despite his attempts to reduce the power of the noble parliaments, he did value his aristocracy. In 1781, he went so far as to make his officer class even more noble: to become a *sous-lieutenant* in the army, cavalry or dragoons, candidates had to prove four 'degrees' of nobility, meaning that their paternal great-grandfather was an aristocrat. A certificate from the royal genealogist Bernard Chérin (who was himself the ennobled son of a merchant) would then be given to their commanding officer. The same conditions were applied to candidates for the École royale militaire, where Napoleon[3] would study from 1784 to 1785. The only way for a

[3] Napoleon was nicknamed 'the corporal', but this was just a term of affec-tion used by the old soldiers he commanded. He was in fact born into a noble Corsican family, and only ever served as an officer.

non-aristocrat to gain access to these privileges was to be the son of a common soldier who had been awarded the Ordre de Saint-Louis, a medal given to exceptionally courageous officers with ten years' experience. As such, the bravest, most experienced NCO had no hope of promotion to officer status or a place at the military academy.

This reinforced elitism in the army must have created tensions in the ranks, but Louis XVI also took steps to lighten the load of the common soldier. For a start, he put an end to dishonest recruitment. From June 1788, recruiting sergeants had to provide a legibly signed contract and a surgeon's medical certificate attesting that a man was not drunk or under duress when he joined up.

At the barracks, conditions were improved – from now on, there were only two common soldiers to a bed instead of three. And to decrease boredom during peacetime, garrison commanders were ordered to create kitchen gardens so that soldiers could plant vegetables. This measure was not restricted to ordinary soldiers – at the Brienne academy, Cadet Bonaparte grew vegetables, too, and showed an early taste for invasions by annexing weaker students' plots.

Many of the young officers who trained in Louis XVI's academies would stay in the army after the Revolution, taking the opportunity for quick promotion when the old royalists fled or were ousted. That was exactly what Napoleon did. And the officers who would later serve alongside him and conquer most of Europe were mostly products of Louis XVI's centres of military excellence.

All this time and effort poured into the military, including France's active participation in the American War of Independence, did not mean that Louis XVI had an excessively belligerent streak. The pride of the nation was at stake, certainly, and Louis was keen to have the best fighters possible, but he did not let short-term political conflicts get in the way of his thirst for progress.

For example, the basic requirement for students wishing to become a naval officer was to master Étienne Bézout's textbook on how to calculate longitude at sea (published in 1769) and his *Complete Mathematics Course for Use by the Navy and the Artillery* (1770). Louis needed his sailors to be able to fire cannons in the right direction, but he was also determined to send French ships to map out all the world's oceans. Before his reign ended, the French navy was heavily present in the Arctic Circle, defining northern shipping routes and surveying fishing grounds in an open challenge to the British fleets.

Louis XVI's attitude to the continuing expeditions of Louis-Antoine de Bougainville (who had first been sponsored by Louis XV) also shows where his priorities lay. When open war broke out between Britain and France on the American continent in 1778, Louis XVI signed a royal order declaring that the French navy should not consider Britain's own famous explorer, James Cook, as an enemy. A message drafted by the Secretary of State for the Navy, Antoine de Sartine, informed Bougainville and all of France's sea captains that:

> Since discoveries ... interest all nations, I have the honour of informing you that the King wishes that, in case of a complete breakdown of relations between France and England, Captain Cook should be treated exactly as if he commanded a ship belonging to a neutral or friendly power.

To Louis XVI, science was more important than war.

He also showed his statesmanlike character when navigator Jean-François de La Pérouse set off around the globe in 1785. La Pérouse had fought against Britain in the Seven Years War and America, but this was a peaceful mission, and Louis ordered him to respect 'savage peoples' (it was much too early for political correctness), and to use weapons only 'as a last resort, only in self-defence, and at a time when restraint would be sure to compromise the safety of French lives and vessels'.

All lives were important to Louis, including those of the common sailors, and the instructions for La Pérouse's voyage stated that: 'His Majesty would regard it as one of the expedition's greatest successes if it could be completed without costing the life of a single man.' In comparison to Napoleon's disregard for individual soldiers' lives a few years later, or even President Mitterand's mission to sink the *Rainbow Warrior* in New Zealand in 1985, Louis XVI comes across as one of the least warlike military leaders France has ever had.

Sadly, La Pérouse was unable to report back on how he had followed his royal instructions. His two ships disappeared, and later expeditions concluded that he had been wrecked in the Solomon Islands in 1788, and that the survivors had been slaughtered by the natives, who don't seem to have known about Louis XVI's peaceable intentions.

According to some witnesses, as Louis XVI was being taken out of his prison cell to be slaughtered by his own natives, his last question to his entourage was: 'Is there any news of La Pérouse?'

V

The French are famous as a nation that questions everything, especially authority. If they had a referendum on any really key issue, it would need three reply boxes: *'Oui'*, *'Non'*, and *'Pourquoi?'*

It is often said this distrust of established facts and opinions dates back to the eighteenth century, when the writings of the Lumières philosophers and a series of scientific leaps made the French people doubt everything. If this was the case, Louis XVI was playing a suicidal game, because he actively encouraged freethinking.

Just before dying in 1788, the Duc de Richelieu, who had lived through the reigns of Louis XIV, XV and XVI, said that: 'Under the first, one dared not speak; under the second, one spoke quietly; and now everyone says everything out loud.'

Loose tongues and loudly expressed opinions were not only a mark of disrespect towards Louis XVI and the monarchy (though that did come into account); they were also a sign that Louis XVI did not see strict censorship as a priority. He could have been forgiven for hunting down the writers, printers and sellers of the scandal sheets that poured mockery and slander on him and his wife – today, the French courts threaten any magazine that prints illegally obtained pictures of a president in his swimsuit, never mind the authors of a pornographic play.

In his memoirs, the politician Étienne-Denis Pasquier, who was arrested during the Revolution and later became Prefect of Police under Napoleon, confirmed that Louis XVI was all for free speech. He wrote that apart from actual enemies of the state...

> ... other citizens enjoyed total liberty; they could speak, they could write ... they could defy authority in complete safety. The press was not legally free, but anything could be published, any audacious rumour could be spread ... One might deny that it was freedom, but one has to agree that it was permissiveness.

Neither during the Revolution nor a decade or so later under Napoleon would there be such freedom.

In a book called *Tableau de Paris*, first published anonymously in Switzerland in 1781, Louis–Sébastien Mercier makes fun of the censors who were meant to stop seditious publications like his being sold in Paris. Their tactic, he says, is to make themselves look efficient by ostentatiously approving 'insignificant books', thereby giving 'a passport to stupidity'. But they don't stop more subversive books being distributed freely. If a writer fears censorship, he simply gets his text published abroad, and when it comes back to Paris, 'the gates of the capital are opened'. Mercier says that satirists even welcome a grumble of disapproval from the censors, because 'forbidden books are sold much more quickly and surely than if they had obtained approval.'

In fact, when *Tableau de Paris* was first imported into France, it was seized by the censors, as was its importer. Hearing about the arrest, Mercier took a copy to the chief censor, Jean-Charles-Pierre Lenoir, saying, 'Monsieur, I hear that you are looking for the author of this work. Well, here is the book, and its author.' The two men had an amiable chat before both Mercier and the importer were allowed to go free, along with their books.

Tableau de Paris wasn't really a dangerous book, though Mercier wrote it as a poison-pen letter about the establishment. It divides Paris into more than 200 categories – professional, social, intellectual and recreational, and includes sketches depicting typical bankers, merchants, the idle rich, fashion addicts, smokers, drinkers and even people who just stare at everyone.

Mercier paints a portrait of a city plagued by charlatan doctors, over-zealous priests, pretentious writers and armies of uniformed servants who are as arrogant as their masters. But he is no more 'dangerous' than Molière a century earlier, who was invited to perform in front of Louis XIV. Mercier mocks university teachers who 'torment their students and earn their hatred' by teaching Latin grammar; he describes a craze amongst frivolous young women for swapping things – hats, dresses, lace – to avoid spending cash; he complains about smoking dens where 'idle workers lazily waste their days' (a pretty accurate description of modern Parisian cafés until the smoking ban); and he warns foreign visitors that the natives aren't always friendly: 'The Parisian does not waste his time, and is hard to pin down. He is polite, but he is not familiar.' Not exactly a call for revolution. Perhaps it was not surprising that the censors treated him as something of a joke.

Louis XVI took a far bigger risk by allowing France's arch troublemaker and champion of free speech, Voltaire, to return to Paris 27 years after he had fled to avoid being imprisoned by

Louis XV. According to Marie-Antoinette's lady-in-waiting Madame Campan, the Queen opposed the idea, because '[Voltaire's] writings were full of principles that directly attacked religion and good morals,' but Louis XVI recognized that the 83-year-old writer, who was dying of prostate cancer, deserved his hour of glory.

On 30 March 1778, Voltaire was paraded through the streets of Paris, cheered by the crowds, and presented with a victor's laurel wreath by the Académie française. He was received as a hero by the Comédie-Française where his last play, *Irène*, was being produced – this was a provocative tragedy about a prince who overthrows a despotic emperor (albeit mainly because he is refused permission to marry the emperor's daughter).

Voltaire, the man who had spent his whole career making fun of the clergy, sneering at aristocrats and calling for a British-style constitutional monarchy was being allowed the kind of triumphal homecoming given to Roman generals returning after a campaign – and all with Louis XVI's approval.

In 1784, Louis XVI allowed another subversive writer the freedom to stage a play that Napoleon later called *'la Révolution en action'*. This was *The Marriage of Figaro*, by Beaumarchais, the former watchmaker and courtier who had disgraced himself under Louis XV, and then become a gun-runner for Louis XVI.

The play takes place in Spain, and depicts a 'mad day' in the life of a servant, Figaro, who is about to marry his beloved Suzanne, when Figaro's master, the Count Almaviva, decides that he is going to reintroduce the *droit de cuissage*, the ancient right of feudal lords to have sex with their vassals' brides. After a long, libidinous chase, the Count is publicly humiliated, has to beg his wife's forgiveness, and Figaro is able to marry his Suzanne. The little man has triumphed over aristocratic privilege.

Beaumarchais wrote the play in 1778, and a reading was staged at the Comédie-Française in 1781, but Louis XVI heard about it and declared that the text was 'awful, and makes fun of everything respectful'. It was, after all, a play about lust, which was not an emotion with which Louis sympathized, and adultery, a sin of which Louis was innocent, unlike almost all his predecessors on the throne and most of his courtiers. It was duly banned.

Beaumarchais did the rounds of the Paris literary *salons*, promising everyone that his play wasn't meant to undermine aristocratic society *en bloc*. In his preface, published in 1785, we get an idea of the kind of things he was saying at the *salons*. It argues that: 'A lord who is immoral enough to want to prostitute all his subordinates to his whims, and who toys with the modesty of his young female vassals, must end up, like this one, being mocked by his servants.'

But Beaumarchais was being disingenuous. The play's famous monologue, one of the longest in pre-revolutionary theatre, is a frontal attack on aristocratic privilege. In Act V, Scene 3, Figaro gives a speech that later inspired the revolutionary Georges Danton to declare that 'Figaro killed the aristocracy.'

Here is the best-known segment of the monologue, addressed to the Count (in his absence, of course):

> Because you're a great lord, you think you're a great genius! Nobility, money, rank, position, they all make you so proud! But what have you done to deserve so much? You took the trouble to be born, that's all. Apart from that, you're a mediocre man. Whereas I, by God, lost amid the obscure masses, I've had to use more knowledge and strategy[4] just to survive than have been used in the last century to govern the whole of Spain.

One phrase alone – 'You took the trouble to be born' – was enough to get the play banned after its initial reading, which probably explains a section later in the monologue, in which Beaumarchais ironizes about censorship. Here, Figaro says

[4] Beaumarchais used *'science et calculs'*, a very modern-sounding combination.

that he has tried to make a living writing plays and has been told that:

> In Madrid, the free sale of texts has been established ... and as long as my writing steers clear of the subjects of authority, religion, politics, morals, people in high places, public borrowing, the Opéra,[5] other shows, or anyone who wants to hold on to anything, then I can print freely, and will only be inspected by three or four censors.

For all his irony about aristocrats and censors, Beaumarchais finally got permission to stage *Le Mariage de Figaro*, which premiered in Paris on 27 April 1784. After his initial objections, Louis XVI had backed down, and thanks to his objections, even contributed to the play's *succès de scandale*. It was a huge hit, and within two years Mozart had turned it into an opera.

The play's reputation nowadays as a political tract ignores the fact that Beaumarchais – who had been ennobled by Louis XV and then stripped of his titles, otherwise he too would have been living a life of privilege – had some purely personal axes to grind. When he began writing it, he was embroiled in a long lawsuit with a wealthy family who were accusing him of forging a will (see Chapter 5). In a way Beaumarchais was lucky that his purely personal resentments struck a chord with the general public – those who could afford a ticket to the Paris theatre, anyway.

VI

It was also under Louis XVI that France's first-ever daily newspaper was founded, the *Journal de Paris*. It was very literary, and its lead articles were often reviews or discussions on art, but its front page always gave the times of sunrise and sunset, the

---

[5] At the time, Marie-Antoinette was criticized for taking part in the immoral goings-on at balls held at the Paris Opéra.

height of the River Seine, and a weather report from the previous day (no doubt intended for readers in the provinces who
would receive their copy late), and there were real news stories.

The first issue, dated 1 January 1777, published two royal
decrees, one 'in favour of the workers and craftsmen of the faubourg Saint-Antoine in Paris' and another 'concerning the free
Royal School of Drawing'. But it also included a letter from
Voltaire, who was still in exile at the time, a dangerous correspondent to publish in your first issue if you're hoping to stay in
business long enough to print number two.

In his letter, Voltaire was not calling for bishops to be publicly
disrobed, or for aristocrats to shorten their names – he begged
the editors to 'tell the public the truth about the pamphlets that
I am supposed to have written ... in which there is not a line
that I have composed'. It was message aimed at Louis XVI,
perhaps – I, Voltaire, am not as satirical as people think.

This first issue had its lighter side, too, and printed a poem
that starts...

> Let's make love, let's make war:
> Both occupations have their attractions.

... as well as a dubious report about a robber called Lefévre
who was allegedly 'resisting arrest' when he stabbed himself –
with two knives, one straight through the heart.

The *Journal de Paris* was no subversive publication. On 13
December 1786, for example, it ran an article rejoicing that
Louis XVI was convening an Assemblée des notables, and said
that the gathering would allow him to 'communicate [to these
decision-makers] the great plans with which His Majesty is
busy, for the good of his state and the relief of his subjects ...
The Nation will note with joy that its sovereign is drawing near
to it and uniting with it more and more closely.' They sound like
words straight out of Louis XVI's mouth.

But the *Journal* can't have been under Louis XVI's thumb,
because on 28 April 1784 it published a long, favourable review

of *The Marriage of Figaro*, saying that the play produced 'a strong sensation thanks to its originality, very good comic intrigues, witty lines, [and] numerous satirical remarks about all classes of society.'[6] The reviewer noted that 'from time to time it excited noises and murmurs' from the audience, no doubt referring both to disapproving aristocrats and disgruntled democrats, and he thought it was over-long, but pronounced the play *'un grand succès'*. All in all, the article reads as if it was written by someone who was completely free to speak his mind.

It is worth noting that the freedom to express ideas in the *Journal de Paris* that was permitted under Louis XVI came to an abrupt end in August 1792, when revolutionaries ransacked the paper's printing press and suspended publication. Not exactly *Liberté*.

By 1786, with Paris swamped in pamphlets about Marie-Antoinette, and his political struggles coming to a head, Louis XVI seems to have started regretting all this freedom of speech.

He wrote to the lawyer Guillaume-Chrétien de Lamoignon de Malesherbes, a senior member of his council of ministers, saying that:

> No doubt the freedom of the press widens the sphere of human knowledge ... but men always go far beyond the point where prudence should stop them. We need not only a police force that is tough on book publication, but also active surveillance of those whose duty it is to examine them, so that bad books get as little publicity as possible.

This seems to be a reference to the lax disapproval that Louis-Sébastien Mercier had received from the censors for his *Tableau de Paris*.

---

[6] Instead of *'classes'*, the writer used the word *'états'*, referring to the three sections of French society: commoners, the clergy and the aristocracy.

Louis XVI's letter sounds draconian, but he knew that Malesherbes was an open-minded man who believed in sharing new ideas. Malesherbes was known as 'the protector of Rousseau', and had permitted the publication of Diderot's free-thinking encyclopedia despite the huge intellectual turmoil it caused, especially about religion (see Chapter 5). Malesherbes was also the brain behind Louis XVI's edict to give religious freedom to Protestants and Jews.

As a younger man, Malesherbes had served under Louis XV, and had once written to him with a series of 'remonstrations', one of which stated that: 'God places the crown on the heads of kings solely in order to protect their subjects' lives, personal freedom and the peaceful ownership of their property.' Malesherbes had assured Louis XV that his remonstrations were intended to protect the monarchy, because 'if they are not listened to by the King, they will be heard in the street, the *salon* and the café' – but this frankness earned Malesherbes a temporary exile from Paris.

And yet this was the man whom Louis XVI appointed as one of his chief ministers. Further proof that he was a monarch in favour of openness and change.

The two men shared so many opinions that in 1792 Malesherbes volunteered to act as Louis XVI's defence counsel during his trial for treason. Louis replied that 'your sacrifice is especially great because you are risking your life and you will not save mine.' Even so, Malesherbes went ahead with the defence, and his reward for daring to speak freely in a revolutionary court was to be guillotined two years after Louis XVI, at the age of 72.

VII

The Revolution is often represented as a cleansing tidal wave of atheism that swept away the antiquated religious beliefs imposed on the people by the clergy and its worldly stooge, Louis XVI. French kings ruled by self-proclaimed 'divine right', so getting rid of the monarchy implied getting rid of God.

But this, like so much about the Revolution, is myth. It is true that the freethinking philosophers were encouraging the intellectual classes to question religion as they knew it, and especially to oppose the right of the Church to possess so much land, to tax the poor, and wield political power. But the vast majority of the French population in 1789 were incapable of reading a page of Diderot's encyclopedia, let alone understanding its complex philosophical vocabulary. And even though *le peuple* were wholly in agreement that the Church's taxes had to be cut, or even abolished, as a whole they were still very religious. They probably would have agreed with the line in Molière's *Dom Juan* (first performed in 1665): *'On n'a pas besoin de lumière, quand on est conduit par le Ciel'* ('One doesn't need light when one is guided by heaven').

It has even been argued that the onslaught of challenging philosophical ideas in eighteenth-century France might have had the opposite effect, and made ordinary people react against modern thinking, in the way that the random splatterings of Jackson Pollock in the 1950s gave way to the pop-art realism of Warhol in the 60s. After a decade of visual anarchy, it was so relaxing to look at a picture of tomato soup.

The *Correspondance littéraire, philosophique et critique* was a highly intellectual magazine, founded in France in 1748. It was originally designed for a select readership of foreign aristocrats and royals (amongst its subscribers were Catherine the Great of Russia, and the rulers of Poland, Sweden and various German states). To protect its freedom of speech, each copy was hand-written, making it a sort of secret dispatch from inside France. By the time Louis XVI came to the throne, one of the editors was the philosopher Diderot, suggesting that the *Correspondance* was no establishment mouthpiece.

In April 1776, a contributor called Jacques–Henri Meister, a friend of the reformer Jacques Necker, wrote that the Jubilee year declared by the Pope 'was celebrated in Paris with a devotion and regularity that would be astonishing in times less corrupt than our own. Does this religious effervescence prove that philosophy has not achieved all the progress it claims for itself?' Diderot might have gnashed his teeth reading that question, but it was published nonetheless.

Meister observed that Parisians seemed to be reacting against 'the philosophers who refuse to recognize any gods other than freedom and net profit' (as well as freethinkers, some 'philosophers' were seen as pragmatists looking to make money out of scientific discoveries). 'It would be amusing,' Meister went on, 'if philosophy had inadvertently helped to reheat religious faith.'

Out in the provinces and in the country, where most French people lived, religion did not need reheating. Religious festivals were heartily observed, partly of course because they were days off work – then, as now, holidaying was France's national sport. In parts of Provence, there were so many saints' festivals, processions and holy days that the year was reduced to about 260 working days.

But these religious festivals were much more than an excuse to laze about at home. There would be processions of crosses, icons and priests through the streets, and at least two masses, as well as rituals to observe. For Fête-Dieu, or Corpus Christi (a moveable feast that usually fell in May or June), country people would cover their houses in flowers and leafy twigs, while in the city they would hang out tapestries and pennants. Towns and villages would be swept clean, and holes in the streets filled in. Ditches and open sewers would be covered in planks to avoid unpleasant accidents during the parade. Then on the big day, bells would ring, and people would join the procession of the great cross and the Holy Sacrament.

According to François-René de Chateaubriand – a French aristocrat who took part in the storming of the Bastille but who later defended the Catholic faith against the revolutionaries – religious processions united all the social classes: 'The humble, the poor, and children' would lead the cortège, while 'judges, soldiers and the powerful' followed. Not forgetting the columns of monks and priests and, in cathedral cities, a bishop, who was forbidden to leave his diocese on that day. Young people would carry baskets of flowers, while children sang and wafted incense. It was, Chateaubriand suggested, a communal celebration untroubled by thoughts of atheism or revolution.

Very similar things happened across France on Assumption Day, Rogations (three days before Ascension) and Ascension Day itself. Religion was fun – the celebrations were theatrical, and not always very religious. In May 1781 a law was passed, forbidding people from 'assembling to throw others into water, play pétanque, bang drums or dance'. In 1782, the Archbishop of Toulouse forbade processions in the evenings because 'scandalous irreverences are committed under cover of darkness.'

But apart from these attempts to protect the decorum of religious ceremonies, the clergy's influence on the laws of the land was weakening in Louis XVI's France. Theoretically, blasphemy was still punishable by death, and according to the letter of the law, anyone who uttered blasphemous words could have their tongue pierced and be sent into a lifetime of slavery on the galley ships. But in practice, under Louis XVI this didn't happen. Religion was having its harsh edges knocked off. At his coronation, Louis XVI even swore that he was independent of the Pope. France was creating its own brand of Catholicism – not exactly modern, but less oppressive than it had been. In everything but taxation, that is.

Aside from the element of fun, French religious festivals of the time were also important to ordinary people because they were an industry. The sweepers and road menders were all paid, as were the musicians, flower sellers, and even the faithful who carried the cross. Innkeepers and food sellers were especially happy, as were the growing numbers of beggars who managed to cadge alms off anyone richer (or drunker) than themselves.

In other words, if offered the choice, ordinary French people in 1789 would probably not have abolished religion. They would definitely have agreed with Louis XVI's plans to end the *dîme*, the tax that fattened up their already bloated bishops and even the priests of relatively small parishes. But if asked to turn their backs on the God who had always been presented to them as the one reliable truth in a world of famine, disease, injustice and overwork, the answer would almost certainly have been a massive '*non, merci*'.

Many French people these days see France in 1789 as a country brimming with freethinking cynics, a population chomping at the bit to tear down the churches and decapitate statues of the Virgin Mary. But in fact, most of Louis XVI's subjects simply aspired to go to church, pray for a decent harvest and then say grace before a hearty meal.

In his above-mentioned article about religious belief, Jacques-Henri Meister of the *Correspondance littéraire* wrote that: 'It has been remarked more than once that ... many things are done out of hatred for those that one wants to do away with, rather than out of affection for those for whom one wants the greatest good.' He seemed to be saying that there were people in France who were against religious ideas themselves, and who therefore wanted to deprive everyone else of any succour (or holiday fun) that religion might bring. The haters were determined to throw the baby Jesus out with the bathwater – abolishing not just religious taxes, but faith itself.

Unluckily for Louis XVI, they would apply the same principle to monarchy. After he had lost his power and most of his privileges, Louis remained popular amongst most French people. But for the more violent factions of the revolutionaries, this wasn't enough. They would demand his head, too.

VIII

In the summer of 1789, Paris would become the blast furnace of the Revolution. The image that has come down to us is of an oppressed mass of skeletal paupers bursting out of their muck-strewn hovels to drag the privileged few down from their gilded carriages.

But a guidebook published in 1787 seems to suggest that life for the less well-off was not all that oppressed and muck-strewn.

Luc-Vincent Thiéry's *Guide des amateurs et des étrangers voyageurs à Paris* (*Guide for Enthusiasts and Foreigners Travelling to Paris*) gives a vivid, and fairly positive, idea of what Paris was actually like just before the Revolution.

Thiéry describes tourist sights like Notre-Dame, the Pont-Neuf, the île Saint-Louis, and dozens of churches, but unlike modern guidebooks, he also goes into great detail about the city's more functional buildings. He lists, for example, 20 hospitals, including those for pregnant women and 'poor found children', a 'medico-electric hospice, institutes for deaf mutes and blind children', and the *'hôpital des incurables'*. He praises 'the instruction to create vast, comfortable infirmaries in the different hospitals', and highlights a hospital for children born with sexually transmitted diseases, created in 1780 because the government had noted that 'all children who were born with venereal infections either died very soon afterwards or ... lived a painful life that usually did not last until puberty'. The city had therefore founded a place for 'these innocent victims' and their mothers. Thiéry describes well-aired rooms equipped with fireplaces and tall candlesticks, chosen so they won't be knocked over and cause a fire. Each mother has her own bed, with two blankets in winter, and the babies have cribs that are cleaned and perfumed regularly, as well as eight to ten nappies a day. Modern mothers in similar circumstances would probably not get better care, or less disapproval. It seemed that Necker's reforms had taken effect.

Thiéry notes other improvements to urban life, like 'new hot baths by the Seine, costing almost nothing, some of them free for the poor', and river water stored in reservoirs which 'thanks to a thousand canals is distributed into all the different districts of the city, cleaning them and providing a prompt remedy for fires'.[7] And Louis XVI was beginning the work that Baron Haussmann would

[7] This is basically the same system as is used today. Paris's street sweepers open valves to send filtered Seine water flowing along the gutters, washing rubbish down into the drains, as well as providing ammunition for drivers who want to splash passers-by.

finish a century later, clearing slums and demolishing shanties on the bridges, bringing 'increasing salubrity thanks to the breezes that can now circulate freely from dawn to dusk', as well as creating boulevards that are 'beautified and carefully maintained, making them an attractive place to walk'. Paris, Thiéry says, is now 'better lit at night ... the streets cleaner and less obstructed'. Obviously, after centuries of almost uncontrolled building, with no sewers and little running water, the work was only just beginning, but there was now light at the end of the street.

Thiéry lists markets, including the new buildings at Les Halles, a whole host of schools, seven public libraries and 30 private ones, and a fascinating variety of administrative offices, including the 'bureau for confiding by domestic servants' – where they could presumably complain about abusive masters.

Thiéry mentions public transport, organized by the Bureau des voitures des environs de Paris, but it is expensive, costing a passenger 15 *sous* per league in a four-seater coach, or eight in a river boat, the equivalent of half a kilo of bread per kilometre – out of reach of the poor.

He even talks about a swimming school, supported by the Académie des sciences, that offers lessons in life-saving, including sessions on how to swim fully-clothed in case one has to jump into the water to make a quick rescue – though these were apparently for men only, as swimmers had to be 'in breeches or trousers', and until the late nineteenth century, it was illegal for Frenchwomen to wear anything but dresses and skirts in public.

Tellingly, standing outside the Théâtre-Français, Thiéry describes 'the marble statue of the immortal Voltaire, a precious work by Monsieur Houdon, the King's sculptor' – so Louis XVI not only allowed the old subversive to return from exile, he even gave permission for him to stand forever in the streets of Paris.

All in all, even if Thiéry is trying to sell Paris to tourists, he presents a picture of a benevolently run city where new improvements were coming every day, the kind of place a foreigner could visit without fear of being lynched for looking too rich by a mob of resentful paupers.

Even Louis-Sébastien Mercier, the author of the above-mentioned *Tableau de Paris*, finds some positive things to say, despite his obvious desire to be seen as a merciless satirist. He ends his book with a section called 'Improvements'. Here, he thanks the city authorities for finally closing the cimetière des Innocents, right next to Les Halles market, which had created 'the least salubrious air in Paris'. He is also glad that the city has cleaned up a sewer near Notre-Dame where 'all the latrines poured out their filth', and 'the infected air ... turned meat bad and discoloured silver and gold'. He congratulates himself, because he had campaigned on these issues and 'by constantly complaining, one makes oneself heard by the men in power'.

Surely it is praise indeed when even the provocative Mercier concedes that Louis XVI 'is being more careful than ever that people should no longer say: "In Paris, everything is done for the great, and nothing for the common people."'

IX

It is an English book that gives the most dispassionate, balanced view of France at the time of the Revolution. This is the impressively named *Travels During the Years 1787, 1788, & 1789: Undertaken More Particularly with a View of Ascertaining the Cultivation, Wealth, Resources, and National Prosperity of the Kingdom of France*, first published in 1792 by Arthur Young. For obvious reasons, it is usually known as *Travels in France*.

Young was a farmer and scientist, interested in agricultural, economic and social reform. He toured England and Ireland widely, writing about how farming could be made more efficient there, before deciding that he ought to take a look across the Channel, too. Serendipitously, he did so just as France's political turmoils were coming to fruition.

More than anything else, Young was interested in France's soil types, crop yields, land prices, livestock pedigrees, and similar agricultural minutiae, but he found the country in such a state of ferment that he could not help diverting from his main task. Even though Young was no revolutionary, he sometimes wrote like one. He was a plain speaker who thought that, as well as informing farmers about their cross-Channel competition, his book might serve as a wake-up call to the British people as a whole, and not just the monarchy. (A year after his French notebooks were published, he brought out a pamphlet called *Example of France, a Warning to Britain*.)

Young had harsh words for almost everything and everybody French, but it was constructive criticism. In the preface to his *Travels in France*, he quoted Jonathan Swift, saying that the reader was free to agree or disagree, but that they should 'believe that I have proceeded at least with partiality, and perhaps with truth'. Even so, Young occasionally comes across as a bit of a jingoist. After visiting Amiens, he advises his readers to 'view the cathedral, said to be built by the English; it is very large, and beautifully light and decorated'.

He sniffs at the quality of the average French country *auberge*. They're cheap and the food is good, he says, but their...

> ... doors give music as well as entrance; the wind whistles through their chinks ... Windows admit rain as well as light; when shut they are not easy to open; and when open not easy to shut. Mops, brooms, and scrubbing-brushes are not in the catalogue of the necessaries of a French inn. Bells there are none; the *fille* must always be bawled for; and when she appears, is neither neat, well dressed, nor handsome.

He clearly didn't fall under the spell of France's rustic charm.

Young goes to Versailles, where he is introduced by a politician friend, Alexandre de la Rochefoucauld,[8] and watches Louis XVI eating (as visitors could in those days). He notes perceptively that: 'During the service the King was seated between his

[8] Rochefoucauld was an aristocratic social reformer who translated the American Constitution into French, and proposed it to France in 1789. He was killed by a gang of *aristo*-hunters in 1792.

two brothers, and seemed by his carriage and inattention to wish himself a-hunting.' Young adds some pertinent advice for Louis XVI: 'To me it would have been a most uncomfortable meal, and were I a sovereign, I would sweep away three-fourths of these stupid forms.' ('Forms' meaning protocols.)

By 1789, this was exactly Louis's problem – he was trapped in the vestiges of his ancestors' traditions like a pear baked on top of a *tarte aux poires*. The conscientious side of him was determined to help his ministers modernize France, dismantle the stagnant parliamentary system, curb Marie-Antoinette's spending, and put an end to the worst follies of etiquette; his weaker side sat eating for the public gallery, wishing he could dash off and chase wild boar.

Young, the practical, democratically inclined English farmer, admits admiration for Louis XVI, who allows almost anybody to come into Versailles and observe the court and the monarchy in operation. It is a sign, he thinks, that the King is still popular:

> It was amusing to see the blackguard figures that were walking uncontrolled about the palace, and even in his bed-chamber; men whose rags betrayed them to be in the last stage of poverty, and I was the only person that stared and wondered how the devil they got there. It is impossible not to like this careless indifference and freedom from suspicion. One loves the master of the house ... for if there was danger of this, the intrusion would be prevented.

Young finds the palace itself less impressive. He laments that the grounds are being left to fall into disrepair (a symptom both of Louis XVI's attempts to save money and the increasing laxity at court): 'The extent and breadth of the canal are nothing to the eye; and it is not in such good repair as a farmer's horse-pond.' And he has a comical dig at Marie-Antoinette's supposedly 'English' garden at le Petit Trianon, which makes the mistake 'of cutting the lawn by too many gravel walks, an error to be seen in almost every garden I have met with in France'.

Leaving the area on his way south to Orléans, Young is astonished by how empty the road is:

> It is a desert compared with those around London. In ten miles we met not one stage or diligence; only two *messageries*, and very few *chaises*; not a tenth of what would have been met had we been leaving London at the same hour. Knowing how great, rich, and important a city Paris is, this circumstance perplexes me much.

The countryside – what interested Young most – is even worse. At one point he exclaims: 'What a miracle, that all this splendour and wealth of the cities in France should be so unconnected with the country!' In the east of France, he walks his horse up a long hill while talking to a peasant woman who describes the terrible tax burden she has to put up with:

> She said her husband had but a morsel of land, one cow and a poor little horse, yet they had a *franchar* (42 lb) of wheat and three chickens to pay as quit-rent to one *Seigneur*, and four *franchar* of oats, one chicken and 1 *sou* to another, besides very heavy *tailles* and other taxes … This woman, at no great distance, might have been taken for sixty or seventy, her figure was so bent, and her face so furrowed and hardened by labour – but she said she was only twenty-eight.

In Dordogne, Young notes that:

> All the country girls and women are without shoes or stockings, and the ploughmen at their work have neither *sabots* nor feet to their stockings. This is a poverty that strikes at the root of national prosperity … The wealth of a nation lies in its circulation and consumption; and the case of poor people abstaining from the use of manufactures of leather and wool ought to be considered as an evil of the first magnitude.

Louis XVI would have agreed – his ministers had tried to improve the roads, both to boost trade and give paying jobs to the poor, and were trying to convince the nobility and the Church to reform taxes. But Young seems to be saying that these good intentions have had little or no effect.

And he has no doubt where the fault lies: 'Whenever you stumble on a *Grand Seigneur*, even one that was worth millions, you are sure to find his property desert.' England at the time was much more densely populated and intensely farmed than France, so Young cannot understand why lazy aristocrats would leave their land and their peasants idle:

> The fields are scenes of pitiable management, as the houses are of misery. Yet all this country [would be] highly improveable, if they knew what to do with it: the property, perhaps, of some of those glittering beings, who figured in the procession the other day at Versailles. Heaven grant me patience while I see a country thus neglected – and forgive me the oaths I swear at the absence and ignorance of the possessors.

Young promises that: 'Oh! If I was the legislator of France for a day, I would make such great lords skip again.'

Which was exactly what Louis XVI had been trying – and failing – to do.

Young meets aristocrats and challenges them face-to-face about all this, and admits that he finds 'an invariable sweetness of disposition [and] mildness of character', but a total unwillingess to face up to the country's problems: 'Tame and elegant, uninteresting and polite ... conversation is like a journey on an endless flat.'

Besides, instead of taking action or decisions, even the men who purport to be doing some kind of business keep stopping for lunch and to preen themselves, habits that infuriate the hard-working Young:

> Dividing the day exactly in halves, destroys it for any expedition, enquiry, or business that demands seven or eight hours

attention, uninterrupted by any calls to the table or the *toilette* ... What is a man good for after his silk breeches and stockings are on, his hat under his arm, and his head *bien poudre*?

But Young reserves his sharpest criticisms for the clergy, who are clearly in need of a dose of weed-killer if France is to survive:

St Germain ... is the richest abbey in France: the abbot has 300,000 *livres* a year. I lose my patience at such revenues being thus bestowed; consistent with the spirit of the tenth century, but not with that of the eighteenth. What a noble farm would the fourth of this income establish! What turnips, what cabbages, what potatoes, what clover, what sheep, what wool! Are not these things better than a fat ecclesiastic?'

Publishing in 1792, Young swore that 'I alter none of these passages', but his notes from 1787 to 1789 contain some remarkably accurate predictions. Talking to less aristocratic people, he hears constant talk about revolution. At a dinner:

One opinion pervaded the whole company, that they are on the eve of some great revolution in the government; that every thing points to it: the confusion in the finances great; with a deficit impossible to provide for ... no minister existing, or to be looked to in or out of power, with such decisive talents as to promise any other remedy than palliative ones: a prince on the throne, with excellent dispositions, but without the resources of a mind that could govern in such a moment without ministers: a court buried in pleasure and dissipation and adding to the distress ... a great ferment amongst all ranks of men, who are eager for some change, without knowing what to look to, or to hope for: and a strong leaven of liberty, increasing every hour since the American revolution – altogether form a combination of circumstances that promise e'er long to ferment into motion.

Young is sympathetic to calls for reform, but is horrified to see that Louis XVI is not clamping down on free speech. At the Palais-Royal in the heart of Paris, he sees printing presses spewing out pamphlets:

> Nineteen-twentieths of these productions are in favour of liberty, and commonly violent against the clergy and nobility ... Is it not wonderful [meaning astonishing], that while the press teems with the most levelling and even seditious principles, that if put in execution would overturn the monarchy, nothing in reply appears, and not the least step is taken by the court to restrain this extreme licentiousness of publication?

It sounds as though Louis XVI's permissiveness has turned into outright submission.

By June 1789, Young was sure that violence was about to erupt. The prices of bread 'the common sort, eaten by the poor ... are beyond their faculties, and occasion great misery'. Meanwhile, Paris's coffee-houses...

> ... are not only crowded within, but other expectant crowds are at the doors and windows, listening to certain orators, who from chairs or tables harangue each his little audience: the eagerness with which they are heard, and the thunder of applause they receive for every sentiment of more than common hardiness or violence against the present government, cannot easily be imagined. I am all amazement at the ministry permitting such nests and hotbeds of sedition and revolt, which disseminate amongst the people, every hour, principles that by and by must be opposed with vigour, and therefore it seems little short of madness to allow the propagation at present.

And still the aristocrats don't see the problem. Young writes about a dinner where 'they ate, and drank, and sat, and walked,

261

loitered, and smirked and smiled, and chatted with that easy indifference, that made me stare at their insipidity.'

He goes to Versailles to attend debates on the crisis, but despairs at the hot air being expended in unproductive arguments: 'The rules and orders of debate in the House of Commons of England ... would have saved them at least a fourth of their time.' Worse, he realizes that the taxing, land-owning classes are refusing to budge: 'The nobility ... are most disgustingly tenacious of all old rights, however hard they may bear on the people; they will not hear of giving way in the least to the spirit of liberty.'

Young is fearful for Louis XVI:

The King, who is personally the honestest man in the world, has but one wish, which is to do right – yet, being without those decisive parts that enable a man to foresee difficulties and to avoid them, finds himself in a moment of such extreme perplexity, that he knows not what council to take refuge in.

And there is little help to be had from Louis's entourage, Young thinks, because his own brothers are scheming against him to protect the status quo, with Marie-Antoinette's connivance: 'The Queen is closely connecting herself with the party of the princes, with the count d'Artois [Louis XVI's brother Charles] at their head.'

The only hopeful sign, in Young's opinion, is that the people he speaks to are not in favour of a wholesale rebellion against Louis XVI: 'They profess that the Kingdom ought to be a monarchy; or, at least, that there ought to be a king.' People want radical reform, not total revolution; they want Louis XVI at the head of a completely renewed form of government.

And at the end of June 1789, with Louis XVI proposing one last attempt to force the nobility and the clergy to give increased powers to the commoners, Young reports that: 'The joy this step occasioned was infinite; the assembly, uniting with the people, all hurried to the château. *Vive le Roi* might have been heard at

Marly [a royal residence near Versailles]: the King and Queen appeared in the balcony, and were received with the loudest shouts of applause.'

As we now know, the joy was short-lived. 'The events that followed', Young confesses, 'were as little to be thought of as of myself being made King of France.'

Chapter 11

LOUIS XVI'S FINAL GAMBLE

'He [Louis XVI] is an honest man, and wishes really to do good, but he has not either genius or education to show the way towards that good which he desires.'

From the diary of Gouverneur Morris, US ambassador to
France 1792–4, who first went to France on business in 1789

I

There are two very contradictory images of Louis XVI as the Revolution approached. On the one hand, the wavering fop, the man who couldn't control his wife's spending, the coward who took refuge from reality by riding off into the forest at every opportunity, and wrote *'Rien'* in his diary for 14 July 1789. On the other, there is the King who tried every means possible – exiling parliament, convening assemblies, offering concessions, changing ministers (he even recalled Necker in August 1788) – in the hope of dragging France over the seemingly impenetrable wall of opposition that the aristocrats had constructed around their privileges.

The problem was that he was both of these men, and everyone knew it. This was why his last attempt to avoid the crisis was huge, ambitious, worthy – and doomed to failure.

Everything started to go fatally wrong for Louis XVI in mid-1788. With the aristocratic parliamentarians resisting change and stirring up popular discontent, the weather tipped the poorer sections of French society into outright despair.

There had been heavy rains and flooding in many parts of France in the autumn of 1787, meaning that fewer crops had been sown. In the Rhône valley, floods had been so bad that mills had been swept away. As a result, hopes were not especially high for the grain harvest of 1788. Then at about 6.30 a.m. on Sunday, 13 July 1788, in a sort of deadly premonition of Bastille Day, a biblical hailstorm hit France, rampaging in the course of four hours from Poitiers in the west of France, along the Loire, across Paris and up to Lille and the Belgian border. Hailstones ranging in size from a walnut to a turkey's egg, often propelled by gusts of wind reaching 150 kph, felled trees, smashed windows, stripped roofs, toppled chimneys and steeples, killed farm animals and of course ruined crops. It was estimated that about 100,000 hectares of land were made unharvestable.

Louis XVI himself was caught in the storm. He had stayed the night at Rambouillet, in his hunting forest near Versailles, and was on his way back on the morning of the thirteenth when, according to his attendant Félix d'Hézecques, he was 'assailed by a terrible hailstorm, the like of which we rarely see. The whole procession was obliged to shelter in the hangars at the village of Trappes, but not before several riders had been injured. The countryside was covered with felled trees and crushed birds and animals.'

Crown agents sent out instructions to farmers to plough up the damaged fields immediately and sow mustard seed, beetroot, cabbages, chicory and turnips – but everyone knew that grain, and therefore bread, was going to be cruelly short. Almost immediately, a new wave of rural emigration began, filling the larger towns, and especially Paris, with hungry, disgruntled paupers.

The bad weather continued. At the end of August 1788, heavy rains forced grape farmers in central France to harvest early. In mid-November, there was widespread frost, damaging fruit trees, as well as the ground crops sown in the ravaged wheat fields. This was the early visiting card of a bitterly cold winter that would see Paris snowbound on New Year's Eve, enduring temperatures of minus 20 °C. Cruellest of all, sudden hard frosts were interspersed with short spells of unseasonably mild weather.

To a highly religious people, it must have seemed as though God was sending them a message about the year to come. It was becoming increasingly clear that the King, previously God's political representative in France, was not going to provide their daily bread in His place.

II

Meanwhile, Louis XVI was still battling to salvage something from the political situation. On 8 August, with horror stories about the plague of hailstones still doing the rounds of France's churches, inns and markets, he announced that he was convening the États généraux. This was the ancient means of consulting the people in times of crisis, whereby representatives of all three of France's estates were called to deliver an opinion on the course of action that a sovereign should take.

Typically, the Paris parliament declared that this session of the États généraux – the first since 1614 – should follow convention and favour the privileged. The noble parliamentarians wanted each of the three estates to have the same number of representatives, even though the lowest class, the *tiers état* or Third Estate, comprised some 96 per cent of the population. In any case, as things stood, the system of voting by estate meant that the nobility and the clergy could outvote two to one any attempt to democratize the tax system, and then claim it as a 'democratic' decision.

Louis XVI defied the parliamentarians, first instructing them to debate whether the number of *tiers état* representatives should be doubled, and then, when they voted against this, by declaring unilaterally that that was how it was going to be. Louis decreed that at the next États généraux, to begin on May Day 1789, there would be at least a thousand delegates, called *députés*,[1] with half of them commoners – he was doubling the *tiers état*'s presence. It was still not fair representation – because of the division into three estates, these 50 per cent of the delegates would still only have 33.3 per cent of the votes while representing 96 per cent of the population, but it was a symbolic move in the right direction. Any vote in favour of the status quo by two estates to one would look dubious if the delegates against were just as numerous as those in favour.

To rub even more salt into the aristocrats' wounds, Louis XVI recalled Jacques Necker yet again to be his Finance Minister. The great reformer, who was still considered a potential saviour by the people, was back, and went straight into action, forbidding the export of grain, subsidizing imports, and even importing a national stock of grain and giving local authorities the power to release it into local markets. It was exactly what the French people wanted – except, of course, for the rich merchants who had hoped to speculate at a time of low supply.

For such a famously weak man, Louis XVI was showing a real talent for political boxing.

On 24 January 1789, in an attempt to rouse public support, Louis published an open letter saying that 'from the extremities of his realm and the least known dwellings, everyone should be sure to send His Majesty their wishes and claims.' At the États généraux, the delegates would, he said, 'advise and assist' him in his politics by expressing 'the desires and complaints of our people, so that by mutual confidence and love between the sovereign and his subjects, the promptest possible remedy may be

[1] The name did not mean that they were subservient to someone, like a sheriff's deputy or a deputy editor. They had been 'deputized' by their electors to serve the state. The same word is used today for French members of parliament.

found for the state's ills, and so that abuses of all sorts may be reformed'.

One thing was certain – the 'desires and complaints' of the aristocrats and the clergy would be that Louis XVI should give up politics and go hunting, because he was trying to hand power to the uppity commoners.

Once again, the selection process for delegates to the États généraux was not going to be totally democratic. The nobles and the clergy were so few in number that they met in large towns and put together a list of likely candidates. There was one democratic change for the clergy – every humble parish priest would now have the chance to vote for a delegate – meaning that the power of the rich, noble bishops was to be greatly reduced.

Meanwhile the *tiers état* had to whittle down about 26 million people to just under 600 delegates. To do so, each town had to elect a representative who would then vote for a district representative, who would in turn vote for a regional representative, who would then have a vote in the election for the actual delegate sent to the États généraux in Versailles. It was a long, tortuous process, which was why the country was given almost five months to carry out the vote.

No one thought to invite women to the États généraux, and they weren't even allowed to vote for delegates – suffrage was restricted to men over the age of 25. What was more, the election of *tiers état* delegates was to be administered by the clergy, who had a vested interest in the result, and voting was to be done after mass, presumably following a sermon about God's wish for a status quo in which bishops always had food on their table and gold on their fingers. It wasn't going to be a secret ballot, either, meaning that anyone voting for a pro–reform candidate would have to do so under the disapproving eyes of the local bigwigs.

The 'wishes, claims, desires and complaints' of the people were to be recorded in *'cahiers de doléances'*, a medieval–sounding name that could be translated as 'grievance notebooks'. In practice they were complaints books. And eventually there would be between 40,000 and 60,000 of them – according to different estimates – written after public meetings to discuss how the people of France envisaged their social and political future.

Many of these *cahiers de doléances* have survived, and they can often be found on the websites of French towns or regions, both as scans of the original pages and in transcripts of the text. There are also thousands of them in the Bibliothèque nationale. They range from long, well-structured treatises on general reforms to 20 lines describing the hard life of a village ploughman. Those bearing signatures show that some of the contributors could barely scratch their surnames, and lists of contributors printed alongside the *doléances* show that some people didn't sign at all, presumably because they were illiterate.

In French history books, these *cahiers* are usually quoted as stinging indictments of everything that was wrong with pre-Revolution France. The vast majority of them abound with tales of privilege, corruption, oppression and abuse. The implication is, of course, that the Revolution couldn't come soon enough.

The weakness with this argument is obvious. *Of course* the *cahiers* describe the terrible inequalities that blighted France in 1789. That was what they were designed to do. If a company chairperson asks for a frank assessment of the problems afflicting the workforce, he or she is not going to hear that everything is wonderful – especially (and this is the key point) if he or she has asked for the assessment precisely because he or she has been trying to improve things, and keeps getting stopped by the overpaid, self-preserving company directors. The complaints will be even more outspoken if the workers know that the idea is to put together an overwhelming list of problems so that the chairperson can force the company directors to give in and accept change.

Surely it is a point in Louis XVI's favour that he commissioned the *cahiers de doléances*. This was free speech at its freest. It was not just a few irritated intellectuals writing obscene plays about the King's sexual problems; this was to be a hard-hitting analysis of genuine everyday problems that affected the well-being and survival of the whole population. In democratic terms, it was much more representative than a yes-no referendum, which is so often presented these days as a victory for the people. Here was a leader saying, 'Go on, say exactly what you think, and no one will get locked up for doing so.' Compare that, for example, with the number of people who would later be guillotined or hacked to bits for criticizing the Revolution.

Complicated though it was, Louis and his ministers tried to make the consultation process as wide as possible – within the bounds of what was considered democratic at the time. At previous États généraux, in 1467 and 1484 for example, delegates had met to discuss all the grievances in the *cahiers* before presenting a summary to the King. This time, though, in theory, each *état* – nobility, clergy and commoners – in every parish was to fill out its own complaints book that would be forwarded to its delegate, who would then produce a list of the most frequent grievances that would be debated in front of the King. In many towns, individual professions were invited to submit their own *cahier* – in Évreux in Normandy, for example, 18 different trades listed their grievances, including butchers, bakers, clockmakers, bailiffs, basket-makers, gardeners, wigmakers and horse renters.

As with the election of delegates, the writing of the *cahiers de doléances* was not what we would now call democratic. For a start, women were excluded, as they had been from becoming delegates – though in reality some women who were heads of their family did get to participate in the meetings. Secondly, the *cahiers* obviously had to be written by someone literate – a village priest, for example, who might be tempted to edit the grievances of his illiterate parishioners to protect himself and the clergy. Many of the discussions to decide what to write were held in churches, priests' houses, or even the local château, so some commoners must have felt as though they were in hostile territory. Lastly, servants, the unemployed and beggars were not invited to offer their opinions on the grounds that they didn't pay tax – which was arch hypocrisy given that the whole of the noble and clerical *états* were tax-exempt and yet had the right to produce their own *cahiers*.

III

Some of the commoners seem to have imagined that Louis XVI was going to wave his magic wand and solve everyone's individual problems: a *cahier* written in the village of Vuzon, near Orléans, denounces the immoral goings-on '*chez* certain residents...where debauched people get together' (these debauched people presumably wrote their own *cahier* about the spoilsports next door). The town of Corbeil asked for its bridge over the Seine to be repaired. In Moux, Burgundy (where *cahier* was misspelled as *cayer*) some parishioners were unhappy that tax collectors had taken away 'the cow whose milk was meant to feed the baby still in the crib'. In Étiolles, now just south of Paris-Orly airport, residents complained about soldiers from a nearby barracks hunting in their fields: 'They come on horseback or in coaches, in all weathers, at any season, into wheat fields that are ready to harvest, into grape vines ready to be picked.' The farmers' main complaint was that they couldn't attack the hunters without fear of being fined. (This, by the way, was where Louis XV used to come hunting, and where his mistress Madame de Pompadour (then Madame d'Étiolles) would lie in wait, hoping to catch his attention.)

Other *cahiers* were much more general and idealistic: in Champmotteaux, near Paris, people hoped that soon 'public worries will dissolve, and fair weather will succeed the storms that have afflicted good citizens' (a poetic reference to both the social situation and the bad weather). In Gouloux, not far from Dijon, residents requested 'the suppression of all exemptions by privilege and ... the equal repartition of a single income tax'. You don't get much more sweeping than that.

Since most people today believe that France was a boiling mass of revolutionary resentment in 1789, it may come as a surprise that one common theme in most of the *cahiers* written by, or on behalf of, the *tiers état* is their desire for a strong monarchy, and their gratitude to the King for asking their opinion. Even though, by definition, the 'grievance notebooks' describe everything that is wrong with France, they also come across as a profession of faith – or hope, in any case – from the commoners that things will be put right by their benevolent King. As the people of the above-mentioned village of Champmotteaux put it, they hoped that after the current problems have been solved: 'the prince so worthy of love will be truly called the father of his people'. In nearby Ballancourt, they predicted (in heavily misspelt French) that 'God will crown His Majesty's good deeds. He [the King] will inspire the zeal, loyalty, respect and love of his subjects, the happiness of his people, and the contentedness and tranquillity of his kingdom.'

Obviously, these pro-monarchy comments could be dismissed as a case of 'flattery will get us everywhere', but at the very least it shows a willingness to take part in the consultation process with the monarch. Ordinary people weren't dismissing it as a pointless exercise, let alone demanding Louis XVI's head on the point of a sword.

The proof that *le peuple* seem to have been aware of what Louis XVI, via his various ministers, had been trying to achieve over the previous years is that the demands made by the *tiers état* in their *cahiers de doléances* matched almost exactly the measures that Necker, Calonne, Brienne and co. had been presenting to parliament. In general, people wanted to improve their life through reform, not revolution.

Most of the commoners were desperate to replace the complex, unfair tax system with a simple per capita income tax and a property tax – without any exemptions for the aristocracy or the clergy. They wanted the *corvée* (free labour provided to the lord or King) to be abolished. They denounced the inefficiency and corruption of judges (many of whom were noble parliamentarians, of course), and demanded an end to all vestiges of feudal law. Peasants wanted the right to hunt and fish on their own land rather than letting noble (and royal) riders come trampling through their crops. Many commoners also hinted politely that the royal family might be able to live off their property rather than receiving money from the state.

Some suggested that noble titles should no longer be inherited, and must be given only for services to the nation. There were also many calls for one-man one-vote (not one-woman) at the États généraux instead of representation according to one's estate.

Clergy-bashing was frequent and varied. There were demands for the Church's money to be spent on charity for the poor. Many thought that all monks and nuns in priories and convents who didn't actually do anything except pray should be asked to take on practical work, like teaching and nursing. Some parishes wanted to elect their priest, which might have given rise to some extreme election promises ('Vote for me and get access to the aristocrats' section of heaven').

Naturally, the *tiers état*'s fiercest criticism of the clergy was aimed at the obscenely rich bishops (it has been said that this was especially the case when poor parish priests transcribed villagers' demands). In Mirabeau, Provence, the *cahier* bristled with fury: 'Of all the abuses that exist in France, the most damaging for the people, the most desperate for the poor, is the immense wealth, the idleness, the exemptions, and the unheard-of luxury enjoyed by the senior clergy. Most of this wealth is made up of the sweat of the people.'

Even so, religion itself did not usually come under attack, and some *cahiers* requested extra holy days and religious processions to ward off the hail and frost that had decimated the previous year's crops.

Tellingly, almost none of the commoners' most frequent *doléances* expressed opposition to what Louis XVI had been trying to do for 15 years or so. If the *tiers état*'s main demands had been enacted, it would have been as though Necker's original plans had finally been voted through – although Louis XVI might have found himself a little poorer than he intended, and

Marie-Antoinette would certainly not have been able to afford any more necklaces for a while.

In short, if the *tiers état* had got their way in May 1789, there would have been no revolution – unless of course the aristocrats and bishops had drawn their swords and bibles and stormed the palace of Versailles. Which was, in fact, more or less what they were about to do.

IV

It would be a mistake to forget the *cahiers de doléances* written by the 4 per cent or so of the population that made up the other two *états*.

The main demands of the nobility were predictable. They wanted their rights to their titles and properties to be confirmed, and for the three estates voting system to be conserved. They also wanted the abolition of *lettres de cachet* – warrants signed by the King that could imprison or exile anyone, including an aristocrat, without trial. This was the weapon that Louis XVI had often used against recalcitrant parliamentarians, so abolishing it would make the Crown even less powerful against militants in favour of the unfair status quo.

Surprisingly, though, there were voices for change even amongst the nobility. Or amongst people who were posing as reformers, anyway.

Louis XVI's cousin, Louis Philippe d'Orléans, the great-grandson of the Philippe d'Orléans who had tasted power as regent for Louis XV, had his eye on the throne in case of a partial revolution. He was now overtly setting himself up as a liberal, a sort of 'people's prince' in favour of constitutional monarchy, and started to conspire actively against Louis XVI. As we shall see, he would later be suspected of organizing some of the riots that led to the downfall of Versailles – indeed, during the Revolution he would change his name to 'Philippe Égalité' and vote in favour of his cousin's execution. Not that it did him much good – he himself was guillotined during la Terreur in 1793.

In 1787, Louis Philippe had called for the États généraux to be convened, claiming this to be a pro-democracy stance. In early 1789, he got his secretary Laclos to pen a 40-page plan advising 'liberal' nobles what to put in their *cahiers* – or rather instructing them: the plan was entitled *Instructions sent by Monsieur the Duc d'Orléans*. Amongst his first suggestions were calls for freedom of expression and a guarantee that no one could be imprisoned without the authority of a judge – this sounds very liberal, but it was no doubt a bit of self-preservation in case Louis XVI took offence at his political manoeuvrings.

Louis Philippe declared himself in favour of fiscal reform – 'income tax will be general and equally applied'. Again, all very liberal, though he specified that reform must be voted by the (non-democratic) États généraux, which would meet regularly to confirm or revoke taxes. He also said that 'in the case of a change of reign, or a regency', the États généraux would be convened 'within six weeks to two months'. What he seemed to be saying was: 'Put me on the throne and you'll have a constitutional monarchy almost immediately.'

However, given that upholding the estates system would assure the clergy and the nobility of victory when any reform was debated, this was fake democracy at its most hypocritical. Louis Philippe's new monarchy or regency would be no more subject to democratic control than Louis XVI was. In fact, the two pro-privilege estates would be much easier to control than the headstrong parliament that was standing up against Louis XVI's reforms.

And some of Louis Philippe's 'instructions' to his peers supported the status quo at its quo-est. As one of the richest men in France, and the owner of the Palais-Royal in central Paris, he advised the nobles to demand that 'all property rights be inviolable, that no one may be deprived of them, even in the public interest, unless he is compensated at the highest price and with minimum delay'. He was determined that no reforms would make him or his class any poorer.

Louis Philippe's influence on the noble estate's *cahiers de doléances* is clear. Many of them made liberal-sounding noises while resisting real change. Some offered to end feudal rights (as long as they were compensated by the peasants concerned); to reduce the number of overpaid, often fake, jobs held by certain nobles (who usually had a decent income from their lands anyway); to encourage free trade and major building projects like roads and canals (which they could invest in). Some aristocrats even said that they would like to be seen as protectors of the poor (the occasional charitable handout made them look good – a policy that Louis Philippe himself adopted during the winter of 1788–9).

In short, a lot of the nobles' 'liberalism' was no more than false electoral promises and fake news.

The clergy, meanwhile, did something similar, reaffirming their key rights while making apparent concessions.

They restated their own importance to the nation – the clergy of Saintonge on the southwest coast warned that 'the throne and the altar share the same foundation; neither can be toppled without the other.'

In Montargis, near Orléans, the clergy's *cahier* opened its chapter on religion with a clause suggesting a backward move: 'Since our holy religion possesses a purity that admits no dilution, let it be requested of the King that, respectful of his sacred vow, he should permit, throughout his kingdom, no public worship other than that of the Catholic religion.' This was an open attack on Louis XVI for allowing Protestants and Jews the freedom to worship.

These same clergymen of Montargis demanded that all schoolteachers should be Catholic, and that authors of blasphemous and immoral books should be subject to 'humiliating punishments'. In the *cahiers*, plenty of priests seized the opportunity to take a swipe at freethinking. In Auch, they moaned that 'a spirit of philosophy and impiety has caused the most lethal attack on faith and morals.'

However, there were also clergymen with more truly Christian concerns. Many offered to pay taxes (as long as the nobles did), called for a clean-up of the justice system, for more free schools, for more vets to be trained so that poor farmers could keep their animals alive, and for quack doctors to be outlawed, to prevent poor, gullible people wasting their money on fake remedies. Many churchmen seemed to have real sympathy for the plight of their poorer flocks – as long as they kept the faith, of course.

V

Women's exclusion from the official process did not stop them publishing some of their own – unofficial – lists of grievances. In the Bibliothèque nationale, there is a *Cahier des doléances des demoiselles*, an anonymous eight-point plan that begins by asking women: 'Should we observe with indifference the advent of this memorable time that is to define for ever the happiness of France?'

It is subtitled 'A speech given by Mademoiselle P..., presiding over the assembly', though it is not clear which assembly this was, or if the text was ever read out in public. No matter: here was a woman saying 'this is how a *cahier de doléances* would look if only we had gender equality.'

The introduction assures men that women can 'focus our minds on other things than frivolities; and women, whom they [men] take too little notice of when it comes to politics, are just as fit to talk about it as they are'.

The author's suggestions include a plea that 'fathers should give the same education to both their sons and daughters', so that 'women of the next generation will be well enough educated to get involved in all occupations, and, without flattering ourselves, things will be all the better for it'.

Things get slightly surreal when the author demands a tax on unmarried men that will be divided between the state and 'poor single girls who have passed the age of 40 and can prove that they truly wanted to get married', but overall it is a simple call for the most basic equal rights.

The Bibliothèque nationale also has a more teasingly written *Cahier des représentations & doléances du beau sexe* (the fair sex), which was published in 1789, and apparently written by women who had been infuriated by the all-male discussions for the official *cahiers de doléances*. It is addressed to the King ('Sire'), and starts by saying that 'we are accused of being chatty … [but] these grievances come after the endless and insolent chattering of the men.'

Its only downfall is that it was obviously written by a bunch of moralizing female aristocrats, and includes a diatribe against 'worldly women [a euphemism for chic ladies of ill repute] and a call for people to attack them in the street and 'cover the carriage, its mistress and her servants in mud'. If these loose women are aristocrats 'out alone, without a male escort or servants, at an hour at which they are abandoned to everything that is most vile and scornful in the class of low-life women', then the authors think they should be sent to a convent for several months. It is a bizarre tirade that might well have been intended as a warning to some of Marie-Antoinette's more shameless friends.

But overall, even these moralizing women are serious in their wish for a better France ('We admit that there are abuses, and they must be reformed') and in their grievance that 'we have been both surprised and humiliated not to be invited to the États généraux.'

VI

In the light of the predictable division along class lines in the official *cahiers de doléances*, the question was: How on earth were the États généraux going to achieve anything?

The equally predictable answer was that they weren't. The social climate was simply too tense for reasoned debate.

Today, on show in the salle du Jeu de paume[2] in Versailles, there are some engravings from 1789 that illustrate this. One

[2] For more about this room's role in the Revolution, see section X below.

shows noble and clerical delegates driving to the États généraux in a luxurious carriage pulled by lions. Its pair is a drawing of *tiers état* delegates in a much simpler vehicle harnessed to a cow and some dogs. Together, they give a neat visual summary of the divisions that the États généraux was going to do nothing to reduce.

In the same room, amongst the marble busts of famous Revolution-era activists, is a severe-looking man in a tight wig and high clerical collar, his mouth clenched above a small but forceful chin. The general impression he creates is one of moral rigidity and impatience. This was an abbot from Chartres called Emmanuel-Joseph Sieyès. In January 1789, when Louis XVI was issuing his call for the *cahiers de doléances* to be written, Sieyès published a well-founded but inflammatory pamphlet called *Qu'est-ce que le tiers état?* (*What is the Third Estate?*). In his view, it meant much more than being neither an aristocrat nor a cleric.

Sieyès was a high-ranking member of the Church – a former chaplain to one of Louis XVI's aunts and an advisor to France's clerical assembly, the body that managed the Church's tax income. But he seems to have grown discontented with life in the establishment, first writing an *Essay on Privileges* in 1788 ('the object of all privileges is to be exempt from the law'), and then his best-known pamphlet that was designed to give the motley mix of commoners in the *tiers état* a sense of shared identity.

The most commonly quoted lines from *Qu'est-ce que le tiers état?* are the opening points in his introduction, which are a typically French exercise in answering one's own rhetorical questions:

1. What is the Third Estate? EVERYTHING.
2. Until now, what has it been in the political hierarchy? NOTHING.
3. What does it want? TO BE SOMETHING.

It is highly effective rhetoric, though, like the chants for a protest march, and must have grabbed the attention of every literate French person who opened it, and every illiterate one who heard about it.

After the introduction, in some 80–odd dense pages (probably beyond the reading ability of most members of the *tiers état*), Sieyès explains his aspirations for a society in which the 4 per cent of nobles and clergy in the population would lose their privileges and the 96 per cent obtain the political rights they deserve. Nobles, he says 'are a burden on the nation', while the *tiers état* has to do 'all the work that maintains society', so that denying them fair representation is 'a social crime'. The only solution, Sieyès said, was to scrap the three estates and have a single electorate, 'the nation', which would make all laws: 'Its will is always legal. It is the law.' The implication was clear – the commoners would take all the decisions.

Sieyès did not say that he wanted to overthrow the monarchy (the word doesn't even appear in the text), and he accuses the nobles of threatening 'the King and the People', so he even seemed to see some common cause between the *tiers état* and Louis XVI. He simply wanted to take privilege out of the political equation, so that the King would implement the commoners' reforms instead of having to bow to the rich parliamentarians' opposition. Which was more or less what Louis XVI had been trying to do for years.

Sieyès took his ideas to their logical conclusion, and warned that it was no use the *tiers état* even participating in the États généraux unless its interests were going to be justly represented: 'By its presence it would only consecrate the oppression of which it would be the eternal victim.' He didn't call for a boycott – on the contrary, he urged delegates to demand fair representation in every vote there. But he was undermining the whole process before it began.

In early 1789, *Qu'est-ce que le tiers état?* became a nationwide bestseller. It didn't bode well for the discussions at Versailles in May.

VII

In April 1789, there was an outbreak of social unrest in Paris that would neatly sum up much of what was to happen later in the year.

After the cruel winter and bad harvests of the previous year, bread prices had risen. As the election of Parisian delegates for the États généraux got under way, there were rumblings of discontent from poor workers that they were not allowed to vote – in Paris, the tax threshold for voters was set higher than elsewhere (for once, low taxes were a disadvantage because they excluded you from the vote). With Sieyès's ideas doing the rounds, and every café and street corner echoing to the sound of political debate, feelings were running high.

On 23 April, one of Paris's best-known industrialists and employers went to speak at a debate held by *tiers état* voters. This was Jean-Baptiste Réveillon, owner of the Paris wallpaper factory that had made the Montgolfier brothers' hot-air balloons and hosted the world's first-ever manned flight.

Réveillon was a poor worker made good. He had started out as a humble carpenter and built up a business that had allowed him to buy a mansion just outside the eastern edge of Paris, with a garden big enough for balloon-testing, and workshops that employed about 350 workers.

One of the secrets of Réveillon's financial success was that he had managed to outmanoeuvre the powerful craftsmen's guilds by saying that his production methods were too new to fit in with their traditional definitions of skilled trades. It was a version of union-busting, and had earned him enemies amongst a well-off and well-organized section of the working population. He had got permission to do this thanks to the royal patronage he earned from the Montgolfiers' airborne exploits, so he was seen as a bit of a '*privilégié*'. Even so, he was known as a fairly benevolent employer, paying decent wages despite ignoring the guilds' set rates.

So when Réveillon stood up to speak about bread prices at the debate on 23 April, his listeners would have known him as a

60-something self-made man who lived in luxury (he was rumoured to have 50,000 books in his library, and thousands of bottles of wine in his cellar), but who prided himself as someone who understood the concerns of the underprivileged. After all, he still lived on site, and saw the poor houses of his workers every time he stepped, or rode, out of his front gate.

There were of course no microphones at the meeting, so not everyone would have heard his every word. And there were hungry, anxious people present, so not everyone would have appreciated the subtleties of his economic arguments.

Today, no one can quite agree what he actually said, but the gist seems to have been that one way to cut the price of bread was to abolish the import duty on grain and open up the market. Supplies would then flood in, and prices would automatically drop. In this way, even the poorest workers at his factory would be able to afford to eat, just as they could back in the days when they earned 15 *sous* instead of the current 25.

To Réveillon, no doubt the key part of his message was 'cut the price of bread'. To the rumour-mongers who left the meeting and started gossiping about him, it was '15 *sous* instead of the current 25'. It was alleged that he wanted to cut wages almost in half.

The upshot was that on 27 April, a crowd of poor Parisians marched towards the Hôtel de Ville (city hall, about a kilometre from Réveillon's factory), shouting amongst other things, 'death to the rich' and 'throw the effing priests in the river'. Outside the Hôtel de Ville, on the place de Grève, where criminals were executed and which has given its name to the modern French language as the word for an industrial strike (*une grève*), an effigy of Réveillon was burned. The mob then returned to Réveillon's factory and tried to storm it, but were stopped by about 50 soldiers.

Next day, a crowd reassembled to protest outside the factory, and were visited by the royal troublemaker Louis Philippe d'Orléans, who gave a speech, threw cash to the crowd and earned himself an ovation before going back to his own life of luxury. Tellingly, it is generally accepted that none of Réveillon's employees were in this crowd – he had probably been able to explain to them how he had been misquoted.

On the evening of 28 April, a carriage belonging to Louis Philippe's wife crossed the army barricade, allowing the mob to break through and enter Réveillon's property. For two hours, rioters rampaged around the compound, destroying everything they could lay their hands on. Furniture, mirrors and doors were smashed or burned, as were Réveillon's stocks of paper, his clothes and his accounts books. They even ripped out his iron banisters and marble fireplaces. (A few days later, while taking refuge in the nearby Bastille, Réveillon issued a statement saying that the estimated cost of repairs to his house was 50,000 to 60,000 *livres* – not a very diplomatic message to broadcast while people were still rioting about bread prices.)

During the riot at the factory, soldiers opened fire on the mob, killing – depending on whom you believe – between 25 and 900 rioters.[3] A dozen or so soldiers were also killed, and about 80 injured. Réveillon and his family were still at home at the time, and had to climb over the wall to escape with their lives.

Réveillon himself was at a loss to understand what had gone wrong. There have since been conspiracy theories that Louis Philippe and/or his secretary Laclos encouraged or even organized the riot. Why else, people ask, did Louis Philippe's carriage emerge unscathed? Why did no one in the crowd attack him after they had been chanting 'death to the rich'? Certainly, at the very least, Louis Philippe's visit to the barricades was a piece of shameless politicking.

But Réveillon may well have been simply a victim of fake news, and an easy target for mob violence, especially if the mob had been incited by the guilds whose financial power Réveillon had undercut. Tellingly, even in modern French historical

---

[3] These days, giving hugely different estimates of numbers of protesters is still common practice in France – the usual phrase is 'X according to the police, Y according to the organizers'.

sources, the element of populist vandalism powered by fake news is often downplayed, probably to avoid sullying the image of the idealistic *peuple* of 1789. In France, the pillaging of France's most famous wallpaper factory is usually referred to neutrally as the 'Réveillon Affair'. In the Larousse online encyclopedia, it gets just three rather misleading lines: 'The wallpaper factory of J-B Réveillon was pillaged and burnt by its workers, who were joined by many workers from the neighbourhood. The army intervention caused 300 deaths.'

In other words, according to this modern encyclopedia, the event was an example of pre-revolutionary terror tactics by Louis XVI's regime.

In a short booklet called the *Exposé justificatif*, written while Réveillon was in hiding at the Bastille, he did his best to defend his name, claiming that he paid most of his workers 30, 35 or 40 *sous* per day, and had only said that he would like them 'to be able to live on 15 *sous* a day'. He argued that during the previous harsh winter, when it was so cold that he had been forced to shut down some of his workshops, 'I kept on ALL the workers without exception, and paid them the same daily rate as before.' Réveillon claimed that: 'Cruel enemies (I don't know who they can be) dared to depict me to the people as a barbarian who puts no value on the sweat of the unfortunate.' He ended his argument for the defence by asking: 'What are my faults? I have never hurt anyone, even the ill-intentioned. I have made people ungrateful, but never poor.'

The unfortunate thing for him was that springtime in Paris in 1789 was not a season for subtle economic debate. Feelings were running much too high. Which is why the États généraux were about to suffer much the same fate as Réveillon's reputation and his factory.

VIII

The night before the delegates were due to parade through Versailles on their way to their first debating session, it was raining heavily. Louis XVI was worried. According to his page, Félix d'Hézecques, 'while getting ready for bed, the King was constantly looking out of the window at the weather. He gave the order that, if it had stopped raining at five in the morning, tapestries should be hung along the route of the procession.' A poignant detail, as though Louis wanted everyone to feel welcome when they visited his home town.

However, the King and his entourage were well aware by now that confrontation was inevitable. As Hézecques describes it (albeit with hindsight and extreme loyalty to Louis XVI): 'Rare were those who came with pure and honest intentions.' He lists the conflicts between the upper and lower clergy, between 'provincial' and Versailles aristocrats, and the *tiers état* and everyone else, before concluding that 'all these delegates, who should have had just one goal, that of supporting the virtuous monarch in his noble projects, brought only their secret hatreds, an unfortunate spirit of division, and all the passions that can grow in the human heart.'

Amongst ordinary people, the sense of expectation was overwhelming. Heralds in violet coats embroidered with royal fleurs-de-lys toured Versailles on white horses, accompanied by troops and trumpeters, to proclaim the opening of the États généraux. Residents had rented out their windows and balconies at extortionate prices to spectators who wanted to watch the King and the delegates parade. Meanwhile delegates from all over the country moved into inns and supporters' houses, and the whole town was abuzz with plots and predictions.

Ceremonies began on 1 May, four days before the official start of the debates – and, coincidentally, one day after George Washington had been sworn in in New York as the first President of the USA (not that the news would have travelled across the Atlantic yet).

On the fourth, which turned out to be rain-free, 1,139 delegates met at the church of Notre-Dame de Versailles, a few streets away from the château. In a diplomatic move, the King and his party went to join them there, riding in a dozen carriages pulled by plumed horses, and preceded by a troop of mounted falconers, their birds on their wrists (perhaps Louis hoped to get in a bit of sparrow-hunting on the way).

The official procession then began, with delegates divided into their estates, parading between ranks of soldiers who were keeping the huge crowds at bay – people from Paris and the whole country had flooded in to attend what everyone recognized as the great showdown that would determine the fate of the nation.

In the cortège, divisions between the factions were clearly visible. The 578 *tiers état* delegates were dressed in simple black suits with short capes, the costume of an ordinary lawyer. They were followed by the 270 nobles in all their finery, with plumed hats, blue coats, and cloaks and waistcoats covered in cloth of gold, many of the men wearing the medals of the noble orders they belonged to. Unlike the *tiers état*, the nobles were allowed to carry swords. The clergy's 291 delegates came next, and were divided between simply dressed parish priests and the high clergy in their surplices and capes, with pride of place given to the venerable 76-year-old Archbishop (and delegate) of Rouen, Dominique de la Rochefoucauld, in his purple robes.

Next came non-delegates, headed by priests from Paris and Versailles who had been invited to give their blessing to the occasion. This was Louis XVI's own idea – on 29 April he had written to the Archbishop of Paris saying that he wanted to 'turn towards God to ask for his assistance and his celestial favour at this great and remarkable assembly of the États généraux', and asking the archbishop to bring along the Holy Sacrament. Louis needed all the help he could get. So on 4 May, everyone saw the Archbishop of Paris solemnly carrying the Holy Sacrament, and sheltering beneath an awning carried by Louis XVI's brothers Charles and Louis Stanislas, and Charles's sons, 13-year-old Louis Antoine and Charles Ferdinand, aged only 11.

Finally it was the turn of the royal couple. Louis XVI had refused the distinction of having his own awning, and walked unshaded, his gold cloak and jewel-encrusted coat glittering in the sun, along with a hat featuring a huge 140-carat diamond called le Régent that both Louis XV and XVI had worn at their coronation, and which Marie-Antoinette had since requisitioned as part of her finery. Now it was back where it belonged.

Next to Louis XVI in the procession came Marie-Antoinette, her silver dress spangled with diamonds and her hair decorated with crown imperials – large, lily-like flowers that are often cultivated because they keep moles away.

According to Félix d'Hézecques, the crowd's sympathies were made very obvious. The *tiers état* were greeted by loud applause that stopped abruptly when the nobles appeared. The only high-ranking delegate to attract any cheers was the self-styled liberal, Louis Philippe, who had decided to parade as part of the cortège of swordless *tiers état* delegates rather than with the royal family (where he might have been asked to help carry the archbishop's awning). Relative silence also greeted the arrival of the clergy, and then, finally, came Louis XVI who 'received a few marks of affection' – a very muted phrase which suggests that Hézecques was shocked by the lack of public enthusiasm for the King. Apparently there were no shouts at all of *'Vive la Reine!'* Marie-Antoinette was greeted with stony silence, or even hissing. She was definitely out of favour.

Apart from Louis Philippe, the bishops and the royal couple, the most noticeable individual in the procession was 51-year-old Michel Gérard from Rennes in Brittany, the only peasant delegate, who chose to parade in his working clothes. The causes he had come to defend were an abolition of the tax on distillers of homemade alcohol and a pay rise for parish priests. He was the only *tiers état* delegate whom Louis XVI had gone to greet personally, an apparently spontaneous and yet hugely symbolic meeting of the highest and lowest members of the social pecking order at the États généraux. It was another sign of the King's almost naive attempt to treat these proceedings as a momentous, yet even-handed, coming-together of the different groups that made up the nation.

The route of the procession led its members two kilometres or so to another church, the cathedral of Saint Louis, where the delegates heard a rousing sermon from the Bishop of Nancy, Anne-Louis-Henri de la Fare. He was a duke, but he believed that the Church should bear its share of the country's financial burdens. He gave a speech contrasting this show of wealth and luxury with the abject living conditions of the peasantry. It apparently sent Louis XVI to sleep, but he was awoken by a thunderous round of applause that shook the more reverential believers in the cathedral – it was the first time anyone had ever clapped a sermon there. Hézecques called the applause a 'lack of respect for the Divinity' and 'the first blow of the axe to the altar'.

The actual opening of the États généraux the next day was no less disrespectful of traditions. It began in an orderly enough fashion, with the delegates taking their places in the debating chamber that had been set up in the Menus-Plaisirs, the rather austere set of buildings that had previously been home to Louis XVI's party accessories. This was where the 1787 Assemblée des notables had taken place.

It could be said, though, that returning there was something of a diplomatic gaffe. The Assemblée des notables had been a much smaller gathering. And two years earlier, the relatively modest, improvised setting had almost been a gesture of humility – the King and his *notables* did not need to meet in palatial surroundings. Now, though, commoners were coming to debate in Versailles. It might have been more tactful to house them in grander surroundings – the Grand Trianon, for example, where Louis XIV used to hold ministerial get-togethers. But that would have meant inviting all the delegates into the palace grounds, a potentially threatening move. The basic problem was, of course, that France had no building for its elected representatives – for the simple reason that it had had no elected representatives.

Paintings show that the debating chamber set up in the Menus-Plaisirs was a vast hall packed with delegates, and it was apparently hard to make oneself heard unless one spoke with a clear, firm voice. On a raised platform at the top of the room stood a throne, under a violet canopy adorned with golden fleurs-de-lys. The *tiers état* delegates were seated in front of the throne, in the centre of the room. Along the wall to the left of the throne were the nobility, and opposite them, the clergy.

When Louis XVI and his family came to take their places on the royal stage, all of them dressed in full regalia to impress on everyone the solemnity of the occasion, Louis noticed that his cousin, Louis Philippe, was sitting out in the chamber, having now joined the noble delegates. The King sent a message asking him to sit with his family. Louis Philippe, typically, refused. The revolt had begun before a single speech had been given.

Louis XVI then welcomed the delegates, saying (by all accounts in a clear, firm voice) that 'the day that my heart has awaited for so long has arrived', repeating his old idea that taxes were felt harshly because of their 'unequal distribution', and recognizing that 'minds are agitated, but an assembly of the representatives of the nation will no doubt heed the counsel of wisdom and prudence'. He ended with a wish that 'a happy harmony may reign in this assembly, and that this time may be forever remembered as one of happiness and prosperity for the Kingdom'.

As he spoke, a ray of sunlight shone through the skylights in the ceiling and lit up the King's face. According to Hézecques, this 'inspired a sentiment of profound veneration in all generous hearts' (and especially the superstitious ones, it is tempting to add). In any case, the speech seemed to unite the room for an instant, and Louis XVI received a hearty ovation.

This was, however, one of the last moments of harmony that the monarchy would enjoy. Louis invited Necker to stand up and outline his proposals on how to stabilize the nation's finances without overtaxing the poor, and the Swiss financier killed off all the goodwill that the King's short speech had earned him by pulling a ream of paper out of his pocket and rambling on in characteristically absurd detail for one and a half hours.

When Necker's voice gave out with the effort of making himself heard, he got a doctor to read the rest of his text – for another hour. What was worse, he seemed to be offering nothing more than a watered-down version of his earlier, radical plans to democratize taxes and voting, with a bottom line that what he needed was 56 million *livres* to pay off the national debt and cure the country's problems.

This was exactly what the delegates did not want to hear. At a time when politics had been distilled into impatient three-line demands like the introduction to Sieyès's *Qu'est-ce que le tiers état?* and when more than 1,000 delegates had come to Versailles armed with their *cahiers* of complaints and reforms, Necker's verbiage made it sound as though nothing was ever going to change.

As the first day's session came to an end with no concrete signs that progress was going to be made, it had become a virtual certainty that pent-up frustrations were about to explode.

IX

From now on, things moved very quickly. Instead of Louis XVI leading the combined delegates in 'happy harmony' to decisions marked by 'wisdom and prudence', the *tiers état* made its bid for power.

The plan was for each estate to read its *cahiers de doléances* individually, then come together for plenary sessions at which issues would be decided according to how each estate voted – that is, the nobles and the clergy could join to outvote the *tiers état* by two estates to one.

However, the *tiers état* had begun their debates early. They had already decided to oppose the usual practice whereby commoners had to kneel when they addressed the King, and Paris delegates had proposed a motion that 'in all political societies, all men are equal' (and, more worryingly in the light of subsequent events, 'the will of everyone shapes the law; public force ensures its execution'). With this spirit of defiance in the air, they were keen to impose their majority, and they moved into the main chamber, calling for the others to join them there, to form a single house with one delegate, one vote. Predictably, both the nobles and the clergy voted not to do so (though by no means unanimously – in a bizarre coincidence, exactly 114 voters from each of the two estates wanted to go and join the *tiers état*).

While delegates from each section of the population carried on talking to themselves, with the *tiers état* becoming increasingly demanding, tragedy struck Louis XVI and Marie-Antoinette. Their seven-year-old son Louis Joseph, the heir to the throne, died. He had been ill for a long time, with (amongst other things) tuberculosis, curvature of the spine and unidentified fevers. He had watched the procession of the delegates from a crib set up on a balcony of the palace of Versailles, waving feebly as his parents passed. After the ceremony, with his condition worsening, he had been sent to the supposedly healthy air of a royal château in the nearby forest of Meudon, where Louis XVI had been riding the ten kilometres to visit him almost every day. He had even gone there immediately after the opening of the États généraux on 5 May. The boy died at one in the morning on 4 June. It must have seemed like a grim omen of what was to come for the monarchy. Louis took mass in private that day, and saw only his immediate entourage. He also asked for audiences with delegates to be postponed for a few days, but the *tiers état* refused, prompting him to ask them: 'Are there no fathers in this assembly?'

Sieyès, the author of *Qu'est-ce le tiers état?*, decided that his fellow commoners had waited long enough, and proposed an ultimatum. The *tiers état* would vote on a new power structure, with or without the other two estates. He called for rebel nobles and clergymen to join the *tiers état* and agree that from now on, all debates would be decided on a one-man, one-vote basis, by a single assembly instead of the three estates. A few reforming clergymen broke ranks, but it was obvious that the bishops and the nobles weren't going to give up their privileges, so the commoners went ahead.

The only real question was what to call their new, single house of parliament. Sieyès suggested 'Assembly of known and veri-fied representatives of the French nation'. A 30-year-old-lawyer called Jean-Joseph Mounier, the delegate who had been sent to ask the clergy to join the debate, had a slightly different sugges-tion: 'Legitimate assembly of representatives of the majority of the nation, acting in the absence of the minority parties'. Fortunately for posterity, the representatives plumped for the much shorter 'Assemblée nationale', which is what the lower house of the French parliament is called today.[4]

Despite the delegates' defiance, the creation of the Assemblée nationale was not an anti-monarchistic move. The delegates invented an oath for themselves, which began very convention-ally: 'We swear to God, to the King and to the Country to fulfil with zeal the functions that we have been given.' (They could have added 'by ourselves'.)

On 20 June, three days after their oath, the members of the new Assemblée nationale arrived to find guards posted in front of locked doors. Foolishly, Louis XVI had reacted by shutting the Menus-Plaisirs. Delegates were told that the building had to be prepared for the next session that the King was going to attend in person. As an excuse, this was about as believable as saying, 'Sorry, I can't vote for tax reform because my arm hurts.'

It seems hard to fathom. Louis XVI, the man who had invited free speech by calling for his people to fill whole books with their complaints and demands, seriously thought that he could silence dissent by denying the delegates a debating chamber. Did he honestly believe that closed doors meant closed mouths? If so, it was a measure both of his naivety and his isolation.

[4] After a few interim name changes – between 1789 and 1799, it would call itself the Assemblée constituante, Assemblée législative, Convention nation-ale, Convention thermidorienne and Directoire, which gives some idea of how the post-revolutionary parliament spent much of its debating time. Though admittedly they did a lot of debating – over those ten years, parlia-ment would meet practically every day, Sundays included.

Louis XVI seems to have believed that everyone would simply get together at the États généraux and calmly agree sensible reforms that he would then implement. He apparently had no inkling that the *tiers état* would come to Versailles intending to scrap their country's law-making process and take power.

Perhaps the biggest problem was that Louis was also being counselled by a Swiss economist who thought that politics was about tables of profit and loss, as well as a gaggle of noble and royal 'advisors' (including his disgruntled wife) who were urging him to show these uppity commoners who was boss.

Sadly, there was no far-sighted politician to advise Louis to go to the new Assemblée and shout, 'Power to the people!' If he had openly declared his support for the *tiers état*, they would probably have carried him to the throne and sworn him in as their spiritual leader.

Louis XVI, though, was not following events closely enough to understand what was going on. Almost every day, he left Versailles, either to visit his son or to go deer hunting, or both – his diary for 3 June read: 'To Meudon on horseback at 4.30 a.m., return by carriage at 10, hunted deer at Marly'. In the first weeks of the États généraux the whole town of Versailles was in uproar, with new political pamphlets appearing every day (Hézecques was horrified to see servants reading them while they stood on duty), but Louis XVI was physically absent half the time, and when present, he often shut himself away (especially just after his son's death and funeral – which took place on the thirteenth).

He may not have realized it, but he had now lost all hold on the reins of power and was slowly but surely toppling from the saddle of monarchy.

X

With their doors closed, the rebel delegates needed a new debating chamber. One of them had an idea. This was a Parisian doctor called Joseph-Ignace Guillotin, who, ironically considering the tool that would later be named after him, had long been a vocal advocate of 'one vote per head'. He suggested going to meet in an indoor tennis court.

This was an interesting choice. The court, known as the salle du Jeu de paume, a name dating from when tennis was played with the palm of one's hand, was tucked away down a side street just a few yards outside the palace fences. The rebel delegates were going to be moving very close to the heart of royal power. Also, the room, although very high-ceilinged, was tiny – little bigger than a modern tennis court. Today, it is open to visitors, and if there are 50 tourists inside, peacefully milling about, it feels full. Guillotin was proposing that 500-odd vociferous delegates would be crammed in there. Even more if nobles and members of the clergy joined them.

Too bad for the town's tennis players – Guillotin was asked to go and prepare the empty room. Being a doctor, he decided on a layout with seats in a semi-circle facing a table, like a public dissection – an apt metaphor for what the delegates were planning to do to the process of government.

There, in the packed, stuffy room, its walls painted black so that players could see the tennis ball more clearly, the delegates swore a famous oath, 'le serment du Jeu de paume', vowing 'never to separate, and to meet wherever circumstances demand, until the constitution of the Kingdom is established and consolidated on firm foundations'.

But even now, they were not planning to do away with Louis XVI. The oath (which was mainly written by the above-mentioned Sieyès and Mounier) began: 'The National Assembly, considering itself summoned to write the Kingdom's constitution, re-establish public order and uphold the true principles of the monarchy ...' And as we all know, the first principle of monarchy is to have a monarch.

On 23 June, Louis XVI made one more half-hearted attempt to prop up the three estates system, apparently because he simply wanted to impose his authority. He went to the freshly prepared Menus-Plaisirs and gave a speech to a combined session of the nobles, clergy and commoners. First he expressed his impatience that no concrete measures to improve the daily life of the people had been decided – 'a perfect agreement should have been born out of simple love for the country, yet a disastrous division is sowing alarm in everyone's minds.' In other words, all they had done for almost two months was argue about voting rights, when the people wanted action. This much was true.

He then ordered that a paper should be read out: 'The King's Intentions'. In this, he promised to let the États généraux establish fairer taxes, to guarantee free speech, put an end to all elements of feudal law, and reform the clergy as long as the central tenets of religion remained intact. It was more or less exactly what the commoners were demanding. But his language was out of date. Jean Sylvain Bailly, a Parisian astronomer and mathematician, and the *tiers état* delegate who had been elected president of the Assemblée nationale, noted in his memoirs that Louis used phrases like 'the King wishes it' and 'the good deeds of the King towards his people', when most of the delegates were now talking about their own rights.

The conclusion to 'The King's Intentions' was almost defiant. Louis informed delegates that 'knowing your *cahiers*, and the perfect agreement between the general wishes of the people and my benevolent intentions ... I will march towards the goal that I wish to attain, with all the courage and firmness that it inspires in me.' It sounded like a threat – coming from the least threatening man in the room.

At the end of the session, Louis told the assembly: 'I order you, *Messieurs*, to separate immediately, and to go tomorrow morning to the chambers that have been assigned to each of your estates so that you can recommence discussions.'

Louis XVI left, and the nobles followed him, as did the bishops. But the commoners and members of the lower clergy stayed put. Even so, workers began removing seats, and a 27-year-old aristocrat called Henri-Évrard de Dreux-Brézé, who had inherited the job of Royal Master of Ceremonies from his father, asked Bailly whether he had heard the King's order to leave the room.

Bailly replied that he could not disband the Assemblée before it had debated what it had just heard. He is usually quoted as telling young Dreux-Brézé: 'The assembled nation cannot receive orders.' But Bailly himself stressed in his memoirs that 'I respected the King too much to give such a reply', and that what he actually said was: '*Monsieur*, the assembly is adjourned after the royal session, and I cannot disband it until it has deliberated on that.'

At this point, another delegate, Honoré Gabriel de Mirabeau, waded in. He was a 40-year-old aristocrat who, according to his own father, was 'as ugly as Satan's son' (he had a giant head and a complexion ravaged by smallpox), and who had been imprisoned at his father's request for debt and eloping with another man's wife. These imprisonments by *lettre de cachet* (royal seal) had predictably turned Mirabeau against royalty. He had tried to get himself elected as a noble delegate, but they had rejected him, so he had joined the *tiers état*, for whom he now considered himself a mouthpiece, thereby ironically proving the aristocrats' arrogant belief that they knew what was best for the common people. Mirabeau would later become a turncoat and a secret advisor to Louis XVI, while remaining a parliamentarian and claiming to support the Revolution.

After Bailly had given his measured reply to Dreux-Brézé, Mirabeau bellowed something along the lines of: 'Tell those who sent you that bayonets have no power against the will of the people!'

In his memoirs, Bailly noted disapprovingly that 'many have approved this reply, but it wasn't a reply. It was an aside that he should not have made ... Had anyone talked about bayonets? Had anyone threatened force? Had Monsieur de Brézé uttered any threat at all? No.'

The true commoner Bailly was respectful of due process, polite and cool-headed, a worthy leader of the new National

Assembly. Hardly surprising that he would be silenced by the guillotine in 1791.

Dreux-Brézé went to Louis to tell him what had just happened, to which Louis replied with a rare bout of swearing: 'Well, if they don't want to leave, then fuck it, let them stay!'[5]

After this failed showdown, some of the nobles decided to join the National Assembly – among them was, of course, the opportunistic Louis Philippe. Meanwhile, in the streets of Versailles, delegates who were known to be against unifying the three estates were insulted or attacked. Arthur Young reports that the Bishop of Beauvais had a stone thrown at his head; the Archbishop of Paris had to change lodgings after all his windows were broken; and the Cardinal de la Rochefoucauld was 'hissed and booed' wherever he went.

Louis XVI realized that matters had got beyond his control and on 27 June 1789 (another day on which he noted *'Rien'* in his diary), he surrendered completely and ordered the remaining clergy and nobles to unite with the others.

On 9 July, the delegates confirmed the status of the National Assembly, and renamed it the Assemblée nationale constituante, since its purpose was to write a new constitution (although in everyday speech it was still usually referred to as the Assemblée nationale, or just Assemblée). The lawyer Mounier presented a long theoretical paper on what constituted a constitution, the key phrase of which was: 'For a constitution to be good, it must be founded on human rights.' (Though, of course, Mounier wrote 'the rights of *men*'.) This was the idea that would lead a month later to the groundbreaking *Déclaration des droits de l'homme et du citoyen* (citizen) for which the French Revolution is famous.

[5] What Louis actually said was something like: *'S'ils ne veulent pas s'en aller, eh bien foutre qu'ils restent!'* Admittedly, the word *'foutre'* is less vulgar than 'fuck', but it is a vulgar verb that describes the same act.

Incidentally, it is often forgotten that both this new constitution and the declaration of human rights were conceived from a monarchistic point of view. Mounier wrote in his paper that:

A constitution that would precisely determine the rights of the monarch and those of the nation would be as useful to the King as it would be to our fellow citizens. He wants his subjects to be happy; he will benefit from their happiness; and when he acts in the name of the laws that he will have agreed with the representatives of his people, then no organization, no individual, whatever their rank and wealth, will dare to oppose his power. The King's lot will be a thousand times more glorious than that of the most absolute despot.

Radical revolutionaries would argue that this was a half-hearted proposal designed to flatter and convince Louis XVI, or that Mounier should have gone the whole nine metres and suggested abolishing the monarchy. But as we have seen from the *cahiers de doléances*, a republic was not what most French people wanted. They wanted a fairer society overseen by a monarch. Mounier was simply respecting the majority view.

Debates about the wording of this new constitution would go on for two more years, long after the storming of the Bastille, but when it was finally voted through in 1791, it was a document designed to set up a constitutional monarchy, with Louis XVI at its head, and with his own head still very much in place.[6]

To sum up, by 9 July 1789, five days before the violent events that are commemorated today as the official start of the Revolution, France had a (more or less) democratically elected parliament, with a majority of non-aristocratic, non-clerical members. The commoners had finally managed to wrest power away from the rich, self-serving magistrates who had resisted all

---

[6] For more details of the first Constitution, see Part III.

the democratic reforms that both Louis XV and Louis XVI had tried to impose on them. The members of the new Assemblée nationale constituante were about to vote on fair taxes, equal representation, free speech and an end to the abuses of privilege, while maintaining a monarchy. Everyone could now calm down and get on with the practical reforms that the country so urgently needed.

And as Bailly had said, they had achieved all this without anyone reaching for their bayonet – indeed, he admitted in his memoirs that at one point armed guards were on their way to oust the delegates from the Menus-Plaisirs, but they had been recalled, presumably by the King. Louis XVI clearly did not want violence in Versailles. In fact, the only fatality during the États généraux had been one delegate who died of apoplexy just before the first debate.

A revolution of sorts had been enacted, bloodlessly. As the French say when they are happy about the result of something, *'Que demande le peuple?'* What more could the people ask for?

Well, that was precisely the problem...

PART III

The Revolution Goes Astray (for the First Time)

'The French mob ... is among the liveliest phenomena of our world. So rapid, audacious; so clear-sighted, inventive, prompt to seize the moment; instinct with life to its finger-ends!'

Thomas Carlyle (1795–1881), safe in London in the 1830s, writing his book *The French Revolution: A History* (1837)

Chapter 12

FRENCH POPULISM
PAR EXCELLENCE

'Quand la lutte s'engage entre le peuple et la Bastille, c'est toujours la Bastille qui finit par avoir tort.'
'When a struggle breaks out between the people and the Bastille, it is always the Bastille that ends up in the wrong.'
Charles de Gaulle (1890–1970), French general and president, in a speech on Bastille Day, 1943

I

As we have seen, in early 1789 there was a window of opportunity for a smooth transition to constitutional change, led by articulate, thoughtful democrats like Bailly and Mounier, who were determined to impose equal rights for all (all males, at least), but who wanted to avoid violence.

However, this window was about to be slammed shut, rather like the falling blade of a guillotine, plummeting France into a period of mob rule, mass panic, civil war and state-endorsed massacre that would continue, with periodic explosions of violence, for almost a hundred years.

The problem was that no one would summon the courage or possess the power to oppose the more violent tendencies of populism. The English traveller Arthur Young attended early sessions of the Assemblée nationale debates in Versailles. He was caught up in the excitement of the fundamental debates going on, and praised the ardour of speakers like Sieyès, Mounier and Mirabeau, but noted something disturbing:

> The spectators in the galleries are allowed to interfere in the debates by clapping their hands, and other noisy expressions of approbation: this is grossly indecent; it is also dangerous; for, if they are permitted to express approbation, they are, by parity of reason, allowed expressions of dissent; and they may hiss as well as clap ... this would be to over-rule the debate and influence the deliberations.

Over the next few years, both in the streets and in the debating chamber, the opinionated, extremist elements of 'the people' would wage a successful campaign of shouting down or physically intimidating the more rational, peaceful reformers.

In this, they would be supported, and even encouraged, by some of the greatest revolutionary 'heroes' like Danton, Robespierre and Marat, who were all rabble-rousers, and all ended up with French blood on their hands. Fittingly perhaps, they were all doomed to fall victim to the violence they encouraged in the mob. Today, the French would be loath to admit it, but what is usually remembered as the most glorious period in their history[1] was in fact a time when a few opportunistic, populist politicians seized power by claiming to be the mouthpiece of *le peuple*, when what the majority of French citizens really wanted was *pain et paix* – bread and peace.

It has always puzzled me why France should have chosen the anniversary of the storming of the Bastille as its national holiday.

---

[1] Apart, perhaps, from the few days in August 1944 during which the Parisians finally rose up and ousted the already teetering Nazi army of occupation.

Admittedly, England commemorates the day when a dragon supposedly got beheaded (or rather, usually forgets to commemorate it). America, on the other hand, which in part served as an example for the French Revolution, never fails to celebrate the adoption of its Declaration of Independence. Every 4 July, Americans are meant to remember the famous sentence 'We hold these Truths to be self-evident, that all Men are created equal, that they are endowed by their Creator with certain unalienable Rights, that among these are Life, Liberty, and the Pursuit of Happiness.' These idealistic sentiments were slightly tainted by the continuation of slavery for almost 90 years and segregation for 100 more, but on 4 July every year, it's the thought that counts. The same cannot really be said of Bastille Day.

Like the Americans, France also adopted a new democratic constitution and a declaration of human rights during its Revolution, but it still chooses to commemorate what in fact was a riot designed to grab a stock of gunpowder held inside a castle. French historians will object that, *non*, it was an attack on a notorious prison, a bastion of royalist authority. But this again is largely fake news – the Bastille was where people were sent by royal *lettres de cachet*, and many of the letters were requested by the prisoners' own aristocratic families, who wanted their errant sons to get a dose of tough love, or to stop them committing more crimes that would dishonour the family name.

On 14 July 1789, there were only seven inmates in the Bastille – four forgers awaiting trial, two men who had been declared insane (including one aristocrat), and a count, Hubert de Solages, who had been sent there at the request of his own family on suspicion of incest with his sister.

Yet, out of all the momentous changes that occurred during the revolutionary years after 1789, this is the event that France has chosen as its greatest national triumph – the morning when disgruntled Parisians took it upon themselves to ignore the fundamental reforms being achieved for them out in the debating halls of Versailles, and decided to start blowing things up.

II

The storming of the Bastille was not even the first event of its kind in Paris that year. As we saw above, a mob had stormed the Réveillon wallpaper factory in April – though it would have been impossible to choose that as the anniversary of the start of the Revolution, because it was little more than misdirected vandalism.

Fearing a repeat of the Réveillon riot, in early July, around 30,000 royal troops were moved into Paris, some of them setting up camp very visibly on the Champ de Mars, by the river where the Eiffel Tower now stands.

On 11 July, Louis XVI sacked his Finance Minister Necker again, less than a year after reinstating him. It is often said that this was because Necker refused to attend the last royal session of the États généraux on 23 June, or that Louis wanted to install a more conservative Finance Minister, but it was also because Necker's dull, purely economic speech during the opening debate had shown that he was badly out of touch with the political climate. Necker was also refusing to work with the new Assemblée – he had to go so that progress with the new constitution could be made.

But by the time news of Necker's dismissal reached Paris the next day, it had been distorted. Instead of the inevitable firing of a man who was resisting change, it was presented as a despotic move by the King who wanted to get rid of the people's champion, the national provider of subsidized grain. Along with the arrival of troops in Paris, it 'proved' that Louis XVI was preparing to stamp out democracy in France.

When this piece of fake news hit the Parisian cafés, where the latest political pamphlets were constantly being dictated and digested, it took very little for the heated atmosphere there to be teased into flames of revolt. A little-known lawyer called Camille Desmoulins, a member of the hot-headed Mirabeau's entourage, is now credited with making the speech that inflamed the mob. It is said that around noon on Sunday, 12 July, he stood on a chair in the Café de Foy,[2] one of the cafés that lined the Palais-Royal gardens (which belonged, incidentally, to the royal troublemaker Louis Philippe), and, with a pistol in one hand and a sword in the other, gave an impromptu speech along the lines of:

> Monsieur Necker has been dismissed. His dismissal is a bell to announce a St Bartholemew's massacre of patriots [a reference to the mass murder of Protestants in Paris in 1572]. Tonight, the Swiss and German battalions [of royal mercenaries] will come out of the Champ-de-Mars to cut our throats. It leaves us with one resource – to take up arms.

This was inflammatory nonsense, a lot like Mirabeau's rant about bayonets a few days earlier. Far from having their throats slit, the patriots were safely installed in Versailles, working on the new constitution. The King's Swiss and German guards were in their barracks, along with their French colleagues, with no orders to massacre anyone.

But when it suits them, people will believe anything. Arthur Young, the English agriculturalist, was in Paris and Versailles at this time, and was generally sympathetic to the Assemblée nationale's aims, but he was appalled by the way fake news about the monarchy was believed in the cafés of the Palais-Royal: 'The reports that were circulated eagerly, tending to show the violent intentions of the court, as if it was bent on the utter extirpation of the French nation ... are perfectly incredible for their gross absurdity: but nothing was so glaringly ridiculous but the mob swallowed it with undiscriminating faith.' He was also 'stunned by the hawkers of seditious pamphlets and descriptions of pretended events, that all tend to keep the people ignorant and alarmed'.

On 12 July, after Camille Desmoulins's speech, an armed but ill-informed mob began parading along the nearby Tuileries

---

[2] After these revolutionary beginnings, in 1790 and 1791, the Café de Foy became a hub for aristocrats who would read out royalist tracts and articles from pro-monarchist newspapers.

gardens, led by men carrying busts of Necker and Louis Philippe. As darkness fell, cavalrymen of the Royal German Regiment came to dispel the crowd, though no one's throat was cut in the process.

Partially fulfilling Desmoulins's prophecy, the Swiss Guards were also sent out into the streets, but their only action was to clash with members of the French Guard when the two royal regiments bumped into each other outside the latter's barracks in the north of Paris.

That night, and during the following day, rioters attacked and burned 40 of the 54 toll booths in the disastrously misconceived Mur des Fermiers généraux, the wall erected in 1784 around the centre of Paris to collect taxes on products brought into the city. With grain scarce and prices high despite Necker's attempt to control them, a tax on wheat was the last thing Paris needed, and the pompous, château-like booths were obvious targets for public resentment.

Just as obvious, but more ill informed, was the attack on the Convent of Saint-Lazare, which was situated near the current railway station of the same name, not far from the barracks of the French Guards. At about 2.30 a.m. on 13 July, around twenty men armed with axes and guns broke into the convent.

Once the first gang had forced its way past the main gate, another twenty-odd men arrived, and began firing their guns into the air. A student came and asked them what they wanted: 'Food and drink,' they answered, so the student opened up a refectory and the men were given meat, bread, wine and cherries. They then threatened to kill him if he didn't give them money. The convent's treasurer came and offered the men a small fortune to leave, but they decided they would rather stay and pillage the place.

Meanwhile, attracted by the sound of gunfire, poor people from the surrounding neighbourhood began a rampage around the corridors of the convent, trashing, burning and stealing, and beating up anyone who stood in their way. The convent's library of some 20,000 books was completely destroyed, as were all the remedies in its dispensary.

The attack is usually explained away by historians as a sort of accident; they say that the rioters were reacting to a rumour that Saint-Lazare was a depot for weapons and grain – implying that the looters were victims of misinformation. But the people who were in the convent at the time describe an outbreak of untamed, random violence. One of the men who lived there even wrote regretfully about the deaths of 'around thirty men and women in the cellar, floating in the wine, drowned after getting drunk', and several who poisoned themselves drinking the spirits in the dispensary.

Predictably, the priests, novices, nuns and philosophy students at Saint-Lazare had no weapons. They did have grain, which was to make bread for the 500 or so members of the community, for a nearby hospital and for distribution to the poor. All this was stolen, along with anything of value that the rioters didn't smash, burn or simply throw out of the windows. A witness called Cousin Jacques lamented after the attack that 'the poor people of the neighbourhood are now deprived for a long time of the abundant help they received [from the convent].'

These eyewitness accounts are collected in a book called *Histoire de Saint-Lazare*, published in 1912 by a certain Eugène Pottet, who had no anti-revolutionary axe to grind – in fact, he says in his introduction to the chapter about the 1789 attack that he believes in the 'progress, true justice and humanity that we owe to the French Revolution'. He is, however, horrified by the senselessness of the attack – 'is it in blood that the ideas of liberty, equality and fraternity must flower?'

It is a question that could be asked of almost everything that was to happen in France over the next four or five years.

III

With even royal troops brawling amongst themselves, it was clearly up to civilians to step in and restore order. The man whose job it now became to keep the peace in Paris was called Jacques de Flesselles. In April 1789, he had been made *prévôt des marchands de Paris* (de facto mayor), replacing a more old-school aristocrat, Louis le Peletier, a former president of the obstructive Paris parliament.

Closer to Necker, Flesselles was a liberal choice. He had been *intendant* (royal administrator) of Lyon for 16 years, during which he had partially democratized the city's income tax system and overseen a boom in its textile industry.

On 13 July 1789, he let 12 of Paris's *électeurs* (men who had voted for the États généraux delegates) come to the Hôtel de Ville (city hall) to join a new municipal council, which elected him president and then demanded the formation of a militia (a *garde bourgeoise*) to protect Paris against mob rule. It was decided that their uniform would be a *cocarde* (rosette) in the city's colours – a blue circle surrounded by red.

That same night, this decision was modified, and white was added between the two colours, forming the now-famous tricolour (which would be adopted as the national flag in 1794). It is usually forgotten, though, that white was then the royal colour. Louis XVI was being symbolically invited to join the new regime.

However, as soon as the formation of this 'guard' was announced, a mob gathered outside the Hôtel de Ville demanding weapons. Apparently fearing that public order was the last thing on his new militia's mind, Flesselles promised (truly or falsely – the debate still rages on) that 12,000 muskets were being sent to arm them. Unsatisfied, a crowd broke into the royal museum of decorative arts, the *garde-meuble royal* (literally, the monarchy's furniture store), on present-day place de la Concorde. Alongside its collection of chairs and tables it held a hoard of historic weapons that were now stolen by the mob. These were quite literally museum pieces, but a mob armed with swords, spears, maces and pikes is a dangerous thing, as Flesselles was soon to find out – to his cost.

In a more orderly fashion, a delegation of formally appointed members of the new militia went to the military hospital at Les

Invalides and demanded their weapons – the governor, a 76-year-old general called Charles François de Virot de Sombreuil, refused, fearing that they were unlikely to be used to appease the climate of violence that was spreading throughout the city. He even got 20 of the hospital's invalids to spend the night of 13–14 July removing the hammers from muskets so that they would be useless. Legend has it that these old soldiers worked extra slowly, thereby making them revolutionary heroes. But given that the armoury at Les Invalides contained 32,000 muskets, even at full speed they would have been hard-pressed to finish.

Early next morning, 14 July, the delegation of militiamen returned, with an armed escort this time, as well as a horde of followers, to repeat their demand for weapons. Sombreuil assured them that he had sent a letter to Versailles asking the King's permission to hand over his muskets. Predictably, the crowd of around 80,000 people surrounding the Invalides didn't want to wait for the morning post, and began to attack the hospital's gates, which were opened without opposition. Either fearing for their lives or supporting the mob's cause, the sentries refused to fire.

The new *garde bourgeoise*, which had been created to maintain public order, was now armed with ancient blades and modern muskets, along with about 20 cannons that had also been taken from the Invalides. All they needed was gunpowder and bullets. And where were they stored? *Ah oui*, an hour's stroll along the river, at the Bastille...

IV

The future *héros de la nation* who were parading around Paris with their mismatched weapons on 14 July 1789 were, it should not be forgotten, meant to be preventing anarchy while the Assemblée nationale constituante finished itemizing the demands in the *cahiers de doléances* and then voted through urgent reforms. In theory, the *garde bourgeoise* was meant to stand side by side with royal troops doing the same peacekeeping job. But for the moment, no royal troops had been ordered to step in.

The only recent use of the army against the people had been to dispel the mob that was trying to stir up trouble in the Tuileries by spreading rumours of an impending massacre. And the regiments of infantry and cavalry encamped on the Champ-de-Mars, literally a ten-minute march from the Invalides, were not sent to protect the weapons store there. Advised that his men would probably refuse to oppose the (enormous) mob, the 67-year-old Swiss general in charge at the Champ-de-Mars, a friend of Marie-Antoinette's called Pierre Victor de Besenval, chose to withdraw his soldiers outside Paris.

The storming of the Bastille (called in French the completely neutral *'prise'*, or 'taking') began, like the Invalides the previous day, with a civilized delegation asking for co-operation from its governor, Bernard-René Jourdan de Launay.[3] A notoriously nervous type, he had already moved his stocks of lead and powder from a store above the entrance gate into an inside courtyard. And like Sombreuil at the Invalides, Launay refused to empty his armoury into the hands of a barely controlled rabble, who had now been joined by some of the people who had ransacked Réveillon's wallpaper factory nearby.

At first, the atmosphere at the Bastille was perfectly cordial, and Launay invited a deputation of citizens inside to share a late breakfast. After all, it had been a restless night for everyone concerned. Predictably, though, when no one emerged from the castle after an hour, a rumour went round that the breakfast guests had been taken prisoner. Even after they came out, full-bellied but empty-handed, feelings were running high.

A second delegation went into the Bastille, and obtained a promise that the governor would not fire the first shot in any

---

[3] Incidentally, Launay had bought the job of governor in 1776 for a massive 300,000 *livres*, mainly because its salary alone was 60,000 p.a. He stayed on long enough to earn his money back more than twice over, though that was probably little consolation for what happened to him on 14 July 1789.

confrontation. But no sooner had they made this pact than three cannons from the Invalides, as well as two antique artillery pieces that had been taken from the *garde-meuble*, were turned on the Bastille's gates. At the same time, rioters began trying to hack their way in with axes.

A five-hour siege ensued, during which the guards returned fire from the castle's turrets. The 32 Swiss Guards and 82 French military invalids on sentry duty killed about a hundred rioters – less than one each. Given that they were firing down on to a compact mob of tens of thousands, this was, by military standards, by no means a murderous riposte. The Bastille also had cannons. Half a dozen volleys of grapeshot (Napoleon's favourite weapon, which he would use against a Paris mob a few years later) would have killed hundreds in just a few minutes, let alone three hours.

Around 3 p.m., a group of official mediators arrived from the Hôtel de Ville, hoping to end the siege peacefully. They were attacked by the mob. More cannons were brought up, and at about 5 p.m., Launay decided to bow to the inevitable and surrender, though only after shouting through a hole in the castle wall that he wanted to be sure that neither he or his men would be executed. According to whom you believe, he either received a guarantee, or didn't.

In any case, if he received a promise, it did not extend to lynching, because several of his soldiers were selected for immediate reprisals. Then, while most of the rioters helped themselves to gunpowder and ammunition, Launay and his troops were marched towards the Hôtel de Ville, being badly manhandled on the way (or not, if you believe those who claim that the Revolution was a demonstration of pure humanitarianism). At one point, Launay seems to have had enough of the mistreatment, because he apparently gave an out-of-work baker a hearty kick in the profiteroles, prompting the mob to shoot and stab him to death, before a butcher carved off his head. This trophy was soon being paraded around the place de Grève on the end of a medieval-style pike.

Launay was not alone for long. In his office at the Bastille, a note had been found. It said 'I am keeping the Parisians amused with rosettes and promises. Hold out until this evening and you will get reinforcements.' It was signed 'Flesselles'.

The note was brought back to the Hôtel de Ville by some of the besiegers and read out before the city council and Flesselles himself. According to a rather partisan author called Philippe le Bas, who published an encyclopedia in 1842, the note 'completed the people's exasperation'. One of the members of the council, which only the day before had elected Flesselles its president, told him: 'Get out, Monsieur de Flesselles. You are a traitor. You have betrayed the nation; the nation abandons you.'

This wasn't exactly fair. Flesselles had been trying to keep weapons out of the hands of excitable rioters. And buoying up the nervous Launay with a jokey note might have prevented the governor of the Bastille from panicking and causing unnecessary bloodshed. At worst, Flesselles was guilty of flippancy and disrespect for the new national rosette.

However, the order to 'get out' was as good as a death sentence. Although some French sources insist that most people in the crowd wanted to escort Flesselles to the Palais-Royal to be tried, he emerged from the relative safety of the Hôtel de Ville into a mob that had just carved off the head of an aristocrat. Within seconds, Flesselles had been shot and decapitated, and his head was on a spike alongside Launay's, being taken on a bird's eye view tour of Paris.

Philippe le Bas concludes his chapter on Flesselles by saying that his 'demise was probably awful, but how can one explain his offences?'

The explanation seems pretty simple. His 'offences' were a combination of aristocratic arrogance, solidarity with a scared colleague, and misinterpreting the mood of ordinary Parisians – all of this in the face of violence from a mob drunk on its first taste of blood and power. The mob were also forgetting the aims of the democrats it had recently elected to the États généraux, who had just managed to persuade the King to reform the country's whole political system.

Interestingly, the Paris riots of 13 and 14 July are what the Assemblée nationale delegate Jean Sylvain Bailly, in his memoirs, calls *'la révolution'*, underlining the fact that this violence was separate from what he and the peaceful democrats were doing out at Versailles.

V

Describing events out in Versailles on 15 July, Bailly records in his memoirs that Louis XVI came to the Assemblée at the members' request, 'without guards and without any accompaniment except his brothers'. Ignoring an armchair that had been placed on a dais as an improvised throne, Louis 'stood, bareheaded' as a sign of respect. He also used the name 'Assemblée nationale', formally acknowledging its status, and did not once refer to 'estates'. All this delighted the delegates, as did his speech. He told them that he had come to...

> ... consult [them] on the most important affairs of state. The most urgent, and the one that most affects my heart, is the terrible disorder that reigns in the capital. The head of the nation comes confidently amongst its representatives to express his sadness and to invite them to find a way of restoring order and calm.

After acknowledging the rapturous applause, and listening to a speech of thanks, Louis XVI informed the Assemblée that he had ordered all his troops out of Paris. It was up to the elected representatives of the people to show that they knew how to govern.

Ten years of political infighting were about to begin. However, for the moment, it was joy and mutual congratulations all round. A group of Assemblée delegates accompanied Louis back – on foot – to the palace, forming a protective cortège, not because a mob wanted to behead him, but to keep his admirers at bay. The King's personal gesture of submission was seen to have saved the nation. Bailly says that he felt 'drunk with an unexpected happiness that put an end to our cruellest worries'.

At 8 p.m. that evening, a group of 94 delegates decided to go to Paris to reassure the citizens that, contrary to the rumours, they weren't about to be attacked by a royal army. Mob rule could end. This procession of politicians included Bailly himself, Sieyès, Mounier, the Archbishop of Paris and the Marquis de La Fayette, one of Louis XVI's army officers who was now vice-president of the Assemblée nationale.

Their arrival in Paris was greeted with unbridled joy. Bailly – who had been appointed the new Mayor of Paris by representatives of its 60 districts – says that the crowds in the street and people at every window were shouting *'Vive la nation! Vive le Roi! Vivent les députés!'* He adds that: 'This triumph was sweet; but if I may say so, we deserved it.'

Armed men were everywhere, 'a forest of rifles', but Bailly (diplomatically) notes that it was 'a militia keeping order, not with force and discipline, but with freedom' – a hint, perhaps, that the mob was still unpredictable.[4]

At the Hôtel de Ville, the Versailles delegates met the Paris council. La Fayette assured the Parisians that 'the King had been misled, but that has changed; he knows our troubles, and will stop them recurring. Bringing words of peace from him, gentlemen, I also hope to bring him the peace that his heart requires.' La Fayette then read out a transcript of the King's speech to the Assemblée, and was cheered. Gérard de

[4] This it certainly was. That same night, a woman dressed in male clothing was brought to the Hôtel de Ville to be hanged for no apparent reason. Bailly managed to save her from the mob, and she was released next day. For the next few days, there was unrest because of rumours that spies were hiding in the Bastille's cellars, and communicating via tunnels with the army. A 'committee' was sent down to inspect the cellars and report that they were empty.

Lally-Tollendal[5] (a noble delegate to the États généraux) told the Paris council that 'we bring you peace on behalf of the King and the Assemblée nationale. You are generous, you are French, you love your wives, your children, your homeland. There are no more bad citizens amongst you … Now peace must be reborn.' It was time to stop the raiding, pillaging and lynching. Lally-Tollendal was cheered to the rafters and carried out on to a balcony to be hailed as a hero.

Back inside the Hôtel de Ville, the aristocratic president of the Assemblée, François de la Rochefoucauld, deflated the *montgolfière* of collective euphoria somewhat by saying that the *garde bourgeoise* had been officially recognized by the King, and that their excesses had been 'pardoned'. At this, Bailly says:

> Several guards came forward and one of them said heatedly that they did not want a pardon, that they did not need it; in serving the nation, they meant to serve the King. His intentions, which were now clear, proved to the whole of France that only *they* had been truly loyal to King and country.

It is worth reiterating this. Bailly does not describe the speaker, but it was almost certainly one of the rioters who had grabbed weapons from the Invalides, stormed the Bastille, and cheered as treacherous heads were impaled on spikes outside the very building where this meeting was being held. This was one of the *cocarde*-wearing militiamen who are regarded today as the real heroes of the Revolution, the noble citizens who took up arms on 14 July 1789, and who toppled the monarchy. And here he was, defiantly defending his actions and yet saying with

---

[5] Gérard was the son of Thomas Arthur de Lally-Tollendal, who was (no doubt falsely) convicted of treason by the Paris parliament and executed outside the Hôtel de Ville in 1766, gagged so that he could not proclaim his innocence. For more details, see *1000 Years of Annoying the French*.

evident sincerity that he and his colleagues had been *serving the King*. His spontaneous outburst seems to prove once and for all that July 1789 was not about ending the monarchy. The mob violence in Paris was mainly inspired by hunger, impatience with politicians and false rumours about an imminent attack by royal troops, but at its heart there was a desire to *protect the King's interests*.

This is the complete opposite of what modern France would have us believe.

VI

On 17 July, Louis XVI proved once again that, despite his failings, he was a pretty courageous man. With an estimated 100,000 armed citizens roaming the streets of Paris, and knowing full well that two of his representatives there had recently been lynched by those same citizens, Louis came to the city – entirely of his own free will.

The previous day, Bailly had been to see him at the palace of Versailles, pushing through a crowd of panicking courtiers before reaching the King, who calmly announced that he intended to go into the capital. Bailly wrote in his memoirs that Louis was 'deeply affected by the murders that the people had committed', but thought that Launay 'deserved his fate' (no doubt because he had allowed the situation to degenerate into chaos, and lost his stock of ammunition). At first, Bailly says, Louis wanted to limit his visit to Notre-Dame and the royal palace at the Tuileries. But Bailly quickly persuaded him that this would not satisfy the people, so Louis agreed: 'I will go to the Hôtel de Ville. When one does something, one must do it completely.'

The King completed his day's work on the sixteenth by acceding to the Assemblée's most recent demands – he sacked all his ministers and recalled Necker yet again. To all intents and purposes, France seemed to be operating as a fully functional constitutional monarchy.

On the morning of 17 July 1789, accompanied by a few soldiers and a deputation of Assemblée members to vouch for his peaceful intent (Bailly says that 'the loyalty of [Paris's] citizens was well known, but ... one could not deny that brigands were operating amongst the good citizens'), Louis XVI was driven to Paris. According to Marie-Antoinette's confidante Madame Campan, as he left Versailles, 'a deathly silence reigned throughout the palace, the fear was extreme; we hardly expected the King to return.'

Louis was met by Mayor Bailly and around 50 city representatives at Chaillot, on the western edge of Paris, opposite where the Eiffel Tower now stands. There, Bailly gave a speech telling the King that in Paris he would 'enjoy the love of his faithful subjects', and that 'neither your people, nor Your Majesty will ever forget this great day. It is the monarchy's most beautiful day. It marks the start of an eternal alliance between the monarch and the people.'

Again, it is timely to remember that this was only three days after the original Bastille Day, and that Bailly was not some nostalgic aristocrat expressing relief that the King had not yet been deposed, imprisoned or executed. He was a commoner, one of the men who had overturned the ancient estates system, and the newly appointed head of the people's council that had seized control of Paris.

Louis XVI replied briefly that he was happy to receive this homage from Paris and its representatives, and then his carriage set off for the five-kilometre ride to the Hôtel de Ville, its whole route lined by massed ranks of men and women armed with rifles, swords, pikes, lances and scythes (Paris was surrounded by small farms). There were, Bailly says, even monks with muskets on their shoulders. For a king accustomed to the protection of his personal guard, it must have been an unnerving spectacle.

As he was crossing the place Louis XV (the present-day Concorde) three musket shots rang out, one of them killing a woman not far from the royal coach, another making a hole in the hat of a *marquis* riding alongside the King. A failed assassination attempt perhaps, though the incident does not seem to have caused much panic, either in the crowd or the royal entourage. By now the city was probably inured to sudden death on the streets. Besides, it must have been hard to hear three shots, because the huge crowd was chanting *'Vive le Roi!'* and *'Vive la nation!'* while trumpets were sounded and cannonades were fired to welcome the royal visitor.

Two kilometres further on, the procession passed a line of cannons guarding the Pont-Neuf, their barrels loaded with flowers – like 1967, it seems that 1789 was a summer of love.

At the Hôtel de Ville, Louis XVI got out of his carriage and was presented with a tricolour *cocarde* that he pinned to his hat. He then walked into the building surrounded by a tight group of citizens who formed a clinking canopy of sword blades over his head – a bizarre and unexpected gesture that apparently did not frighten Louis.

Inside the council chamber, he was greeted with applause and *'Vive le Roi!'* before taking his seat on a throne and being hailed by the city representatives as *'Notre roi, notre père!'* A councillor called Louis de Corny, a former cavalryman who had served in the American War and taken part in the storming of the Bastille, proposed a motion to commission a statue of Louis XVI, inscribed with the words 'Restorer of public liberty and father of the French'. This suggestion was greeted, Bailly says, 'with universal acclamation', and a vote was taken to erect the statue *on the ruins of the Bastille.*

The crowd outside was chanting the King's name, so he went to a window, wearing his hat with the *cocarde nationale*, a sight that, according to Bailly, 'provoked cheers and applause in the square, in the nearby streets, as far as he could be seen'. As Louis left the building, the cheers were even louder than when he arrived, because he had proved that he accepted the changes that had been forced upon him. He was escorted out of the city and back to Versailles, through crowds that were now pointing their muskets, blades and pikes down towards the ground as a gesture of peace.

As soon as Louis arrived home, Marie-Antoinette and their children rushed to embrace him. According to Madame Campan, he repeated several times that 'happily, no blood was spilt'.

Once again, let us not forget that Louis XVI had voluntarily offered himself up, with almost no guards, to the armed crowds that had stormed the Invalides and the Bastille just three days earlier. His denigrators say that it was mere resignation that took him to Paris to be paraded around like a tame bear. In his diary, he wrote simply *'Voyage à Paris à l'Hôtel de Ville.'* For once his bland indifference reads like extreme bravery.

Chapter 13

FRANCE PERFECTS
ITS TALENT FOR FAKE NEWS

'Thus it is in revolutions. One rascal writes and an hundred thousand
fools believe.'

Arthur Young (1741–1820), in his book
Travels in France (1792)

I

While the Paris council set about disarming the mob by
offering to buy back weapons, and the Assemblée nationale constituante continued its work in Versailles on a new constitution, news of events in the capital spread across the country.

Often, this caused similar outbreaks of violence in smaller
towns. The travelling British farmer Arthur Young arrived at an
inn in Strasbourg on the morning of 20 July to find people discussing the storming of the Bastille and the lack of intervention
from royal troops. That same night, he watched a mob break
into the city's *hôtel de ville*: 'From that minute, a shower of case-
ments, sashes, shutters, chairs, tables, sofas, books, papers, pictures, etc. rained incessantly from all the windows of the house
... which was then succeeded by tiles, skirting boards, banisters,
framework, and every part of the building that force could
detach.' He adds that 'they destroyed all the public archives, the

streets for some way around strewed with papers.' Meanwhile, Young says, 'the troops, both horse and foot, were quiet spectators.' All the soldiers did, he says, was guard churches and public buildings to stop the damage spreading.

In other large towns, Louis XVI's administrators, the *intendants*, handed over control more peacefully. Within days, people's committees had taken over Marseille, Rouen, Strasbourg, Nantes and the towns along the Loire Valley. By 20 July, in Lyon, Bordeaux, Nancy, Limoges and Amiens, power was being shared by royal and popular administrators. In a few places, like Lille, Toulouse and Grenoble, the status quo was maintained.

Almost everywhere, both in towns under the control of people's committees and those where royal administrators were hanging on, militias were formed to keep the peace. Everyone was afraid of food riots, wanton destruction of shops (especially bakeries) and flour mills, and that stocks of grain intended for the poor or to be released on to the market to reduce prices would be stolen.

French historians often point out that these local militias were organized by *les notables* – prominent citizens such as lawyers, administrators, businessmen, landowners and leaders of the clergy. Their commanders would have been a mixture of aristocrats and *bourgeois*, all of them from the wealthier, more educated classes. The implication is, of course, that they weren't really *people's* militias – they were there to protect the establishment. But even today, it is a sad fact that education and wealth are closely correlated, and in eighteenth-century France, as we have seen in earlier chapters, if you weren't rich, noble, male or or all of those, your chances of getting a decent education were practically zero. Sifting truth from rumour and maintaining calm were therefore inevitably tasks that fell to the educated upper echelons of the community. You could say – and it is often said – that the members of the Assemblée nationale were all *notables*, too, but they were perfectly capable of defending the people's interests and working for democracy.

In any case, peacekeeping militias were urgently needed because, by 20 July, France was descending (or rising) into mass hysteria.

With partial, garbled, contradictory accounts of events in Paris circulating by word of mouth, the country succumbed to what has become known as 'la Grande Peur', or 'the Great Fear'. (This is not to be confused with 'la Terreur', which would strike later, and be much more justified.) The name seems to have been chosen by French historians as an excuse, or at least an explanation, for uncontrolled mob brutality. Rather like the people who voted for Brexit because they truly believed that Brussels dictated the shape of bananas in British supermarkets, the implication is that the perpetrators of the violence of July and August 1789 were victims of misinformation and/or their cruel lack of a decent education. In 1989, on the bicentenary of the Revolution, an American food historian called Mary Matossian went even further and suggested that la Grande Peur (and, incidentally, the Salem witch-hunt of 1692–3) had been caused by the LSD-like effect of microtoxins in badly kept rye flour. But surely a much more credible cause for the outbreak of mob violence across France in July 1789 was a mixture of hunger, resentment and a feeling that if the Parisians can do it, *pourquoi pas nous aussi?*

French historians usually say that the Grande Peur was a rural phenomenon, because much of the violence that summer was done to châteaux, which were usually situated outside towns. But in truth, fear spread almost everywhere. From small villages to the largest cities, in inns and cafés, at toll gates and markets, rumours were repeated about revolutionary hordes, royalist armies or just plain 'brigands' being on their way to kill everyone.[1]

---

[1] There are echoes of this fear in the French national anthem, which was written in 1792. It asks: 'Do you hear the roar of fierce soldiers in our country-side? They have come to cut the throats of your sons and your women.'

Vivid accounts of non-existent battles and massacres did the rounds. There were also rumours that aristocratic landowners were either burning crops or hoarding grain to increase the price of flour and bread.

Travelling through Alsace, Arthur Young heard a story that 'the Queen had a plot, nearly on the point of execution, to blow up the National Assembly by a mine and to march the army instantly to massacre all Paris.' In Dijon, he was told that Marie-Antoinette had been convicted of a plot to poison the King. There was a common belief, supported by seditious pamphlets, that the Queen was the lover of her husband's cousin Louis Philippe, and wanted to put him on the throne. Another rumour during the Grande Peur was that Louis XVI's brother Charles had assembled an army and was preparing to sweep across France. In the southwest, people even thought the English were invading to conquer Aquitaine, as they had done in the fourteenth century.

All across France, gangs of peasants erected roadblocks and threatened anyone who wasn't wearing a tricolour *cocarde* or who looked or spoke like a *seigneur*. Riding though the Vosges, Arthur Young was accosted by a group of men. Rather rashly, he asked them, 'Suppose I am a *seigneur*, what then, my friends?' and was told, 'Why, be hanged, for that most likely is what you deserve.' He immediately bought himself a *cocarde*, but while he was riding it blew off his hat into a river, and he was soon stopped again. This time, he assured the crowd that he was just an English traveller, but they accused him of being a *seigneur* in disguise, and he only escaped unscathed by giving a speech about the English tax system, in which the rich were subject to window tax, and even paid 'for the liberty to kill their own partridges'. After he shouted, *'Vive le tiers état!'* he says they 'seemed to think that I might be an honest fellow'.

Real aristocrats were not so lucky. Young was told in the Besançon region of eastern France that:

Many chateaus have been burnt, others plundered, the *seigneurs* hunted down like wild beasts, their wives and daughters ravished ... and all their property destroyed: and these abominations not inflicted on marked persons, who were odious for their former conduct ... but an indiscriminating blind rage for the love of plunder.

At an inn he spoke to men who had received letters from Mâcon, Lyon, the Auvergne and other regions saying that 'similar commotions and mischiefs were perpetrating everywhere; and that it was expected they would pervade the whole kingdom'.

However, it wasn't always random violence – when pillaging a château, peasants often grabbed anything that looked like a landowner's deed, tax-collection register or list of tenants, and threw them on bonfires, as if to destroy the last traces of feudalism.

Young was horrified that wherever he went in late July and early August 1789 there were no reliable sources of information that might have eased the tensions. At a café in Dijon, he had to wait an hour to get a look at the only newspaper. Elsewhere, he found either no papers at all, editions that were two weeks old, or copies of the *Gazette de France*, the official royalist paper that no one believed. Fearful gossip was filling the information vacuum and whipping the population into a frenzy of violence.

II

In Paris, however, the general mood amongst ordinary people was not fear. It was one of suspicion, accusation and bloody revenge.

Stories about people hoarding grain and/or guns were so rife that rumour-peddlers coming to the Hôtel de Ville with accusations were threatened with imprisonment if their story turned out to be false. Guards had to be sent to protect a convent in Montmartre from a rabble that was accusing the abbess of hiding a stock of weapons – luckily for her, an inspection proved the rumour to be unfounded. According to the American businessman (and later ambassador) Gouverneur Morris, between 14 and 22 July the Marquis de La Fayette and his men saved 17 people from Parisian lynch mobs.

The former *intendant* (royal administrator) of Paris, Louis Bénigne François Bertier de Sauvigny, was not so lucky. On 20 July, he was grabbed by a crowd in Compiègne, to the north of Paris. They had been told that he was a wanted man in Paris, although Bailly wrote in his memoirs that this was not true: Bertier 'was not accused by the city of Paris, and there was no reason to hold him prisoner'. The Paris council sent guards to bring Bertier into the city for his own protection.

Two days later, peasants in Viry, to the south of Paris, performed a more violent citizen's arrest on Bertier's father-in-law, who was hiding out at a friend's country house. This was 74-year-old Joseph Foullon de Doué, who had very briefly been Finance Minister after Necker's dismissal on 11 July. There was a rumour going around accusing Foullon of suggesting that if people had no bread, they should eat hay or grass (a precursor to the fake news that Marie-Antoinette recommended cake).

The peasants at Viry therefore beat up the old man, stuffed hay in his mouth, fitted him out with collars of nettles and thistles, and marched him to Paris with a bale of hay strapped to his back, giving him only vinegar to quench his thirst. Amazingly, Foullon survived the march, and arrived at the Hôtel de Ville at around 5 a.m. on 22 July, much to the embarrassment of the Paris council, who quickly convened to issue a statement saying that people suspected of treason should simply be made 'prisoners in the hands of the nation' – again, Bailly says that this was for Foullon's own protection.

News of Foullon's presence spread, and a crowd filled the square in front of the Hôtel de Ville, calling for him to be hanged. Bailly tried to calm them, but eventually they burst into the building and demanded an instant trial. The councillors objected that this was illegal, and Foullon was grabbed, taken outside and hanged from the nearest lamp post. The rope broke twice, so finally he was decapitated and his head stuck on a pike, after the fashion of the time. His body was mutilated and dragged through the streets.

Unfortunately for Bertier, he was just arriving in Paris under escort, en route to the Hôtel de Ville. His guards were having to beg and cajole their way through armed hordes baying for Bertier's blood. When his father-in-law's head was brandished at the carriage, the guards told Bertier it was probably Launay, the governor of the Bastille.

At the Hôtel de Ville, Bailly questioned Bertier, before dictating a document guaranteeing his safety. However, Bailly says, 'Howls were heard in the square ... The tumult that had reigned there for so long turned into fury and revolt.' Bailly consulted the council, who agreed that Bertier should be taken to prison, and that his guards 'would answer to the nation and the city of Paris' for his safety. What this seems to have meant is 'we've got to get him out of here and it's not our fault if something unpleasant happens to him on the way.'

Predictably, as soon as the guards took Bertier outside, he was grabbed by the mob and strung up from a lamp post. A soldier came into the council chamber a few minutes later, carrying a bloody piece of meat, and announced, 'This is Bertier's heart.' His head, meanwhile, had joined that of his father-in-law as part of a roving horror show doing the rounds of Paris.

In a book called *La Chute de la monarchie* (*The Fall of the Monarchy*), written in 1972 and still studied by French history students today, there is a timeline of the Revolution which drily states for 22 July 1789 that: 'Bertier de Sauvigny, *intendant* of Paris, was hanged by the people.'

The suggestion seems to be that during the Revolution, 'the people' represented justice. For at least this one French historian, collectively *'le peuple'* was 'right', and had the authority to hang anyone it wanted. But this is clearly a detached, romanticized view of 1789. At the time, we know from Bailly and others that the lynching of Bertier was carried out against the express instructions of the people's elected council of Paris. Bailly, its leader, was horrified by the violence. He said of Foullon and Bertier's killings that they 'sullied the Revolution'.

What is clear from Bailly's record of events is that he and his fellow councillors realized that, to their shame, they could not control 'the people'. Bailly concludes his account of 22 July by saying: 'What kind of magistrature lacks the authority to stop crimes committed before its very eyes!'

This mob violence (or justified popular vengeance, depending on how you interpret it) all over France taught the men at the Hôtel de Ville, the members of the Assemblée, and Louis XVI and his court, a very simple lesson: 'the people' were going to be a menace.

For the moment, the lynchers, pillagers and *aristo*-hunters were prepared to side with the *notables* (including many aristocrats) who had taken power under cover of the tricolour *cocarde*. In most towns, the armed crowds had been given the status of an official people's guard. But if the hordes of pike-toting citizens weren't satisfied with the reforms that were promised, or became impatient to see concrete results, they were going to turn nasty, and the men forming the new regime would end up on the same lamp posts as Foullon and Bertier.

In short, after a brief period of idealism, the new politicians understood that it was necessary to harness this potential violence in favour of the Revolution. They had to endorse the mob for fear of becoming its new victim.

Mob violence didn't always go unpunished. In the town of Cluny, in central France, around thirty peasants were hanged for looting. It was also said that the soldier who had ripped out Bertier's heart was executed that same night by his horrified comrades-in-arms. But this kind of punishment was rare. The new councils and the Assemblée had to be careful not to be seen as supporters of the *aristos*. The regime therefore began to pay lip service to the idea that the people's militias, including lynch mobs, were entirely made up of good citizens who wanted to defend their nation against reactionaries and traitors. Even

Bailly becomes a little ambivalent about the Paris mob, at one point calling them 'generous citizens who have become warriors'. The new ruling class began to suffer from a kind of *'Grande Peur de la Grande Peur'* – a fear of the people.

In the following few years, what this would mean for France was that any aspiring politician who claimed to be on the side of a murderous mob could grab power. The mass guillotinings, massacres of political prisoners and general climate of violence – collectively known as la Terreur – which was to reign in France until 1794 would simply be a state-sanctioned version of la Grande Peur.

III

Understandably, amongst the rich and privileged, the general reaction to the people's Grande Peur was Grande Panique. They started to run for their lives. Louis XVI's brother Charles was one of the first to leave the country, and had fled Paris on 16 July 1789. He had been opposed to the whole idea of abolishing the system of the three estates, and had plotted to have Necker removed from office when the Swiss economist proposed to reduce aristocratic and royal privileges. Arthur Young reports that one day, Charles saw Madame Necker walking in Versailles and began hissing at her. It is usually said that Charles left France on the insistence of Louis XVI and their brother Louis Stanislas, so that there would at least be one heir to the throne out of reach of the revolutionaries. Charles went first to Italy to stay with his in-laws (his wife was the daughter of the King of Sardinia), and then toured Europe trying to raise a counter-revolutionary army – thereby endangering Louis XVI's life.

Other prominent aristocrats who left France around this time were Victor-François de Broglie, commander of the royal troops, whom Louis XVI had appointed Minister of War only a few days earlier; Charles-Eugène de Lorraine, who led the troops that confronted a Paris mob on 12 July; Louis Joseph de Bourbon, one of Louis XVI's cousins (not to be confused with the so-called 'democrat' Louis Philippe), who would later go to Germany and help to raise a counter-revolutionary army; Louis Joseph's son, Louis Henri de Bourbon, and grandson, the 17-year-old Louis d'Enghien (who would later be executed by Napoleon Bonaparte on spurious treason charges); and Yolande de Polignac, Marie-Antoinette's confidante and 'co-star' in pornographic plays, who was a hate figure for many people, a living symbol of the Queen's excesses.

Marie-Antoinette confided to Yolande that she was 'terrified' for her own safety. She knew that she was in imminent danger of attack by anyone who believed the stories circulating about her. Marie-Antoinette was also afraid of being locked up in a convent. This was a serious prospect, because errant French females were often sent away to live like nuns as punishment. Adulterous wives could be imprisoned for two years in a convent, and if their husband died during that period, the unfortunate woman would stay cloistered for life. There was talk amongst Assemblée delegates of preparing an apartment for Marie-Antoinette at the Val-de-Grâce convent hospital in Paris, supposedly for her own protection, but surely also as penance for her formerly extravagant (and allegedly adulterous) lifestyle. In the summer of 1789 she and Louis wondered about fleeing to the heavily garrisoned town of Metz in the east of France, but in the end they decided to stay in Versailles and continue to represent the monarchy.

For the moment, Louis XVI's brother Louis Stanislas also decided to remain in Versailles, even though he was fiercely opposed to the idea of the Assemblée nationale, and was constantly urging the King to stand up to the democrats – not particularly helpful, or wise, advice.

Meanwhile, many aristocrats who hadn't nailed their colours to the revolutionary flagpole by becoming Assemblée delegates, especially those who had been living in vulnerable rural châteaux, grabbed what they could and headed for the nearest border. The great emigration of some 140,000 French men, women and children had begun.

IV

The Assemblée reacted to events with a similar sense of urgency. In modern France, nothing official happens in August unless there is a national emergency, at which point politicians will make a big show of interrupting their well-earned holidays to save the nation. But back in 1789, deliberations on the new constitution suddenly became more focused, as delegates tried to show that they were determined to deliver concrete results as well as ideals.

The debate during '*la nuit du 4 août*' has gone down in revolutionary legend as one of the key moments in the founding of a democratic republic. During the night of 4–5 August, there was an emergency session to discuss the abolition of all remaining feudal rights. Some of the most radical proposals were put forward by aristocrats like the Duc d'Aiguillon, who called for all *droits seigneuraux*, or lords' rights, to be scrapped. These included symbolic privileges like the best pew in church and being bowed to by peasants, as well as the rights to demand taxes from tenants, to force them to use the lord's windmill, and de facto control over food prices, because lords were allowed to sell their produce early, at a higher price, before their tenants' harvests were released on to the market.

The Bishop of Chartres, another aristocrat, suggested abolishing the landlords' exclusive right to hunt on their land. Other delegates demanded democratic moves such as sharing the Church's wealth with the poor and making all legal processes free of charge.

One of the most vital reforms was suggested by yet another member of the privileged classes, the Vicomte Alexandre de Beauharnais,[2] who proposed allowing commoners access to all posts in civil, religious and military institutions. He would later

---

[2] He was the first husband of Napoleon's famous wife Joséphine, and father of two children by her.

command a revolutionary army and be guillotined for losing a battle.

It was not until mid-September that the Assemblée finally compressed all its ideas from 4–5 August into a highly legalistic-sounding 18-point plan. Almost all the above-mentioned privileges were to be abolished, though in the end some were watered down. For example, the *dîmes* (clerical taxes) were still payable if they covered clergymen's salaries or were used to finance seminaries, hospitals or religious schools. Worse, landlords would be able to buy back certain privileges like the right to tax their tenants. In effect, of the truly feudal privileges, only the physical servitude of the *corvée* (obligatory labour for the lord or the Church) and the *mainmorte* (whereby lords inherited their tenants' belongings) were abolished outright.

Nevertheless, it was still a daring set of decrees that would have been unimaginable just a few weeks earlier.

Another momentous decision taken on the night of 4 August 1789 was that the new Constitution would be prefaced by a declaration of citizens' fundamental rights. Between 20 and 26 August, delegates debated what these should be. Partly inspired by the American Declaration of Independence of 1776 (13 of the Assemblée's aristocratic delegates, including La Fayette, had been officers there during the American War), partly by the Lumières philosophers' notions of individual freedom, the resulting, and highly succinct, 17-article text is still part of the French Constitution today.

La Déclaration des droits de l'homme et du citoyen de 1789[3] contained such famous clauses as 'Men are born and remain free and equal in law', 'The law must be the same for all', 'The free communication of thoughts and opinions is one of the most precious rights of Man', 'No man may be accused, arrested or

---

[3] As we shall see later, those masculine nouns, *homme* and *citoyen*, would have a disastrously negative impact on women's rights under the Revolution. See Chapter 21.

imprisoned except in cases determined by law, and in the ways decreed by law' (a reaction to the recent lynchings), and article 17, which was added under pressure from fearful aristocratic delegates: 'Property is an inviolable and sacred right, and no one may be deprived of it, unless public necessity, affirmed by law, clearly demands it, and on condition that fair compensation is given in advance' – a pretty clear attempt to stop the looting of châteaux.

On 26 August, the delegates turned to the draft of the Constitution itself, setting out the Assemblée's power to make the laws that would be ratified (no longer proposed) by the King, as well as its sole right to fix income taxes and budgets. The Constitution would undergo many changes over the following years, but that August, its basic demands were established. The key phrase in the draft was: 'There is in France no authority superior to the law; the King reigns only by law.' It was the end of *'Qui veut le roy, si veut la loy.'* The King was to stay on, but as a second-class citizen, subject to the Assemblée.

All in all, the mob violence of the early summer seemed to have produced some startlingly rapid political results. The only problem was that, for the moment at least, it was all talk. By the end of the summer, the law on the abolition of feudal rights had not been published; the *Declaration of Men's and Citizens' Rights* was not finalized; and the Constitution still needed honing down from sweeping idealism into a practical working document.

The first of these ground-breaking texts to be ready for public distribution was the law abolishing feudal rights. This announcement was due for publication on 18 September. People accused Louis XVI of holding things up for almost a month by not signing the decree. In private, he had raised objections to the law, saying that he did not agree with 'the despoiling of my clergy and my nobility'. In a letter to the Archbishop of Arles, he wrote that he would not 'surrender to this enthusiasm that has seized all the orders [of society]'.

The job of printing the text of the law was given to the royal press and, somehow or other, the documents did not get sent out to the towns and villages where the laws were meant to be enacted, which was a pity because it would have brought some positive, and non-fake, news to the poor.

Again, Louis XVI was blamed for this hiccup – more petty delaying tactics. But the official excuse given for the holdup was that the Assemblée had ordered the documents to be *printed*, but had not given the order to *distribute* them.

In any case, not until 3 November would the law abolishing the ancient privileges of the aristocracy and the clergy be published. Even watered down, it still freed whole swathes of the population from at least some of their taxes (and many peasants would subsequently take this as a hint that they didn't need to pay any tax at all). It also opened the way for commoners to become judges, bishops, officers and administrators of all sorts, and allowed peasants to hunt any wild animals that strayed into their paths (a right that is still enjoyed today, making country walks in France dangerous for most of the year).

And yet again, these reforms were sanctioned by the King – the document ended with a note to the effect that 'the King commands that the above orders be printed'. The new anti-feudal law also acknowledged his status – article 17 'solemnly proclaims King Louis XVI as Restorer of French liberty'. On paper at least, he was playing his role as a second-class citizen, and the constitutional monarchy was still functioning.

Chapter 14

THE SUN GOES DOWN ON VERSAILLES

'Il s'est trouvé des méchants qui ont fait soulever le peuple, et les excès où il s'est porté les jours derniers sont leur ouvrage. Il ne faut pas en vouloir au peuple.'

'There were some nasty rogues who made the people rise up, and the recent excesses are their fault. We mustn't blame the people.'

Louis XVI explaining mob violence to his son in October 1789

I

If the delays in signing and publishing the feudalism laws were deliberate on Louis XVI's part, it was a foolish move. His usually laconic diary (which shows that he continued hunting merrily throughout the summer of 1789, after the events of 14–17 July) becomes almost wordy in early October. On the fifth, he notes that a hunt was 'interrupted by events'. On the following day, he records a 'departure to Paris at twelve-thirty, visit to the Hôtel de Ville, supper and bed at the Tuileries'.

Thanks to a mixture of personal courage and tactical resignation, Louis XVI had so far managed to ride the wave of Revolution. He was still held in high personal esteem by the vast majority of his subjects. In Paris he had been cheered by the people who stormed the Bastille; at least one of the scare stories during the Grande Peur had been about an attempt on his life; and no one was accusing him of trying to overthrow the Assemblée, even if his brothers, his wife and several of his cousins were considered suspect. As Madame Campan put it in her memoirs, as the summer of 1789 came to an end, 'the people still spoke of the King with love, and seemed to think that, thanks to his character, he would favour the wish of the nation to reform what they called the abuses.' He was still part of the revolutionary process, and, in public anyway, approved of most of it.

As summer turned into autumn, though, with the new laws marooned at the printer's, Louis XVI was seen by some as partially guilty of delaying practical solutions to the everyday problems that were crippling France. After the riots of July, food prices had not come down. On the contrary, some grain merchants were scared of sending their supplies to market, in case it was all stolen by the mob. Many employers, too, had shut up shop for fear of looting, or because their former workers were out on the streets carrying muskets. Many domestic servants had no one to serve. As a result, by October, the poor and hungry were poorer, hungrier – and angrier. And, despite the general goodwill towards him, some of the resentment was directed at Louis XVI.

The events of *'les 5 et 6 octobre 1789'* are usually presented by French historians as a tipping point in the Revolution – a 20-kilometre women's march from Paris to Versailles to fetch the King. This, so the legend has it, was when the female half of *le peuple* took the Revolution in hand, forcing Louis XVI to come into the city and face up to his daily responsibilities amongst his people, instead of hiding away in his palace.

As with most tales of revolutionary heroism, that is at best a partial truth. In fact, protesting had started a day earlier, when some women traders from Les Halles market marched the 600 metres to the gardens of the Palais-Royal, where they knew that vocal and influential men gathered to drink, give speeches and write pamphlets. There, the women made their own, loud and vulgar voices heard about the scarcity of bread despite a good grain harvest.

Predictably, rumours about the food shortage were doing the rounds. It was alleged that vast stores of grain, flour and bread were being hidden from the people to starve them into submission. Some of those rumours had almost certainly passed through, or even originated at, the cafés of the Palais-Royal. And it is often said that, on 4 October, the male agitators there saw the group of angry women and had the eighteenth-century equivalent of a lightbulb moment – a candle moment. Here was a chance to stir up even more trouble.

Fortunately for the rumour-mongers, a few days previously, Louis XVI had committed a major political blunder. He had summoned a regiment of 5,000 soldiers to guard him and his entourage at Versailles. Understandable, perhaps, given that Marie-Antoinette could not walk in her own gardens without fear of being insulted or worse, and that many former palace servants were now to be seen touting pikes and muskets in the town's streets.

The soldiers summoned to Versailles were all French, but they belonged to the régiment de Flandres, a Belgian-sounding name, and people were highly suspicious of foreign troops thanks to the presence of the Swiss and German guards in Paris during the July events.

Even less prudently, on 1 October, Louis XVI allowed his regular *gardes du corps* to throw a huge banquet for the newly arrived officers in the palace theatre – 240 slap-up dinners in Versailles at a time of chronic food shortages in Paris. It was to be a case of nibbling while Paris burned with resentment.

Piling on the provocation, the *gardes du corps* invited only officers who were known to have little or no sympathy for the Revolution. Many French soldiers had already defected to the improvised revolutionary forces; others had stayed on in the army but were in favour of reform, but this banquet was to be a get-together for the royalist faithful.

A Parisian newspaper called *Le Courrier de Versailles à Paris et de Paris à Versailles* gave a vivid account of the evening. The paper was pro-Revolution but claimed to report 'in a spirit of peace and conciliation', and its account rings true. There is no sensationalism or outrage, as there often was in partisan publications at the time. 'The room was lit as it had been during the greatest parties,' the *Courrier* reported, there was an orchestra, and the event was attended by 'the most beautiful women of the court and the town [who] provided very agreeable distractions'.

Soldiers being soldiers, they got royally drunk, and when Louis XVI put in an appearance after a day's deer hunting, along with Marie-Antoinette, they were hailed with shouts and toasts of *'Vive le Roi!'* and *'Vive la Reine!'* The *Courrier de Versaill*es said that the toasts to the King were performed 'with the honours of war, the drawn sword in one hand, the glass in the other'. One brave voice proposed a toast to the nation, a revolutionary idea, but was shouted down. At one point, someone yelled out, 'Down with the tricolour *cocarde!*' and any man who was wearing it was forced to take it off, or replace it with a white, royalist, rosette, or even the black of Austria and Marie-Antoinette.

To crown the evening of royalist sentiments, a few soldiers climbed on to the balcony of the banqueting hall to wave the white *cocarde*.

After the dinner was over, the soldiers went out on to the terrace to shout royalist slogans, and, according to the *Courrier de Versailles*, 'make madness and music', much to the annoyance of all the townspeople within earshot (and no doubt of Louis XVI himself, who was not a party animal).

By 3 October, highly detailed – often strategically exaggerated – accounts of the banquet had reached Paris. Less scrupulous newspapers and pamphlets than the *Courrier de Versailles* gave lavish descriptions of an *'orgie des gardes du corps'* during which, so it was claimed in the provocative, anti-monarchist paper *L'Ami du peuple*, the tricolour *cocarde* had been trampled[1] underfoot by royalist troops who, it was widely assumed, had been brought to Versailles to overpower the Assemblée and then attack Paris.

Even the fair-minded Bailly reported in his memoirs (no doubt quoting sources he read at the time) that 'officers vomited terrible imprecations against the Assemblée nationale, and anxiety reigned in Versailles until fatigue and drunkenness reduced their perpetrators to incapacity.'

The implication was that a royal *coup d'état* had been narrowly avoided, or was being plotted in the barracks at Versailles. A whole new scare story had been created, and Louis XVI's months of diplomacy had been undone by one over-indulgent French *soirée*.

II

With feelings about this 'orgy' running high in Paris on 4 October, it was not difficult to whip up support for a larger demonstration the following day. Who did the whipping has been a subject of contention ever since. Some allege that radical factions based at Palais-Royal, unhappy with the Assemblée's allegiance to the King, seized the chance to make their move. Others see it as the work of Louis XVI's cousin Louis Philippe d'Orléans and his supporters – Madame Campan describes being threatened by some of them just before the events in question. Given that the Palais-Royal belonged to Louis Philippe, his hangers-on would certainly have been present when the women arrived. But there is of course a valid argument for saying that it was the women market traders themselves who decided to organize a much bigger demonstration. Many of them were members of the guild of female market traders, the

[1] This trampling is usually reported as undisputable fact in modern French history books.

Dames de la Halle (women of the market hall) – so they were already an organized body.[2]

On 5 October, a Monday morning, women from Les Halles and the faubourg Saint-Antoine (just beyond the Bastille) began to gather outside the Hôtel de Ville, defying the pouring rain.

Contrary to common belief, they were there not to demonstrate against Louis XVI or his soldiers, but to remind the Paris councillors of their duty to provide for its citizens. According to Mayor Bailly himself, they wanted to 'complain to the representatives of the community about the negligence and ineptitude regarding food supplies'. At the start of the day, it was the newly appointed democrats rather than the King who were being told to face up to their responsibilities.

Once this crowd of women had formed, armed men began to join in, and they squared up to the guards who were blocking the entrance to the city hall. After a short struggle, the men managed to force the gate. According to Bailly (who wasn't yet present himself) the women objected to this male intervention, and said that all they wanted was to obtain assurances from the councillors. Some of the women even formed a barricade on the steps and 'managed to let in only members of their own sex, and to keep out men who tried to accompany them'.

Unfortunately, there were plenty of men with more than bread on their minds. A group of them managed to smash open a side entrance and, according to Bailly, emptied the Hôtel de Ville's armoury, stole 200,000 *livres* (a huge amount of cash) from the treasury, and 'were stopped when, torch in hand, they were about to set light to the most combustible parts of the building'. Without this last-minute intervention, 5 October 1789 would be remembered for a far less defensible version of the storming of the Bastille, directed this time against the bastion of Paris's new democratic council.

---

[2] The irony here is that the Revolution abolished their guild, along with other trades' closed shops, depriving these women – now seen as revolutionary heroines – of a status they cherished.

The *Courrier de Versailles* summed up these events in dramatic fashion: 'Our Hôtel de Ville has been pillaged! Disorder! Confusion! Armed women! The people have turned against the people!' (And this was a pro-revolutionary newspaper, not a disapproving royalist pamphlet.)

It was more proof that *le peuple* was no unified, heroic force for justice, despite what modern French historians might tell us.

By now, some women had decided to march out to Versailles to see Louis XVI. This was, for the moment at least, not an aggressive move. The Dames de la Halle had a semi-official role as spokeswomen for the people, and would regularly go to plead with the King, or congratulate the royal couple on a new baby. As we saw earlier, after the birth of her first son, Marie-Antoinette had been less than amused to receive a spontaneous visit from some Paris market fishwives.

As recently as 25 August, a large crowd of women market traders had been to Versailles to attend the annual party for the festival of St Louis. Bailly went with them, and was delighted by the joyfulness of the whole occasion. He and some of the women were received by Louis XVI in his bedroom (though not in his bed – this wasn't Louis XV), and Bailly describes how he 'presented the King with a superb bouquet that the market women had given me for His Majesty. It was wrapped in a gauze veil, on which was inscribed, in gold letters, "To Louis XVI, the best of kings".' The visitors were then taken to see Marie-Antoinette, Louis XVI's aunts, and practically the whole family. It was apparently all very cordial, even if Marie-Antoinette herself was still thought of by most common people as an over-privileged foreigner.

So this women's march to Versailles on 5 October was a conventional monarchist gesture. Obtaining no satisfaction from lesser authorities, the Dames de la Halle were simply going to see the man in charge. Besides, under the old absolute monarchy, the King had usually had stocks of wheat at his disposal, to be released on to the market during a shortage. Louis XVI was still a genuine source of hope during a famine.

Several thousand women began the five-hour march to Versailles. Estimates vary between five and ten thousand. Given these numbers, it is doubtful that they were all market traders. And breaking even more with tradition, they brought along a couple of cannons that they had 'liberated' from outside the Hôtel de Ville. Many were also armed with pikes.

It is often alleged that this all-female procession was infiltrated by men in drag. If this was true, it is hard to imagine why the men would have bothered. If they thought the women wouldn't notice, they were almost certainly mistaken – for one thing, razors at the time were not as efficient as they are today, or as frequently used. If the men wanted to fool observers into thinking that it was an all-female march, again why would they bother? Until that point, no mob had shown any such scruples.

It is true that the most famous illustration of the march, a primitively drawn colour print, shows some very masculine-looking *dames*, including one who seems to have a moustache. More importantly, the drawing suggests that, whether their intentions were peaceful or not, and whatever their real gender, the women presented a frightening spectacle – almost every one of them is armed with a pike, musket, sword, axe, scythe, club or cannon.

The only unarmed marcher visible in the drawing is a chic and reluctant-looking lady, who is being 'helped' along, with a marcher's arm round her waist and a guiding hand clamped to her wrist. The Dames de la Halle were apparently determined that female citizens of all classes should support their demands for food.

One thing that no illustrations of the march show – perhaps in an attempt to mythologize the joyous event – is the hardship and dirt that the women must have suffered that day. With little or nothing to eat or drink, they dragged their weapons, their long skirts, and in many cases their children, through 20 kilometres of mud, as the heavens poured chilly autumnal rain on their heads. These were desperate people at the end of their tether who, so far, had been let down by the Revolution.

III

Most accounts are adamant that the procession was greeted by the people of Versailles with cries of *'Vivent les Parisiennes!'* (a shout often repeated by modern Parisian men, but for different reasons). However, the *Journal de Paris* says that 'the avenues and streets were full of terrified people running in all directions.' This sounds credible – the arrival of the marchers was like something out of la Grande Peur. There are not many towns that would be pleased to see a several-thousand-strong armed mob approaching, unless they were expecting an army of liberation. And Versailles didn't need liberating. It was the seat of a functioning, reasonably democratic government.

The women marched straight to the palace, and while most of them rested in the place des Armes, by the royal stables, a small deputation went into the Assemblée building, where the delegates had been discussing a letter that they had received from Louis XVI about the anti-feudal laws that he was being asked to sign. 'It is not that they all represent my idea of perfection,' the King had written almost wittily, 'but I think it would be praiseworthy of me not to delay my acceptance of the present wishes of the representatives of the nation.' In government, it seemed that all was harmony.

Suddenly, in burst about twenty women, to the disbelief of the male-only delegates. Typically, though, the women were no longer alone. A man was now proclaiming himself their 'orator', and addressed the startled Assemblée. This was a 25-year-old bailiff called Stanislas Maillard. An ambitious opportunist, he had been one of the men who arrested Launay, the governor of the Bastille, and had since appointed himself 'Captain of the Bastille Volunteers'.[3]

Maillard informed the Assemblée delegates that 'we [clearly he had elected himself an honorary woman] have come to demand bread and to punish those who insulted the patriotic

---

[3] He would later be accused of organizing massacres in September 1792.

344

cocarde.' Given that the women themselves had only ever mentioned food, he was already overstepping the mark.

According to the president of the Assemblée, Jean-Joseph Mounier – the man who had drafted the new Constitution – Maillard and another self-appointed male spokesman also repeated a rumour that a miller was being paid 200 *livres* per day *not* to make flour, and that 'the aristocrats want to starve us to death.'

The delegates shouted, 'Name him!' and received a hesitant reply from the two 'spokesmen' about having heard the story from some women who in turn had heard that it was a clergyman – probably the Archbishop of Paris. This was met with howls of disbelief from the Assemblée delegates.

As Maillard began shouting demands and threats, Mounier replied calmly that 'the only way to get more bread is to re-establish order. The more you massacre, the less bread there will be.' He then gave orders that the Parisian women (and their male hangers-on) should be given food and drink.

It was quickly decided that Mounier should lead a deputation of women, along with Maillard, to see the King and request food aid for Paris. The canny Mounier also decided to take along the draft Constitution and the *Declaration of Men's and Citizens' Rights*, thinking that this turn of events might force Louis into ratifying them at last. Even when faced by the hectoring 'Captain of the Bastille Volunteers', here was a calmer, more principled mind working for democracy.

Despite being president of the new Assemblée, or rather because he respected its due processes, Mounier was obliged to obey protocol, and had no power to march over to the palace and demand an audience with the King – especially if he wanted to bring along several angry demonstrators. He therefore negotiated a group visit for himself, Maillard the mansplainer, and five women.

In his memoirs, Mounier describes walking through the rain-swept streets of Versailles and seeing the crowds of women outside the palace 'among whom mingled a certain number of men, most of them in rags, a ferocious look in their eyes, gesturing menacingly and shouting horribly'. These were not the alleged transvestites who had marched with the women – since then, hearing about the women's march, a predominantly masculine Parisian mob had followed on. These men, Mounier saw, were armed with 'guns, old pikes, axes, iron bars and long poles mounted with sword or knife blades'.

A few of the men decided to accompany Mounier and his deputation, but they were mistaken for an attack mob and dispersed by royal sentries. Mounier tried again, and this time he was recognized and 'received with honour', though as the lines opened to receive him and his companions, the crowd surged forward and almost broke into the palace. The situation was on a knife edge.

Inside, Mounier told Louis XVI about 'the terrible situation in Paris, these women's complaints, the promise we gave them to make every effort, along with His Majesty, to supply Paris with food, and our pleas that they should withdraw in peace and commit no violence'. Louis expressed his sympathy, and the women present, Mounier said, were 'moved'. One of them, a 17-year-old girl, had already fainted at the shock of meeting the King.

While Louis signed the Assemblée's promise of food aid, and gave instructions for several wagonloads of bread to be sent to Paris (a gesture that would be quoted by agitators as proof that the food shortage was deliberate), Mounier played his political trump card. He told some of the King's advisors that it was now or never if Louis was going to sign the Constitution and the *Declaration of Men's and Citizens' Rights*. Any further delay, he said, would be taken as a refusal and 'would ignite the fury of the Parisians'. On the other hand, if Louis signed, 'it would be announced to the people as an act of benevolence, and would dispel the unrest'.

It was an astute piece of political blackmail, and Louis immediately went into a meeting with his advisors to decide how to react. At the end of this, he gave what Mounier calls 'pure and simple acceptance'.

Suddenly, France had a new democratic Constitution and its citizens (the males, at least) had a written guarantee of their fundamental human rights. All this and a promise of food to ease the shortages in Paris.

Mission accomplished, *n'est-ce pas?*

IV

It is often said that it was during this October confrontation in Versailles that Marie-Antoinette delivered her famous line: 'Let them eat cake.' In French, she is supposed to have suggested that poor people should turn to *brioche* – bread with added eggs, butter, milk and sugar – if they couldn't get bread.

But this was just another of the scurrilous rumours about the *Autrichienne* that people wanted to believe. In fact, the quip was doing the rounds well before Marie-Antoinette was born. In his autobiography, *Les Confessions*, Jean-Jacques Rousseau describes how he was feeling hungry one day in 1736 when he remembered 'the solution suggested by a great princess, who was told that the peasants had no bread, and answered: Then why don't they eat *brioche?*' His *Confessions* were published in 1782, seven years before October 1789. Of course it is possible that Marie-Antoinette revived Rousseau's old joke, but given the political tensions of 1789, it is highly unlikely that she would have done so, and there are no eyewitness accounts of her making the remark.

The truth was that Marie-Antoinette inspired so much bad feeling that it was easy to pin the tasteless joke on her. This distrust of royal attitudes to baked goods might also explain why, when the women emerged from the palace to break the good news to their fellow marchers, they were accused of lying about the promise of bread, and threatened with lynching. They had to beg to be let back in so that the King could give them written proof that they were telling the truth.

Sadly, while Mounier and co. had been inside (incidentally, he never mentions Maillard entering the palace), violence had already broken out. This was partly Louis XVI's fault because the meeting with his advisors had taken four hours, more than enough time to read the 30-odd clauses in the declarations he was meant to sign. In fact, he and his counsellors had been discussing whether to make a run for it. Reports were coming in that some of the women outside were saying they intended to return to Paris with Marie-Antoinette's head on a pike, and a *cocarde* made out of her entrails. They were threats that had to be taken seriously.

The King's advisors urged him to leave immediately for the garrison town of Metz. Typically he hesitated, and then declared that he refused to become a 'fugitive king'. Meanwhile, coaches had been ordered from the stables, so that at least Marie-Antoinette and the children could escape. These had been stopped by the crowds, but there were other means of transport within the palace grounds, and the Queen could have been spirited out via a distant rear entrance without running the gauntlet of the mob. However, Marie-Antoinette decided that she should stay by her husband's side. Later, Louis would admit that he regretted this missed opportunity. But for now, despite the noise of shooting outside, the King and Queen stayed in their palace.

During these overlong deliberations, an order had been given for the royal troops to withdraw in the hope that this would calm the mob. As they left the scene, they were fired upon by members of the Versailles people's militia (supposedly a peacekeeping force) and, according to Mounier, 'several men and several horses were wounded'.

While Mounier sat waiting for a reply to his requests, he was being given regular updates on the situation in the streets. Many marchers had taken refuge in churches or had been invited in by townspeople, but there were still plenty of violent-looking protesters gathered at the palace gates, apparently looking for trouble. The account in his memoirs of all this remains factual until his frustration bursts through and he expresses his amazement that the situation had been allowed to get out of hand: 'Women, whose numbers had been vastly exaggerated! Followed by a few vile brigands! ... It should have been so easy to repulse them.'

To avoid a large-scale confrontation between royal troops and armed citizens, what was needed was a large peacekeeping force. And at last, some time between nine and ten o'clock, Mounier received word that they were on their way.

Back in Paris, the city council had been disastrously slow to react to the news that several thousand armed Parisians – of both genders – were marching towards the royal palace and the seat of government. It was almost inevitable that there would be violence, possibly a miniature civil war if Louis XVI's recently arrived troops waded in.

There was, in theory at least, a solution to the dilemma. This was the city's section of the Garde nationale that had now been formed, and hurriedly trained, by the Marquis de La Fayette, hero of the American War. Soon after the attacks on the Invalides and the Bastille, and the Grande Peur, the Assemblée had called for volunteers from the spontaneously formed people's militias to create a National Guard that would prevent future unrest. The Assemblée had inserted a clause into their draft *Declaration of Men's and Citizens' Rights*: 'The guarantee of men's and citizens' rights necessitates the formation of a public army.'

Louis XVI had appointed La Fayette as head of the Paris branch of this new National Guard, and he had taken charge of about 10,000 men whose job was to keep the peace, a difficult job given that they were outnumbered about ten to one by other armed citizens. After the lynchings of Foullon and Berthier, La Fayette had resigned, but been pressed upon to take up his post again. There probably weren't many candidates for such an impossible job.

During the pillaging of the Hôtel de Ville on 5 October, La Fayette did not arrive *in situ* until about two in the afternoon, when there was still a large, volatile crowd in the square demanding food and action. He then refused to march out to Versailles until he received an official order from the city council – which couldn't be given until Mayor Bailly arrived. Bailly didn't turn up until 4 p.m., so several more hours were lost, a delay that has since caused royalist sympathizers to accuse him of plotting against Louis XVI.

Once La Fayette had assembled several thousand National Guards, he marched them from Paris to Versailles, posted them outside the palace, and then went straight to bed. Or so it is often alleged.

Apparently unconcerned by the furious mob now filling the town, he assured first Mounier and then Louis XVI that his men had all sworn allegiance to the King and would 'tolerate no violence'. He was, he told Mounier at about 3 a.m., 'certain of general tranquillity'; he was going to 'retire for some rest' and Mounier should do the same. Again, this insouciance has earned La Fayette the fury of the royalists, who dubbed him 'General Morpheus', after the Greek god of dreams.

Louis then met Mounier again, and promised him that 'I have no intention of leaving, and will never distance myself from the Assemblée nationale.' Mounier knew that this was to dispel a rumour now circulating around Versailles that the royal family were about to flee to Metz.

As everyone except La Fayette expected, at about four in the morning, an armed crowd broke into the palace.

First they went to the royal guards' barracks, cut a few throats and dragged about 15 men to the palace gates. Some of these were lynched; others were kept alive while the mob discussed how best to kill them. Meanwhile, unhindered by La Fayette's men, intruders entered the palace grounds through gates that had been left open, killing two guards and taking one of the bodies to be beheaded with an axe below Louis XVI's bedroom window. The murderous mob then flooded up the main staircase into the palace, heading for Marie-Antoinette's apartment.

It was widely rumoured at the time that the attack was led by Louis XVI's cousin Louis Philippe. There were reports that he had been seen that night in the palace, wearing a woman's coat and hat, and shouting, 'We're going to kill the Queen!' The rumours were almost certainly more fake news, because Louis Philippe didn't need to take the risk of leading a mob. As a supposed revolutionary sympathizer, he was in a strong enough position to seize power as regent, whether Marie-Antoinette was dead or alive.

There are many accounts of heroic royal guards barring the door to the Queen's apartments, shouting to wake everyone up as they were stabbed and slashed at by the intruders. One of these, Miomandre de Sainte-Marie, later claimed that he tried to reason with the attackers, telling them, 'My friends! You love the King!' But they attacked him and he was forced to fall back, shouting to the Queen's ladies-in-waiting, 'I am alone against two hundred tigers!'

Luckily for Marie-Antoinette, she had been lying half-awake on her bed and, along with her two children, was whisked away to the King's apartment via a hidden staircase that Louis had had installed so that his occasional visits to his wife's bed would be less public and embarrassing.

It is a testament to the enduring personal respect felt for Louis XVI that the royal family actually found refuge in his bedroom. The mob got as far as an antechamber, and disarmed the guards, but then a royal attendant came and ordered them, in the name of the King, to stand down. And, probably to his surprise, they obeyed. For the moment, at least, Marie-Antoinette's head was going to stay attached to her body.

Meanwhile, La Fayette had got out of bed and was urging his men to resist. Reminding them of their oath of allegiance, he rushed around rallying the defences, and ordering the National Guard to take control of the situation. They stopped thieves who were emptying the royal stables, saved some royal guards from being burned alive, and even killed a few of the 'brigands'.

With order restored and dawn breaking, the crowd outside the palace began calling for Louis XVI and Marie-Antoinette to show themselves. Marie-Antoinette was terrified she would be used for musket practice, but she appeared at the King's side, to be met by cries of *'Vive le Roi!'* (not *'la Reine'*, of course). Louis XVI was in shock, so La Fayette made a speech, promising everyone that the King was going to do everything he could to provide food for Paris.

According to most accounts, it was at this time that the crowd began to chant: *'Le Roi à Paris!'* Louis must have known that this was more than an invitation to drop by for breakfast, but he appeared on the balcony again and announced: 'My friends, I will go to Paris with my wife and my children. It is to the love of my subjects that I entrust that which I hold most precious.' This was a cue for more cries of *'Vive le Roi!'* and even a few of *'Vive la Reine!'* The mood, it seemed, had changed.

The Assemblée convened early and decided to send a message of support to the King. Thirty-six delegates came to the palace and delivered a formal promise whereby 'the Assemblée has just voted unanimously to declare the King inseparable from the representatives of the nation.' Despite the tumultuous events of the past 24 hours, the democratic government still saw itself as part of a constitutional monarchy. As one of the delegates put it, 'The ship of state maintains its course, no matter what gusts of wind assail it.'

Intentionally or not, this was a partial quotation of Paris's motto: *'Fluctuat nec mergitur'*, which could be translated as 'It gets tossed about, but has never sunk'. What had just happened was the equivalent of this unsinkable Parisian vessel sailing out to Versailles and ramming it amidships. The Assemblée delegates were still sounding optimistic, but their civilized, respectful version of a democratic constitutional monarchy had just been holed below the waterline.

V

At about half past midday on 6 October 1789, the Assemblée was debating recent developments when those present were informed that a procession was going past the building. The delegates went outside to see the royal family setting off for Paris. According to Mounier's eyewitness account, the carriage was preceded by two women, each waving a guard's head on their pike.[4] Other women were holding up loaves of bread, suggesting that the two types of trophy were somehow equivalent. And as if it was all just a surreal, gigantic picnic, there were some 50 or 60 wagons loaded with bread and flour, and people were singing a folk song with the chorus *'Nous ramenons le boulanger, la boulangère et le petit mitron'* ('We're bringing back the baker, his wife and the baker's boy') – a witty reference to the King, Queen and four-year-old Dauphin.

This motley cortège was under the escort of La Fayette and his men, who had supposedly come to Versailles to protect the royal family and the Assemblée from any disruption at the hands of the rioters. Now they were, according to Mounier, 'firing their weapons, as if they had just won a victory'. Some of the royal guards who had been saved from the lynch mob were walking near the front of the procession, dressed in National Guard jackets. The guards too had become trophies.

Mounier ends his account of the day by expressing his shame that the Assemblée had not used their power to defend Louis XVI – they had allowed him 'to leave accompanied by the murderers of his servants'. Mounier says that many ordinary *Versaillais* were waking up to the idea that their *raison d'être* (and in many cases their source of income) was being confiscated. The Parisians were reassuring them, 'Don't worry, he'll be back.' Probably, though, many *Versaillais* already suspected that this was just another piece of fake news.

These few tumultuous hours had brought about momentous changes. The previous day, Louis had been hunting in the forest at Meudon (a good day, 'shot 81 pieces', before he was 'interrupted by events'); Marie-Antoinette had been in her rural idyll

---

[4] In the event, the heads would not be carried all the way to Paris that day. They did not arrive there until the following day, and the carriers were arrested.

at le Petit Trianon (with, it was said, her alleged lover, Fersen), while the Assemblée calmly debated their reforms. Old and new Versailles, standing shoulder to shoulder, had been patiently forging the new France with their politely worded speeches and co-signed decrees. Already, the exchanges between King and Assemblée had become a new form of Versailles etiquette, with rules being obeyed on both sides, and every word and gesture calculated to promote progress.

Then, surging out of the Parisian mud and rain, an armed crowd had stabbed and battered its way through all the decorum. In the space of just a few hours, the 160-year reign of Versailles had been terminated. Mob rule had won. And the mob was only just discovering its own strength.

PART IV

Towards Terror Firma

'*La folie de la Révolution fut de vouloir instituer la vertu sur la terre.
Quand on veut rendre les hommes bons et sages, libres, modérés, généreux,
on est amené fatalement à vouloir les tuer tous.*'
'The madness of the Revolution was to try to instigate virtue on
Earth. When one wants to make men good and wise, moderate and
generous, inevitably one wants to kill them all.'
Anatole France (1844–1924), French writer, in his book
Les Opinions de M. Jérôme Coignard

'*A quoi devons-nous la liberté, sinon aux émeutes populaires?*'
'To what do we owe our freedom, if not to riots by the people?'
Jean-Paul Marat (1743–93),
French journalist and politician, in a speech to the Assemblée

Chapter 15

A SHORT HONEYMOON
IN PARIS

'Les témoignages d'affection et de fidélité que j'ai reçus des habitants de ma bonne ville de Paris ... me détermine à y fixer mon séjour le plus habituel.'
'The declarations of affection and loyalty that I have received from the residents of my good city of Paris ... have convinced me to make it my most regular residence.'

Louis XVI, in a letter to the Assemblée nationale,
8 October 1789

I

Geographically speaking, the French monarchy had gone full circle. More than a century earlier, Louis XIV had emigrated to Versailles in order to free himself from Parisian schemers. Now the royal family was back by the River Seine, hemmed in more tightly by political rivals than the Sun King had ever been.

Although Louis XVI was by nature indecisive, he seems to have accepted very quickly that the journey to Paris was not just a day trip. The family moved into the palace at the Tuileries,[1]

---

[1] After the Revolution, the palais des Tuileries would be the Paris residence of Louis XVI's brothers – Kings Louis XVIII and Charles X, his second cousin King Louis-Philippe, and the two emperors Napoleon Bonaparte and Napoléon III. It was dynamited and burned by rebelling Parisians in 1871.

which had been one of Louis XIV's homes, but which had been neglected since the early 1700s. In October 1789, its gardens were hunting grounds for prostitutes, and various parts of the palace were squatted by a hundred-odd idle staff, actors (a theatre had been opened in the building by Marie-Antoinette's hairdresser Léonard, under the patronage of Louis XVI's brother Louis Stanislas), and a 70-year-old countess.

Fortunately, the countess had refurbished a wing of the palace for herself, and she was now evicted from her apartments to make way for the rightful owners. Although she must have owed a fortune in rent arrears, Louis bought all her furnishings for the generous sum of 117,000 *livres*.

Of the royals who now moved into the Tuileries, only Marie-Antoinette would have felt somewhat at home – she still had a pied-à-terre there from the time when she used to come into Paris for plays and parties.

The royal family's reception in Paris that first day must have been nerve-racking, but by all accounts they put on a brave face. They were being shown off like famous guests at a drinks party whose hosts drag them around the room, introducing them to anyone and everyone.

Mayor Bailly met the royal party when it arrived in Paris, as he had done for Louis XVI's solo visit on 17 July. He presented the King with the keys to the city, and said that it was a *'beau jour'* because the sovereign was finally returning to Paris after so long away in Versailles. Louis replied that he 'always felt pleasure and trust amongst the citizens of his good city of Paris'.

Next they were taken to the Hôtel de Ville, where Bailly repeated the King's words to the assembled councillors and spectators, provoking applause and cries of *'Vive le Roi!'* However, he had forgotten to mention 'trust', and Marie-Antoinette corrected him – a diplomatic but ultimately misguided interruption.

To great cheers, it was then announced that the Assemblée nationale would also move to Paris. The delegates were still determined to stay welded to the monarchy, and Louis XVI's abduction did not mean that the new government was going to give up its work.

Moreau de Saint-Méry, who had been president of the Paris council from 1 July to 18 September, and who was now the Assemblée member for the island of Martinique, gave a speech telling Louis XVI: 'You have just strengthened your attachment to us by adopting the Constitution that will form a double bond between the nation and the throne.' He also tried to console Louis for his sudden change of residence, saying that 'when a beloved father is summoned by the desires of an immense family, he naturally chooses the place where the greatest number of his children are living.' The King, whose ancestor Louis XIV had moved out of the family home in Paris, was still seen as the father of the nation, and apparently he had now come back to babysit.[2]

Life for Louis XVI and his family soon settled into a downsized normality. Furnishings and personal effects were brought from Versailles, as were staff, including Madame Campan and Léonard, Marie-Antoinette's hairdresser (though the styles he created were nowhere near as extravagant as before). The family dined twice a week in public, and attended public mass, as they had always done. Marie-Antoinette's friend and confidante, Madame de Lamballe, came to live at the palace and would give glittering *soirées*, but Marie-Antoinette usually stayed away, now acutely aware of the damage that could be done by stories of her enjoying herself too much in aristocratic company.

Louis was allowed to go out hunting almost as often as he wanted. As early as 12 October, less than a week after the abduction, his diary mentions 'deer hunting at Port-Royal' (on the southern outskirts of Paris). In 1790 alone, he lists 130 days of hunting, almost back to the numbers before the Revolution.

---

[2] Not all Saint-Méry's speeches were so warm-hearted. A slave owner, in May 1791 he proposed to prolong slavery, and then boycotted the Assemblée because of its vote to give equal rights to freed slaves in France's colonies.

And when he wasn't chasing or shooting wildlife, he would go riding several times a week, often accompanied only by his closest entourage, and without guards (the royal family was now being guarded – and watched – by members of the Garde nationale).

This freedom of movement has given rise to plenty of speculation about why the royal family did not take the opportunity to make their escape in late 1789 or early 1790. Louis could have ridden off in hunting garb, while Marie-Antoinette and the children were spirited away in disguise to meet him in the forest, where a carriage could have whisked them all to freedom. This would have been even simpler in June and July 1790, when the whole family was permitted to leave the centre of Paris and move into the château de Saint-Cloud,[3] one of their traditional summer residences.

The usual reason given for missing the opportunity to escape is not just Louis XVI's notorious indecisiveness. First of all, he was afraid of abandoning his aged aunts to the mob; and part of him still hoped that the Assemblée would manage to restore peace, and allow France to settle into a calm and benevolent constitutional monarchy.

On the other hand, Marie-Antoinette was under constant pressure from friends and enemies alike to return to Austria on her own. She was tempted – she thought that if she fled, leaving behind a message to the effect that she wanted to free her husband of the burden of such an unpopular wife, Louis XVI's personal reputation might be enhanced, and the monarchy reinforced. This, though, would have meant leaving behind her children, or at the very least her four-year-old son, the heir to

[3] Like the Tuileries palace, the château de Saint-Cloud was to become a casualty of the Siege of Paris of 1870–71. When the Prussian army set up its HQ there in October 1870, French cannons destroyed the sixteenth-century château.

the throne. In the end, she told the courtier Jacques-Mathieu Augeard that 'my duty is to die at the feet of the King.'[4]

While the royal family were in residence at the Tuileries, they received plenty of moral support from aristocrats living in Paris (of whom there were still plenty – the exodus had only just begun). Royalist visitors would often make a show of bravado, arriving with bouquets of fleurs-de-lys or wearing white ribbons as symbols of their solidarity. Louis XVI and Marie-Antoinette knew, though, that these same people would not be so foolhardy out in the streets, where roving gangs were challenging anyone who did not sport the tricolour *cocarde*.

In her memoirs, Madame Campan criticizes these Parisian aristocrats, saying that in some ways they made things worse for the royal family by showing that strong monarchist opposition to the concept of *'la nation'* was still rife in Paris. Even worse, she says, these people were foolishly indiscreet at home or in the houses of people of a like mind: 'They spoke out, they had discussions at table, without thinking that the servants belonged to the enemy army.' In a city where rumour ruled, loose talk really could cost lives.

This was the main difference between life at Versailles and its downscaled equivalent in Paris – ordinary Parisians were everywhere, and plenty of them were distrustful, defiant or downright hostile. As we saw earlier, in the years leading up to 1789, security at Versailles had become notoriously lax, so that people could wander relatively freely around the grounds and even in the palace, but most of these intruders had been reverential, in awe or just curious – the exceptions being the increasing number of people who came to insult Marie-Antoinette. Now, though, at the Tuileries, the balance of power had changed. Parisians seemed to believe that they owned the royal family. The atmosphere became zoo-like.

---

[4] As things turned out, of course, the time and place of her death wasn't a choice she was going to be offered.

Louis XVI's sister Élisabeth had to move out of her rooms on the ground floor of the Tuileries because of people staring in through her windows. Madame Campan tells the story of a group of women coming to the terrace outside Marie-Antoinette's apartment, and shouting for her to show herself. When the Queen obeyed, she was subjected to a public debating session (as Madame Campan puts it, 'in these groups there are always orators'). The Queen would have to learn to love Parisians, she was told. Marie-Antoinette assured them that she always had. 'But on 14 July you wanted to besiege and bombard the city.' Marie-Antoinette calmly answered that she understood why the women should believe this: there had been many rumours to this effect. They were false but it was understandable that they should be believed, 'and that was what caused the people's unhappiness'.

A woman then called out in German, but Marie-Antoinette replied that she 'had become so French that she had forgotten her native tongue'.

After applauding this short masterclass in diplomacy, the women asked the Queen to give them the ribbons and flowers on her hat, which she did. And according to Madame Campan, they stayed on the terrace for half an hour, happily chanting, 'Long live our good Queen!'

Marie-Antoinette must have found scenes like this simultaneously reassuring and terrifying. She was almost literally buying her survival with submissive words and a handful of ribbons.

II

Even now, though, there were signs that peaceful political change would continue unabated. Confirming that it saw itself as part of the constitutional monarchy, the Assemblée moved into the riding school in the Tuileries – a long, high-vaulted building with terrible acoustics but plenty of room for delegates and a public audience.

It was laid out rather like a theatre, with an orator's platform at one end, facing the president's desk, and rows of seats along the side walls. The more radical delegates sat on the benches to the president's left, the more conservative on his right. This division (the origin of the terms left and right in politics) had first arisen over the issue of whether to give the King a veto on laws voted by the Assemblée. Those in favour had gathered on the right of the chamber. And they had won (for the moment, at least).

Spectators were seated at each end of the room, and in a public gallery running around the chamber above the debating area. The Assemblée's sessions became a Parisian spectator sport, and audience participation started to play an increasing role in decision-making – with predictably populist consequences, as we shall see.

Groundbreaking decisions continued to pour out: in September 1789, a lawyer called Jacques-Guillaume Thouret proposed a quaint but impractical plan to divide France into 80 equally-sized square *départements*, each split into nine square *communes* which in turn would contain nine square *cantons*. These were to be the nation's new administrative units. It quickly dawned on the delegates that some of these communes would contain nothing but trees or mountains, while others would be home to several towns, and that France is not square, so some of the *départements* on the outer edges would consist of small portions of a square. On Thouret's map, a tiny northwestern corner of Brittany consisting largely of open sea would have formed a whole *département*. This geographical naivety was no doubt a symptom of the Assemblée's boundless idealism, and Thouret's grid was soon replaced by a more workable system whereby 83 *départements* were founded along the rough outlines of the old pre-revolutionary *provinces*.

More radically still, in November 1789, the Assemblée requisitioned all the Church's wealth and property, to pay off the nation's debts. In return, the state agreed to maintain the buildings and pay the clergy's salaries, starting with a decent minimum wage for the humblest priests (1,200 *livres* per year), rising to generous but reduced salaries for bishops (50,000 *livres* for Paris, 20,000 for the others).[5] Even more radically, commoners could now become bishops, and would have to be elected by their local councils, and from now on, there would be only 83 of them, one per *département*, as opposed to more than 130 before. All monastic orders were abolished unless they were involved in education or charitable work. After some prevarication, Louis XVI approved all these measures.

In June 1790, democracy took a huge symbolic step forward when the Assemblée voted to abolish the hereditary aristocracy. The law listed the titles that were to be deleted from the records forever: *marquis, chevalier, écuyer, comte, vicomte, messire, prince, baron, vidame, noble* and *duc*, as well as *monseigneur* and forms of address such as *excellence* and *éminence*. From now on, no one was to have a coat of arms, and 'no French citizen may call themselves anything other than their family name.' The writer Beaumarchais was humble Pierre-Augustin Caron again, and although the famous Marquis de La Fayette became plain old Gilbert du Motier, he declared his support for the abolition of titles. The opinionated delegate Mirabeau (previously a *comte*) was furious when the papers immediately started calling him Riqueti (his family name), and shouted at journalists attending

[5] This generous offer was withdrawn in 1795 when the state decided that it would no longer pay any clergymen.

[6] Predictably, taking away the badges of recognition from France's establishment was not something they would put up with for very long. In practice, La Fayette was still known by his noble title, as were Mirabeau and others. In 1808 the Emperor Napoleon Bonaparte created his own aristocracy, and in 1814, on the temporary restoration of the monarchy, both royal and imperial aristocratic names were formally recognized. In the mid-nineteenth century, under Napoléon III, any self-important family would add a noble 'de' in front of their name if they thought they deserved it. Today, the aristocratic 'de' is worn as proudly as it was in 1789.

the Assemblée that this sudden change had 'disoriented Europe'. Modest he was not.[6]

Ominously, this anti-aristocratic policy inspired a popular engraving that showed four peasants with wooden flails triumphantly smashing and trampling badges of rank that have been thrown to the ground – coats of arms, swords, uniforms and bishop's mitres. It did not require a huge leap of imagination to picture the people inside them getting a beating, too.

Yet again, though, Louis XVI himself avoided hostility. He signed the relevant decrees, and he had always been known by his first name, so the rule about aristocratic titles did not affect him. Besides, as the Constitution had more and more clauses added to it, not one of these questioned the King's role. It was clear that a majority of the Assemblée, and the nation at large, still wanted a monarch.

III

By now the anniversary of the upheavals of 1789 was approaching. In the year since 14 July, the symbol of the Bastille had taken root in the public imagination. Memories of the day of rioting had been cleansed of violence and turned into a fashion accessory: in the street, people wore images of the Bastille on brooches and belt buckles, or sewn on their hat. If the political climate had been completely settled, Marie-Antoinette's more daring friends might well have had their hair styled in a Bastille *coiffe*, no doubt complete with collapsible towers.

And what many French people conveniently ignore is that on 14 July 1790, the first anniversary of Bastille Day, the celebrations were led by Louis XVI. In Paris, the date was marked by a huge public party, with the King as its star guest.

The choice of date was proof that politicians were yielding to populism. It was a message to *le peuple* from the new establishment – 'We're with you!' (Subtext: 'So please don't riot again and kick us out of power.')

But this *fête de la Fédération* on 14 July 1790 was also a celebration in honour of the constitutional monarchy and the reforms it had achieved. The citizens of Paris were invited to congratulate themselves for installing a new regime that was working. The Revolution was a year old; democratic change had been achieved; privilege was dead (or mortally wounded); no more radical upheavals were necessary.

In fact, the 14 July celebration was not the first of its kind. In the preceding months, there had been similar festivities in Dijon, Brittany, Anjou and Alsace. On 30 May, the city of Lyon had held a *fête de la Fédération* at which the National Guard and elected officials swore to 'protect with all our power the Constitution of the realm, and to be faithful to the nation, the law and the King'.

Paris decided not to be outdone, and selected 14 July as the next suitable date. The plan was to turn the whole of the Champ-de-Mars – the large park that now contains the Eiffel Tower – into an arena, with a raised 'altar of the nation' surrounded by earthwork terraces designed to hold about 100,000 spectators, most of them elected (male) officials from all over the country.

When the underpaid labourers got behind with the job and threatened to go on strike, Louis XVI and La Fayette both came along to put in some symbolic spadework, a brilliant PR move that attracted hordes of volunteers. In a rare show of national unity, it was said that rich and poor, common and noble, men and women all worked together to prepare the site for the national celebration.

Louis XVI's diary for 14 July 1790 is laconic but descriptive: 'Ceremony of the Federation at the Champ-de-Mars; departure at noon, it started at 3.30, dined at seven.'

He and the family drove into town from Saint-Cloud, where they were spending the summer, a six-kilometre trip that took hours because of the hordes of cheering spectators. Elected officials had arrived from all the new *départements*, and it was estimated that the streets were thronged with 400,000 people. Madame Campan was astonished by the joyful fervour of the crowd: 'They loved the Constitution as much as the King, the King as much as the Constitution, and it was impossible in their hearts to separate one from the other.'

At the Champ-de-Mars, Louis was taken through an *arc de triomphe* to a throne on the central platform. With the ceremony's key figure in place, Talleyrand, the young (atheist) Bishop of Autun, one of the prime movers in the recent dismantling of the clergy, held probably the most gigantic communal mass ever seen in France. He told the crowd: 'You are united and will remain so, whatever happens. Glory to God, to France and to the King!'

La Fayette made a dramatic arrival in the arena on a white horse, at the head of an army of 18,000 National Guards, to swear allegiance on behalf of 'his' men to the Constitution, the Assemblée and the King. The president of the Assemblée, Charles-François de Bonnay,[7] did likewise, and then it was Louis XVI's turn.

Although it would have been almost impossible to hear Louis XVI above the noise of the crowd, it was officially recorded that he vowed: 'I, King of the French,[8] swear to use the power that is delegated to me by the constitutional law of the state to protect the Constitution decreed by the National Assembly and accepted by me, and to execute its laws.' He was publicly confirming his status as the constitutional monarch, and hundreds of thousands of spectators were deliriously happy about it.

A painting by Charles Thévenin, completed in 1796 and now in Paris's Musée Carnavalet, shows the immense crowd, with regional delegates waving their banners, a row of impeccably uniformed National Guards lining the passage from the *arc de*

---

[7] A fairly anonymous noble delegate – at that time presidents of the Assemblée held office by rote, for only two weeks or so.

[8] Constitutionally, he was no longer 'King of France' and, by making this vow, acknowledged the fact.

triomphe to the altar, and in the foreground, a group of people apparently hugging each other in delight. And this mood of celebration lasted for days afterwards, with dances, firework displays and a regatta on the Seine.

In Chévenet's painting, only the sombre, stormy sky casts a cloud over the communal festivities. This was a realistic touch – as the ceremony came to an end and Louis XVI was driven home to his seven o'clock dinner, it began to rain. But the clouds were also symbolic. Working in 1796, the painter was well aware that the *fête de la Fédération* had been the joyful highpoint of the constitutional regime. As the crowds celebrated on 14 July 1790, they were being watched by ambitious, cynical tacticians. A political hurricane was being brewed in the cafés of the Palais-Royal, by royalist exiles abroad plotting an armed return to France, and even on the benches of the Assemblée itself. When the storm hit, it would sweep all unity and celebration away.

Chapter 16

A DOUBLE-HEADED THREAT

'Ne pouvant fortifier la justice, ils ont justifié la force.'
'Unable to fortify justice, [men] have justified force.'
Blaise Pascal (1623–62), French philosopher, in his
Pensées, published posthumously in 1669

I

Today, in the château de Versailles, there is a head-and-shoulders marble bust of Louis XVI standing in the Œil de Bœuf,[1] the anteroom to his apartments. This was where visitors would wait to be admitted to his presence. It is a spacious room decorated with a golden fresco of cavorting nymphs, presumably to keep people amused while they waited. The room has eight doors, showing that it was something of a crossroads at the heart of the palace. Today, the bust of Louis XVI stands by one of these doors, gazing genially at the herds of modern intruders who tramp through his former home, taking photos of

---

[1] The 'Bull's Eye' room is named after the oval window at one end. In fact, though, there is another oval in the wall opposite the window for symmetry's sake. The room should therefore be called the 'Œils de bœuf', plural. And before anyone objects: although the plural of '*œil*' is '*yeux*', the plural of '*œil de bœuf*' is irregular: '*œils de bœuf*'.

themselves. He is smiling, his head slightly uplifted in a gesture of apparent optimism. On the base of the sculpture is a signature: 'Loudon, 1790'.

Admittedly, the bust might well have been begun before the political upheavals of 1789, but the fact that it was completed, and then added to the royal collection, shows that Louis XVI still had reasons to be cheerful in 1790.

He wasn't alone. The general ambience of optimism and contentment reigning in France at the end of 1790 – amongst those who weren't plotting to spoil the mood, anyway – can be gauged from an almanac for 1791 published in Versailles. This was a town that had lost most of its status, and a large slice of its income, since October 1789, so one might expect its almanac to be a doom-laden catalogue of recriminations.

The publisher, a certain Blaizot, lists himself as a 'bookseller to the King and Queen', so we can assume that the Revolution had reduced his takings. He admits in his introduction that 'the almanac we present to the public today can have nothing in common with its predecessors except the name.' But he seems to have accepted his losses in surprisingly good heart. He writes that 'today a new order of things calls all citizens to take part in the administration. Let each person become more interested in educating themselves, either to be more useful to society, or to manage their own affairs in a way beneficial to others.'

This, Blaizot says, is what he is doing with his almanac, which is a 260-page compendium of everything you need to know about the town of Versailles and its surroundings. It gives the names and job titles of all those elected to serve the new *département* of Seine-et-Oise and its capital, Versailles. The book also describes every major public building in the region (including the palace, inside and out), and provides lists of schools, churches, public baths, theatres and the like, the times of sunrise and sunset for every day of the year, and even the dates of eclipses of the sun and moon.

The palace is described as though the royal family still lived there (that section of the book was probably reprinted virtually as before), but elsewhere the Revolution has made its mark. We are told, for example, that it is impossible to name people serving in the royal households, because 'Their Majesties are proposing to establish a new order in their houses.' The same goes for the King's secretaries of state, who are being replaced by elected officials.

The clearest sign that the author in no way resents the new status quo is a section at the end of the almanac called 'An Idea of the New Constitution of the French Empire'. Here, Blaizot tells his readers that 'we are already beginning to feel the benefits of the new order of things that promises France a solid and durable happiness.'

He explains exactly why, giving a potted history of the change-over from the three *états* to the Assemblée, and stressing that political decisions now rest in the hands of those elected by 'the nation'. The King effectively has no more power – he cannot propose laws, cannot veto them, and even if he objects to an idea, the third time the Assemblée sends him a bill to be signed, it automatically becomes law.

Blaizot is scathing about the former system of monarchy: under the Sun King Louis XIV 'the brilliance of royalty and literature covered the scars and concealed the bankruptcy of the French nation', he says. And he has nothing but harsh words for the old elitism: 'France ... had a class of demi-gods and a mass of semi-savages. The aristocracy fed the arrogance of the former.'

Now, though, everything is unity: 'France forms a single state, a single territory, a single everything, governed by the same principles and the same laws, by the King, supreme head of the Nation, imposed upon and governed by the legislative assembly that is the sovereign representative of the Nation.' Blaizot concludes: 'Who in France cannot love such a solid, happy order? Who in France will not play their part in making this order yet more solid and happy?'

It could be argued that this 'bookseller to the King and Queen' was a Versailles royalist pleading for Louis XVI to be left with at least some vestiges of power and status. But his criticisms of Louis XIV and the aristocratic elitists seem to rule this out, as does his tone of genuine excitement about the new democracy and what its elected officials are going to achieve. This 1791 yearbook for Versailles seems to be predicting a rosy future for the region's citizens – albeit, of course, those who can read and afford a 260-odd page book.

II

However, behind the scenes, there was growing discontent on both sides of the political spectrum. Although many aristocrats were emigrating, plenty stayed on, often still in positions of power and influence, awaiting their chance to step in and give the plebs a kicking, either metaphorical or physical. Meanwhile, it was clear to the poorest members of French society that the Assemblée was not going far or fast enough with its reforms.

Take, for example, the confiscation of land and property from the Church, the nobility and the Crown. Louis XVI lost his châteaux at Marly, near Versailles, and La Muette on the western edge of Paris (which today houses the OECD) but he was spared homelessness. He got to keep most of his châteaux in and around Paris – Versailles, the Tuileries, Saint-Cloud, Rambouillet, Saint-Germain-en-Laye and Compiègne, as well as the attached hunting forests and farmland, a rich source of income. For symbolic reasons, the Assemblée could have gone further.

The mass confiscation of property was first voted in November 1789, and the new French state suddenly became the owner of churches, abbeys, convents, châteaux (and all the artworks inside them), as well as highly valuable fields, forests and urban land. A month later, it was decided that a large proportion of this would be sold to the people, to balance the national books. It was the kind of money tree that modern governments dream of, and should have helped to lift the rural poor clear of the danger of starvation.

Yet the sale was a total shambles. For a start, only the rich could hope to bid for a château or a productive farm. Furthermore, properties were auctioned off, which was fair enough, but purchases were to be paid for over 12 years, at a price fixed in a specially created revolutionary currency, the long since forgotten *assignat*. This was paper money backed by the value of the new national assets. The scheme was opposed by Jacques Necker, who was still nominally Louis XVI's Finance Minister, but a powerless figure. Necker's warnings were ignored by the Assemblée.

Unfortunately (though perhaps predictably), with the national assets about to be sold off, and the currency's capital thereby depleted, the *assignat* lost 5 per cent of its value as soon as it was issued. When the Assemblée tried to shore things up by printing more *assignats* and using them to pay the nation's bills, the new currency plummeted again, and by late 1791 had lost half its original worth. In 1793, refusal to accept payment in *assignats* was made punishable by the death penalty, but none of this did any good, and the currency eventually became totally valueless in early 1796.

At the time, patriots blamed foreign intervention – and it was true that forged banknotes were being made in Britain, Germany, Belgium and Switzerland. But the fact is that the French state issued about 45 billion *livres* of *assignats*, whereas the total value of the confiscated assets backing up the currency was only about three billion. It was a bubble designed to burst.

The result of this debacle was that the privileged few who had bought the national assets at fixed *assignat* prices were gifted with bargains comparable to the oil refineries snapped up for a handful of dollars in post-Soviet Russia. The Revolution that was meant to eradicate privilege had dropped a windfall into the laps of the rich bourgeoisie and the remaining nobles. The wealth of the nation had been redistributed to the wealthy.

To cap it all, after the restoration of the monarchy in 1825, a law was passed – the so-called '*loi du milliard*' or 'billion law'

– giving compensation to all the aristocratic and royal émigrés who had lost property in the great confiscation. The money did not cover their true losses, but still cost the French state a billion francs. Amongst those who accepted payouts were the future King Louis-Philippe (the son of Louis XVI's conspirator cousin), the Marquis de La Fayette and the aristocratic atheist Bishop Talleyrand.

The effect of this botched sell-off was all too visible to the poorer citizens who had hoped to receive their slice of the national pie. Many of the large buildings bought by speculators were pulled to pieces and sold as construction materials. This provided labouring work, but once the stone and the lead roofing was gone, little or nothing was left of an abbey or a château that would have been a source of longer-term employment. And all the profits had disappeared into the pocket of the new owner.

Modern France is still rich in historical buildings, but it could be vastly richer. Just like the dissolution of the English monasteries by Henry VIII, France's property confiscation condemned some jewels of religious architecture to the scrap heap.

The abbey of Jumièges on the Seine in Normandy was a typical example. Its eleventh-century walls, a thirteenth-century choir, a honeycomb of Gothic cloisters and a seventeenth-century library were smashed down and sold off as builders' supplies. Robbed of their valuable lead roof, medieval frescoes mouldered and disappeared in the rain.

Similarly, the thirteenth-century buildings of the abbey of Savigny, on the Brittany–Normandy border, were stripped of their artworks and decorations and then dynamited, the ancient stones sold as masonry. The lost treasures there included a 70-metre steeple and 76 ancient stained-glass windows. Almost pathetically, a surviving archway and a few fragments of wall were declared national monuments in 1924.

In Paris, the church of Saint-Paul-des-Champs, near the place des Vosges, was completely torn down. This was a fifteenth-century building with seventh-century foundations, where several kings of France had been baptized. The church and its cemetery were sold to speculators and wiped off the map.

Former royal homes didn't fare much better. The château of Marly near Versailles, for example, was bought by an industrialist who turned it into a cotton mill. When he went bankrupt, Louis XIV's former home was demolished for its stone and lead.

If all this destruction had in some way helped the poor, other than providing them with temporary labour, it would seem more excusable. In the event, though, what it boiled down to was national treasures being more or less given away to rich vandals.

III

At the same time, not everyone in the Assemblée or the nation at large was happy with the elitism evident in the ever-evolving Constitution. This was particularly true for the clauses about private property being 'inviolable', and 'fair and pre-emptive compensation' being paid for any further confiscations. The rich were locking down their strong boxes with the aid of the supposedly democratic state.

This Constitution also stated that the King's person was 'inviolable and sacred' and that 'royalty ... is hereditary, and passed in the reigning race from male to male, by order of birth'.[2] In other words, in many people's eyes the Revolution had effectively come to a halt. It was just a matter of moving the chess pieces about the board; none could be taken off. Understandably, after the initial feeling in 1789 that anything was possible, some of the more republican Assemblée delegates were feeling increasingly frustrated.

[2] When the first Constitution was eventually published in September 1791 it would also state that 'women and their descendants [were] perpetually excluded' from the French throne.

Probably the man who was infuriating the radicals the most was the Marquis de La Fayette. After his dramatic performance at the *fête de la Fédération* in July 1790, the dashing young general (he was still only 32) began to cultivate his image as a kind of national protector, making public appearances and issuing declarations. On 9 October 1790, for example, he turned up with a delegation of his troops to congratulate the municipal council of Paris on its new permanent status – as if it needed his blessing. He had already made a famous speech to the Assemblée saying that: 'For the Revolution, disorder was necessary, because the old order was nothing but servitude, and in that case, insurrection is the holiest of duties. But for the sake of the Constitution, the new order must become firmer, and laws must be respected.' Now La Fayette urged the Assemblée to support martial law (imposed by him and his troops) to protect the monarchy, which felt to some veterans of 1789 like a return to the Ancien Régime.

La Fayette's enemies resorted to the tactics that had been so successfully used against Marie-Antoinette – fake news. And to make it all credible, they linked his name with hers. One 16-page scandal sheet called *La Confession de Marie-Antoinette* depicted the Queen admitting that she was controlling the young general and that 'it was necessary to use all the ruses that a woman, and especially a German woman, has at her disposal ... As my official lover, he courts me continuously, he screws me morning and night, which only attaches him to me even more.' Barely credible stuff, but damaging all the same, especially because the pamphlet boasted that it would reveal Marie-Antoinette's 'loves and intrigues with Monsieur de La Fayette and the principal members of the Assemblée nationale, and ... her counter-revolutionary projects.'

Another, even longer, pamphlet involving these alleged lovers was called *The Loving Evenings of General Motier* [La Fayette's common name as a citizen] *and Beautiful Antoinette, by the Austrian's Little Spaniel*. Its 32 pages described intimate, treasonable conversations taking place over three evenings, the last of which is cut short because La Fayette becomes impotent.

Worse, though, were supposedly more credible sources such as the 'newspaper' *L'Ami du peuple*, which was regularly pasted up on the walls of Paris. More political in tone than the outright scandal sheets, it stated overtly that La Fayette was Marie-Antoinette's lover and suggested that he was 'in a plot with enemies of the Revolution'.

However, the reality was that Marie-Antoinette despised and distrusted La Fayette, blaming him at least in part for not preventing the attack on Versailles in October 1790, as well as her subsequent kidnap by the Parisians.

It was true that La Fayette was in close contact with royalist agitators, some of whom were still active in the supposedly revolutionary French army. In February 1791, he wrote a letter to a pro-royalist general, boasting that 'I am violently attacked by all party leaders, who see me as an incorruptible, fearless obstacle, and the chief aim of any ill-intentioned project is to get rid of me.' It was arrogant but true. As we shall see later, these attacks on La Fayette were not just barbs aimed at a conservative political figure, they were also designed to undermine the head of the National Guard, thereby opening the way for violence.

Bizarrely, one of La Fayette's most virulent critics was a man whose ideas were very similar to his. Mirabeau, the highly vocal delegate of the Assemblée nationale, had first made his presence felt during the États généraux of May 1789. Although by birth a count, Mirabeau became a delegate in the *tiers état*, and quickly emerged as one of the nation's greatest (and loudest) orators. One of the prime movers in the drafting of the *Declaration of Men's and Citizens' Rights*, he was also a proponent of the constitutional monarchy, and seems to have waged a campaign against La Fayette for purely personal reasons – it was impossible to have two national heroes. What's more, La Fayette was handsome, slim and had fought battles, whereas Mirabeau was ugly and his main contact with soldiers had been while locked up in prison as a younger man for debts and adultery.

Mirabeau accused La Fayette (privately, at least), of wanting to become a kind of dictator – 'the all-powerful intermediary between the monarch and his subjects', whereas he, Mirabeau, swore 'to maintain the monarchist government, and [saw] dictatorship under a king as a crime'. We know this because Mirabeau wrote it in one of the secret communiqués that he had begun to send to Louis XVI, keeping him informed of everything that was being said in Parisian political circles. Shockingly, despite his public role as the people's champion, Mirabeau was a royal spy, and was receiving payment in gold for his services.

However, we also know from the papers discovered after his death that Mirabeau never promised to work for counter-revolution. He was trying to convince Louis to accept a British-style constitutional monarchy, and wrote that he wanted to be 'the defender of monarchic power regulated by laws, and the apostle of liberty guaranteed by monarchic power'.

When Mirabeau died suddenly in April 1791, aged only 42, he was so popular with the people that some suspected that he had been poisoned by enemies of the Revolution. His body was ceremoniously entombed in the Panthéon, which was converted in his honour into the resting place of France's heroes (and a small number of heroines), the role that it still plays today. However, when copies of his illicit correspondence with Louis XVI were found in November 1792, his remains were removed and reburied nearby. His sister then had them exhumed and taken to the cimetière de Clamart which was decommissioned soon afterwards, to make way rather aptly for Paris's amphitheatre for anatomical dissection. Bodies that were not claimed by the families of the deceased were sent to the Paris catacombs, which is probably where Mirabeau's bones now lie, amongst the anonymous piles of skulls, femurs and ribs that form one of the city's most popular tourist attractions.

Somewhat mistakenly, the discovery of his letters to Louis XVI, many of them actually urging the King to continue working with the Assemblée, was seized upon by opponents of constitutional monarchy as evidence of Mirabeau's involvement in a counter-revolutionary conspiracy.

Sadly for France, there were plenty of conspiracy theorists who were only too keen to misinterpret facts to whip up public paranoia and unleash the violence that had been kept – more or less – in check since October 1790.

IV

The various factions at work during the ten or so years of the French Revolution seem to have divided and subdivided until they were as thinly sliced as a courgette in a Parisian kitchen. It was almost as though a new political movement emerged every time two or more politicians got together for a glass of wine. Reading histories of the Revolution, one comes across the Cordeliers, Girondins, Jacobins, Indulgents, Feuillants, Montagnards, Hébertistes, Fédérés, Exagérés, and Enragés, as well as the 48 *sections révolutionnaires de Paris*, the new neighbourhood committees who threw their weight behind one faction or another. The political arena was like a gladiatorial tournament, with everyone fighting each other.

It's very similar in France today – fortunately without the guillotinings. After every election, some ambitious candidate declares that their party was at fault and forms a new one, based around guess-whom. President Macron was one of these break-away politicians – jumping ship from the Socialists in April 2016, he formed his party, La République en marche. He won the presidential election of May 2017, and by July some of the party members were already reported to be splitting off into a new faction, Démocratie en marche. In French politics, there seems to be no concept of broad consensus – if you don't agree with every single word of your party's creed, you just form a new party, with yourself as leader.

This process began during the Revolution, when political clubs and factions were jostling for power, usually as instruments of one man's ego.[3] Each one of these claimed to represent universal truth, and refused to recognize any plurality of opinion – all those who didn't agree with them entirely were tarred with the same brush. Or, as it would eventually turn out, decapitated with the same guillotine.

This was why, to the more radical republicans, everyone with an ounce of sympathy for the King was branded an outright traitor. Those in favour of a constitutional monarchy were dubbed, scathingly, *'monarchiens'* – an adjective that neatly combines *'monarchie'* with *'chien'* (dog). It was the same trick that people had used when they called Marie-Antoinette *'l'Autrichienne'*. And *'monarchien'* is a label that is still used in modern French history books, despite its disparaging overtones, to describe the democrats like Bailly, Mounier, La Fayette and (posthumously) Mirabeau, even though they were supporting peaceful reform that might have avoided massacres and civil war.

At this point in the Revolution, when the monarchy was coming under its first concentrated attack, the most outspoken radicals were larger-than-life figures who have gone down in history because of their violent deaths – Marat, Danton and Robespierre, to name just the most famous.

Jean-Paul Marat was perhaps the most vitriolic critic of the *monarchiens*. He is best known for being murdered in his bathtub – and when one reads his writings, it seems fitting that he is remembered for his bloody demise.

Like Necker, Marat was Swiss, but shared none of his compatriot's love of order and harmony. He was born in 1743, trained as a doctor, and in the early 1770s practised in Newcastle, England, taking on both human and animal patients to earn a living. At the same time he wrote philosophical treatises inspired by Rousseau, the main thrust of his thought being to attack anyone he didn't agree with. In one of his essays Marat took a sideswipe at 'the inconsequential Voltaire', earning himself a

[3] They were almost all men.

stinging rebuke from the master. Voltaire wrote an article lambasting Marat's lack of focus on his own ideas: 'One should not, as you do, stray off one's subject to go and provoke brawls in the street.' A fitting remark given Marat's later taste for stirring up riots.

In 1776 Marat moved to France and, thanks to a recommendation from one of his aristocratic patients, got a job as physician to the guards of Louis XVI's brother Charles. This prestigious position attracted even more aristocratic patients, and soon Marat was a rich man. He spent some of his income on a physics laboratory where he conducted experiments on electricity, fire and light, publishing his ideas in a series of papers, one of which attempted (and, according to France's Académie des sciences, failed) to disprove the theories of Newton. Marat's wealth had done nothing to mellow his argumentative nature.

By the early 1780s, Marat was a comfortable member of France's establishment – a wealthy doctor and self-appointed philosopher, participating (albeit inefficiently) in Louis XVI's programme to develop the sciences, and profiting from the patronage of royals and aristocrats. According to some historians, he was even sleeping with the wife of his original aristocratic benefactor.

However, after he gave up his job with the royal guards to devote himself to science, Marat's income seems to have plummeted, and in 1785 he got embroiled in a battle with the tax authorities. He wrote to them claiming that he should be exempt from *capitation* (poll tax) 'because I am like all foreigners who travel and spend money to inform themselves'. He also complained about 'the bad faith of people who have abused my trust and forced me to adopt the strictest frugality'. Resentment against the establishment was brewing. The answer came back from the royal taxman: pay up. It was enough to turn anyone against the monarchy.

In August 1789, Marat pitched into the revolutionary debate with a pamphlet entitled *Le Moniteur patriote*, a violent attack on the moderation shown by Assemblée delegates like Mounier who were looking for a way to ensure 'the people's happiness'. Pouring scorn on such woolly concepts as happiness, Marat said that the Assemblée's draft Constitution contained 'illusory, dangerous, shameful, alarming measures' which meant that it should be 'rejected with indignation by every true Frenchman'. These 'worthy delegates' were leaving power in the hands of the King, who would treat the people 'like a herd of animals'. Marat reminded his readers that 'the blood of traitors is still steaming', while hinting that the Assemblée were 'enemies of the state' and 'false patriots'. Polite debates about how best to manage the peaceful transition to democracy were clearly not Marat's thing.

He followed this up with the regular publication of *L'Ami du peuple*, a sort of rabble-rousing tabloid newspaper that he wrote, financed and had pasted up on the walls of Paris. In these tracts he mixed truly democratic ideas like the need to abolish slavery in the colonies (Marat's political ideas were egalitarian, even if his instincts were murderous) with attacks on anyone he perceived to be an 'enemy of the Revolution', calls for La Fayette's heart to be ripped out, and accusations that Louis XVI had 'caused 15 million people to die of poverty and starvation' and 'had the throats of thousands of defenders of the nation cut in order to re-establish depotism'. One of the most famous lines from *L'Ami du peuple* was Marat's assertion that: 'It is by violence that liberty must be established.'

With these bloodthirsty rants being posted all over Paris practically every day from September 1789 to September 1792, it is hardly surprising that the Assemblée and La Fayette's National Guard had their work cut out keeping the peace.

V

Until 1787, Georges Jacques Danton was a relatively humble lawyer's clerk from eastern France. Then he married the daughter of a rich Parisian café and cabaret owner – who was also a royal tax collector. This match brought a dowry of 20,000 *livres* with which the 27-year-old Danton bought a post as a lawyer.[4] Like Marat, Danton was a beneficiary of the royal regime that he would later turn against.

When the Revolution began, Danton was living in the cour du Commerce Saint-André, a small passageway off the boulevard Saint-Germain. It is now full of tourist restaurants, but in 1789 it was a hotbed of revolutionary activity. Marat's *Ami du peuple* was printed there, and, coincidentally or not, it was in a workshop in this passageway that the prototype of the guillotine would later be tested on sheep.

This neighbourhood of central Paris, where poor workers lived alongside *petit bourgeois* intellectuals like Danton, was one of the most active during the events of the early Revolution. This was when Danton seized his chance to gain prominence. He was by all accounts a natural orator, with a loud voice and commanding physical presence. Like Mirabeau, he possessed a gift for snappy phrases, sarcastic put-downs and dramatic gestures. Also like Mirabeau, he was a profoundly ugly man. As a baby, he had been gored by a bull, deforming his upper lip. He had also had his nose broken, and bore the scars of childhood smallpox. His grimacing face alone was almost enough to silence his opponents.

In early 1789 Danton began attending neighbourhood political meetings. These would later be formalized into the club des Cordeliers, which took its name from the nearby monastery of the same name, which had been requisitioned by revolutionaries. As its logo, the club chose an open eye, deeming itself 'the wide-open eye of revolutionary vigilance'. As such, it issued

[4] The full price of this position was 78,000 *livres*, which Danton arranged to pay off in instalments. He made the final payments thanks to bribes paid to him by Louis XVI, via the royal spy Mirabeau, who wanted to convince some of the more virulent revolutionaries not to be too anti-monarchistic.

statements, launched petitions and organized the occasional riot. It was overtly against the moderate Bailly's mayorship of Paris and La Fayette's rule of law.

Danton became the club's natural leader, though he usually managed to stay out of the riots that his speeches incited – perhaps because of the bribes he was receiving from Mirabeau. For example, Danton took no part in the events of 14 July 1789, even though he had stood on a table at a meeting the previous day and given a rousing speech to a crowd of hungry, angry workers. He urged them to take up arms and 'push back the 15,000 brigands amassed in Montmartre and the 30,000 men ready to descend upon Paris, pillage the city and cut its citizens' throats'.

That day, 13 July 1789, as the cheers rang out and his audience went off to find weapons, a lawyer called Christophe Lavaux came over to speak to Danton. Lavaux was an old friend who had come to the Paris bar at the same time as Danton, but had known nothing about his political activities. In his memoirs, Lavaux wrote that Danton had previously possessed 'a just mind, and a gentle, modest, silent character', and that ambition must have transformed him.

Lavaux told Danton that he was wrong about the invading royal armies – he had just come from Versailles, and everything there was proceeding calmly. Danton replied furiously: 'You don't understand a thing. The people have risen up against despotism ... The throne has been overturned, and your estate is finished.' (Lavaux was an aristocrat.)

Lavaux warned Danton that his troublemaking would lead him to the scaffold. Danton dismissed this idea, but after that day, every time the two met, Danton would taunt Lavaux, telling him 'you'll be hanged' or 'you'll be guillotined'. Lavaux always replied, 'Not before you.'

In the end, Lavaux was right, and Danton would eventually fall victim to the reign of terror that he was to instigate, but not before thousands of others had been massacred with, at the very least, Danton's tacit consent.

VI

Danton's great rival in the extreme republican ranks was a very different man – Maximilien de Robespierre.[5] If Danton was a bellowing grizzly bear, Robespierre was a cat, which was how his contemporaries described him. He had a small, pleasant face, with a pointed nose and watchful eyes, and, like all felines, was capable of seeming sleek and imperturbable, only to lash out suddenly with deadly claws. In Robespierre's case, these were verbal or political, and aimed straight at the throat.

Robespierre is probably the Revolution's most controversial figure. He is viewed either as an idealist, the man who finally turned the woolly compromises of the Constitution into true revolution, or as a power-mad, guillotine-wielding dictator.

His supporters have plenty of exemplary quotations to choose from. Reading them, one would think that Robespierre had nothing but democratic ideals and the well-being of France at heart as he guillotined his way through his opponents. In his very last speech to parliament in July 1794, he said that: 'The French Revolution is the first to be founded on theories of human rights and the principles of justice. Other revolutions required only ambition. Ours imposes virtue.' Fine words, the only problem being that France at the time was in the grip of the Terreur imposed by an all-powerful state police, with thousands being executed after show trials, and the speech was given a day before Robespierre tried to organize the armed overthrow of the government by the Paris mob.

A biography, written in 1795 by a royalist clergyman called Liévin-Bonaventure Proyart, and called *The Life and Crimes of Robespierre, Nicknamed the Tyrant, from His Birth to His Death*

---

[5] Despite his 'de', Robespierre was not noble. His family name was originally spelt Derobespierre, and he separated out the two parts, apparently in an effort to make himself look noble – a strange gesture at such a time. Either that, or he wanted to make sure he was known as 'Robespierre', and not the more aristocratic-sounding 'Derobespierre'.

– so we know where the author's sympathies lie – begins by saying that Robespierre was someone whom 'monsters, less monstrous than he, called the Tyrant'. Even his supporters were terrified of him.

Robespierre was born in Arras in northern France in 1758, the bastard son of a lawyer and a brewer's daughter. His father abandoned his family when Maximilien was small and his mother died soon afterwards, leaving the boy to be raised by his maternal grandfather. A studious pupil, when he was ten he won a scholarship to go to the collège Louis-le-Grand in Paris, one of the best schools in France, financed by the King. Here he gained a reputation as a brilliant student but a loner, often lost in his own musings.

Liévin-Bonaventure Proyart's biography includes an eye-witness account of a ceremony held in Paris to greet Louis XVI shortly after his coronation, for which Robespierre was selected to read out a Latin verse written by one of his teachers. 'I remember that the King looked down benevolently on the young Monster,' Proyart wrote, 'who, although raised in the King's house, would one day strike him with the first dagger blow.' After qualifying as a lawyer and returning to Arras, like Danton, Robespierre seized the opportunity to go into politics in 1789. He wrote the *cahier de doléances* for a local cobblers' guild, and was elected a *tiers état* delegate.

He threw himself into the Assemblée's debates, expressing some truly idealistic opinions – he spoke out in favour of universal suffrage (including for women), against slavery, and even against the death penalty that he would use so freely later. He was one of the delegates who accompanied Louis XVI into Paris on 17 July 1789.

It is no surprise that the young Robespierre features prominently in the painter Jacques-Louis David's official depiction of the historic Jeu de paume oath of 20 June 1789, clasping his hands dramatically to his chest and gazing towards heaven (or the curved ceiling anyway). Typically, Robespierre stands alone in the drawing, while most of the other men are shaking

Above: The women's march from Paris to Versailles on 5 October 1789. In fact, they were probably less heavily armed than this, and had to struggle through mud and torrential rain. Also, it is often forgotten that the *Parisiennes* originally went to Versailles to ask Louis XVI's help in obtaining bread, not to demand his head.

Left: The marquis de La Fayette, whose National Guard failed to keep the peace during the Revolution. He is often accused of fighting his own personal battle rather than supporting political change. Note the revolutionary rosette, the '*cocarde*', on his hat, held almost out of view.

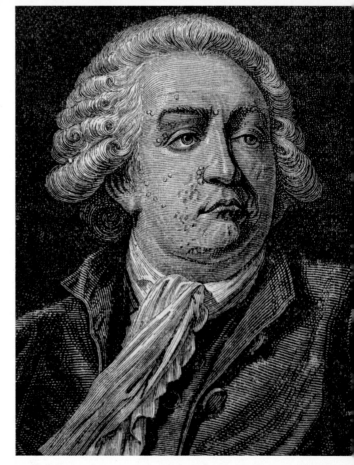

Above: Paris, 14 July 1790, the celebration of the first anniversary of Bastille Day. King Louis XVI was the guest of honour at the ceremony, and received an oath of allegiance from politicians and the National Guard. France was still very much a functioning monarchy.

Right: Honoré de Mirabeau, one of the early revolutionary hotheads, was an aristocrat who became anti-authoritarian after being imprisoned for debt and adultery as a young man. However, he later turned into a royalist spy, passing messages to Louis XVI and trying to curb anti-royalist fervour in parliament.

Right: The Constitution of 1791 – signed by Louis XVI 'J'accepte.' It affirmed the position of the King as head of a new, almost democratic constitutional monarchy. The Constitution included the 'Declaration of Men's and Citizens' Rights' (the French Revolution accorded very few new rights to women).

DÉCRET
DE L'ASSEMBLÉE NATIONALE.
Du *trois Septembre* 1791.

La Constitution française.
Declaration des droits de l'homme et du Citoyen.

Les Représentans du Peuple Français, constitués en Assemblée Nationale, considérant que l'ignorance, l'oubli ou le mépris des droits de l'homme sont les seules causes des malheurs publics et de la Corruption des Gouvernemens, ont résolu d'exposer, dans une Déclaration solennelle, les droits naturels, inaliénables et sacrés de l'homme, afin que cette déclaration, constamment présente à tous les Membres du Corps social, leur rappelle sans cesse leurs droits et leurs devoirs; afin que les actes du pouvoir législatif et ceux du pouvoir

Sans culotte Parisien.

Left: A 'sans-culotte'. This nickname implies that they were bare-bottomed, but in fact it described poorer people who did not wear the tight breeches and stockings of the rich. Instead they sported long, loose trousers. Gangs of them would patrol the streets of Paris, challenging anyone who did not wear the revolutionary rosette.

Above: The three most famous revolutionary politicians, Georges-Jacques Danton, Jean-Paul Marat and Maximilien de Robespierre. Three men who called for violence, only to die violently themselves.

Left: Marat's free newspaper, *L'Ami du peuple* ('The People's Friend'), written and published by him from September 1789 to September 1792. Almost every day, populist outrage, calls for riots and assassinations, and (frequently fake) news about the Revolution were pasted up on Paris's walls.

Nº. C. X X.

L'AMI DU PEUPLE,

O U

LE PUBLICISTE PARISIEN,

JOURNAL POLITIQUE ET IMPARTIAL;

Par M. Marat, *Auteur de* l'Offrande a' *la* Patrie, *du* Moniteur, *et du* Plan de Constitution, *etc.*

Vitam impendere vero.

DU MARDI 1 JUIN 1790.

Arrêtés relatifs au soulagement des pauvres nationaux, et au renvoi des mendians étrangers. — Observations à ce sujet. — Arrêtés relatifs à la réforme du clergé. — Réflexions sur la proclamation du Roi.

ASSEMBLÉE NATIONALE.

Séance du 3o mai 1790.

L'assemblée, après avoir ouï le rapport du comité de mendicité, a arrêté qu'il sera établi de nouveaux (1) ateliers dans Paris,

(1) Il existe actuellement au fauxbourg St.-Martin, maison des Récollets, une manufacture montée

Above: September 1792, the massacre of 'immoral' women at La Salpêtrière prison, Paris. Most of the victims were prostitutes or adulterous wives. Ironically, before being hacked and beaten to death, many of the women were raped by their supposedly moralistic executioners. The massacres went largely uncondemned by the revolutionary authorities.

Right: March 1792, Louis XVI (still nominally King) inspects the proposed design of the guillotine. Legend has it that he suggested the more efficient, angled blade for this humane, 'egalitarian' method of execution. Not that it helped him: his execution in 1793 was botched, the blade passing through the base of his skull and mutilating his lower jaw.

Above: Louis XVI's execution, on 21 January 1793 in the place de la Révolution (now place de la Concorde) in Paris. He was allowed to ride to the scaffold in a closed carriage, partly out of a fear that royalists might attempt a last-minute rescue.

Right: 16 October, 1793. Marie-Antoinette sketched en route to the guillotine by Jacques-Louis David. She was driven through the streets to the scaffold on an open cart, like a common prisoner, her hands tied. The former Queen's body was buried in a mass grave, her detached head placed between her legs.

Left: The writer Olympe de Gouges, who campaigned against slavery, and wrote the 'Declaration of the Rights of Women and Female Citizens', a demand for equal rights to education, property and free speech for women. These demands were largely ignored by the revolutionary government, and in 1793 she was guillotined for criticizing Marat and Robespierre for their bloodthirstiness.

Above: During the '*Terreur*' of 1793-94, thousands of supposed counter-revolutionaries were massacred in western France. A favourite technique in Nantes was drowning, wittily renamed 'vertical deportation', or when naked men and women were tied together, a 'republican wedding'.

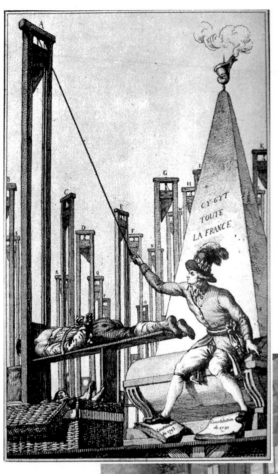

Left: A satirical engraving of 1794: Robespierre is depicted hard at work, purging his critics as he tramples on the Constitution. The gravestone reads 'here lies all of France.' In total, during outbreaks of *La Terreur*, around 300,000 French citizens were killed by over-zealous revolutionaries.

Below: In 1799, with the Revolution stalling, a young revolutionary general called Napoleon Bonaparte stepped into the power vacuum. Soon afterwards, France had an emperor who was just as absolutist as King Louis XVI or his predecessors had even been.

hands, embracing or gesturing towards Bailly as he swears allegiance to the nation.

Robespierre did not content himself with being the MP for humble Arras. He was also busy manoeuvring himself to become the leader and spokesman of one of Paris's influential political clubs, the Jacobins, named after the convent near the Tuileries palace where it met. Initially founded by a group of moderate Bretons, Robespierre brought in members from all over France, and turned it into a full-blown opposition party that held a sort of alternative Assemblée in the chapter house and library of the former convent.

Robespierre is often credited with inventing the slogan '*Liberté, Égalité, Fraternité*' during a speech in which he proposed sewing a motto on the uniforms of the National Guard. Originally, though, the full slogan was '*Liberté, Égalité, Fraternité ou la Mort*' – 'or Death', as though fraternity might be swapped for violence if the wearer of the badge felt like it. And once Robespierre rose to power, 'Liberty, Equality, Death' would become a tragically accurate slogan.

VII

While republicans like Marat, Danton and Robespierre were sniping at the moderate constitutionalists, or *monarchiens*, from one side, equally ambitious royalists were doing so on the other flank.

Some of these were acting with the approval of the royal family, who were all getting increasingly nervous in their Parisian palace, surrounded by scheming politicians and disrespectful citizens. By the end of 1790, Louis himself was finally beginning to look for a way to escape – not necessarily from France, because he still felt the need to be the figurehead for 'his' people, but from Paris. As the endless debates about the Constitution dragged on, he was becoming convinced that the new mode of government could not survive, and that his only hope was to be ready to set up an alternative regime (preferably a return to his own benevolent rule, of course) before the republican hotheads could grab power.

Inevitably, Parisians got wind of the King's wish to escape (Marat was constantly warning about it), and Louis was forbidden from returning to Saint-Cloud, even after he wrote a letter to the Assemblée promising them that the Constitution 'made him happy'. Hemmed in by suspicious National Guards, Louis XVI was getting scared.

One of the King's staunchest supporters, and a man who was proving that he knew how to quieten a mob, was a general with the quaint name François-Claude-Amour de Bouillé, the commander of the army guarding France's eastern border, and its main garrison in Metz. Bouillé proved his mettle in August 1790 when soldiers in Nancy mutinied, having got it into their heads that their officers were stealing their pay. La Fayette, the man with nominal responsibility for law and order, sent a general to deal with the rebellion, but he was locked up by the mutineers. Bouillé then marched over from Metz with some 5,000 soldiers and fought his way into the town, a battle that caused around 300 dead and wounded. After a court martial, 72 men were jailed, 41 condemned to be galley slaves for 30 years (an effective death sentence) and 22 were hanged. One unfortunate soldier was broken on the wheel – by all accounts the last person to suffer this brutal punishment in mainland France before the more humane, though equally deadly, guillotine was introduced.

Bouillé's intervention was the kind of firm action that royalists had been calling for since July 1789. Now, though, all it did was create martyrs. In Paris, Marat began writing about 'the assassin Bouillé' and the 'killers of the garrison and citizens of Nancy', as if the whole town had been massacred by royalist forces (a fate Marat was constantly predicting for Paris).

The Nancy affair also revealed the fatal divisions in the Assemblée. After offering Bouillé its congratulations in September 1790, a year later, delegates were hailing the Nancy mutineers as national heroes. It seemed that Louis was right to be losing confidence in the peaceful transition to democracy.

General Bouillé, meanwhile, kept his job, as well as a firm command over his army of loyal soldiers, and Louis XVI knew that he had a valuable – if inflammatory – supporter in the east of France, waiting to step in and clip revolutionary wings.

VIII

In theory, Louis XVI's brothers and cousins were supposed to be organizing rescue parties, but in fact some of them were wondering how they could wangle their own way on to the throne. Not all of these supposed allies were hoping to protect Louis from the mob surrounding his palace.

Louis gave the job of attracting help from abroad to one of his closest political allies, Louis Charles Auguste Le Tonnelier de Breteuil, former ambassador to Russia, Sweden and Austria. Breteuil had very briefly served as Louis XVI's Chief Minister in July 1789, but emigrated to Switzerland just after the storming of the Bastille. In November 1790, Louis managed to get a letter, written in his own hand, to Breteuil, asking him to plead his cause with Austria and all the German states. The letter gave Breteuil the power to 'deal with foreign courts and propose in [Louis XVI's] name all measures that might re-establish royal authority and the tranquillity of the Kingdom'.

However, Breteuil was a 60-year-old ambassador, and quickly discovered that he was competing for attention with younger men of action who were offering to fight.

As mentioned earlier, Louis XVI's youngest brother, Charles, was amongst the first royalists to leave France. He escaped on 16 July 1789, and made his way to Turin, home of his wife's father, the King of Sardinia (the Italian island was not at that time considered beautiful or sophisticated enough to warrant a royal palace). There, Charles set up a committee to plot counter-revolution, along with Louis Joseph, Prince de Condé, a grandson of Louis XIV who had seen military service in Germany as a younger man.

Back in France, Louis XVI heard that this Turin committee was planning to capture Alsace on the eastern border – and maybe grant the province independence. Louis got a letter to his brother explaining that rumours like this, whether true or not, did his cause no good at all. Whether Charles was deliberately putting his brother's life at risk, or hoping to grab a chunk of France for himself, is not entirely clear.

In any case, Charles and Condé turned for help to Marie-Antoinette's younger brother, Leopold,[6] who was now Holy Roman Emperor. A conference was organized at Pillnitz in Saxony, with King Friedrich Wilhelm II of Prussia, an arch-conservative who was known to be against anything to do with modern Lumières-style thinking.

Charles and Condé did their best to convince the two monarchs to invade France, and smash what they predicted to be an unmotivated, ill-organized revolutionary army. The invasion plan had been drawn up by Bouillé, the man who broke the Nancy mutiny, and who had joined this ex-pat campaign to 'liberate' France.

However, Leopold told them that an invasion would put his sister's life in danger – and that of Louis XVI of course. Leopold was also sure that Britain would not join a war against revolutionary France because the British were too happy to see chaos reigning on the other side of the Channel (and in fact, Leopold himself was not unhappy to see France's military power diminished). Prussia, meanwhile, had recently got embroiled unprofitably in wars in Belgium and Russia, and Friedrich Wilhelm was not keen to start fighting again.

So all Charles and Condé obtained was a written warning to the French not to harm the royal family. Like most written warnings, it was decidedly unthreatening. 'The situation in which His Majesty the King of France currently finds himself is a matter of common interest to all the sovereigns of Europe,'

[6] Her elder brother Joseph, the man who had come to Versailles to give marriage counselling, had died in 1790 aged only 48.

Leopold and Friedrich Wilhelm declared. They called for the preservation of 'a monarchist government that respects the rights of sovereigns and the well-being of the French'. And in case this did not happen, they would 'give their troops orders to stay within range to take action'.

Predictably, this was a major disappointment to Charles, Condé and Bouillé, especially the last two who were hoping to ride away from Pillnitz to collect the Austrian and Prussian armies. Even so, despite its lack of truly threatening language, the so-called 'Declaration of Pillnitz' was seized upon by French republicans as yet another sign that the monarchy had to end.

All this convinced Marie-Antoinette that, whether an army came to rescue the family or not, they had to escape. While Louis XVI increasingly dithered and lamented the injustice of his fate, she worked with her close friend and alleged former lover, Fersen, on practical plans. The first of these was to order a six-seater carriage – a *berline* – complete with a larder, cooking utensils, a foldaway dining table and leather chamber pots. To disguise its true purpose, the carriage was ordered in the name of a German baroness, Theophila von Korff (usually called 'de Korff' in French sources), who 'was planning to travel to Russia'.

As the carriage builders and leather workers got started on the commission, a showdown between the extreme republican and royalist factions in Paris made the need to escape even more urgent.

Chapter 17

THE KING AND QUEEN TRY TO TAKE FRENCH LEAVE

'D'après ... l'impossibilité où le Roi se trouve à présent d'opérer le bien et d'empêcher le mal qui se commet, est-il étonnant que le Roi ait cherché à recouvrir sa liberté et à se mettre en sûreté avec sa famille?'

'Given the King's present situation, in which he finds it impossible either to do good or to prevent evil from being committed, is it surprising that the King has sought to take back his freedom and seek safety with his family?'

Louis XVI, in a letter to the French people.
He left the handwritten document on his bed when
he fled from Paris on 20 June 1791

I

The tensions between moderates and extremists at the Assemblée, and between monarchist sympathizers and outright royalists, seem to have crystallized on a single, eventful day in 1791.

On the morning of 28 February, a Monday, about 1,200 men and women set out from Paris's faubourg Saint-Antoine, the neighbourhood around the Bastille, to attack the château de Vincennes, a fourteenth-century castle a five-kilometre walk away. They were led by the *commandant général* of the faubourg Saint-Antoine, a brewer and chemist called Antoine Joseph

Santerre, who had been elected a general after his exploits during the storming of the Bastille, when he had commandeered fire pumps to spurt inflammable phosphorus at the prison walls.

Now Santerre was staging a repeat of that siege at Vincennes, which, it has to be said, looked rather like the Bastille, with its tall, medieval dungeon and high battlements. Vincennes, like the Bastille, had been a royal prison under Louis XV, and its inmates had included the Marquis de Sade, the politician Mirabeau, and the subversive writer Diderot. More recently, it had been converted into attractive private apartments that were granted as favours by Louis XVI. However, in November 1790 it had been requisitioned as a *'bien national'* (national asset) and there were plans to turn it back into a prison, under revolutionary control this time.

This was the problem: by now there was so much disagreement and distrust between the moderate reformists, like La Fayette, Mirabeau and Bailly, and the Marat-style republicans, like the rising stars Robespierre and Danton, that this revolutionary prison had become suspect. It was easy to convince the workers of the faubourg Saint-Antoine that the prison would house anyone who criticized the new Constitution. According to another rumour, Vincennes was already being used as a counter-revolutionary headquarters. Santerre told his improvised army that it had to be demolished.

A contemporary engraving shows men and women apparently hacking at the castle walls with pickaxes and sticks. Unlike the storming of the Bastille, the attackers had no cannons – it was going to take them a long time.

Back in Paris, La Fayette received news of the slow-motion demolition, and at about 3 p.m. he arrived with his National Guard. Respecting due process, he received confirmation from the Mayor of Vincennes that he did not want his town's château to be destroyed, and duly marched into the castle, where his men quickly quelled the attack. He took 60 people into custody for resisting, and marched back to Paris.

Once calm had been restored, La Fayette went to yell at Santerre, accusing him of shooting at his aide-de-camp Desmottes during the resistance. Santerre denied it, and was backed up by his men, but arriving back in Paris, La Fayette found the gate locked (probably by Santerre's men), and had to force his way through. As he marched along the rue du Faubourg Saint-Antoine, shots rang out, apparently aimed both at Desmottes and La Fayette, and one of the National Guards had to prod his bayonet at a man who tried to trip up La Fayette's horse with a pole. It was factional warfare in the streets.

Meanwhile, another château was also under siege. This was the royal palace of the Tuileries, where a small army of around 500 men suddenly appeared at about 9 p.m., most of them dressed in black cloaks and carrying easily concealed weapons such as daggers and pistols. According to the memoirs of a certain Marquis de Ferrières, they were 'nobles or enemies of the Revolution', and told the palace guards that La Fayette had been killed in Vincennes, and that his soldiers needed reinforcements. They, the men in cloaks, would stay and protect the King.

Just then, a soldier arrived at the palace with news that La Fayette was safe, and the King was warned that a crowd of armed men had invaded his palace. Louis XVI came to talk to the intruders, who told him that there was an uprising in Paris and that *le peuple* were cutting each other's throats in the faubourg Saint-Antoine. 'Sire,' one of them said, 'your nobility has rushed to your sacred person to defend it.'

Louis apparently replied, 'Your zeal is indiscreet. Give up your weapons and withdraw. I am safe amongst the National Guard.' (That last sentence sounds very much like an official statement added later.) La Fayette arrived, and, according to the Marquis de Ferrières, 'reproached the nobles in barely controlled terms' – it had been a long day for the young general. His men forced the intruders to hand over their weapons, and a collection of hunting knives, swordsticks and curious daggers with snakes' tongue blades was piled into two large baskets. The humiliated noblemen were then made to leave the palace through a jostling, insult-hurling guard of honour of La Fayette's troops. Seven of the intruders were taken into custody for resisting.

A day of double revolt had come to an end with no loss of human life, the only damage some displaced stones at the château de Vincennes, and the punctured pride of a few hundred noblemen who had performed a polite storming of the Tuileries palace.

The fallout, though, was much more damaging. Accusations were soon being hurled in all directions.

According to the Marquis de Ferrières, a pro-revolutionary despite his aristocratic title, the noblemen knew about the plan to attack Vincennes and wanted to 'take advantage of the absence of Monsieur de La Fayette, abduct the King and take him to Metz. But the riot at Vincennes was over much sooner than the aristocrats expected.'

La Fayette's supporters accused Santerre of being in league with the nobles. Others maintained that Santerre had mounted the pointless attack on Vincennes to lure La Fayette into a trap and assassinate him.

A pro-Constitution newspaper called *Le Journal des clubs* accused Marat of provoking the Vincennes riot to cause violence and discontent: 'Marat ... wants to dive into the purest blood of the citizens.'

Typically, Marat interpreted the whole day as a counter-revolutionary plot. Vincennes, he said, was set up by La Fayette on the advice of Mirabeau 'to distract the people by some cleverly organized event', so that the King could escape. This, he warned, would have been followed by an invasion of France: 'The conspirators and their Austrian friends are only waiting for the flight of the royal family to come and cut our throats.'

Whatever the truth behind 28 February 1791, one key aspect of the day's events must have struck Louis XVI: castles and palaces were being attacked again. And this time, it was not a simple matter of the mob versus royal guards – it was everyone against everyone else, and he, Louis, was trapped in the middle of the mêlée.

II

A swift succession of events in early 1791 precipitated the royal escape attempt.

On 19 February, before the attacks on Vincennes and the Tuileries, Louis XVI's aunts Adelaïde and Victoire, known as Mesdames, had left Paris, supposedly on a pilgrimage to Rome. Completely undisguised and in a magnificent royal carriage, they were stopped by suspicious officials at Chalon-sur-Saône, 340 kilometres southeast of Paris, and had to send a message to Louis, begging him to intervene. He wrote to the Assemblée, saying he was 'convinced that they [his aunts] cannot be deprived of the liberty that everyone possesses to go where he wants ... even though it is with great repugnance that I view their separation from me'. After due deliberation in the Assemblée, and pressure from monarchist delegates, Mesdames were allowed to proceed.

Louis had always told Marie-Antoinette that he was afraid of what would happen to his aunts if he fled Paris and left them behind. That obstacle had now been overcome.

Mesdames's trip to Rome did nothing to silence the conspiracy theorists, of course, who began to circulate the story that Louis Stanislas, the older of the King's two brothers, was about to follow his aunts out of the country. On 22 February, a mob gathered outside Louis Stanislas's home at the palais du Luxembourg. He came out and swore that he would never abandon his brother, but they forced him to go to the Tuileries and make the promise in person to Louis XVI. It is easy to imagine the two men's private conversation: 'Whatever we promise, they won't believe us, so why continue?'

Then on 2 April 1791 came a previously mentioned political blow: Mirabeau died. Since his early days as a revolutionary hothead, the ugly count had mellowed into a royal spy and manipulator, Louis XVI's inside man at the Assemblée.

His death at 42, either from heart disease or the effects of his debauched lifestyle, was a setback to the royals. In the increasingly gladiatorial atmosphere of the Assemblée, his loud voice would be sorely missed.

Finally, on 18 April, the royal family was prevented from going to celebrate Easter at the château de Saint-Cloud, their refuge just outside Paris. As soon as the carriages arrived to pick them up from the Tuileries, a mob formed, shouting that the King was trying to escape. La Fayette ordered his men to force a passage for the royal cortège, but they refused. Some of the National Guards climbed up on to the carriage and shouted accusations and insults through the windows, while members of the crowd attacked royal servants.

Marie-Antoinette fled back into the Tuileries with her son, but Louis sat for one and three-quarter hours in the carriage, waiting for the deadlock to be resolved, occasionally poking his head out the window to complain that: 'It would be surprising if, after giving freedom to the nation, I were[1] not free myself.' Mayor Bailly came and pleaded with the people to calm down, but was ignored. Eventually Louis had to give in and return to his palatial prison.

For once, Louis XVI's diary entry sounded almost angry. He wrote: 'Leaving for Saint-Cloud at 11.30, they prevented us.' Next day, he went to the Assemblée to express his dissatisfaction at greater length. He told delegates that he had given in to this illegal demonstration 'because I was afraid of provoking acts of punishment against a misinformed crowd that thinks it is defending laws when it is breaking them'. Even so, he stressed that 'it is important for the Nation to prove that I am free.'

For Marat, this whole affair was a godsend. He published a tract haranguing the King: 'Do the people not know that you planned to go from Saint-Cloud to Compiègne [north of Paris]

---

[1] In the French version of this sentence, Louis remembered to use the imperfect subjunctive, *'je fusse'*, a linguistic nicety that wasn't going to win over semi-literate revolutionaries.

and thence to the border?' And in *L'Ami du peuple* he repeated his theory about an invasion: 'Parisians! You will be the executioners of three million of your brothers if you are mad enough to let him [the King] outside your walls.'

For weeks afterwards, debate about the Easter carriage standoff raged at the Assemblée, in political clubs and the streets of Paris, with La Fayette's hold on law and order weakening all the time.

It is almost certain that the Easter trip to Saint-Cloud was not a real escape attempt – for one thing, the anonymous six-seater carriage had not been delivered yet – but it might well have been a sort of dummy run. If so, it had proved a terrifying failure.

III

Louis XVI and Marie-Antoinette must have realized that the Parisians were not trying to make them stay simply out of respect for the constitutional monarchy. Thanks to Marat et al., ordinary people were seriously afraid that a vengeful royalist army would come marauding into France as soon as the royal family had left. Marie-Antoinette seems to have been all for this idea, and wrote to her brother Leopold that: 'Armed force has destroyed everything. Only armed force can repair it.' Louis, though, was against excessive violence, as he always had been, and planned only to put himself into the safe hands of General Bouillé, the commander of the eastern army. For this reason, Louis code-named the escape operation 'voyage to Montmédy', referring to a castle near the northeastern border of France, 80 kilometres from the royalist stronghold of Metz. In the event, the royal party would be stopped 50 kilometres short of their destination, at a village called Varennes-en-Argonne.

The so-called *'fuite[2] de Varennes'* is one of those events, like the Battle of Waterloo, that the French like to analyse minute by

---

[2] *Fuite* is the noun from the verb *fuir*, to flee, though aptly enough it also means a leak.

minute. And just like Waterloo, its outcome hung on a series of mistakes, misunderstandings and missed opportunities. Napoleon himself used to enjoy answering all the 'what-ifs' about the *fuite de Varennes*, and telling people what he would have done to speed the King's departure – even though Louis XVI's eventual execution would create the vacuum that allowed Napoleon to step in and seize power.

The first hitch in the escape plan came when the devout Louis XVI refused to run away on 19 June because it was a Sunday, as though escaping would count as working on the Sabbath.

Hitch *deux* came when, at about 11. 30 p.m. on Monday 20 June, as Louis XVI performed his reduced but still semi-public *coucher*, La Fayette arrived to pay his respects. The impatient King, desperate to close his bedcurtains and sneak away, had to pretend that he was in no hurry to go to sleep.

Meanwhile, Marie-Antoinette's Swedish friend, Axel de Fersen, was driving a small carriage around the back streets outside the Tuileries. He had already picked up Louis XVI's sister, Élisabeth, and his two children, the six-year-old Louis Charles and 12-year-old Marie-Thérèse. At last, at about half past midnight, Louis XVI and Marie-Antoinette stole out of side entrances at the Tuileries, and joined the party.

Fersen drove them unopposed outside the city gates, where the six-seater *berline* was waiting. Here, the protagonists assumed their fake identities: Louis was Monsieur Durand, a servant of the supposed owner of the carriage, Madame de Korff (who was played by the Marquise de Tourzel, the governess of the royal children); Marie-Antoinette was Madame Rochet, governess of Madame de Korff's children, who were of course played by Marie-Thérèse and Louis Charles (though he was disguised as a girl); Élisabeth was Rosalie,[3] Madame de Korff's

---

[3] Was it a coincidence that Élisabeth's assumed name was the same as the educational nun in Abbé Joseph Reyre's novel *L'École des jeunes demoiselles*, discussed in Chapter 10?

companion. All the participants in this role-play were dressed in the appropriate clothing for their character. The three former royal bodyguards, in the lackeys' seats outside, wore servants' livery – unfortunately, it was the bright yellow of the royal-blooded Bourbon-Condé family, the feudal lords of large swathes of the northeast of France, through which they would be travelling.

When the *berline* finally set off – after a tearful farewell between Marie-Antoinette and Fersen (Louis had forbidden the Swede from accompanying them any further so that his escape plan should bear no foreign fingerprints) – it was almost two hours behind schedule, a delay that would prove fatal.

The plan was for the anonymous coach to proceed unobtrusively through the night, and meet up with a military escort at a village called Somme-Vesle, about 180 kilometres from Paris. It was thought that a gathering of royal troops nearer the capital would arouse too much suspicion. In another of the what-ifs, the command of this military escort had been given to a relatively inexperienced 29-year-old colonel, Claude-Antoine-Gabriel de Choiseul. Again, the reason for this was discretion – General Bouillé himself was too well known a figure to be seen hanging around mysteriously at night.

For some inexplicable reason, Choiseul had Marie-Antoinette's hairdresser, Léonard, with him. Perhaps the Queen wanted to look her best when she arrived at Montmédy the next day to start her new life as a counter-revolutionary avenger. Between them, the two men seem to have decided that, with no sign of the royal coach after several hours of fruitless waiting (the *berline* was now four hours behind schedule), the escape had been called off. Choiseul told his men to stand down, and sent messengers along the whole route to Montmédy spreading the misinformation.

By this time, the empty beds at the Tuileries had been discovered, and the alarm raised. La Fayette immediately dispatched riders towards the northeast with warnings to local officials to watch out for the King. When the *berline* reached the meeting point at Somme-Vesle in the late afternoon, La Fayette's men were about two hours behind them.

In any case, the royal fugitives had now been spotted. The landlord of a coaching inn just short of Varennes, a man called Jean-Baptiste Drouet, had spent some time in Versailles, and later claimed to have recognized Marie-Antoinette, before comparing the face of Louis XVI with his picture on an *assignat* note (though that may have been a pro-revolutionary afterthought, to give favourable publicity to the ailing currency). Drouet watched the *berline* head off towards Varennes, alerted some of his townspeople, and followed.

Arriving at Varennes at about 11 p.m., almost 24 hours since leaving the Tuileries, Louis and Marie-Antoinette were again surprised to find no troops waiting as arranged. Even worse, they couldn't find the change of horses that had been arranged there (they were in fact waiting on the other side of a bridge). As the royal party dithered, Drouet was calling out the local National Guardsmen, who overturned a wagon to block the bridge, and had the church bells rung to alert the population.

The fugitives must have guessed that the bells were tolling for them as a group of patriotic drinkers from the local inn, the Bras d'Or (Golden Arm), performed a kind of citizen's arrest, ordering them to get out of the *berline* and wait in the house of the aptly named grocer, Jean-Baptiste Sauce, who was also the town's *procureur* (prosecutor).

Here, Louis and Marie-Antoinette came within minutes of escaping. Monsieur Sauce examined their passports and accepted them as genuine. He was about to let them leave when Drouet stepped in to prevent it. A judge arrived, a man called Jacques Destez, who had also worked in Versailles.[4] Seeing the King, he instantly bowed and gasped the royal term of respect: 'Sire!'

---

[4] If nothing else, this proves what a great source of employment Versailles had been when Louis XVI lived there.

Louis might well have been wise to reply something along the lines of, 'Sorry, you must have the wrong chap. I am humble Monsieur Durand, and I demand that you let us continue our journey.' Instead he clicked out of character, admitting, 'Yes, it's me, the King. And here are the Queen and the royal family. I have come to live amongst you.'

If Marie-Antoinette slapped her forehead and collapsed despairingly into an armchair at this point, it has not been recorded.

As the crowd outside the Sauce residence grew, and the bells began to ring across the whole region, two new escape routes opened up. First the Duc de Choiseul arrived with a detachment of troops, and offered to fight his way out, escorting the royal party to safety. Then at about 5.30 a.m., a lieutenant called Rohrig came to report that he had 60 hussars nearby, ready to force their way into Varennes. Both times, Louis XVI refused, saying that he did not want force to be used. Some say this was proof of his indecisiveness, others that he wanted to preserve at all costs his reputation as the benevolent father of the nation. Either way, he was condemning himself to remain a prisoner of a patriotic mob, thereby putting himself, and especially the unpopular Marie-Antoinette, in danger of lynching.

By eight the next morning, La Fayette's envoys had brought orders for the royal family to be arrested and escorted back to Paris. The long return journey began. It had taken less than 24 hours to drive to Varennes, but the exhausted fugitives now had to endure a four-day trip in the other direction.

All along the route, and at every overnight stop, hostile crowds yelled accusations of treason. The weather had suddenly turned hot, and the dry roads disgorged clouds of choking dust, but the royals were ordered to keep their windows open so that everyone could see them as they progressed at walking pace. It is said that spiteful observers blew pipe smoke into the carriage.

Two Assemblée delegates were sent out to meet the party, and squeezed into the already cramped carriage. As soon as they arrived, Louis XVI's sister Élisabeth assured them that 'the King did not want to leave the country' (she said simply *'sortir'*, a verb implying 'go outside the border'). Louis XVI's first words to the politicians were to confirm this: 'No, *Messieurs*, I wasn't leaving the country, I have declared this, and it is true.' He was intensely aware of the need to avoid any suggestion of foreign collusion.

Arriving at the outskirts of Paris at around 6 p.m. on 25 June, the carriage met the ominous welcome that La Fayette had prepared, no doubt to express his personal sense of betrayal. The National Guard lined the streets, holding back an almost totally silent crowd. An order had been issued: 'Anyone who applauds the King will be beaten. Anyone who insults him will be hanged.'

Not that this imposed silence would have comforted the royal family. A contemporary picture of the arrival in Paris shows the carriage with pike- and scythe-wielding patriots riding on the roof. And when the cortège reached the Tuileries some two hours later, mob rule finally broke out – the crowd began to roar insults, and Marie-Antoinette had to be pulled free as people tried to grab her.

The only consolation in La Fayette's order that anyone insulting the King would be hanged was that it revealed the moderate Assemblée's face-saving strategy concerning the *fuite de Varennes*. As early as the morning after their escape, Bailly and co. had issued a statement saying that Louis XVI had been 'kidnapped'. This was to be their method of clinging on to their hopes of a constitutional monarchy: it wasn't the King's fault.

Meanwhile, though, with republicans like Danton and Robespierre shouting 'treason!' and calling for a republic, and the Marat wing of public opinion howling for royal blood, Louis XVI was suspended from his role as monarch.

His failed escape had thrust him one step closer to the scaffold.

IV

The Louis XVI of 1791 is generally presented as at best a political irrelevancy, at worst a traitor and instigator of civil war. But the handwritten letter that was found lying on his empty bed on the morning of 21 June 1791 gives a very different idea of the man.

Spread across 16 pages of cramped double columns, and headed *'Déclaration de Louis XVI à tous les Français à sa sortie de Paris'* ('Declaration by Louis XVI to all French people on his leaving Paris'), it is a detailed account of his thoughts about the state of the nation as he decided that he could no longer remain a prisoner in his own palace.

Louis had apparently spent several days working on the text, and had asked his brother Louis Stanislas to draft an initial version. This his brother had done, but Louis thought it too aggressive – Louis Stanislas had always been a stalwart opponent of Necker, the Assemblée and any compromise on taxes. Louis XVI therefore rewrote the letter himself, doubling it in length.

Incidentally, Louis Stanislas escaped successfully on the day of the King and Queen's aborted trip to Varennes. His *fuite* was easier – he fled on horseback, leaving his estranged wife to fend for herself.[5] To prepare for the long journey, he had been prac-tising horseriding, which he had previously given up because of his burgeoning obesity. He made it to Belgium and set about plotting the counter-revolution with Marie-Antoinette's brother Leopold.

The letter found on Louis XVI's bed on 21 June 1791 was a sort of manifesto, divided into sections – Justice, Domestic Administration, Foreign Affairs, Finances – like one of Necker's reports. It began (with Louis talking about himself in the third person, as though the monarch were an abstract entity): 'As long as the King could hope to see order and the happiness of the Kingdom reborn thanks to the measures used by the Assemblée nationale, and by his residence near this Assemblée in the capital of the Kingdom, no personal sacrifice was too much.'

[5] His wife, Marie-Joséphine, emigrated with her *lectrice* (reader) and lover, Jeanne-Marguerite de Gourbillon, and the two women travelled Europe together until Marie-Joséphine's death in England in 1810.

Not even the lack of hunting had bothered him, it seemed. Now, though, he had realized that the constitutional monarchy would not work:

> Today, the only reward for all these sacrifices is to see the destruction of royalty, to see all powers ignored, properties violated, personal safety put at risk everywhere, crimes being left unpunished, and complete anarchy establishing itself above the law, with the show of authority that the new Constitution authorizes proving insufficient to repair a single one of the wrongs that have been inflicted upon the Kingdom.

Here, he was right – if 500 aristocrats armed with daggers had been able to get inside the Tuileries, what hope was there against a 10,000-strong Paris mob? There was no security in Paris.

But Louis XVI's concerns went beyond fears for his own life, or annoyance that he had been robbed of his ancestral powers. Despite his reputation for indifference, his letter showed that he was just as lucid about political developments as anyone in the Assemblée. He saw all too clearly that the tide had turned:

> The nearer the Assemblée gets to the end of its task [of actually publishing the Constitution], the more one sees wise people being discredited, and every day increases the number of measures that can only make the process of government more difficult or even impossible, and inspire distrust and opposition towards it. Rules that are meant to soothe the wounds that are still bleeding in several provinces only increase worries and cause discontent. The 'clubs' dominate everything and invade everything; the thousands of libellous and incendiary newspapers and pamphlets only echo what the clubs are saying, and manipulate people's minds along the path they want them to follow.

Louis proposed political changes, mainly to give himself more power, to prevent the 'loss of Royal Majesty in the eyes of the people', and to give the country a central authority that it now lacked. He also begged the people to 'return to your King, he will always be your father, your best friend', a sentiment that was out of date, at least with ordinary Parisians, who were controlling much of what went on politically in the nation. But the letter proved that Louis wasn't just running for his life and planning to return with a conquering army to teach the plebs a lesson – he truly seemed to care about the state of the nation, and understood how it was being run (or not run).

The trouble was that the letter also showed his naivety. A more practised politician would have entrusted someone to print the text and have copies pasted on every wall in Paris on 21 June. They would not have left it on a bed in the vague hope that a sympathizer might pass it on. They would also have made it shorter – several of the 16 pages are given over to a self-pitying regurgitation of events since the États généraux.

In the event, almost no one read the King's long, heartfelt 'Declaration to all French people'. It was suppressed by his own sympathizers in the Assemblée because it would have contradicted their story about a kidnapping. No kidnapper would give the abductee time to write a 16-page ransom note.

And in any case, the wordy royal manifesto was irrelevant. To the majority of French people, terrified of invasion, only one word mattered: Varennes.

V

From now on, violence was inevitable – in fact, for everyone except Louis XVI and the moderates hoping to impose their new Constitution, violence was *necessary*.

If Louis XVI's brothers were to hold on to their status (and palaces), they needed to storm back into France and, whether Louis survived or not, re-establish the monarchy by force. The aristocracy, both those in exile and those who had stayed on, were in the same boat.

The republicans, meanwhile, needed riots and unrest so that La Fayette, Bailly and the so-called '*monarchiens*' would be completely discredited, and they (people like Danton and Robespierre) could seize power.

Unsurprisingly given this requirement for violence, within days of the return from Varennes there was a massacre in Paris.

As the nation approached the second anniversary of Bastille Day, much less harmoniously than a year earlier, the Assemblée debated whether to reinstate the King as head of the constitutional monarchy. Robespierre (who had begun coming to debates finely dressed and with powdered hair, as if preparing for greater things) gave a fiery speech against the 'inviolability' of the monarch:

> If the King called down upon the nation all the horrors of a civil and foreign war; if at the head of an army of rebels and foreigners, he came to ravage his own country and bury freedom and the happiness of the whole world beneath its ruins, would he be inviolable?

This was not at all what Louis XVI had done, or was planning to do, but Robespierre demanded that the question be put to the nation. It was an early example of the referendum tactic – not content with the decision of a democratically elected parliament, a dissenter wanted to ask 'the people' – who can be manipulated with some well-placed fake news.

A young delegate called Antoine Barnave, who had been one of the men sent to meet the royal coach on its return from Varennes, and who according to his detractors was in love with Marie-Antoinette, gave a long, impassioned speech to the Assemblée in favour of continuing with the constitutional process: 'All government, to be good, must embrace the principle of stability. Otherwise, instead of happiness, all it has to offer is endless change.' He took a swipe at 'some men whose intentions I do not wish to call into question' (ahem), but who 'seek to impose the politics of fiction, because it is easier to do that than to contribute truly and positively to the well-being of the nation'.

Barnave was applauded by the majority of the Assemblée, and won the day – not that it helped his career. Dubbed 'Monsieur Deux-Visages' ('Two-Faces') by his opponents, he would be forced out of Parisian politics, accused of treason and guillotined in November 1793.

After this sitting of the Assemblée, Robespierre emerged from the building and addressed a crowd that had gathered in the street: 'My friends, all is lost, the King is saved.'

This crowd then toured the city, forcing theatres to close their doors – purely, it seems, to disrupt everyday life amongst the leisured classes – then went to the Jacobins club (Robespierre's group) and demanded that a petition be drawn up, calling for Louis XVI's immediate abdication.

Robespierre was against this move, because he feared it would give La Fayette's National Guard an excuse to suppress opposition by force, but Danton stepped in and helped to write a new version of the petition. It was agreed that a massive demonstration would be held the next day, 17 July, on the ruins of the Bastille.

Predictably, despite having contributed to the climate of unrest, the big names were absent that day: Robespierre because of his opposition to the petition, and Danton because he had been warned to stay away. He spent the day in the country.

Meanwhile, La Fayette and Bailly had had time to do their own petitioning. Posters were put up calling for order. Bailly warned that 'foreigners, no doubt paid to agitate good citizens, have recently arrived in Paris'.

That evening, 16 July, the Assemblée reinstated the King as constitutional monarch, and the republicans were more determined than ever to hold their demonstration. They tried to gather at the Bastille, but it was being patrolled by wary National Guardsmen, so they went to the Champ-de-Mars, where the *fête de la Fédération* had been celebrated the previous year, and where the 'altar of the nation' still stood as a monument to the great oath of allegiance to King and country that had been taken that day.

Bizarrely, two men were discovered skulking under the altar, drilling holes in the planks. When they were arrested, they claimed to have been trying to look up ladies' dresses, and were released (apparently in eighteenth-century France that was not a crime worth worrying about). But the mob had other ideas. Accused of spying for the royalists, one of the men was beaten to death, the other half-hanged from a lamp post, then decapitated. As befitted the new Parisian fashion, their heads were stuck on pikes and paraded around the streets.

With some 20,000 people in the stadium at the Champ-de-Mars, and a mass petition-signing in full swing, the Assemblée decided that it was time to take control. After all, despite what Robespierre said, his followers were rebels, calling for revolt against a decision of the Assemblée. Martial order was voted, and La Fayette and Bailly (in his capacity as Mayor of Paris) were sent to disperse the crowd.

La Fayette was shot at, but was obviously getting used to being used for target practice, and did not react. His troops took up positions around the Champ-de-Mars. Bailly's guardsmen marched into the Champ-de-Mars and were fired upon. They riposted, killing somewhere between ten and 400 demonstrators – according to the pro-royalist press, barely a dozen people were shot, whereas Marat's *Ami du peuple* claimed that 400 bodies had been dumped in the Seine, and that Bailly had helped to cover up the massacre by hastening the departure of the corpses downriver.

Most contemporary accounts agreed on around 50 deaths that day. But the casualties didn't stop there. *L'Ami du peuple* was banned, and Marat had to go into hiding. Danton fled to England, where he would stay until mid-September. A few organizers of the 17 July 1791 demonstration were arrested.

In political terms, the losers were the moderates. The advocates of mob rule achieved their goal: La Fayette, the figurehead of the National Guard, became a figure of hate. His house was attacked, and he would resign in October and take refuge in his château in Auvergne (which had not been requisitioned or demolished). Bailly was not so lucky. He withdrew from politics in November, and exiled himself to Nancy, but his role in the 17 July massacre was never forgotten, and he was eventually brought back to Paris and executed for treason in November 1793, by a guillotine specially set up for him on the edge of the Champ-de-Mars.

One of La Fayette's last acts at the Assemblée was an attempt to bring peace and harmony to the nation. In early September 1791, the delegates announced that their Constitution was finally ready to be published (not that it had changed much since its last manifestation). Louis XVI sent a letter to the Assemblée saying that he would come and 'pronounce [his] solemn acceptance'. A delegation of 60 delegates went to the Tuileries to thank him, and at La Fayette's insistence, they proposed a complete amnesty for all acts committed since the beginning of the Revolution (including, presumably, La Fayette's own violent interventions). Louis told the delegates: 'This day will be remembered in history. I wish that it should end discord, unite everyone and that we should all be one.'[6]

On 14 September 1791, after some discussion as to whether delegates should stand up, sit down or kneel in his presence (in the end it was each to his own), Louis XVI came to the Assemblée for the Constitution-signing ceremony.

He swore his allegiance to 'the nation and the law', and vowed to 'use all the power that has been delegated to me to uphold the Constitution decreed by the Assemblée nationale constituante, and to have its laws carried out'.

After the ceremony, Louis was escorted back to the Tuileries by cheering crowds and celebratory cannon fire. For once, there was a party mood in Paris, and people heard more cries of *'Vive le Roi!'* than 'Traitor!' Apparently, Louis wasn't the only one

[6] This outbreak of triple repetition may have been a case of 'Louis doth protest too much, methinks' – by now, he probably didn't believe that unity was possible.

who wanted peace restored to the streets of Paris. Meanwhile, copies of the Constitution were dispatched to be read out across the nation.

Soon everyone in France would learn that the country now had 'no authority superior to the law', and that the King was subject to that law. The aristocracy and the clergy no longer held any privileges. All political matters were to be decided by the elected Assemblée. Suffrage was not yet universal – it was limited to male taxpayers aged over 25 who had lived in their place of residence for a year (only about 15 per cent of the population) – but in theory at least, all French citizens were now equal before the law, and taxes were in the process of being democratized (especially because peasants had largely stopped paying their landlords anyway).

The moderate, *monarchien* majority in the Assemblée patted itself on the back and declared that its work was done. The Assemblée constituante changed its name to the Assemblée législative, a body that would be entirely devoted to passing new laws within the Constitution. All the unpleasantness of the past two years or so could be forgotten, including any unfortunate lynchings or massacres there might have been, and the royal family's escape attempt (or rather 'kidnapping'). The slate was wiped clean. The Revolution was complete.

In fact, though, the self-congratulatory regime was closing its eyes to the guillotine blade now rushing down towards its neck.

Chapter 18

'THE HOMELAND IS IN DANGER'

'Louis XVI va livrer nos cités aux fers ensanglantés des despotes de l'Europe.'
'Louis XVI is going to hand over our towns to the bloody blades of the
despots of Europe.'

From a petition delivered to the Assemblée législative on
31 July 1792 by the revolutionary committee of the
neighbourhood of Mauconseil in Paris

I

Louis XVI has always been accused of hypocrisy. His die-hard
opponents say that he never wanted any democratization of
France, and that he was only ever paying lip service to reform,
while waiting for the chance to escape and join up with a counter-revolutionary army. As we have seen, this is largely untrue.
Or rather, it was untrue until 1791. After Varennes, fearing more
than ever for his safety and that of his family, Louis seems to
have started playing at Monsieur Deux-Visages.

There is a letter from Louis XVI to King Friedrich Wilhelm of
Prussia that bears no date. Some historians claim it was written
in December 1790, before the *fuite de Varennes*. If this is true, it
proves that Louis was being totally two-faced long before he tried
to escape, which strengthens the republicans' argument – he was,

they can say, always unworthy of the Assemblée's trust. However, it is also argued (more convincingly)[1] that the letter was written in December 1791, when Louis had given up any real hope of a workable constitutional regime and lasting peace in France.

In the letter, Louis complains that 'despite my acceptance of the new Constitution, agitators are openly plotting to destroy all vestiges of the monarchy'. He reveals that he has written to Russia, Spain and Sweden, to suggest 'a congress of the principal powers of Europe, supported by an army, as the best means of stopping the agitators here, providing the means to establish a more desirable order, and preventing the evil that afflicts us here from spreading to the other European states'.

He doesn't say that he wants to reverse all the democratic reforms in the Constitution or overthrow the Assemblée, but it is an open call to invade France. By the end of 1791, his two brothers were putting together an army in Koblenz, on the Rhine, which was ruled over by an uncle of theirs, Clemens Wenzeslaus von Sachsen (the brother-in-law of one of Louis XV's sons). In Turin, meanwhile, their cousin Louis Joseph de Condé was doing the same. Some 140,000 French citizens had emigrated since the beginning of the Revolution, many of them aristocrats who had served in the army or were now willing to fight; there were also whole regiments of soldiers still loyal to the King.

In November 1791, the new Assemblée législative voted in favour of drastic punitive action against anyone who proved their treachery by staying out of the country after the end of the year. Those who did so would be under sentence of death and dispossession if they returned to France.

In December, Louis XVI paid lip service to this new law by warning Clemens Wenzeslaus von Sachsen that: 'If by 15

---

[1] The letter contains a reference to a General Heymann, who hadn't arrived in Prussia until July 1791.

January, he [Clemens] does not prevent all gatherings and all hostile actions by French citizens who have taken refuge in his dominions, then I will regard him as an enemy of France.' Louis promised the Assemblée that: 'I will make a similar declaration to all those who favour gatherings that threaten the tranquillity of the Kingdom.'

The delegates naturally assumed that last sentence referred to the Austrians and Prussians, though in Louis XVI's mind, it must have applied more to the Parisians. In any case, he was now telling the Assemblée one thing while plotting the opposite with his supporters abroad.

By now, the French political and military establishment was one huge knot of interwoven conspiracies.

Although logic dictated that France had to repel the counter-revolutionaries, Marat and the extreme republicans opposed military action. Marat's line was simple: if the King and the *monarchiens* were in favour of war, even a defensive one, it had to be part of a counter-revolutionary plot. In this, he wasn't entirely wrong, but he went further and depicted Louis XVI as a bloodthirsty warmonger. Rather unconvincingly, he wrote that the King's passion for hunting revealed a murderous streak: 'His fiery temperament has always guided him towards violent measures.'

Meanwhile, the political opponents of the Constitution fought for supremacy by bombarding their political clubs with speeches. One of the chief warmongers was the Assemblée delegate Jacques Pierre Brissot, a former secretary to Louis XVI's cousin Louis Philippe, who was at the storming of the Bastille, and who had written the petition calling for Louis XVI's abdication after the Champ-de-Mars massacres. He now called war a 'crusade for universal liberty' that would encourage the subjects of other monarchies to revolt.

Robespierre poured scorn on this idea: 'You will lead our triumphant army into all our neighbouring countries, you will set up municipalities, councils, national assemblies everywhere ...

Under your leadership, our generals will be missionaries of the Constitution ... No one likes armed missionaries.'[2]

Of course the battle of words was not just about war: it was about who could be the 'purest' republican, and who could best represent what *le peuple* wanted. Then, as now, the politicians were all lecturing the people on what they wanted, as were *Ami du peuple*-style newspapers with names like *L'Orateur du peuple*, *Le Réveil du peuple* (*The People's Wake-up Call*), *Le Tribun du peuple* and *Le Journal de la vérité* (*The Newspaper of Truth*, the ancestor of *Pravda*). And, of course, they were all debating about who would succeed the King and the pro-Constitution Assemblée when the reactionary duo were inevitably overthrown.

France declared war on 20 April 1792 – though only on the Austrians, who were now led by Marie-Antoinette's nephew, Franz II, after the death of her brother Leopold in March 1792. An outright war against all France's monarchist neighbours was thought too ambitious.

The Austrians controlled the Low Countries, and it was here that the French revolutionary army proved how low the country's morale had fallen, and how undisciplined its people had become.

On 29 April, a French general called Théodore Dillon was patrolling on the Belgian border near Lille when he met an Austrian army. There was a brief skirmish, but Dillon was under orders to avoid an outright battle, so he ordered his men to retreat. However, they panicked and stampeded. When Dillon tried to restore order, one of his own men shot him in the shoulder. The fleeing soldiers finally arrived back within the safety of Lille, only to see Dillon being brought in, wounded. Accusing him of treason for ordering the retreat, the soldiers shot and bayoneted him to death, before dragging his body to the central square and throwing it on a bonfire. They also hanged his second-in-command and cut the throats of several prisoners.

---

[2] Robespierre seems to have given Napoleon Bonaparte ideas, because that was *exactly* what he would start doing a few years later.

If the French troops were meant to be 'armed missionaries', it was for the church of mob rule.

II

La Fayette, meanwhile, had been recalled from his short exile. He was put in charge of the 25,000 better-disciplined troops based in Metz, but he fared little better than Dillon. Like the murdered general, La Fayette was patrolling the Belgian border when he was twice surprised by smaller but more efficient Austrian forces. He quickly decided that this war was a losing game, and that he would do better to join the web of conspiracies in Paris on the side of the constitutional monarchy (and, of course, on his own side, too).

On 16 June 1792, he wrote an open letter to the Assemblée, with a copy to Louis XVI, effectively presenting himself (supported by his army) as a national saviour, as if France didn't already have enough of those. 'France is threatened from without, and agitated within,' La Fayette wrote perceptively. 'Enemies within, drunk with fanaticism and pride, promise false hopes and fatigue us with their insolent malevolence. You must repress them.' This was where he (and his army) came in.

> I can reply to those who pretend to suspect me: ' ... Let us see in this moment of crisis who is the most inflexible in their principles, the most stubborn in their resistance, and who will confront most bravely the obstacles and dangers that traitors are hiding from their country.' ... How could I wait any longer before fulfilling this duty?

La Fayette's letter showed that he understood the need for stability to be re-established, but it was an open threat to impose personal martial law, and as such it infuriated the Assemblée, as well as playing right into the hands of the republicans, who could point yet again to the danger of monarchist tyranny.

Predictably, the letter was immediately seized upon as an excuse for a mob to attack the royal palace at the Tuileries.

This was not entirely La Fayette's fault. Louis XVI was refusing to sign a new law establishing a force of 20,000 armed volunteers who were to be recruited in the provinces and brought to Paris as additional protection against riots and/or a foreign invasion. This measure was unpopular with almost everyone – monarchists thought it was an excuse to increase the size of the mobs, while republicans condemned it as a new monarchist army. However, as soon as Louis XVI vetoed the law, it suddenly became popular with the republicans. It was more proof that neither he nor the Assemblée could do anything right, in republican eyes at least.

On 20 June 1792, around 10,000 Parisians forced their way into the palais des Tuileries, enraged (or so we are told) about this veto and La Fayette's letter. The mob got into the palace without any opposition because the National Guard was under the command of Antoine Joseph Santerre, one of the men implicated in the rioting at Vincennes in February 1791, who now effectively gave the demonstrators an armed escort into the King's apartments.

It was exactly what the royal family had been afraid of – a horde of pike-wielding Parisians rampaging into their home, one of them carrying an effigy of Marie-Antionette hanging from a lamp post. According to one account, the invaders were so unwashed that the royals smelt them coming. The Queen wisely crept out of the palace via a side entrance while intruders tried to smash down the door to her son's bedroom with axes.

It was Louis XVI, wearing an extra-thick waistcoat in case he was stabbed, who confronted the mob, sitting impassively as a pike was thrust towards him. On its blade was a red revolutionary bonnet. Even though it was too small, he perched it on top of his powdered head.

A butcher-turned-revolutionary called Louis Legendre, who had taken part in the October 1789 march to Versailles, yelled at the King: '*Monsieur*, you are treacherous! You have always lied to us, and you are lying to us now!'

Louis was apparently taken aback by the use of *'Monsieur'* instead of *'Votre Majesté'* or *'Sire'*, but kept his calm and agreed to drink a toast to the nation. He also explained to the intruders that his veto of the law on priests was within the Constitution, which he was upholding as he had promised to do. His impassive demeanour and willingness to talk quietened the crowds, especially after a soldier performed a primitive lie-detector test, putting his hand over the King's heart to see whether it was beating abnormally fast – it wasn't.

Louis had to put up with this treatment for two hours before help arrived, in the shape of the Mayor of Paris, Jérôme Pétion, a republican who had in fact been one of the instigators of the riot, and some National Guards who were actually willing to clear the palace of intruders. If Pétion had hoped to arrive too late to stop a royal lynching, he was disappointed. Almost every door in the palace had been smashed in, but the Queen had escaped with her children and the King was engaged in calm debate with the rioters, a revolutionary bonnet on his (as yet) still-attached head.

Louis XVI had saved the monarchy, but only for a few weeks.

III

La Fayette's offer of help turned out to be a damp squib – most of his army refused to march from Metz to the capital, and he arrived in Compiègne, to the north of Paris, with just a small force of loyal troops. When he offered to smuggle the royal family out to Compiègne and thence to safety, Louis XVI didn't believe he was capable of pulling it off.

As summer set in, the royals feared the worst. Louis XVI began reading the life story of King Charles I of England, who had lost his head in 1649. Readers of France's many newspapers were force-fed a diet of unsettling news – shortages of coffee, sugar and soap had provoked a renewal of the attacks on shops, while out in the country, gangs of so-called *'taxateurs'* ('taxers') were grabbing grain from markets and warehouses. All over France, châteaux were burning again.

The political agitators were constantly fanning the flames of discontent, with Marat warning that: 'The atrocious Assemblée, free of all reins, will carry on its machinations in the dark and march with giant steps towards the fatal time when it will declare the counter-revolution.' He was losing patience with relatively moderate republicans like Robespierre who were waiting for the right time to bring down the pro-monarchy Assemblée. For Marat, the solution was quick and simple:

> After the massacre at the Champ-de-Mars, if I had found 2,000 men boiling with the same rage that was tearing my breast, I would have led them to stab the general [La Fayette] amongst his battalions of brigands, burn the despot [Louis XVI] in his palace and impale our atrocious representatives [the Assemblée] in their seats.

In the end, despite such bloody threats being pasted up on the walls of Paris, the death knell for the monarchy came not from France but from the émigrés in Germany.

In May 1792, Louis XVI had sent a writer called Jacques Mallet du Pan, a Protestant pastor's son and advocate of the constitutional monarchy, to Koblenz to meet the French counter-revolutionaries gathered there, and put together some kind of manifesto of their intentions. As a moderate, Mallet du Pan was no doubt chosen because he was likely to produce something fairly diplomatic that expressed a desire to restore law and order while upholding the constitutional monarchy – nothing that would put Louis XVI's life and status at risk.

Unfortunately, Mallet du Pan's mission was hijacked by an arch-royalist called Jérôme-Joseph Geoffroy de Limon and a French diplomat by the name of Jean-Joachim Pellenc, who was an agent in the pay of the Austrians. Together these two conjured up what has become known as the *Brunswick Manifesto*, an open letter to the people of France so inflammatory that it was almost guaranteed to rouse the Parisian mob to hysteria – and, of course, get Marat, Robespierre et al. dancing for joy.

After calling on all French soldiers to 'return to their former loyalty and submit immediately to the King, their legitimate sovereign', the *Manifesto* ordered the people of Paris to do the same, and warned the Assemblée and all other elected representatives in France that they would be 'judged militarily, without hope of pardon' if they failed to show the royal family due respect. On top of this:

> If the Tuileries palace is entered or insulted, or the slightest violence or insult is committed against Their Majesties ... exemplary, unforgettable vengeance will be exacted, and the city of Paris will be subjected to military action and total subversion, and those guilty of revolt given the punishments they deserve.

Signed Karl Wilhelm Ferdinand, Duke of Brunswick, the head of the Prussian army, it was published in Koblenz on 25 July 1792, and appeared in France's official government newspaper the *Moniteur universel* on 3 August.

It was exactly what Louis XVI's enemies had been waiting for.

IV

Calls to put the monarchy out of its misery had been coming thick and fast. In early July the Assemblée had drawn up the measures to be taken in case a warning had to be issued: *'Citoyens, la Patrie est en danger'* ('Citizens, the homeland is in danger'). One of these measures was that 'all citizens able to carry weapons ... should be permanently on duty'. In Paris, they didn't need to be asked twice. Also, after the warning, wearing any colours except the tricolour *cocarde* would be punishable by death. Political opposition, even symbolic, would be over.

On 11 July, as Austrian troops marauded on the Franco-Belgian border, the warning was given, and the streets of Paris were suddenly full of armed men and women. That same day,

Robespierre gave a speech to the club des Jacobins, denouncing the 'enemies who guide us' (Louis XVI and the Assemblée), explaining that 'the tyrants have only pretended to declare war on their accomplices and allies' and accusing 'the men who are so-called representatives of the people' of being 'wholly occupied with impoverishing them and cutting their throats'. This was a message to be sent out to the provinces, summoning the army of volunteers that Louis XVI had tried to veto. Robespierre had now openly elected himself head of the mob.

Soon, large groups of volunteers from Brittany and Marseille appeared in the city. Officially, they were invited to the third anniversary of the storming of the Bastille, but everyone knew what their real purpose was. Louis XVI attended the commemoration, and gave the oath to the nation, but unlike 1790, there were few if any shouts of *'Vive le Roi!'* and Marie-Antoinette stayed away.

The Assemblée was trying to prove that it had the national crisis in hand, but power was being snatched away every day. On 29 July, Robespierre gave a speech demanding its dissolution, on the grounds that it had betrayed France. On 31 July, 47 out of the 48 *sections* (neighbourhood revolutionary committees) of Paris sent a petition to the Assemblée demanding an end to the monarchy. The Mauconseil[3] *section* added its powerful warning that: 'Louis XVI is going to hand over our towns to the bloody blades of the despots of Europe.'

With rumours flying around that the Tuileries were about to be attacked again, on 9 August, the Parisian republicans made their move and formed the Commune insurrectionnelle, a self-appointed group of committees replacing the elected Paris council. Many of the members had belonged to the official council, but they now gave themselves new powers, and appointed the chief intruder of 20 June, Santerre, as head of

---

[3] In August 1792, the neighbourhood would change its name from Mauconseil (which sounds like 'bad advice') to Bon-Conseil. It is now the highly trendy area of Montorgueil.

the city's National Guard, after the previous incumbent had been 'unfortunately' shot and killed leaving a meeting with the Commune insurrectionnelle. Robespierre, who would soon emerge as head of one of the Commune's committees, wrote to a friend saying that 'the Revolution is about to pick up speed.'

At midnight on 9 August, the Quinze-Vingts section of Paris, to the southeast of the Bastille, sounded its bells, the signal to gather for the final attack on the monarchy. Crowds began to muster around the Tuileries, as about 1,000 members of Louis XVI's loyal Swiss Guards and 300 armed aristocrats took up defensive positions in and around the palace. National Guards were also on duty there, but their allegiance was made clear when Louis went out to speak to them, and was jeered and insulted.

By 5 a.m., some 20,000 armed insurgents were at the palace gates, some of them manning cannons, and the people inside were panicking. Marie-Antoinette was arguing in favour of a pitched battle, which would almost certainly have resulted in mass slaughter of the defenders and their royal charges. In the end, Louis agreed to take refuge in the nearby Assemblée, where delegates had gone into emergency session. Announcing his departure from the palace, he said: *'Marchons'* ('Let's walk/ march'), inadvertently – or maybe ironically – quoting the chorus of a new song that was becoming popular amongst the republicans, the *'Marseillaise'* (see next chapter).

After crossing the Tuileries garden, a dangerous ordeal because insurgents were now everywhere, and the sun was rising, the royal family arrived in the Assemblée chamber, and Louis informed the delegates that: 'I have come here to avoid a great crime, and I shall always believe myself safe with my family amongst the representatives of the nation.' As the Constitution forbade debates in the presence of the King, the refugees were then put inside a small area reserved for the *logotachygraphe* (stenographer) behind the president of the Assemblée's seat. They stayed there all day, listening to musket and cannon fire outside, and frantic decision-making in the chamber, with many of the republican delegates taking the opportunity to insult the royal family.

Time and again throughout the morning, 'citizens' came in to address the Assemblée, and were allowed to interrupt proceedings. One of these deputations informed the delegates that they, the citizens, were 'the new magistrates of the people' and that, as legislators, 'it is now up to us to support the people'. They were in effect announcing that the Assemblée had been deposed. Finally, Pierre Vergniaud, its president, yielded to the obvious and declared that there had arisen in the nation 'a wish for the revocation of the authority delegated to Louis XVI', so that he was 'suspended from his functions'.

Louis XVI was now jobless.

He was also homeless, because outside the overheated (literally and metaphorically) debating chamber, the Tuileries palace was being ransacked.[4]

The Swiss Guards shot about 200 of the intruders before they were overwhelmed, and about 300 of them died in battle or were stabbed and beaten to death after surrendering. Around 60 of the Swiss were taken into custody and marched to the Hôtel de Ville, where they were killed. Very quickly, heads and body parts began appearing on pikes in the streets of Paris.

Of the armed aristocrats who had come to protect the King, around 100 died, but 200 or so managed to slip away unharmed in their civilian clothes. The royal family, meanwhile, were taken to the nearby couvent des Feuillants, effectively under arrest. Three days later they would be transferred to Temple prison.

---

[4] Strangely, it was noted by Louise-Élisabeth de Tourzel, the royal children's governess, that almost nothing was stolen from the palace on 10 August. The only exception was 'the theft of the wine and liqueurs, of which not a bottle was left'. She adds that the personal effects of the royal family were not taken until curators were sent in to protect and catalogue them, at which point everything disappeared.

As the blood began to sink into the carpets and wallpapers of the Tuileries, one optimistic Assemblée delegate gave a speech, saying, 'The people are not bloodthirsty. Not only will it be possible, it will be easy to bring the citizens who are now massing back to law, justice and reason.'

He could not have been more wrong.

V

Since the Assemblée did not have the right to rule alone, it was announced that a new parliament would be elected, called the Convention nationale (the name that Robespierre had been using). The Convention would decide on the measures necessary to 'assure the sovereignty of the people'. It was not hard to guess that those would exclude any form of monarchy.

This new parliament was touted as the first truly democratic government of France. Gone were the vestiges of the three estates, gone were the monarchists, gone was the Constitution that had preserved old privileges. The partial revolution was over. At last, real democracy had been achieved, and the people would be governed by 749 men who represented their real interests – because this, everyone was told, was a parliament elected by universal suffrage.

However, to vote in the 1792 elections, one had to be male, aged over 21, living at the same address for a year, and 'not in a state of servitude'. This meant that servants, valets, maids or anyone whose job was lowly enough for them to accept accommodation and food in lieu of part of their wages, including many farm workers, were denied the vote. So much for democracy.

In addition to this, the final turnout was less than 12 per cent of the electorate. So much for a mandate. What was more, in the light of recent events, almost none of the candidates were moderates – they were mostly the 'patriots' who had been most outspoken against the Assemblée.

Interestingly, one of the few former Assemblée delegates elected to the Convention was a citizen called Philippe Égalité

– this was Louis XVI's cousin Louis Philippe, who had 'gone on a diplomatic mission to London' after the Versailles march of October 1789, but was now back in Paris, and had been keeping his head down, awaiting political developments. He adopted his new egalitarian name, and was elected as the Convention nationale's representative for the Seine, choosing to sit with the extreme republicans like Robespierre and Danton. Though as we shall see, this show of revolutionary fervour would not spare him from the guillotine.

The key question about this second Revolution is: did the events of 10 August 1792, when the people took power away from the 'treacherous despots' who had supposedly invited foreign armies to invade the country and cut citizens' throats, finally introduce true *Liberté, Égalité* and *Fraternité*?

The answer is: No, and it wasn't really intended to. This seems to be where the Revolution went definitively wrong.

Before 10 August 1792, its leaders had been aiming – in theory at least – to make the country a fairer place, mostly via polite, interminable debates. In the eighteenth century even more than now, the French loved an intellectual discussion, so it was a very gradual process. Open debate usually leads to compromise, which meant that their initial ideals had been watered down considerably by pressure from the more privileged members of the Assemblée. This explained why the first, imperfect Constitution had taken so long to complete.

But overall, the elected members of the Assemblée nationale constituante and its successor the Assemblée législative had come close to achieving the impossible – combining the more benevolent aspects of the monarchy with the demands of the poor, underpaid, overtaxed masses. The constitutional monarchy had been plodding slowly along a path of peaceful reform, with the King accepting his reduced powers. Even if he was only paying lip service to these changes, this was all that mattered. He could complain all he wanted in private, but he was publicly respecting the new regime, and helping to make it work.

Now, though, as of August 1792, French politics had been hijacked by political animals with very different ideals. Shouting, 'We are the people!' what these politicians really wanted was a violent uprising that would deliver absolute power into their hands. There were some (mainly non-Parisian) members of the new Convention nationale who thought that economic reforms were more important than social revenge, but they would soon be ousted. Very quickly, the reins of power would be seized by the Parisian agitators.

The Commune insurrectionnelle's decision to invite armed volunteers into Paris, and to allow all Parisians to bear arms, was not taken so that the new regime would organize colourful parades. Appointing a known troublemaker like Santerre to lead the Paris National Guard was a guarantee of indiscipline and violence. In early September, Paris even named Marat one of the administrators of its police force, which was like choosing an arsonist to guard a gunpowder factory.

With Marat's newspaper *L'Ami du peuple* telling everyone that 'all the heads of the great must be felled', and one of the Paris sections (Poissonnière, to the north of the city centre) announcing openly that it was necessary to 'bring prompt justice to all the wrong-doers and conspirators held in the prisons', the new regime was definitely not going to be about tolerance and forgiveness.

Parisian politicians like Robespierre and Danton, who had kept their heads down during the uprising of 10 August – no doubt to avoid charges that they had sanctioned violent rebellion and massacres – now assumed office. Both of them were elected to the new Convention, and Danton, who until now had been little more than a rabblerouser in the political clubs, was made Minister of Justice. On 25 August, he gave a speech saying that 'No nation on earth obtains freedom without combat. You have traitors among you. Oh, without them, the combat would be over.' He also suggested that house-to-house searches should be made, to look for hidden weapons and arrest 'suspects'. The call to violent oppression could not have been clearer.

At the same time, coincidentally or not, rumours began to circulate about royalist prisoners plotting counter-revolution in their Parisian cells.

VI

On 2 September, the killing of political opponents began.

In Paris, the first victims were a group of 19 priests who had refused to take the oath of allegiance to the (now defunct) Constitution. Tried by a 'people's commission', one after the other they received the verdict '*à la Force*', meaning that they should be taken to the Force prison (ironically, one of those recently modernized and made more comfortable by Louis XVI). However, as soon as each priest was taken away by his guards, he was piked and bayonetted to death in the street.

In the couvent des Carmes, a convent in the southwest of Paris that had been converted into a prison, a three-day killing spree began, during which 115 priests were taken into the convent gardens and shot, stabbed or beaten to death. Amongst these were an archbishop, two bishops, and one priest called Guillaume-Antoine Delfaud who had been a delegate at the États généraux and supported the *tiers état*'s call for a democratic government.

On that same day, around 1,500 armed men from the Paris *sections* marched into Bicêtre prison hospital, just outside southern Paris, where many of the patients were vagrants, sufferers from advanced syphilis, homosexuals and children convicted of petty street crimes. It was rumoured that a large stock of counter-revolutionary weapons was hidden there. None were found, but the invaders clubbed about a hundred prisoners to death, many of them children.

Similar scenes were enacted across Paris, in the Conciergerie and Grand Châtelet prisons, either with or without kangaroo courts.

On the evening of 2 September, the populist politicians seem to have decided that they needed to take credit for this sudden increase in judicial efficiency. A *'comité de surveillance'* ('surveillance committee'), set up at the Hôtel de Ville in Paris to make sure that the city was behaving with enough revolutionary fervour, published a circular addressed to their 'brothers in all the departments of France'. It revealed 'a terrible plot, organized by the royal court, to cut the throats of all French patriots, a plot in which a large number of members of the Assemblée nationale are implicated', and announced that 'a large number of ferocious conspirators held in the prisons have been put to death by the people, acts of justice which seemed indispensable.' The circular then suggested that 'the nation ... will no doubt adopt this useful and necessary method at once.' The document was signed, amongst others, by Marat and later countersigned by Danton, the Minister of Justice.

Unsurprisingly, the massacres continued.

On 3 September, a group of men who had perpetrated the Bicêtre killings the day before arrived at the Salpêtrière prison hospital on the right bank of the Seine, which held 186 women, most of them prostitutes or wives accused of adultery. Two men from the revolutionary committee of the Finistère section of Paris, which included Salpêtrière, came and gave the order for the women to be removed from their cells and taken into the large courtyard (which can still be visited today). Then while their names were read out from the prison register, about 130 of the women were brought forward to be bludgeoned, hacked and stabbed to death. One can only conclude that sex outside marriage was proof of counter-revolutionary sympathies, although if that was true, it is hard to explain why about 30 of the women were raped before being killed.

At the Force prison in the Marais, hearings continued for several days, with over 160 prisoners receiving instantly executed death penalties. One of these was Marie-Antoinette's close friend, Marie-Thérèse, Princesse de Lamballe. Ordered to reveal details of the royal couple's dealings with foreign powers, she refused, and was 'released' into the street. There, she was bludgeoned to the ground, stabbed and beaten to death, and then her body was stripped naked. Her head was sawn off, and her heart ripped out, and they were paraded through the streets, along with the rest of her corpse. The head made its way on a pike through the Marais as far as the Temple prison, where Marie-Antoinette was in custody with her family. There, the severed head was held up to the windows, while members of the mob ordered the Queen to kiss her alleged lesbian lover. The shutters were closed, and Marie-Antoinette never saw her friend's remains, but she fainted all the same.

Interestingly, at one point, Lamballe's head was given to a sculptress to make a wax effigy. Marie Grosholtz was a young artist who would later make the death masks of Louis XVI, Marie-Antoinette and Robespierre,[5] before going to London and opening a waxworks museum, under her married name, Madame Tussaud. The museum would include a 'Chamber of Horrors' depicting the violence of the Revolution.

Either spontaneously or in reaction to the *comité de surveillance*'s circular, massacres spread all across France, and wherever aristocrats, recalcitrant priests, former royal soldiers or unpopular prisoners of some other sort could be found, they were put to death. Perhaps appropriately, the biggest massacre outside Paris (for the moment, at least) took place in Versailles, where on 9 September 1792 a group of 50 prisoners were on their way from Orléans to Paris, under escort by the National Guard. Alerted about their arrival, in all likelihood by Danton himself, an armed Parisian mob was waiting for them at a crossroads. The escort miraculously disappeared and 43 of the prisoners were hacked to death, among them a former Minister of War, a former Minister of Foreign Affairs, the ex-royal governor of Paris and a bishop. Nine men managed to escape, but a further 13 prisoners being held in the Queen's former stables were not so lucky.

---

[5] Though given the speed with which these three decapitated heads were disposed of, it has often been said that their 'death masks' are fake.

By the end of the day, the railings outside the château de Versailles were host to an exhibition of severed heads.

It is almost impossible to know how many prisoners were killed by mobs during September 1792, but most current estimates put the number at about 1,200 in Paris and around 150 in the provinces. Approximately half of these were inmates being held for non-revolutionary crimes. On top of the prison massacres, there were also plenty of random lynchings and disappearances, and of course the sheer terror that must have been felt by every prisoner in almost every jail, waiting to hear the mob arrive to do their 'revolutionary duty'.

VII

There has been a great deal of soul-searching in France about who exactly carried out these massacres. Individual names of the men who chaired the kangaroo courts, led the mobs or severed the heads have been bandied about, as if to contradict the idea that large numbers of the French – and especially Parisian – population were psychopaths. But as we have seen, in the late 1780s and early 1790s it was not difficult to find people willing to murder anyone who looked too rich or wore the wrong uniform. It was a class war, and the formerly downtrodden masses had been provided with weapons and told to fight it.

As with all groups and factions involved in the French Revolution, the killers have been given a name – the *septembriseurs* (*briser* meaning to smash). Among them, the subgroup who preferred to bludgeon rather than stab or shoot their victims are known as *bûcheurs*, a pun on *boucher* (butcher) adapted from *bûche*, the word for a log.

Their numbers are impossible to calculate, because there were often several thousand people gathered outside a prison, either taking part in the killing and mutilation, or just watching. Many of them were in uniform, either as National Guards or armed volunteers. In any case, most of the people wielding their weapons, or cheering on the killers, would have argued that they were helping to save the nation. Some actually went and demanded payment from the Parisian authorities for their work. A political ally of Robespierre's called Jacques-Nicolas Baillaud-Varenne, a member of the Paris Commune insurrectionnelle, gave a speech calling the killers his *ouvriers* (labourers).

Most accounts of mob violence in Paris refer to the famous '*sans-culottes*' ('without breeches'), so called not because they were so poor that they went around bare-buttocked, but because they wore long, loose trousers rather than the tighter knee breeches and stockings favoured by the middle and upper classes. Wearing these long trousers, often accessorized with a tricolour *cocarde*, red bonnet and long, pointed pike, provided a sort of mass anonymity. They were '*le peuple*', the group that politicians portrayed as the innocent, spontaneously reacting tools of public opinion – or what the politicians wanted public opinion to be. As one Assemblée[6] delegate said after going to the Abbaye prison to try and pacify the mob, 'The people are over-excited to the point where they will listen to no one.' This was not quite true – they were listening to the politicians who were stirring up their paranoia.

Whoever did the actual killing in September 1792, the blame has to be laid at the feet of these politicians who were now playing a vicious game of 'more populist than thou'.

In the Assemblée, the delegates seemed to be falling over themselves to be understanding about the massacres. Even before the more radical Convention nationale took over, the new extreme republican sympathies in parliament were already making themselves felt.

As early as the night of 2 September, a delegate reported to a late-night sitting that he wanted to stress. . .

---

[6] The Convention nationale would not start officially until 21 September.

... an important fact in defence of the honour of the people. In the prisons, the people organized tribunals of twelve persons ... After asking each prisoner several questions, the judges put their hands on his head and asked, 'Do you believe that in our conscience we can free this gentleman?' If the answer was yes, the accused was released, and went out to meet the pikes.

According to the delegate, this apparently constituted an 'honourable' trial.

On 3 September, the Minister of the Interior, Jean-Marie Roland, spoke at great length about the events, and seemed to announce a shameless cover-up:

Yesterday was a day over which it is probably best to draw a veil. I know that the people, terrible in their justice, have carried out a sort of justice. They do not attack everything that attracts their fury; they direct it towards those whom they believe to have avoided for too long the sword of the law, and who, because of the present dangers, must be sacrificed without delay.

He talked about 'justified anger' and 'indignation taken to its extreme'. The implication was that populist massacres were all right.

There were a few dissenting voices. On 3 September, Armand de Kersaint, the member for Seine-et-Oise, spoke out against this populism. He harangued the Assemblée:

Public disorder is the fruit of errors, and you know how avidly your enemies have seized this means of misleading the people. It is up to you to tell them the truth. At this very moment, the public is probably being fed exaggerated news, and it must be contradicted. By this means, hopefully we can stop the civic unrest in Paris.

Kersaint was much too forthright to last – he would be guillotined the following year.

Not surprisingly, in their tower at the Temple prison, the royal family were in constant fear for their lives, and it is said that Louis XVI turned pale and started trembling as soon as he heard cannon fire on the night of 2 September. When the mob arrived with the Princesse de Lamballe's severed head, they tried to enter the Temple and were only turned back by a brave *commissaire*, a representative of Paris's Bondy *section* called François Daujon, who told the crowd that Marie-Antoinette's head 'did not belong to them'. (He could have added 'yet'.)

The September massacre season ended a few days after it began, but then the new Convention nationale was sworn in, its first act to declare the end of the monarchy and the beginning of a new 'era of the French'. In true populist fashion, it announced that the last five days of the year (or six in a leap year) would henceforth be holidays known as the *jours sansculottides*.

Sadly for Louis XVI, with the *sans-culottes* needing some positive news amidst setbacks in the war against Prussians and the Austrians, the new masters of the nation chose him as the next target in their populist agenda.

Chapter 19

IF YOU CAN KEEP YOUR HEAD ...

'Le sang, même celui des coupables, versé avec cruauté et profusion, souille éternellement les révolutions.'
'Blood, even that of the guilty, if shed cruelly and profusely, sullies revolutions for ever.'

Olympe de Gouges (1748–93), French writer who was
guillotined for demanding equal rights for women

I

To step outside the political turmoil for a moment, it is perhaps important to list a few French innovations of 1792. These give an idea of the spirit of change in the country. And at least two of them were to have fatal consequences for Louis XVI and many others.

The first, and quaintest, of these was the new calendar. As soon as the Convention nationale opened, it declared that from 21 September 1792 all official documents should be dated 'Year One of the French Republic'. Until then, 1792 had been known in revolutionary circles as 'Year Four of Liberty', dating back to 1789, but now it was decided that 'under the Constitution, the people did not have real liberty'. The calendar was therefore decreed to have restarted, and work began on freeing the days, years and months of their historical baggage. From September

1792 on, there would be no reference to Christianity or even Ancient Rome.

Three members of the Convention, headed by a man called Gilbert Romme (who would later be accused of treason and stab himself to death on the way to the scaffold), were commissioned to draw up the new calendar. This they did with the help of a poet called Philippe-François-Nazaire Fabre (later charged with fraud, and guillotined) and a former royal gardener called André Thouin, who miraculously survived into old age.

This poetic, rustic input was designed to instil citizens of the new Republic with a knowledge of Nature, and 'to make the people love fields'.

The 12 months were therefore renamed to represent events of the farming year. Then, as now, in practical terms, the French year began in September, and the first month (22 September–21 October) was called *vendémiaire*, from *vendanges*, meaning grape harvest. Others were *pluviôse*, the month of rain in January and February, *floréal* for flowering in April and May, and *thermidor*, which sounds like the time for cooking lobsters but was in fact the month of summer heat.

Wishing to free themselves entirely from the past, and impose a new era of Lumières logic, the commission decided that each month should have only 30 days. This is why the above-mentioned *sansculottides* holidays were needed at the end of each year.

The most confusing elements of the calendar were the days of the week. For a start, there were ten of them, from *primidi* to *decadi*. The most obvious result of this was a ten-day week, a recipe for disaster with French people who are so fond of their weekends. This was no doubt the reason why the calendar would last less than 15 years.

In addition, each day had its own name, in a perverse and impossible-to-remember imitation of the old saints' calendar. That former system had, the commission said, been 'a catalogue of lies and dupery'. Instead, they gave each day a new rustic name. Pearls amongst these (and 'Pearl' wasn't one of them, because mollusc farmers were excluded from the calendar) included Donkey (6 October), Celery (23 October), Spade (20 December), Dung (28 December), Broccoli (31 January), Tuna (15 March), Pitchfork (8 June), Watering Can (28 July), Lentil (10 August) and Basket (16 September). The list proves that it was quite difficult to find 360 recognizable terms related to food production, and that the commission was sometimes forced to scrape the bottom of the barrel – which, by the way, was 21 October.

As one can imagine, the calendar was rarely used except in the most official documents, and it was being ignored long before it was actually discontinued. No French builder ever told a customer: 'There's no way we can finish by Cucumber. But we should have it done by Artichoke. Bean at the very latest.' And even revolutionary records never used the day's names. The first year of the new calendar (22 September 1792) became known as *1 vendémiaire an I*.

Despite the fact that ordinary people rarely if ever used it, the calendar was an indication of how keenly the new French government of September 1792 felt the need for complete change. And the ominous date in this new calendar that Louis XVI would have to beware of was Moss, in year two, otherwise known as *2 pluviôse an II*. It was creeping ever closer.

II

The next innovation of 1792 was the national anthem. Unlike the calendar, this was not a celebration of France's foodstuffs and farming implements. The *'Marseillaise'* was a battle hymn that expressed the fears early in the year when, as the song says, everyone expected foreign royalist invaders to come and 'cut the throats of [their] sons and companions'.[1]

It was written during the night of 25–26 April 1792 by a military engineer called Claude Joseph Rouget de Lisle, who was

---

[1] The French word is *'compagne'*, which means female partner. As with so much in the French Revolution, the viewpoint is steadfastly male.

serving in Strasbourg, on the French–German border, a town that expected to be besieged by Austrian and Prussian armies at any moment. The Mayor of Strasbourg, a friend of de Lisle's from the Freemasons who possessed a decent tenor voice, sang it at his house the following day, and the mayor's sister thought it 'catchy and with a certain originality'. She arranged it for voice and harpsichord and it quickly became a hit all over France, under the name of 'War Song for the Rhine Army'.

The hymn got its modern name when the armed volunteers summoned by the Paris Commune arrived in the city in July 1792. The contingent from Marseille arrived singing the new song.

The words were perfectly suited to the job that the volunteers had been brought in to do – oversee the fall of the monarchy. The first verse, the only one usually sung, calls on the 'children of the homeland' to form an army and march against tyranny, so that 'impure blood' will run in the fields. The second begins by insulting the invading army: 'What does this horde of slaves, traitors and conspiring kings want?' and ends with the answer: 'They dare to dream of throwing us back into our former slavery.'

Throughout seven verses (it was a productive night), Rouget de Lisle encouraged all patriotic citizens to repel the 'bloody despots', 'accomplices of Bouillé' (the royalist general who put down a mutiny in Nancy) and all traitors who, like 'tigers, without pity, tear the breasts of their mothers'. He also suggested that the French, as 'magnanimous warriors', might 'spare sad victims', but that part of the song seems to have been forgotten.

Practically every verse drips with blood and vengeance, which was definitely the theme in France from the time the song was written until at least 1795, when it was officially adopted as the national anthem. This was not reassuring for Louis XVI and the royal family, or anyone who dared to utter opposition to the Convention's more radical members.

Rouget de Lisle himself does not seem to have been anti-monarchist. On 10 August 1792, he was sacked from the army for expressing sympathy for the royal family, and was later imprisoned, before serving again to repel a counter-revolutionary army that invaded Brittany in 1795.

In the days before royalties, Rouget de Lisle never made a fortune for his song, and even spent some time in a debtors' prison in his sixties. He wrote throughout his life, penning such ditties as 'A Hymn to Reason' and 'The First Song of the Industrialists', though none of these caught on like the '*Marseillaise*'.

Ironically, one of his later compositions was addressed to Louis XVI's brother, Louis Stanislas, who came to the throne in 1814 as Louis XVIII when the monarchy was restored after the fall of Napoleon. This was called '*Vive le Roi!*' – a war cry that Rouget de Lisle's lyrics call:

> *Noble cri de la vieille France,*
> *Cri d'espérance,*
> *De bonheur, d'amour et de foi,*
> *Trop longtemps étouffé par le crime...*

> ('Noble cry of old France,
> Cry of hope,
> Of happiness, love and faith,
> Too long suppressed by crime.')

The song ends with a wish that 'France and its king should be happy together, and from their shared happiness our own will be born.'

Unfortunately, even this obsequiousness did not find favour with Louis XVIII, and Rouget de Lisle was denied the rare distinction of writing two national anthems for opposing regimes. But it is amusing to think that the French Republic's national anthem was in fact written by an apparently raving royalist. Not that this would have been much of a consolation for Louis XVI and moderate politicians back in 1792, trapped in the era when France was divided along the strict lines drawn out by the '*Marseillaise*', between 'traitors' and vengeful 'patriots'.

III

The third innovation from this period is one in which Louis XVI, who had always been fascinated by machines, played a part. It is the guillotine.

The contraption that would become a sad symbol of this period of the Revolution was not invented by the French. Decapitation machines had existed for centuries, with Halifax in northern England laying claim to Europe's earliest mechanical gibbet, dating back to at least 1286.[2]

Joseph-Ignace Guillotin, a doctor from Saintes in the southwest of France, and a delegate at the first Assemblée nationale, probably knew nothing about Halifax when he first suggested a swift method of execution during a speech to parliament in October 1789. His was a humanitarian idea – previously, being beheaded by a drunken executioner wielding a heavy, often blunt axe was not a tidy process. Swords were lighter and more accurate but often broke. And those were the lucky victims. Beheading was reserved for the upper classes, whereas less privileged criminals would be broken on the wheel, burned, slowly hanged or dismembered. Guillotin's idea was to extend the democratic ideals of the Revolution to execution – one punishment for all. He also proposed that the ignominy of the punishment should end with the victims' death, and that bodies should be given to their families and buried without any mention of how they came to be in the grave. All in all, a thoughtful man.

Unfortunately Guillotin spoilt the effect of all this humanism with a joke. He promised the Assemblée that his idea would result in swift, efficient executions: 'With my machine, I can cut off your head in the wink of an eye and you won't feel a thing.' He got a laugh, but his fellow delegates were so shocked by his levity that they called a halt to the debate.

---

[2] For more details on the guillotine's historic origins, see *1000 Years of Annoying the French*.

When discussions resumed, Guillotin's suggestion was accepted, and on 21 January 1790, Louis XVI signed the decree formalizing the use of a new execution machine. In a tragic coincidence (or a humorous one, depending on how much of a revolutionary you are), this was exactly three years before he would be guillotined.

Tests on sheep and human corpses were carried out, some of them in a workshop in the tiny alleyway where Marat was printing his exhortations to massacre and Danton was writing his inflammatory speeches. A melting pot of murderous thoughts.

It is said, though not attested, that in early March 1792, Louis XVI attended a meeting at the Tuileries to discuss the design of the guillotine, and actually helped to perfect it. At first, a scythe-like curved blade was envisaged, or a simple horizontal one. But Louis, the amateur engineer, apparently argued that an oblique cutting edge would be more efficient. If this story is true, it suggests that he had no inkling that he faced execution, and that he was much more scared of lynching by the mob. Either that, or he wanted to make sure that his eventual demise would be as painless as possible. In any case, on 25 March 1792, Louis XVI appended his signature to the Assemblée's decree authorizing the creation of this new execution machine.

Exactly a month later, it claimed its first head, when a mugger called Nicolas Jacques Pelletier was executed on the place de Grève, outside the Hôtel de Ville in Paris. The large crowd, used to long, gruesome executions or mass lynchings, was apparently disappointed, and cries were heard of 'give us back the gallows!' Within months, the sheer number of prisoners lining up to take their turn on the 'national razor' would be enough to satisfy the most bloodthirsty crowd.

When it was first used, the machine had no official name. Several people were vying for credit for its development. There was an architect called Pierre Giraud and a German harpsichord builder called Johann Tobias Schmidt (who made the prototype). For a while, it was known as the *louisette*, in honour of Antoine Louis, a surgeon who had had been involved in the project since it was first mooted. But Guillotin's joke was apparently too good to be forgotten, and even inspired a song with the catchy title: 'On the Inimitable Head-Cutting Machine of Doctor Guillotin Called the Guillotine'. The label stuck, and the humanitarian doctor was so horrified to hear his name attached to an engine of death that he more or less withdrew from political life, devoting the rest of his life to healing rather than beheading.

The only sign that Louis XVI felt at all uncomfortable about this technological innovation came in July 1792. Johann Tobias Schmidt sent a letter to the King on the fifth, requesting a royal patent for a *machine à décapiter*, along with a drawing of his design. However, his application was returned to him on the twenty-fourth with a handwritten note from Clément Félix Champion de Villeneuve, whom Louis XVI had just chosen as his Minister of the Interior. Villeneuve was no doubt express-ing the King's opinion when he wrote that 'it is repugnant to humanity to grant a patent for a discovery of this type,' and he advised Schmidt to ask the government instead. A sly hint, perhaps, at what Louis XVI thought of the government by that time, mere weeks before his palace was stormed and his reign was brought to a violent end.

IV

Almost as soon as the guillotine was oiled and sharpened, politi-cal executions began.

In the wake of the riot at the Tuileries on 10 August 1792, amongst its other activities, the Paris Commune insurrection-nelle had decreed that its *sections* could set up a Revolutionary Tribunal with powers to arrest, condemn and execute anyone suspected of counter-revolutionary activities. As such, the exist-ing legal system was completely bypassed.

Robespierre was by this time the head of the place de Vendôme *section*, which renamed itself ominously the *section des piques* in honour of the heads being toted around on pointed sticks. This was the neighbourhood just a stroll from the Tuileries palace and the Convention's debating chamber, a highly convenient power base.

The self-appointed defenders of the nation at the new Tribunal révolutionnaire quickly began to arrest the men who would become the first purely political victims of the guillotine.

Louis Collenot d'Angremont had joined the royal court as language teacher to Marie-Antoinette, and written an English-teaching book and a French grammar while in her service. In 1789, he took on a very different job, as head of the *bureau militaire* of the National Guard.

It was in this capacity that Angremont was accused of managing a network of about 1,500 royal sympathizers who were paid to disrupt anti-royalist demonstrations. (If disruption really was the objective, he was certainly not very good at his job.) The key accusation was that Angremont's men had actually instigated the violence that led to the deaths of several hundred rioters on 10 August. This was barely credible, but predictably, after a two-day trial, he was found guilty, and guillotined five hours after the verdict was pronounced, on the evening of 21 August.

Next up was one of his supposed accomplices, Arnaud de la Porte, a former Minister of the Navy and Minister of the King's Household, who had been in charge of Louis XVI's civil list income. He was accused of paying Angremont's 1,500 sympathizers, at a cost of 200,000 *livres* per month, a shockingly large sum. He was also charged with financing royalist pamphlets – including some that had criticized Robespierre's Jacobins club. The Jacobins were not forgiving enemies, and Arnaud de la Porte was found guilty and guillotined on 24 August.

The third victim of this new tribunal was perhaps the most indicative of the way France was now heading. Barnabé Farmian Durosoy had not been involved in paying conspirators or infiltrators. His only crime was to write and publish a newspaper, the *Gazette de Paris*, that supported the idea of constitutional monarchy.

It was true that seditious publications had been banned during Louis XVI's reign, but as we saw earlier, his censors had been increasingly lax. Under the Assemblée, Marat had had to move his printing presses around the city to avoid confiscation, and had gone into hiding after some of his most bloodthirsty incitements to violence. But until 1792 there had been no suggestion that newspaper publishers should be executed for their opinions. Now, though, the crackdown on freedom of speech was beginning, engineered by politicians who were touting *Liberté* as one of their slogans.

Durosoy, who used the pen name of Du Rozoy, had written a scathing article after the 10 August storming of the Tuileries, condemning the mob and those who controlled it – 'those who deliberate' and 'those who cut throats'. He described the politicians and agitators who 'write, debate, slander, sharpen daggers, distribute bullets, give orders, meet, and increase the price paid for denouncements, crimes, scandal sheets and poisons'. This (largely accurate) conspiracy theory got him arrested by the Tribunal révolutionnaire, and executed on the evening of 25 August, three and a half hours after the end of his trial.

Large crowds gathered for these executions, to boo the 'traitors' and shout *'Vive la nation!'* as the bloodied heads were held up for their approval. Just a few days into the campaign to stamp out freedom of thought, Paris was getting a taste for these public shows. Angremont's execution was even given extra atmosphere, being held by torchlight.

However, as we saw in the previous chapter, even these swift trials did not satisfy the thirst for traitors' blood, which was why the prison massacres happened. Then in November 1792 came the promise of a show trial to delight the most impatient revolutionary.

V

Ever since 1789, Louis XVI had been playing a dangerous game, performing his role in the constitutional monarchy while maintaining a constant correspondence with royalist émigrés. Although some of his letters had been pleas to tone down counter-revolutionary activity, merely staying in contact was tantamount to treason.

By autumn 1792, the counter-revolutionary armies had begun to retreat. After meeting some fierce resistance on the Belgian and German borders of France, the Prussians and Austrians had apparently decided that it was not going to be the walkover they had hoped for, and their monarchistic ardour cooled. French revolutionary troops even occupied parts of Belgium and the Rhineland. It looked as though the *'Patrie'* was no longer *'en danger'*.

Louis XVI might have been able to breathe a sigh of relief, but then one of his old acquaintances came forward to drop a bombshell.

A locksmith called François Gamain revealed that he had installed a hidden safe in the Tuileries palace, behind some panelling in the corridor that led from Louis XVI's apartment to his son's room. According to Gamain, he didn't know what the safe was for, but once the job was done, Louis gave him some poisoned wine in an attempt to protect the secret. Gamain swore in a statement that he had only survived by vomiting up everything he had eaten and drunk that day, but had since been so ill that there was 'no hope that his health would ever recover sufficiently for him to go about his work and meet the needs of his family'.[3]

The poisoning story sounds highly implausible. For a start, Louis XVI was not in the habit of handing glasses of wine to anyone. They were usually handed to him. And if someone had to be poisoned, would the King really do it himself? Furthermore, the royal family was surrounded by faithful servants and advisors who knew a whole multitude of secrets, and the Gamains had been in their service for years. They had moved to Versailles while Louis XIV was still on the throne, and François Gamain's father and uncles had all worked for the royal family. As a younger man, Louis XVI had studied locksmithing with François, and probably never dreamt that his old tutor would denounce him to his political enemies.

---

[3] This heavy hint was taken, and Gamain was given a job as a 'municipal officer' in Versailles.

What Louis probably didn't know was that since the royal family had been moved into Paris, François Gamain had been elected to the Versailles council, and had even joined the committee that was set up there to make sure that all royal statues and inscriptions were taken off public buildings. Out of touch with what was going on in his old home town, Louis had simply chosen the wrong locksmith for his secret job.

When the safe was unlocked, it was found to contain boxfuls of explosively compromising documents. Whether they were all genuine or not (and the authenticity of some or all of them has been disputed), the evidence that Louis XVI had had a secret communications network was enough to get him formally accused of treason.

It was always clear that the trial was going to be a foregone conclusion. On 3 December, Robespierre gave a famous speech at the Convention, reminding members of the execution of Charles I of England and stating that 'the crimes of kings engender all other crimes'. According to Robespierre, France did not even have to try Louis, because 'he is already condemned'. And anyway, a trial would be a political mistake: 'If Louis can be presumed innocent, what is the Revolution?' After a short hypocritical digression about how he personally opposed the death penalty, Robespierre came to his conclusion: this was not the time for the 'peaceful people' to be their generous selves, and 'Louis must die so that the nation can live.'

On 6 December, the preparations for a guilty verdict continued. After debating why the Minister of the Interior, Jean-Marie Roland, was not making sure that Paris was amply supplied with food,[4] the Convention turned to the subject of the King's treachery.

[4] Reading the parliamentary archives, it sounds as though food shortages in the capital were partially caused by bad management and even fraud, but Roland's defenders stoked the fires of paranoia by accusing 'agents of bankers in Vienna, Berlin, London and Madrid'.

Marat, who was now serving as a member of parliament, did not mince his words. First he played the 'if you don't agree with me, you're a traitor' card, warning his colleagues about 'the formerly privileged class of ex-nobles, ex-financiers, ex-snobs, ex-bible-bashers, of whom some still sit amongst you'. He said that the easiest way 'to identify the traitors in this assembly' was for parliament to decree that 'the death of the tyrant [Louis XVI] should be voted openly, and each person's vote published'.

A member called Pierre Bourbotte[5] took up this call, and added that it was imperative to try the King and 'pronounce the death sentence against him the next day'.

When Pierre-Louis Manuel, who had been imprisoned in the Bastille for seditious publications in 1786, and was no friend of the monarchy, objected that 'you cannot pre-judge that Louis will be condemned to death', he was shouted down,[6] and it was decided that a commission of 21 members of the Convention would draft a list of Louis's 'crimes', and that he would then be summoned to the debating chamber to answer the charges. The following day, each member would step forward and publicly pronounce a verdict.

At the end of the minutes of that day's proceedings, a member called Nicolas-Marie Quinette (a baron turned republican) reminded the house that 'the insurrection of 10 August overthrew the regime that was killing liberty. Louis XVI should have been killed at that time, on the wreckage of his throne.'

Things were not looking promising for Louis.

---

[5] Like so many who demanded the use of the guillotine, Bourbotte became one of its victims in June 1795.

[6] Manuel was another of the politicians who were too fair-minded to survive. He was guillotined in November 1793.

Chapter 20

CRIMES AND PUNISHMENTS

'Je m'arrête devant l'histoire. Songez qu'elle jugera votre jugement et que le sien sera celui des siècles.'
'I conclude in full view of history. Remember that it will judge your verdict, and that its judgement will be that of the centuries.'

    Raymond de Sèze (1748–1828), French lawyer, defending
        Louis XVI before the Convention nationale

I

On Tuesday, 11 December 1792, before Louis XVI (now known as Louis Capet, a name that referred back to the medieval royal family, of which the Bourbons were a branch) was summoned from his cell at the Temple prison, members of the Convention were allowed to suggest new accusations against him. These included 'dictating laws to the nation', 'paying for scandal sheets, pamphlets and newspapers to pervert public opinion' and 'using [his] popularity as a means to enslave the people'. There were so many charges that even Marat called for restraint. Besides, he, like his more extreme colleagues, wanted to get on with condemning Louis to death.

When Citizen Capet was brought into the chamber, and allowed to sit down in the armchair from which he had given his speech ratifying the Constitution just over a year earlier, he was told that 'the French people accuse you of committing a multitude of crimes to establish your tyranny, while destroying its freedom.'

Like many of the people who would later be brought before revolutionary tribunals, Louis stayed calm and rational in the face of often absurd charges. When accused of 'marching an army against the people' and only withdrawing it 'when the storming of the Bastille and the general insurrection showed you that the people were victorious', Louis replied: 'At that time I was allowed to march troops where I wanted.'

Accused of allowing the tricolour *cocarde* to be 'trampled … during orgies in your presence', he simply stated that 'it didn't happen in my presence'.

For all the charges relating to the political decisions he had taken since late 1789, he rightly reminded his audience that they had been overseen by the Assemblée and that he had only been acting within the Constitution.

But when it came to the accusations of conspiring with counter-revolutionary armies and paying agents in France, Louis was on much shakier ground. He claimed that he had 'disowned all the actions of [his] brothers', that 'all diplomatic correspondence went via ministers', and that 'the idea of counter-revolution never entered my head', but the charges piled up, as did damning letters supposedly in his handwriting. One after the other, Louis maintained that he didn't recognize the documents, but after a dozen or so, he finally lapsed into tired denials: 'don't recognize it', 'not at all', 'same as before', *'non'*.

The onslaught only ended when Louis asked for a lawyer, and was allowed to withdraw. Three counsels were appointed, but Louis must have felt that they would have to be magicians to get him a reprieve.

On 26 December,[1] Louis was brought back to the Convention to answer the charges. Faced with so much evidence, his lawyers

---

[1] One can't fault the Convention's work ethic. There was a parliamentary session on Christmas Day, and New Year's Day.

seem to have decided that their only hope was to protest their client's good character, claim a mistrial and plead for mercy.

After Louis announced simply that 'my counsel will read my defence', Raymond de Sèze, a count who had represented Marie-Antoinette in the necklace affair of 1785, gave a long, impassioned speech addressed diplomatically to the 'citizen representatives of the nation'.

He argued that Louis was 'only a man … he can no longer inspire any fear', so that 'this is the time when you owe him not only more justice but more, if I may say so, favour.' In any case, the charges against him were misguided, because Louis had simply been the head of the regime in power at the time. As Sèze put it, 'Nations are sovereign. They are free to give themselves the government that seems appropriate … But a great nation cannot exercise its own sovereignty. It has to delegate it, and this delegation leads it either to give itself a king or to create a republic.' In short, Louis just happened to be that delegate, and was, in a way, the ultimate victim of the monarchy.

It was an ingenious intellectual argument, though not one likely to find favour with Robespierre, Marat and the like.

After refuting most of the charges on the grounds that Louis was only doing exactly what the Assemblée and the Constitution had empowered him to do, Sèze played his rhetorical trump card:

> You want to decide the fate of Louis, but you yourselves are the accusers. You want to decide the fate of Louis, but you have already announced your decision. You want to decide the fate of Louis, but your opinions are already known all over Europe. Louis seems to be the only Frenchman for whom there is no law.

Next, Sèze launched into a long, detailed denial, charge by charge, letter by letter, of all the accusations against Louis, and reminded everyone that he had been trying to reduce taxes and improve democracy even before the États généraux, but this claim only produced 'murmurs on the extreme left and in the public gallery'.

Louis was asked if he had anything to add and after saying, rather pointlessly, that his defence lawyer had been speaking the truth, he simply denied that he had ever wanted to 'spill the people's blood'.

As soon as the accused and his lawyers left the debating chamber, the Convention erupted into a violent argument as to whether the verdict should be pronounced immediately or not, with calls for moderates, including the president of the session, who was vainly trying to maintain order, to be sent *'à l'Abbaye'* – to one of the prisons where inmates had been massacred. Finally, members voted to allow time for the speech for the defence to be printed, so that the public could read it.

On 14 January, the Convention returned to the 'Louis Capet' question, and would stick with it for the following three days, expending most of their energies on points of order. The majority of these concerned not what the verdict would be – that was a foregone conclusion – but how it should be pronounced, and whether parliament had the right to condemn a former king to death without consulting the people. Opinions were split along predictable political lines – in the eyes of Robespierre's supporters, there was no need to prevaricate; they should start sharpening the blade. The moderates either wanted to give members the option to vote for imprisonment instead of the guillotine, or to allow an appeal process. Some in-betweeners argued in favour of delaying any execution until the verdict could be ratified by a referendum.

On 15 January, members were called out one by one to answer yes or no, whether Louis was guilty of 'conspiring against public liberty and attacks on the security of the state': 673 out of 718 said simply *'oui'*. The same process was used to decide whether a verdict should be ratified by the people: 423 voted *'non'*.

On 16 January, after hearing a complaint that a moderate, Charles de Villette, had received a death threat as he entered the chamber – 'if he did not vote for the death of Louis, he would be massacred' – members voted on the punishment that would be meted out to the former King.

Of 726 members of the Convention present, 387 voted for an immediate execution, 44 for a death sentence to be delayed until further debate had taken place, 290 for imprisonment and/or banishment, with five abstentions (Charles de Villette, by the way, voted for imprisonment).[2] When a stay of execution was put to the vote, there was a majority of 60 against it.

Instead of a simple answer to the question about punishment, most speakers gave a short speech. Or, in Robespierre's case, a long one, after he had insisted 'I don't like long speeches about obvious questions.' He declared himself 'inflexible towards tyrants because I am sympathetic towards the oppressed', reminded everyone that 'the people has ordered me to judge', and voted for death.

Danton kept it short and sweet and voted 'death for the tyrant'.

Marat said he was convinced that 'Louis was the main author of ... all the massacres that have sullied France since the start of the Revolution' and voted for 'death for the tyrant within 24 hours'.

Louis XVI's own cousin, Louis Philippe, alias 'Égalité (formerly d'Orléans)' assured the house that: 'Solely concerned with my duty, and convinced that all those who have attacked or will attack the sovereignty of the people deserve death, I vote for death.' With family like that, Louis needed no enemies.

II

On the morning of Monday, 21 January 1793, security in Paris was at a maximum. The city gates were closed, and the streets were lined with some 80,000 soldiers and National Guards.

---

[2] After the vote, several members who had called for the death penalty were threatened by royalists, and one, Louis-Michel Lepeletier de Saint-Fargeau, was murdered during dinner the day before Louis XVI's execution.

Cannons were set up at key locations. All the shops were closed. Louis XVI was driven in a carriage (he was spared the usual indignity of riding, backwards, on an open cart) escorted by the commander of the National Guard, Santerre, the man implicated in the riots at Vincennes and the Champ-de-Mars, and 200 of his men. It took the carriage more than an hour to cover the three kilometres or so from the Temple prison to the place de la Révolution (formerly the place Louis XV, and today place de la Concorde), because the cortège took a long route along the wide boulevards, where there was more room for the military escort.

As his carriage entered the square, Louis broke off from reciting psalms and said, 'We've arrived, if I'm not mistaken.' Some 23 years earlier, this had been the site of a tragedy for Louis, when the firework display to celebrate his wedding had caused a stampede that killed more than 100 people. Now the crowd was much more orderly – mainly thanks to 20,000 armed men in tight ranks holding back a mass of mostly silent spectators.

After initially refusing to have his hands tied, Louis relented when one of the five executioners offered to bind them with his handkerchief rather than a rope. His hair was then quickly cut and the collar ripped from his shirt.

Up on the red-painted scaffold, Louis tried to make a speech to the crowd. Asking for the drums to be silenced, he walked to the edge of the platform and said something along the lines of: 'I am innocent of all the crimes of which I am accused. I pray to God that the blood you are about to spill will never fall on France.' He was interrupted as the drums started up again, and the executioners laid him on the bench and closed the wooden collar around his neck.

Louis struggled as the blade came down, and by all reports it did not sever his neck. It cut through the back of his skull and into his jaw. The technology clearly had not yet been perfected after all.

Even so, the guillotine had done its job, as had the Convention nationale. At the age of 39, the 'tyrant' was dead.

These days, the execution of Louis XVI is seen as just one step in the Revolution, alongside the storming of the Bastille, the march to Versailles and the attack on the Tuileries. In revolutions, people die, and the winners take revenge on the losers.

In Louis XVI's case, though, it seems valid to ask why he should have been executed. There was, of course, the danger of counter-revolution, but more than 300 members of the Convention had proposed a solution to this – lock him up, and if France is invaded again, put him to death. A royal hostage might have been a greater protection for France, unless Louis XVI's brothers had decided that they preferred to get him out of the way so that they could claim the crown. But reading the minutes of the Convention's debates, security wasn't the issue – it was revenge for 'despotism', 'tyranny' and the suffering that the monarchy had imposed on 'the people'.

The real question is: was this fair?

It is true that the aristocratic landowners, including the royal family, had taxed and worked generations of poor workers into early graves, while keeping non-aristocrats away from all the best-paid, most prestigious jobs in the land. For centuries, France had tolerated a monstrously unfair status quo.

However, as we have seen, almost as soon as he became king, and mature enough to see beyond his locksmithing and hunting, Louis XVI had set about changing this situation. Slowly and partially, it was true, but peacefully. And it was the aristocrats, not Louis himself, who had scuppered his attempts to make taxation fairer. After he commissioned the *cahiers de doléances* and convened the États généraux and inadvertently triggered the Revolution, he had played the game and worked with the new, more democratic, parliament to create a constitutional monarchy. Again, it was aristocrats within the Assemblée who watered down the reforms, causing the collapse of that regime. And it seems credible that it was only once Louis felt totally unsafe that he began communicating in earnest with the people, including foreign monarchs, who wanted to help save his life.

To use a modern analogy, imagine a vast company owned by a billionaire who inherited it from his father. He loves his luxury, spends too much time on his yacht, and his wife is famous for her obscenely expensive collection of shoes and diamonds. Even so, he decides that the company should pay decent wages to its rank and file. He also wants to get ordinary workers involved in the company's decision-making process, because despite the company's vast assets, its results are not looking healthy, and the owner realizes that new input is needed.

He invests in training, and opens a state-of the-art research-and-development department to guarantee the company's long-term future. He reduces workers' hours. He even proposes to cut directors' salaries and pensions, including his own.

But every time he puts his plans to the board of directors, they vote him down. Understandably, perhaps, given what they stand to lose, but unforgivably. He tinkers with the details, makes compromises, but always gets the same answer: *non*. Even though the workers are calling for an all-out strike, and the company's results are getting worse, the overpaid board members vote *non*.

The strike happens, and the owner decides to sit down with the workers. Together, they begin to hammer out a solution that hands most of the shares over to the rank and file, while keeping the owner on as honorary chairman. The negotiations are ponderous, and members of the board are constantly throwing spanners into the works, but the company truly is changing, and the workers' voices are being heard.

The question is this: Why would the workers then kill the man who was trying to sort things out?

They almost certainly wouldn't.

So the second question is: Who would want to kill the owner, along with anyone who dares to suggest that he is not such a bad guy despite what his family has been doing for generations?

The answer seems to be: People who do not want to see a peaceful, negotiated solution, and who desire violence because it suits their purpose, which is to grab the company for themselves. And for the most part, these people would not be ordinary workers – they would be political ideologists who have decided that their ideas are more important than the ultimate fate of the company they are claiming to save.

This analogy would explain the murderous round of accusations and killings that followed Louis XVI's death. Instead of bringing closure to the Revolution, the King's execution seems to have confirmed to the more ambitious politicians that no head was sacred, and that the guillotine knew no limits. A purge of all the non-radicals could begin.

III

The Convention nationale had always been split into factions. There were, of course, factions within factions, and political 'clubs' constantly breaking away from each other, but at the time of the vote on Louis XVI's fate, the main divisions were these...

On the right of the house, literally and politically, were the so-called 'Girondins', a name inspired by the fact that many of them came from the Gironde region around Bordeaux in the southwest of France. They were mostly staunch believers in the Revolution, but wanted to limit dangerous confrontations. Many of them had tried to prop up the ailing constitutional monarchy, and believed in the rule of law. Most of them asked for Louis XVI's death sentence to be delayed.

To the left, on the highest benches in parliament, sat the 'Montagnards', the 'Mountainmen', occupying the revolutionary high ground. They were mostly Parisians, and claimed to represent the radical spirit of the storming of the Bastille. They had opposed the Constitution, and had wanted to use any means possible to overthrow the moderate Assemblée and install what they saw as democracy – the rule of 'the people'. It was the firebrand speeches of Montagnards like Robespierre, Danton and Marat that whipped up the mobs to invade the Tuileries and put an end to the constitutional monarchy. They voted for immediate death for Louis XVI.

In the centre sat what became known as the 'Plaine', a group seen as flat and unimaginative by both sides. Many of them came from the wealthier bourgeois areas of Paris, and from financial and legal backgrounds. They believed in the Revolution, but wanted compromise, and did not see the point in trying and executing Louis XVI. Because they seemed to be bogged down in moderation, they were nicknamed the 'Marais', a reference to the flat area of central Paris, but which also meant marshland. One Montagnard called Pierre Joseph Duhem famously said that 'the Marais toads are raising their heads. Good! They'll be easier to cut off.' The Plaine was in the majority in the Convention, but it wasn't a unified group, and so did not vote en bloc for or against Louis XVI's death.

After the King's execution, using the favourite tactic of a dictatorship – 'if you don't agree with us, you're a traitor' – the Montagnards kept up the pace of their own revolution, aiming to oust all moderates from power. In March 1793, at Danton's suggestion, the Tribunal revolutionnaire, originally set up in 1792, was made permanent and given sweeping powers to 'uncover all counter-revolutionary enterprises, all attacks on liberty, equality, unity and the indivisibility of the republic, interior and exterior security, and all plots to re-establish the monarchy, or establish any authority that attacks liberty, equality and the sovereignty of the people'. The tribunal's decisions would be subject to no appeal, and one of the first was that anyone bearing arms against the republic or wearing the white royal rosette should be executed within 24 hours.

Political opposition was at an end.

Marat took up his poison pen against the moderates, publishing a paper urging his parliamentary colleagues to 'arrest all the enemies of our Revolution and everyone suspect. Let us exterminate without pity all the conspirators if we are not to be exterminated ourselves.' These conspirators were easy to find, he said:

Counter-revolution is in the government, in the Convention ...
Criminal delegates are pulling the strings of the plot that they
have organized with the hordes of despots who are coming to
cut our throats ... All the disloyal members who neglected their
duty by opposing the death of the tyrant ... are traitors, royalists and incompetents.'

It was what has since become another classic dictatorial tactic
– pointing at the enemy within.

When Marat's tract was read out in full in parliament, about a
hundred Montagnards stood up and pledged their support for it
(including some who weren't even members of the Convention
but somehow got their names into the minutes). The Girondins
managed to have Marat arrested for slander against parliamentarians, but he was found innocent by his allies on the
Revolutionary Tribunal, and carried through the streets of Paris
in triumph.

The moderates were broken, and all that was needed was a
mob to do the mopping up. On 31 May 1793, after a day of
unrest in Paris during which alarm bells had been rung as if to
announce an invasion, the city's *sections* sent deputations to the
Convention to ask what they were going to do about the imminent danger. Danton greeted them by saying that the people
'hate cowardly moderation that will bring back tyranny' and,
to cheers from the public gallery, announced: 'The people will
carry out a general insurrection to regain its liberty.'

The message was clear, and on 2 June, the Parisians returned
to the Convention, this time with tens of thousands of National
Guards (who, by surrounding parliament, were in theory themselves committing counter-revolution). The crowd demanded
that 29 leaders of the Girondins be arrested. When the chairman of the session tried to evacuate the chamber, the National
Guard threatened the members with cannons. The Girondins
had no choice but to submit to house arrest.

None of these men were really counter-revolutionaries. Many
were devout republicans and revolutionaries. They included

Jacques Pierre Brissot, a veteran of the Bastille (both as a prisoner and a stormer), Jérôme Pétion, one of the two delegates sent to fetch the royal family after the escape to Varennes, and Pierre Victurnien Vergniaud, one of the men who had argued most strongly in favour of war against the potential Austrian invaders. Several of the Girondins managed to get out of Paris and take refuge in the provinces, but 21 of them would be dead within months, including the three men mentioned above.

IV

This was also the ideal time to finish off the royal family. Philippe Égalité's double-dealing days came to an end on the scaffold in November 1793 after his son, the future King Louis-Philippe, joined the émigré army; Louis XVI's sister Élisabeth was brought before the Revolutionary Tribunal in March 1794, accused of being the 'sister of a tyrant'. She replied: 'If my brother had been a tyrant, you wouldn't be where you are now.' A week after her thirtieth birthday, she was taken to the guillotine and executed last in a batch of 25. It was only while standing in line that she learnt that her sister-in-law, Marie-Antoinette, had met the same fate a few months earlier, in October 1793.

Marie-Antoinette had always been the revolutionaries' favourite enemy, the living symbol of everything that was wrong with the privileged society of the Ancien Régime. The *Autrichienne* must have known that her fate was sealed as soon as Louis XVI lost his head – after all, he had actually been popular with ordinary people. And when her time came, it was as an explicit move on the part of the radical members of the Convention to fire up public opinion. In March 1793, Robespierre told his colleagues that 'the time has come for patriots to rekindle the vigorous and undying hatred that they have shown for the name of kings.' After the punishment of one tyrant (Louis), he said:

> Are we going to tolerate that another person, no less guilty, no less accused by the nation … should sit peacefully here? … A

great republic, outraged by so much insolence ... expects from you the initiative that will revive in all hearts a holy antipathy for royalty, and give new energy to public morale.

In short, executing Marie-Antoinette would make the politicians more popular.

Interrogated before her trial, she was asked such leading questions as: 'Was it you who taught Louis Capet the art of profound duplicity with which he duped the good people of France for so long?' (To which she defiantly replied that 'the people have been duped, cruelly, but not by my husband or me.') She was also accused of 'dilapidating the wealth of France' (which was true), encouraging Louis to veto laws (no doubt also true), and 'wanting to destroy liberty by climbing back on to the throne over the corpses of patriots' – to which she answered: 'We didn't need to climb back on to the throne because we were there already.' This was clearly one defendant who knew she stood no chance of being found not guilty.

The trial itself on 14 October 1793 was even more surreal, and degenerated into a pure show of hatred. A former member of the Versailles National Guard gave descriptions of 'orgies' (meaning debauched feasts) at the palace that he had in fact not seen with his own eyes. Another witness testified to finding wine bottles under Marie-Antoinette's bed in the Tuileries in August 1792, proving that she had got the Swiss Guards drunk so that they would commit a massacre. Hearing these accusations, she remained fairly impassive, shaking her white-haired head, or denying any knowledge of events.

She only lost her cool when more vicious allegations were made. Citing a list of pornographic pamphlets, the Convention member Jacques-René Hébert (who would himself be purged and guillotined five months later) accused Marie-Antoinette of putting her son to bed between herself and his aunt Élisabeth before indulging in 'frenetic debauchery'. Marie-Antoinette's horrified response has often been quoted: *'J'en appelle à toutes les mères!'* – 'I call all mothers as my witness!' It earned her so many cheers of support from women in the public gallery that the proceedings had to be suspended. But only for a short while – in all, Marie-Antoinette spent more than 30 hours over two days, sitting on a wooden chair in her patched black widow's dress, listening to a torrent of allegations. At the end of her hearing on 15 October she was asked if she had anything more to say and replied: 'I was just the wife of Louis XVI.' Which was, in truth, what the whole trial came down to.

After waiting in an anteroom until almost 4 a.m., she was called back into the courtroom to hear the guilty verdict. Some say that she expected to be banished. But the judge, Antoine Quentin Fouquier-Tinville, had known all along that he was going to pronounce the death penalty.[3]

Unlike Louis, on the morning of 16 October 1793 Marie-Antoinette had her hands tied behind her back as she was lifted on to the open cart that carried her the short drive across the river from the Conciergerie to the place de la Révolution. This time, only 30,000 soldiers were needed to line the route – no one expected an attempt to save her life. The crowd watching the *Autrichienne* was much more aggressive and disdainful than those who had seen Louis drive by ten months earlier. This was pure revenge.

By all accounts, Marie-Antoinette followed her husband to the guillotine resignedly, her last words being an apology when she stepped on the executioner's foot as she climbed the steps to the scaffold: 'I'm sorry, I didn't do it deliberately.' If he forgave her, he was probably the only one in the whole square that day.

Her surviving son, the Dauphin Louis Charles, hailed by royalists as Louis XVII on the death of his father, was not put on trial. Separated from Marie-Antoinette in July 1793 to be educated as an 'ordinary citizen' (that is, by a semi-literate tutor), he was made to sign a statement alleging incest by his mother. After

[3] He would receive the same sentence 18 months later.

Marie-Antoinette's execution he spent several months living in a dank, windowless cell where almost no one spoke to him and he contracted scabies and tuberculosis. He died in June 1795, aged ten.

His sister, Marie-Thérèse, was luckier. Kept as a potential hostage, in December 1795 she was exchanged for six French prisoners and sent to live with her mother's family in Vienna. There, she was greeted as a heroine by French émigrés, including her uncles, but regarded them as traitors for failing to save her father. Napoleon Bonaparte would later call her 'the only man in the Bourbon family'.

V

Meanwhile, the radicalized Convention was now spending much of its time discussing alleged plots instead of social progress. Parallel committees were formed – the Comité de salut public (public salvation), which oversaw all major domestic and foreign polices and would quickly be dominated by Robespierre and his allies; and the Comité de sûreté générale (general security), which already existed but was now turned into a sort of high-speed prosecution service, its dozen or so members able to issue arrest warrants from Paris for suspected traitors anywhere in France.

In September 1793, the *loi des suspects* was passed, listing the types of French people who should be considered possible enemies of the state. They included all citizens who 'by their conduct, their contacts, their words or their writings, have shown themselves to be partisans of tyranny'. There were many specific categories, notably returning émigrés and their families, but the Paris Commune authorities came up with a neat generalization when they specified that they would be hunting down 'all those who, having done nothing against liberty, have done nothing for it, either'. In other words, France had just invented the thought police.

Possible 'enemies of liberty' were either put on record as suspect and kept under surveillance (it is estimated that the list ran to some 300,000 names), or arrested and tried – the only two verdicts of a trial being either complete acquittal or execution. Almost everyone in France now went in fear of his or her life. This was la Terreur, or one of them, anyway.[4]

Because if that wasn't terrifying enough, in June 1794 Robespierre and his allies passed another law making the accusation and execution process even more efficient. They felt that too many people were clogging up the prisons, many of them using this time to prepare their defence. From now on, the Revolutionary Tribunal would not need to hear the accused's defence. According to the new law, known as the *loi de prairial* (after the revolutionary name for June), to be an 'enemy of the people', it was now enough to 'disparage the Convention', to 'inspire discouragement', 'deprave morals or corrupt the public conscience'. Proof of these crimes could be 'oral or written', and 'every citizen has the right to seize conspirators and counter-revolutionaries, and accuse them'.

From now on, a misplaced joke, a murmured complaint, or just annoying your neighbour could cost you your head. In the six weeks after the passing of this law, the Paris Revolutionary Tribunal was able to guillotine as many people – more than 1,200 – as it had in the previous 14 months.

While Robespierre was busy pruning away his political rivals, including those in the Convention more radical than he was (one of his sayings from this time was 'all factions must die at

---

[4] The Larousse encyclopedia lists at least three. It says that strictly speaking the first was the short period in August–September 1792 between the storming of the Tuileries and the prison massacres. The second (the one mentioned above) was the main Terreur, from September 1793–July 1794, though from April 1794 onwards it was the Grande Terreur. Larousse also says that Terreur 'reappeared periodically'. However, the word Terreur is most commonly used to describe any period during the Revolution when there were purges of those suspected of not being revolutionary enough, and that policy will be adopted here. Distinctions seem pedantic.

the same stroke'),[5] the Sûreté générale concentrated on eliminating all sources of dissent in the general population. If the guillotine wasn't quick enough, there were other methods – in Lyon, for example, more than 1,800 people were blown to bits with cannons.

Estimates vary widely as to the number of people summarily executed during the Terreur – it is a very sensitive political subject in France, and many records were destroyed during the 1871 Commune in Paris (a sort of aftershock of the Revolution; see Chapter 22). However, it can be safely said that, not counting the deaths in the civil war in western France (see this chapter, section VIII), probably more than 40,000 people were put to death during the whole Revolution, the majority between 1793 and 1795, during the 'second', violent Revolution after the attempt at a constitutional monarchy had failed. Of those, about half were given a trial, and the rest were either lynched or executed on mere suspicion.

Many of those killed were not even political – during the Terreur, just being a common criminal was enough to make you a counter-revolutionary. At a time of war and potential famine, theft, forgery or fraud were capital crimes. It is thought that only about 20 per cent of the Terreur's victims were aristocrats, returning émigrés or the political opponents of the radical republicans.

Amongst the more famous heads to be held up to the Paris crowds over the months following the purge of the Girondins were well-known founders of the Revolution such as Jean Sylvain Bailly, the first Mayor of Paris; Antoine Barnave, the second delegate sent to meet the Varennes fugitives; Camille Desmoulins,

---

[5] It is sometimes said that Robespierre's growing irritability and bloodthirstiness was caused by illness, probably chronic constipation. And it is interesting, if anecdotal, that all the most fiery revolutionary speakers had physical problems – Marat his skin disease, Mirabeau his outsized head, Danton a squashed nose and deformed lip.

one of the first to call for Revolution in 1789 (his wife Lucille was also guillotined a week later); Madame du Barry, the last official mistress of Louis XV; the chemist Antoine Lavoisier, who has gone down in scientific history for his discovery that matter conserves its mass when it changes state (but he had also once been a tax collector for Louis XVI); Chrétien de Malesherbes, a lawyer who had supported Diderot's *Encyclopédie*, and tried to defend Louis XVI; and Olympe de Gouges, a female writer who dared to criticize the Terreur and who had provocatively penned a Declaration of Women's Rights. (For more about women's struggles during the Revolution see Chapter 21.)

Amongst those who escaped the guillotine was Jean-Joseph Mounier, one of the creators of France's *Declaration of Men's and Citizens' Rights*. Still aged only 30, he fled to Switzerland after Louis XVI was taken to Paris in October 1789. There, he wrote a book condemning what he called the 'populist tyranny' wielded by the men who destroyed the constitutional monarchy. In *Research into the Causes that Prevented the French People from Becoming Free*, published in 1792, he told the populists that: 'You have dishonoured the names of patriotism and liberty, using them as a pretext for the most terrible outrages.' Wisely, he stayed out of France until 1801, and on his return Napoleon Bonaparte recognized his political talents and made him a Counsellor of State.

VI

However, as Pierre Vergniaud (the man who had declared that 'the homeland is in danger') said, revolution 'devours its children', and the most famous advocates of death for traitors also met a bloody end.

Marat was spared a fatal encounter with the guillotine, but did not escape a blade. During the summer of 1793, he had become an absentee from the Convention, not out of weakening revolutionary fervour, but because the skin condition from which he suffered became so acute that he now spent most of his time in a copper bath full of sulphur water.[6] It is probably going too far to say that his madly itching dermatitis was one of the things that made him so violently resentful towards everyone in France except the scrofulous poor, but, as we have seen, his voice had always been one of the loudest calling for blood to be spilt, and in July 1793, his words came back to bite him.

After the Girondins were forced out of the Convention in June 1793, and several of them executed, a group of them took refuge in Normandy, where they began to hold meetings denouncing the new radicalism in the Convention. One of them, Jean-Pascal Rouyer, is quoted as saying: 'Cut off Marat's head and the nation will be saved.'

In the audience at that meeting was a 24-year-old noblewoman called Marie-Anne-Charlotte de Corday d'Armont (usually abbreviated now as Charlotte Corday), who decided to go and save the nation herself – perhaps encouraged to do so by the Girondin fugitives. She went to Paris and, learning that Marat was shut away at home in his bathtub, sent him a note telling him that she wanted to 'reveal secrets that are vital for the salvation of the Republic'.

Marat clearly couldn't resist a young woman with traitors to denounce, and on the evening of 13 July 1793, she was let into his bathroom, where she pulled out a knife that she had hidden up her sleeve, and stabbed him in the chest.

She did not try to run away, and when searched, was found to be carrying a long political tract, which began by denouncing the Terreur: 'There are factions breaking up everywhere, with the Montagnards winning thanks to crimes and oppression, and a few monsters soaked in our blood are organizing these detestable plots.' The tract referred to Danton, Robespierre and Marat as 'brigands sitting on a bloody throne' and urged all citizens to rise up against them.

---

[6] The iconic painting of Marat's corpse in the bath by Jacques-Louis David was highly idealized. David, a Montagnard and member of the Comité de sûreté générale, made his friend's skin almost as white as the towel on his head, but in reality it would have been blotched and inflamed.

In the Convention the next day, a supporter of Marat demanded a law that would discourage any future murder attempts on politicians by sentencing the killers to 'the most terrible suffering' – they wanted a return to the days before Guillotin, before Louis XVI even, when murderers were publicly tortured. A committee was duly set up to define the new punishment. In terms of humanity, the Revolution was going backwards.

Four days later, Charlotte de Corday d'Armont was guillotined. According to eyewitnesses, when her head fell into the basket, one of the carpenters who had worked on the scaffold, a fan of Marat called Legros (Fat man), picked it up and slapped her face – causing her to blush. There was such an outcry from the spectators about this lack of respect that Legros was arrested and sentenced to three months in prison.

Today a heroic statue of Danton greets everyone who comes out of the Paris Métro at Odéon.[7] On its base is an inscription: *'Après le pain, l'éducation est le premier besoin du peuple'* ('After bread, education is the most basic need of the people'). A noble phrase to be remembered by.

It is hardly surprising that the city of Paris, choosing an inscription when they erected the monument in 1891, didn't select one of Danton's less idealistic sayings, like: 'What do I care if people call me a drinker of blood? Let's drink the blood of the enemies of humanity!' (He was referring to the Dutch and the British, as well as French 'traitors' who argued against war.) In his early career, he had been a staunch advocate of 'chop off his head first, ask questions later'. According to Danton mark 1, blood was the people's most basic need, not bread.

But in mid-1793, after so many fiery speeches at political meetings and in the Convention, he lost much of his radical ardour. The realities of government seemed to hit home. He

---

[7] Admittedly, people who take the exit leading directly to the Faculté de médecine might miss him.

tried to prevent the storming of the Convention by the Paris *sections* on 31 May 1793; he was said to have left some of the arrested Girondins loosely guarded so that they could escape; and as de facto head of the Comité de salut public he began secret negotiations with the Austrians to give them Marie-Antoinette and thereby make peace with one of the countries threatening to invade France. In short, Danton had mutated into something of a moderate – and it was at this time that he gave his idealistic speech demanding free education for all children.

After the death of his wife in the summer of 1793, he married their 16-year-old babysitter, and she seems to have drained him of all his remaining political energy. He even stopped going to the Convention, and asked to be excused from the Comité de salut public. He returned to the fray later, but only to speak out against the Terreur, telling the Convention: 'I ask that we stop the blood-letting,' while also opposing one of Robespierre's purges of radicals in the parliament.

This mixture of weakness and opposition to Robespierre was fatal, and on 2 April 1794, Danton was accused of treason. When members of the Convention demanded that he be allowed to defend himself in the house, Robespierre objected, saying that he was an 'idol that has been rotten for a long time'.

During his trial, Danton was apparently on great oratorial form again, and so effective that his speeches were expunged from the record. Nothing could be allowed to undermine the pre-decided guilty verdict.

On the evening of 5 April, Danton met the same fate as the King he had helped to condemn to death. By the time he climbed up to the guillotine, the scaffold was already soaked with the blood of his allies who had been put on trial at the same time. His last words were said to have been: 'Don't forget to show my head to the crowd. It is worth seeing.'

But the words he spoke as his cart passed Robespierre's house in the rue Saint-Honoré, on its way to the place de la Révolution, were just as memorable. He shouted: 'Robespierre, you'll be following me! Your house will be demolished!'

The second part of his prediction was wrong, and the house can still be seen today (though Danton was certainly speaking metaphorically), but the first would come true within four months.

Robespierre finally became entangled in the web of his own conspiracies in July 1794 (or *thermidor an II* as it was now officially known). With various factions in the two main Comités (salut and sûreté) at loggerheads, he announced that he was going to overhaul them both and give salut authority over sûreté. His dictatorial attitude over this and other matters finally stirred the neutrals in the so-called 'Plaine' of the Convention into action, and when a member called Louis Louchet demanded his arrest, the house voted in favour.

Furious, Robespierre called the chairman of the session 'president of the assassins', but every time he tried to give a speech, he was prevented, with shouts of 'Down with the tyrant!' Finally, he and four other members, including his younger brother Augustin, were arrested, and taken away.

There had already been unrest in Paris over rumours that Robespierre, the representative of the *sans-culottes*, was at risk, and the Paris Commune immediately convened at the Hôtel de Ville and voted to organize a general insurrection. They sounded the alarm bells and forbade the governors of all Paris's jails from locking up Robespierre and his colleagues.

The Commune asked Robespierre to lead their insurrection and promised to take the Convention by force. They had more than 2,000 men with cannons gathered outside the Hôtel de Ville. But, ever the politician, Robespierre refused to lead what was in effect a counter-revolutionary revolt, and instead agreed to set up an 'executive committee' in which he, wisely, would not take part in person.

Robespierre, his brother and their three arrested colleagues were holed up in the Hôtel de Ville, contemplating how best to grab power back without being accused of treason, when a force of National Guards and police loyal to the Convention stormed in – the 2,000 insurgents outside had since got bored or frightened and gone home.

Robespierre was in the process of signing an order to his Paris *section*, the *piques*, to help him 'save the nation', when he was interrupted – at the bottom of the page, one can see the partial signature 'Ro'. As the Convention forces entered the building, Augustin threw himself out of a window and broke his leg, and Robespierre – depending on the account one believes – either shot himself in the mouth, or was hit by a gendarme's bullet. In any case, he survived, with a broken jaw and a gaping hole in his cheek.

The next day, Robespierre and 21 of his closest political allies were guillotined, followed, over the next few days, by a further 83 supporters. To Robespierre, in terrible pain, unable to speak, the blade must have brought relief.

The Robespierriste faction that had sought to divide and rule was united in the communal grave at the cimetière des Errancis, in the northwest of Paris, alongside more than 1,000 other victims of the guillotine, including one of the most famous, Élisabeth, the sister of Louis XVI.

Sadly for France, the death of the main instigators of violence was by no means the end of the bloodshed.

VIII

The Chouans are usually dismissed these days as reactionary troublemakers. This was the collective name given to the people who rebelled against the revolutionary regime between 1792 and 1794, most of them in Brittany and the Vendée, just to the south of the Loire.

In the French collective imagination (except in Brittany and the Vendée), they are regarded as people who simply failed to understand progress, as if they had opposed the invention of the wheel or been scared of curdling milk into cheese. Either that, or as a bunch of bigots manipulated by the last remnants of the dying Church. On the other hand, the people who opposed

– and eventually massacred – the Chouans are usually referred to as 'patriots'.

The name itself – Chouans, a western French patois name for owls – comes from the nickname of a Breton salt smuggler called Jean Cottereau (under the monarchy, salt was subject to the *gabelle* tax, so was ripe for black-market trading). Jean and his two brothers were known to use an owl's hoot as a signal during their illegal outings. Jean Cottereau is often said to have opposed the Revolution because the abolition of the *gabelle* robbed him of his smuggling income. However, he also reacted to the botched selling-off of national assets, and allegedly tried to burn down the house of a wealthy mayor who had benefited from the scheme.

In any case, Jean 'Chouan' Cottereau was just one of hundreds of thousands of men across France who objected to the announcement in August 1792 that conscription was to be introduced, to replenish the armies resisting foreign and royalist invasion. Men like Cottereau refused to fight for a revolution they didn't believe in, especially because high-ups in the revolutionary administration were going to be exempt from conscription – it was a case of everyone is *égal*, but some are more *égal*[8] than others.

What was more, as we saw in Chapter 10, in 1789 the French were generally religious people. This was especially true of the massive peasant population. Even though they disapproved of the opulent lifestyles enjoyed by bishops and abbots, and didn't want to pay the Church's taxes, they were unhappy when their parish priests were threatened with imprisonment or violence if they refused to swear allegiance to the intellectuals in Paris – and some 80 per cent of the Breton clergy refused to take the oath.

In the summer of 1792, even before the introduction of conscription, there were minor rebellions all over western France, mainly by groups of peasants who marched into towns to attack National Guards or army garrisons. At this point, most of the

---

[8] Grammar pedants may rightly object that in the plural this should be *égaux*.

uprisings were successfully put down by the better-armed revolutionary forces.

But as of February 1793, the rebels became more organized – sometimes, but not always, thanks to overtly royalist agitators – and conducted guerrilla operations during which they would storm a town jail to release prisoners, attack a small garrison of National Guards, or ambush the *commissaires* sent to impose conscription.

Attacks on large Breton towns like Nantes and Vannes failed, but further south in the Vendée, the rebel guerrillas combined to form an army of some 30,000 armed men, who were often accompanied by their whole family to avoid reprisals. They marched north to join the Bretons, and fought their way successfully as far as Granville, on the border with Normandy, and Le Mans, 200 kilometres west of Paris.

However, forced to be constantly on the move, carrying their wounded with them, suffering from waterborne diseases like dysentery and typhus, and provided with no reinforcements or supplies, by the end of 1793, the rebels were seriously weakened, with only 20,000 armed troops. It took just two defeats to finish them off.

On 10 December, the rebels captured Le Mans and moved into many of the houses, glad for the food and shelter. But within two days, three republican armies converged on them, and only half of the rebels were able to escape – the rest were trapped in the town, where they were wiped out by street fighting, cannon fire and summary justice. Republican troops chased the fleeing rebels westwards, killing anyone they caught. Somewhere between 6,000 and 20,000 rebels died (according to reports on different sides), around half of them during the fighting in Le Mans and the rest afterwards. It is thought that about half of the dead were women and children. A revolutionary *commissaire* called Benaben described women and their daughters being raped and killed, their corpses being stripped naked and laid out with their legs spread.

The republican armies lost only a hundred or so men.

The final mopping-up operation came ten days later, near a town called Savenay, 30 kilometres west of Nantes, where 18,000 republicans trapped the 2,000 or so rebels who had not managed to cross the Loire to relative safety in the Vendée. As one of the republican generals, Jean-Baptiste Kléber, described it in his memoirs:

> Each column went in a different direction to pursue the rebels. The carnage became horrible. Everywhere one saw only piles of bodies ... Thousands of prisoners of all ages and sexes were captured and taken behind the lines. The representatives of the people tried them before the revolutionary tribunals, and France, indeed the whole of Europe, knows the atrocities committed against those poor people.

Less humanely, another general, François Joseph Westermann, wrote to Paris, boasting:

> There are so many [bodies] that in several places, they form pyramids. We are shooting people endlessly at Savenay, because all the time brigands are arriving, claiming that they want to be taken prisoner ... We don't take prisoners, because we would have to give them the bread of liberty, and because pity is not revolutionary.

This was not entirely true: although 2,000 or so men were executed around Savenay, about 1,600 women and children were spared. Kléber, who had not taken part in Westermann's activities, argued that they should be released, but he was ignored and the captives were marched to prison in Nantes.

The town on the Loire had already been set up as a sort of outpost of the Tribunal révolutionnaire. It was occupied by revolutionary police, and from November to mid-December 1793, 144 people were tried and guillotined for sympathizing with the rebels. As of late December the tribunal went into overdrive, and from 29 December to 25 January, more than 1,900 people were condemned to death.

By the time the 1,600 arrived from Savernay, Nantes was already overflowing with prisoners, most of them crowded into a coffee warehouse by the river that had been requisitioned and turned into a jail. In all, it housed about 9,000 inmates, of all ages and sexes. With no sanitary arrangements, typhus broke out, and prisoners began dying in droves. A resident of the town sent a letter to the town hall, complaining that 'there is a smell so fetid that several of our brothers who were on guard there have died.'

Inside, it was much worse, and a certain Dr Thomas, who bravely ventured in, reported seeing 'skeletons of children still clenched to the breasts of the skeletons that had been their mothers'. Even before the prisoners began dying of disease, hunger and cold had taken their toll.

The head of the revolutionary authorities in Nantes, a man called Jean-Baptiste Carrier, one of the more radical members of the Convention who had helped to set up the Tribunal révolutionnaire, ordered a clean-up – by the prisoners who were still able to stand. Bodies were gathered and carted off to a quarry. Straw in which people had been sleeping – and defecating – was burnt or doused with acid.

But there remained one more element of the clean-up to be completed – the prisoners themselves. Carrier ordered their elimination.

An estimated 2,000 men were taken in batches to the quarry where they had buried their comrades. There they were lined up and shot. Victims who did not die after the first bullet were either finished off with rifle butts or had to wait while a musket was reloaded.

A less noisy, and cheaper, method of extermination was decided upon for an estimated 4,000 or so more: drowning. The technique was first tried out on 25 October 1793, on 90 priests who had refused to take the oath of allegiance to the republic. They were herded on to a small sailing boat into which holes had been bored. It was towed out into the fast-flowing Loire, where it promptly sank. Three priests who were rescued by sailors on a passing ship were taken back into custody and drowned the next day.

Encouraged by the successful experiment, Carrier's men applied the technique to non-clerical prisoners, who were tied up in pairs, often attached to a heavy stone, and herded on to holed boats. Sometimes the boats were intact, and were sailed out to an island where they were scuppered. Prisoners who didn't drown quickly enough were stabbed or shot. Women were usually stripped naked before the execution, and some of them were tied to naked men, forming what was jokingly referred to as a 'revolutionary wedding'. Everyone was robbed of their valuables.

On 26 December 1793, Commissaire Benaben wrote a report to the authorities saying that:

> The brigands sometimes complained that they were starving to death, but they won't be able to say they're dying of thirst. Today we gave a drink to about 1,200. I don't know who thought up this punishment, but it is much quicker than the guillotine, which now seems to be reserved for cutting off the heads of aristocrats, priests and those who, thanks to their former rank, had a great influence over the people.

The Assemblée's democratic decree that everyone should suffer the same – humane – death penalty had been overturned. The new regime of fanatics had introduced a system of privilege in death, with cold-blooded brutal massacre the punishment for being 'uninfluential'.

As with almost all statistics relating to the Revolution, and especially its bloodier aspects, estimates of the number of people drowned vary depending on whether the statistics come from revolutionary or royalist/Chouan sources. The likely figure was something like 4,000, though the numbers seem less important than the way in which one group of French people treated another, all – supposedly – in the name of *Liberté, Égalité* and *Fraternité*.

Nantes and Le Mans were not the only scenes of these massacres. In the Anjou region, another 7,000 or so people were shot or guillotined in the same period, while some 2,000 died in prison. An early-twentieth-century historian called Émile Gabory, who wrote seven books listing every battle, skirmish and heated argument during the Chouans' uprising, even alleged that in the town of Angers, the skins of some rebels were cured and made into cavalrymen's trousers. If this is true, France had descended into savagery bordering on genocide.

And in fact, the revolutionaries had more or less announced it as such. When the Vendéens first revolted in 1793, the Convention voted that 'combustible materials should be sent into the Vendée so that forests, coppices and heathland can be burnt ... Crops will be cut down ... and livestock seized.'

At the end of that year, a general called Louis-Marie Turreau was sent to the Vendée to stifle all remaining elements of rebellion. He wrote to Paris asking for guidance: 'You must decide in advance the fate of the women and children I encounter in this rebellious region. If I am to put them all to the sword, I cannot carry out such a measure without an order covering my responsibility.' He received no reply, but the fact that he asked the question suggests what kind of informal instructions he had received.

So, as Turreau described in his memoirs, 'taking instructions from several decrees by the Convention', he issued orders to his men:

All brigands found carrying arms, or who have carried them to revolt against their country will be bayoneted. The same action will be taken against girls, women and children in the same situation. Those who are merely suspected will not be spared either ... All villages, farms, woods, brushland, and anything that can be burnt will be set on fire, but only after any food there has been taken away.

He added that all orders to kill or burn should come from a general, but this part of his instructions seems to have been forgotten, and the armies invading the Vendée killed, raped and pillaged their way across the region, earning themselves the name *'colonnes infernales'*.

There was fierce resistance from guerrilla groups – Jean 'Chouan' Cottereau was killed during one such skirmish in July 1794, and one of his brothers shot himself while hiding in a church. But most of the deaths during this campaign happened outside combat. Of Cottereau's immediate family, only one brother survived – his two sisters and one brother were guillotined.

As usual, estimates vary, but it is thought that in around four months, the *colonnes infernales* killed some 50,000 people. They also 'requisitioned' 45,000 animals, 1,800 barrels of wine, 12,000 tonnes of grain, 60 tonnes of iron, 40 tonnes of church bells, and – most bizarrely – about 400 kilos of metal stripped from tombs. By comparison, the English invaders during the Hundred Years War had been well-behaved tourists.

When the Convention overthrew Robespierre and put an end to the Terreur in 1794, it fudged the issue of these massacres. A few generals were replaced, a couple of them were briefly imprisoned, and perversely, Jean-Baptiste Carrier, the Nantes mass-murderer, testified against General Turreau. Carrier was guillotined in December 1794, largely as a scapegoat, after some of his accomplices turned against him. Turreau, meanwhile, enjoyed a colourful career. He was made ambassador to the United States, and on returning to France, decided to support the restoration of the monarchy under Louis XVIII in 1814. After that, he had a change of heart and switched sides to back Napoleon Bonaparte. Not exactly a man of principle.

There are always sociopathic individuals who will take advantage of any conflict, but the carnage of 1793 and 1794, both the barbarous massacres and the clinical guillotinings, was inflicted by tens of thousands of French people on their fellow citizens. The conclusion when reading about all the sadism and bloodshed is simple: if the constitutional monarchy of 1789 had been preserved, almost none of these killings would have happened. Even if Louis XVI were held personally responsible for every single death from starvation, poverty and overwork during his whole regime, he would have been a less bloody tyrant than the men who engineered his final downfall and instigated the Terreur.

And the worst thing is that, when one looks closely at who was better off in France after the Terreur, it really seems as if, contrary to revolutionary myth, the killing was all for nothing. Not only was the country left permanently scarred by civil war, the old social divisions were as strong as ever.

PART V

Plus Ça Change, Plus C'est la Même Chose

Chapter 21

HOW THE REVOLUTION FAILED TO HELP THE POOR, WOMEN AND SLAVES

'La femme a le droit de monter sur l'échafaud; elle doit avoir également celui de monter à la tribune.'
'A woman has the right to ascend to the scaffold; she must also have the right to ascend to the political rostrum.'

               Olympe de Gouges (1748–93), who was guillotined for
               writing the *Declaration of the Rights of Women
               and the Female Citizen*

I

One of the angriest poems written by Arthur Rimbaud, France's archetypal *poète maudit*, is called 'Les Pauvres à l'église' ('Poor People in Church'). It is a half-disdainful, half-pitying description of a congregation in his home town of Charleville-Mézières in the northeast of France. Amongst its harshest lines are these:

Heureux, humiliés comme des chiens battus,
Les Pauvres au bon Dieu, le patron et le sire
Tendent leurs oremus risibles et têtus.

Aux femmes, c'est bien bon de faire des bancs lisses,
Après les six jours noirs où Dieu les fait souffrir...

Dehors, le froid, la faim, l'homme en ribote:
C'est bon. Encore une heure; après, les maux sans noms!

(Happy, humiliated like abused dogs,
The poor offer up to God, the master and the lord,
Their laughable, stubborn Latin prayers.

To the women, it feels good to rub the pews smooth,
After the six black days during which God has made them
suffer...

Outside, everything is cold and hunger, men on the booze:
All right. Another hour, and then it's back to nameless ills.)

This is not just a tirade against religion as the opium (or
absinthe) of the people. It is also about the drudge of daily life
for the poorer citizens of France. And it was written sometime
in 1870 or 1871. Clearly the Revolution had not freed the poor
from the poverty and slavery of the Ancien Régime.

In 1793, after the fall of the constitutional monarchy, the
Convention declared itself the champion of ordinary *peuple* and
drafted a new Constitution. This guaranteed freedom of religion
and freedom of speech; it formalized the presumption of innocence until proven guilty, promised material help for the poor
and affordable education for all, and banned anyone from profiting from public service. It also strayed into flagrant populism,
specifying that the people could revise or scrap the Constitution
whenever they wanted, because 'no generation may impose its
laws on the following generation'. Not only that, insurrection
was 'for the people, and for each section of the people, the most
sacred of rights and the most indispensable of duties'. All in all,
a recipe for continuing anarchy on the streets of Paris.

Fortunately, perhaps, the Constitution of '93 was never applied because under the Terreur, Robespierre et al. decided that presumption of innocence, freedom of speech and freedom in general could wait. In any case, it was all about politics, not about everyday life.

In the first period after the constitutional monarchy, precious little help was given to the poor. Thanks to a decree passed in November 1793, they were now allowed to call everyone in France *'tu'* instead of *'vous'*, but that was probably of little consolation when no one would sell you food, whatever you called them. Because conditions for the poor were as bad as, if not worse than, before the Revolution.

The revolutionary currency, the *assignat*, had proved a total disaster. As we saw earlier, the only people to benefit from it were the rich speculators who bought up the clergy's seized assets for fixed *assignat* prices, with 12 years to pay. And as its value plummeted, in real terms their mortgages got cheaper and cheaper. Before the currency was finally scrapped in February 1796, at a ceremony in which banknotes and their printing plates were publicly burned in Paris's place Vendôme, it had fallen to about 3 per cent of its original value.

But the real value was already zero, or worse. Long before February 1796, people who had issued loans in *assignats* were desperate *not* to be paid back. As one man put it, 'your debtor pays his debt, and bankrupts you'. Under the Terreur, the Convention made it punishable by death to refuse to accept *assignats*, or to trade in precious metals – making things even more punitive than during the bad old days of the John Law and the Regent Philippe d'Orléans – but in any case, if there was nothing for sale, no one could be accused of refusing to take *assignats*.

Meanwhile, industry ground to a halt. To take one bald statistic, in France, coal production fell from 725,000 tonnes in 1789 to only 250,000 in 1795. Why dig it out if no one could buy it? Unemployment in that sector naturally rose in the same proportions. Factories and fields lost men to conscription, slowing down all sorts of production. The cessation of trade with Britain also meant that new industrial machines were not available in France. The luxury industries had all but ceased to exist, as their former clients fled the country or hid their wealth. Further afield, the valuable sugar resources from Haiti were under threat both from British invaders and a slave rebellion (of which, more in section IV of this chapter).

Thanks to all the above, and the sudden obsession amongst men with spending their time on politics or getting jobs in the new administrations, rather than doing productive work, in 1795, the economy was at a standstill.

Inflation was also taking its toll. To combat this, in September 1793, the Convention imposed maximum prices on essentials, and decreed that only 1790 prices could be charged for: 'bread, meat, wine, grain, flour, vegetables, fruit, butter, vinegar, cider, eau-de-vie, coal, oil, soap, salt, meat[1] and fish, honey, sugar, paper, hemp, wool, leather, iron and steel, copper, sheets, canvas and all fabrics except silk'. Things were so bad that lingerie was not considered essential.

To add to the poor's woes, the harvest of 1794 was a failure all over France, and the winter of 1794–5 harsher than any in living memory. When the maximum-price law was repealed in late 1794, in an attempt to encourage merchants to inject more food into the market, *Fraternité* did not kick in, and speculation became rife. Farmers stockpiled their produce wherever possible, waiting for prices to rise (and making sure they had something to eat for themselves). Grain merchants imported food and charged whatever they pleased.

In 1795, an anonymous correspondent wrote to the Convention giving an example of how this affected even a relatively well-off French family. He described a man who had retired before 1790 with an annual pension of 3,000 *livres*, enough to live simply but

---

[1] Hunger was apparently making the politicians repeat themselves.

comfortably. Back then, a pound of flour had cost him one tenth of a *livre*. But now a farmer was telling the pensioner: 'Give me two and a half *livres* for one pound' – a 25-fold increase.

With starvation threatening the population, just as in 1789, hordes of beggars and unemployed people moved into the bigger towns in search of work and food. The government was forced to impose rationing. It also spent vast amounts of state money buying food at high prices from speculators in order to keep the markets supplied.

Paris was richer and reasonably well supplied compared to some other regions of the country, but the city's political *sections* began to petition the Convention for help. In 1795, one of these petitioners, an anonymous writer, gave a harrowing portrait of the city, describing a street in which 'within ten minutes [he saw] seven unfortunates fainting, and a child at the nipple dying on its mother's breast which had dried up, while near a sewer a woman was fighting a dog for a bone'. It seems hard to believe that this was happening in *every* street, but conditions were certainly terrible, especially for the refugees from out of town, who were excluded from the rationing system.

Meanwhile, the petitioner says he saw 'caterers' tables where epicureans were gathered, surrounded by the sobs and tears of despair, calmly studying the art of eating'. He accuses one of them: 'But your children have nothing to eat!' To which the glutton replies, 'So what? Tomorrow I'm getting divorced.'

It all sounds very Dickensian, fact mixed with fiction and sentiment, but the *sections* were doing more than write. There were food riots in Paris, Rouen and Amiens, and the Convention was so frightened of a repeat of 1789 (this time aimed at itself, rather than the monarchy), that in March 1795, Emmanuel-Joseph Sieyès, one of the idealists of the États généraux, championed a law condemning to death anyone opposed to the Convention.

This threat did not discourage the Parisians, and on 1 April, the Convention was invaded by demonstrators demanding food – coincidentally, just as members were congratulating themselves on the success of their rationing programme. The invasion was short-lived, though, and the insurgents were evicted by a combination of political promises and National Guards from the richer parts of Paris.

However, starvation did not magically disappear, and on 20 May 1795, the protesters returned in force. The Convention had been forewarned by posters and pamphlets announcing the attack, and had posted armed men all around the building, but the protesters broke through and began smashing down locked doors with axes, in a repeat of the invasion of the Tuileries on 10 August 1792. This time, instead of *'Vive la nation!'* they were shouting, 'Bread and the Constitution of 1793!' They finally managed to fight their way into the debating chamber, stabbed one of the members, beheaded him and stuck his head on a pike.

Clearly, the people had decided that, even with the King dispatched, the Revolution was doing them no good at all. A few radical members of the Convention, the remnants of the Montagnards, who were now wittily calling themselves the 'Crête' ('Crest'), seized their opportunity, went to the rostrum and declared that they would implement all of the people's demands.

But then troops and National Guards burst in, ordering the 'armed citizens' to withdraw – and, now heavily outnumbered and outgunned, they obeyed. The embarrassed Crête members were arrested[2] and taken away, and now it was the turn of the Convention's right wing to use the opportunity for a clear-out. The National Guard was purged of men with *sans-culottes* leanings, revolutionary committees were abolished, and weapons were confiscated from everyone in the city's *sections* who didn't have a good excuse for bearing them. It was the end

---

[2] Six of the Crête were condemned to death, and all stabbed themselves on the way to the scaffold (prisoner searches were apparently not standard in eighteenth-century France). Three managed to commit suicide, but the others, bleeding profusely, were taken to the guillotine and finished off.

of the people's army that had existed on and off in Paris since July 1789.

Politically, things also changed, and not necessarily for the good of ordinary people. In August 1795, yet another Constitution was published. There was a subtle change to its name. This one was called *The Declaration of the Rights and Duties of Men and Citizens*. That extra word, 'Duties', reflected a new conservatism. This Constitution retained many of the revolutionary ideas of 1789 – 'equality means that the law is the same for all'; 'do to others the good that you would wish to receive'; 'no one can be prevented from saying, writing, printing or publishing their thoughts' – as well as creating new national holidays to replace the old religious ones, giving people a right to appeal legal decisions, and promising primary school education for all in 'reading, writing, elements of calculation and morals'.

That last word seems to be key. From now on, moral behaviour was the citizen's main duty: 'No one is a good citizen if he is not a good son, good father, good brother, good friend, or good husband.' Male supremacy was being reinforced in almost biblical language.

And unlike in 1793, being a 'good' citizen did not mean fighting for one's rights – a key clause was: 'Any armed gathering is an attack on the Constitution.' The good citizen would shut up, sit tight and let parliament get on with its job.

This conservatism was underlined by the creation of a ruling 'Directoire' ('Board of directors') of five men aged over 40 who would be appointed by parliament from amongst MPs or ministers, with one of them being replaced every year. Compare this concentration of power to the original Assemblée nationale's system of electing a president who served as little more than a chairman of debates, and held the position for a few weeks at most. The Directoire was a sort of five-headed king, a post-revolutionary Hydra.

The new Constitution also divided the French parliament into two houses, *à l'anglaise*. The lower house, the Conseil des

Cinq-Cents (the Council of the 500), was to be elected by male taxpayers aged over 30 who had been in France for more than ten years. With around 60 per cent of the male population aged under 30, that was handing the country over to comfortably-off, middle-aged men. The decisions of the 500 would be ratified by an upper house, the Conseil des Anciens (Old Men's Council), which consisted of 250 MPs aged over 40 who had resided in France for no less than 15 years. They were to sport a fancy uniform of a tall, ribboned hat and a red cloak with gold tassels, making themselves look like velvety political lampstands.

It all sounds very stodgy and bourgeois, and it was. The new elite was stamping its authority on France. The aristocrats had been dispossessed. Their assets, and those of the Church, had been sold cheaply to the bourgeoisie. Populist politicians had wiped each other out in factional wars. Into the vacuum stepped the merchants, lawyers, landowners and their like. They might be relatively cash poor because of the dire state of the nation's finances, but they were property rich, and ready to get their hands on the reins of power and steer the economy to their advantage. They didn't want the monarchy to return because now France was their oyster, so they were able to write some radical-sounding clauses into their Constitution, thereby reassuring the people that the Revolution was still going ahead. But while the poor wondered where their next loaf was coming from, and how much it would cost, the new privileged elite (an aristocracy in all but name) could rub its hands together and look forward to a bright, profitable future.

In short, by ending the constitutional monarchy, the *sans-culottes* had given themselves a right royal kick in the revolutionary pants.

II

'Any woman who deals with matters outside her sphere of knowledge and duty is no more than a schemer,' Marie-Antoinette once told her lady-in-waiting Madame Campan. She was being ironic about the negativity aimed at her when she tried to inter-vene in French politics. And although the revolutionaries did not agree with her politics, there were many people in France who shared her frustration – the women.

As we have seen in earlier chapters, women did their fair share of France's everyday work, especially in the country – we saw Arthur Young, the itinerant British agronomist, meeting a woman so worn out by hard labour that she looked 70 when she was only 28. Then there were the *cahiers de doléances* written by women to underline their anger at being excluded from the process of writing these official communiqués from the people to the King. But neither work nor complaining won them any real political recognition during the French Revolution. It seems strange – the movement that was meant to free all ordi-nary people from tyranny forgot half the population.

The 1795 Constitution and its all-male definition of the 'good citizen' was merely the confirmation of the misogyny at the heart of the Revolution, which, let's not forget, boasted about its 'fraternity', not its humanity, solidarity or any other gender-neutral concept that would have included the female half of the population.

The Ancien Régime had been notoriously sexist – all its administrators were male, and the only way a woman could exercise any real influence was either by holding a *salon* where the most brilliant male minds would deign to speak to women on equal terms, as long as the women were either beautiful, rich, aristocratic or all of those. Alternatively, some women, like the official mistresses of Louis XIV and Louis XV, or Madame Necker, the wife of Louis XVI's Finance Minister, exercised influence through their well-placed partners.

The Lumières philosophers might have been expected to enlighten men as to women's untapped potential. Voltaire, for example, was the long-time partner of one of France's most brilliant mathematicians and physicists, Émilie du Châtelet, who translated Newton's theories from Latin into French and wrote an analysis of Leibniz's philosophy. But that didn't make him any less misogynistic. The entry *'Femme'* in Voltaire's *Dictionnaire philosophique* of 1764 makes enlightening reading:

> It is not surprising that in every country, man has made himself the master of women, since everything is based on his strength. He is usually far superior to women, both in body and mind. There have been very knowledgeable women, and great women warriors, but there has never been a woman inventor. Their skill usually lies in social exchange and decoration. Generally speaking, they are designed to mollify the behaviour of men.

He does note that there have been queens in what he calls 'female strongholds' such as England, Spain and Naples, and female regents in France, but 'in no republic have they ever played the smallest role in government, and they have never reigned over an elected regime'.

QED for Voltaire, and, it seems for most of the supposedly modern male thinkers of his era. In *Émile, ou De l'éducation*, the social revolutionary Jean-Jacques Rousseau's treatise on education, he wanted the girl to become 'gentle and self-effacing'. He also said that: 'Almost all little girls hate learning to read and write; but they are always willing to learn how to hold a needle.'

Diderot's *Encyclopédie* was fairer-minded: 'The education of women has been so severely neglected in all civilized nations that it is surprising to find so many women who have excelled by their erudition and their works.' The entry for *'Femme'* in volume 6 is open-minded enough to quote Anna Maria van Shurman, a seventeenth-century Dutch painter and thinker, who...

> ... posed the question: is the study of the arts suited to Christian women? She maintains the affirmative ... based on the notion that studying the arts informs them, and gives a wisdom that one cannot obtain via the dangerous route of experience. But one may question whether this precocious caution does not rob them of some of their innocence. What one can say in favour of

the study of science and the arts is that it seems certain that it will distract women from their penchant for immorality.

In other words: Look at this atlas, *ma chérie*, and it just might stop you from turning into a harlot.

The *Encyclopédie* has a separate entry for *'Femme'* as in 'Wife', which merely hammers home the message:

Even if husband and wife have the same interests in being together, it is essential that authority be given to one or the other; and the laws of civilized nations, and the customs of Europe, give this authority unanimously and definitively to the male, as he is gifted with the greater strength of body and mind, contributes more to the common good, in both human and sacred affairs, so that a wife must of necessity be subordinate to her husband and obey his orders in all domestic affairs. That is the sentiment of both modern and ancient thinkers on jurisprudence, and the formal decision of lawmakers.

Reading this, one almost expects the paragraph to end with something like: 'Now, *Madame*, don't you think you ought to stop reading and go and make dinner?'

When the Revolution came, there were of course women who saw the opportunity to end sexual privileges, as well as the economic ones.

Louise-Félicité de Kéralio was 30 when the Revolution broke out (according to France's Bibliothèque nationale – other sources make her 32). Her father was a tutor at the École militaire in Paris, and made sure she received a good education. She wrote a history of Elizabeth I's reign in England, which earned her the accolade of being hailed France's first *historienne* (female historian). She also translated John Howard's study of the conditions in France's prisons into French. In 1786, she set up a press in the basement of her parents' home and published five volumes of a *Collection of the Best French Works Written by*

Women.[3] This at a time when it was illegal for women to own a printing works.

The Revolution radicalized her still further, and in 1789 she founded a newspaper – *Le Journal d'État et du citoyen*, thereby becoming France's first-ever female editor-in-chief. In one of her earliest editions, on 20 August 1789, Kéralio lambasted the Abbé de Sieyès for excluding women from the political process: 'We don't understand what he means when he says that not all citizens can take an active part in the formation of a government's powers … At such a time, let us avoid reducing anyone, no matter whom, to humiliating uselessness.' (She does slightly weaken her point by saying that women are useful because they can exercise influence 'amongst their servants', but this was still pretty radical stuff.)

She did not confine herself to sexual politics. Her newspaper was a political journal with a female editor – *Égalité* at work. It commented on all the reforms being carried out in the new Assemblée, and suggested many others, even speculating about a republic well before the monarchy actually fell. The paper carried on throughout the Revolution, under different titles (*Le Mercure national* and *Le Journal général de l'Europe*), though Kéralio herself stepped down in 1791, after marrying and getting pregnant unfashionably late, well over 30.

However, she remained politically active in the Société fraternelle des patriotes de l'un et l'autre sexe (Fraternal Society of Patriots of Both Sexes), which had been founded by a male schoolteacher called Claude Dansard. Again, this was not a society founded to defend women's rights, simply a platform where women's opinions were equally valued. The Society did demand equal education for women, and reforms to the marriage laws, but in essence it was just one of the many Parisian clubs where political ideas were debated. Again, it was *Égalité* in action.

[3] Inevitably, almost all the women she listed were of aristocratic origin.

Louise-Félicité de Kéralio's husband, Pierre-François-Joseph Robert, was elected to the Convention, and served as one of the radicals on the Montagne. But the couple avoided the purges during and after the Terreur because in early 1793 Robert was sent to Brussels as a *commissaire* to the northeastern army. He later backed Napoleon, and they had to take refuge when Louis XVIII was placed on the throne. Choosing to remain in exile, Louise-Félicité de Kéralio wrote novels and travel books and died peacefully in Belgium at the ripe old age of 66.

One of Kéralio's co-members in the Société fraternelle des patriotes de l'un et l'autre sexe was a Dutch-woman called Etta Palm d'Aelders. At the time of the Revolution she was a well-established Paris society widow with a *salon* of her own, where she met influential men, some of whom became her lovers. She claimed to be a *baronne* but was in fact the daughter of a wallpaper seller from Groningen.

She rode the wave of 1789 successfully, attracting the new breed of influential man like Marat to her drawing room. A self-made woman, aged 46 when the Bastille was stormed, she was inspired by the climate of (supposed) *Liberté* to defend women's rights.

In 1790 she gave a speech at the Société patriotique des Amis de la Liberté, one of Paris's best-attended political debating clubs, 'on the injustice of laws in favour of men, at women's expense'. After wittily excusing herself for speaking imperfect French ('I consulted the dictionary in my heart more than that of the Académie') she lectured the *messieurs* present about justice, which, she said 'must be the first virtue of free men, and justice demands that laws should be shared by all beings, just like the air and the sun'. She called marriage being 'delivered to a despot', and suggested that from now on, if the law was changed, women could be 'your willing companions and not your slaves'. She also argued that women's ambitions should be recognized: 'Do you think that our desire for success and fame is less strong than yours?' Not at all, she informed them, asking,

'Why should we not be given the same education and means to achieve them?'

The speech was apparently well received in some revolutionary circles, because in 1791 it earned her a *médaille nationale*, awarded by the town of Creil-sur-Oise, just outside Paris.

Again, like Louise-Félicité de Kéralio, Etta Palm d'Aelders did not confine herself to women's rights. She wrote and spoke about all aspects of the Revolution, wanting to be treated by men as a political equal. But she kept up her campaign against the laws that forbade women from getting elected to any administration. On 1 April 1792, she went to the Assemblée, 'accompanied by a few other ladies', according to the minutes of the parliamentary session. There, she gave a speech calling for wives to have the same rights as husbands, suggesting that women should be allowed to perform both civil and military functions, and demanding equal education opportunities for girls. Eloquently, she told the 'fathers of the nation' that 'justice, the sister of liberty, demands equal rights for all individuals, regardless of their sex.'

Without quoting the speech itself (Palm d'Aelders published it herself later), the minutes outlined her ideas in detail and summed them up pretty equitably – 'Women have shared the dangers of the Revolution, why should they not share its advantages?' – before giving the president's disappointing reply: 'The Assemblée will avoid, when making laws, as is its duty, anything that could cause [the women's] regrets and tears.' In other words, leave it in our capable male hands, dearie.

After this, Etta Palm d'Aelders seems to have got bogged down in scandal. She had long been providing the French government with information about Dutch ex-pats in Paris, and was now accused of spying for the Prussians. When she published a book of her patriotic and feminist speeches in 1793, she prefaced it with a reply to the 'atrocious calumnies' aimed at her by, amongst others, Louise-Félicité de Kéralio. Despite the suspicions against her, she was sent to Holland to report back on French émigrés, but was caught and imprisoned by the Dutch, and died soon after her release in 1799.

III

There were of course many other women demanding equal rights from the men with their hands on power. In May 1793, Pauline Léon (a *chocolatière*) and Claire Lacombe (an actress) founded the Société des républicaines révolutionnaires, a women-only political group. Its avowed aim was 'to take up arms in the defence of the nation', and article 1 of its statutes was that 'women citizens are free to take up arms or not'. They wanted to go and fight for the Revolution in the Vendée.

Never afraid of controversy, Claire Lacombe even went to the Convention in October 1793 and threatened the men: 'Our rights are those of the people, and if we are oppressed, we know how to oppose repression with resistance.'

Shortly afterwards, she was arrested for trying to force the women market traders – the Dames de la Halle who had marched to Versailles in October 1789 – to wear the red republican bonnet. Ironically, perhaps, the women objected that it was a male-only hat and complained to the authorities.

Finally reacting to all this feminism, at the end of October 1793 the Convention held a debate about whether women should be allowed to form political groups. Louis-Joseph Charlier[4] (who had presided over the Convention during Marie-Antoinette's trial days earlier) defended them, telling his colleagues that 'unless you contest that women belong to the human race, how can you take away this right?' But he was outvoted, and women were (in theory at least) silenced.

Undeterred, Claire Lacombe carried on her campaign for equal rights, but after being arrested yet again in 1794, and imprisoned for a year, she finally decided that it was safer to withdraw from politics and return to acting.

---

[4] He committed suicide in 1797 at the age of 42, considering the Revolution a failure.

That was probably a wise decision, considering the fate of the most famous of the revolutionary feminists, Olympe de Gouges.[5] A writer, she came up with some of the best-known quotes in support of her cause, including its pithiest: 'Women, isn't it high time that we too held a revolution?'

The daughter of a butcher (although it was rumoured that she was the illegitimate offspring of a *marquis*), she was married off at 17, and widowed a year later, in 1766. Adopting a noble *de* in front of her maiden name, she began a relationship with a noble member of the naval administration, entered refined Parisian circles, and started a theatre company.

One of her earliest plays apparently attracted death threats – *Zamire and Mirza, or The Lucky Shipwreck*, accepted by the Théâtre-Français in 1785, was about the horrors of slavery, and certain powerful men with vested interests in the Caribbean were unhappy. They came close to getting her locked up in the Bastille for subversion, and managed to have the play banned until 1789.

Even before the Revolution, though, Gouges was campaigning for reform of all sorts. She published an anonymous *Letter to the People* in 1788, suggesting that the well-off pay a voluntary income tax to ease the pressure on the government and protect the poor from famine. She was fairly moderate in her politics, and supported the idea of a constitutional monarchy. At the beginning, she even backed the three estates system that had prevented democratic change in France for centuries.

When Revolution came, she joined clubs like the Société patriotique des Amis de la Liberté, and continued to write provocative plays like *Les Démocrates et les aristocrates, ou Les Curieux du Champ de Mars*, which depicted a group of people

---

[5] To British readers, the most famous would probably be the English ex-pat Mary Wollstonecraft, who wrote *Vindication of the Rights of Woman* in 1792 and spent 1793–5 in France. But she was a peripheral figure in the Revolution, and compromised her integrity by failing to condemn the Terreur in her book *An Historical and Moral View of the French Revolution*.

of all classes at the 1790 *fête de la Fédération* commemorating the anniversary of the storming of the Bastille. The play showed social barriers breaking down thanks to the Revolution, and the possibility of real national unity. Again, a moderate, humane voice.

In 1791 Gouges penned her most famous text, the *Déclaration des droits de la femme et de la citoyenne*, a reaction to the male-only declaration at the heart of the new Constitution. Her text opens with the forceful line: 'Man, are you capable of being just?' and goes on, 'Tell me, who gave you the sovereign right to oppress my sex?' Clearly she had had enough of moderation.

Her *Déclaration* does not demand separate laws in favour of women (apart from a mother's freedom to name and shame the father of an illegitimate baby), just equal rights to education, property, the vote, jobs and free speech. Many of her 17 clauses are more or less repeats of the official Constitution, with '*l'homme*' and '*le citoyen*' replaced by '*la femme et l'homme*' and '*la citoyenne et le citoyen*'. Her most famous clause is number 10, in which she demands: 'A woman has the right to ascend to the scaffold; she must also have the right to ascend to the political rostrum.' All in all, it is a very reasonable list of requests to enjoy both the same rights and duties as men.

Sadly, it remained unpublished, and therefore unacknowledged by the male politicians, but Gouges did manage to obtain a measure of equality when she successfully lobbied for women to play an official role in the third anniversary celebrations of Bastille Day in 1792.

Now, though, she began to annoy some dangerous people. A few months after the prison massacres of September 1792, which were overtly supported or tacitly approved by powerful figures like Danton, Robespierre and Marat, she signed a poster condemning the violence: 'Blood, even that of the guilty, if shed cruelly and profusely, sullies revolutions for ever.'

As the Terreur gained speed and heads began to roll, she did not hesitate to criticize the culprits openly, calling Marat 'an abortion of humanity' and Robespierre 'loathsome, a disgrace to the Revolution'. On 19 July 1793, she published – and signed – a pamphlet warning about a new dictatorship, lamenting that so many peasants were being sent away to war, and calling for a vote on whether France should return to a more stable, peaceful constitutional monarchy. 'I would be delighted to live under a republican government,' she wrote, but 'look how our finances are exhausted, look at the complete downfall of France, look at these treacherous bloodthirsty men.'

Coming from a man, this would have been bad enough, but a woman? It gave the powers that be the perfect opportunity to silence the troublemakeress. She was summarily tried for treason on 2 November 1793 and guillotined the following day – only the second woman to have the honour of 'ascending the scaffold', after Marie-Antoinette.

After her death, the propaganda poured out against her and women in general – the newspaper *Le Moniteur* warned its female readers: 'She [Olympe de Gouges] wanted to be a man of state, and it appears that the law has punished this female conspirator for forgetting the virtues appropriate to her sex.'

Pierre-Gaspard Chaumette, the public prosecutor for Paris, wrote a lecture to women saying that: 'The man–woman, the impudent Olympe de Gouges, the first to set up women's societies, abandoned the care of her household to go into politics, and committed crimes.' Talking of the women who were demanding equal rights, he went on: 'All these immoral beings have been eliminated by the avenging blade of the law, and you want to imitate them? No, you will only be worthy of esteem if you force yourselves to be what Nature intended.' (Chaumette, by the way, was guillotined in April 1794, not for blatant sexism but on trumped-up charges of being an English spy.)

Given that last quotation, it is probably pointless to ask the question: Did these women achieve any semblance of equal rights? The obvious answer is no. After all, we have already seen the flagrantly phallocentric Constitution of 1795. The Revolution might have been about *Liberté*, but women were not included.

There is a more detailed answer than 'no', however, and it makes depressing reading. Over the course of the Revolution, the male politicians consciously and repeatedly resisted all calls to give *citoyennes* their due.

There were some minor advances in gender politics: in April 1791, daughters obtained the right to inherit as much as their brothers. In September 1792, divorce was authorized, including for incompatibility and by mutual agreement, or if the husband was mad, absent or a criminal. Women over 21 were also given leave to marry whom they wanted without parental consent (though with parental consent they could be married off at only 13). At the same time, women were given permission to sign legal documents as witnesses.

But apart from those concessions, the Revolution was one long campaign to enforce male supremacy. To quote just the main anti-equality measures:

On 27 August 1789, during the constitutional monarchy, the *loi salique* was confirmed, meaning that France would never have a queen.

On 22 December 1789, women were excluded from voting (along with the poorest men). Only one delegate at the Assemblée defended women's right to vote – an aristocratic mathematician called Nicolas de Condorcet, who was purged from the government in 1793, and later found dead in his prison cell.

As we saw above, in October 1793, all women's political *sociétés* were dissolved by order of the Convention.

On 20 December 1793, a 'large number of women' came to the Convention to protest that their husbands had been imprisoned without trial, and that they were 'all good citizens'. The women quite reasonably suggested that commissions should be set up 'to examine the causes of these arrests and restore liberty to those who deserve it'. Robespierre dismissively addressed his colleagues: 'If you see so many women in this chamber, can you believe that all their husbands are patriots? Probably not, and you must conclude that on the contrary, they are aristocrats.'

According to the minutes of the session, this provoked 'shouts by these women', and the president ordered any woman making noise to be arrested. The warning was stark: shut up and go home where you belong – or else.

The final nails in the female coffin came in 1795. On 23 May, there were so many women protesting in the streets about the lack of food that parliament voted a law banning women from attending political meetings, and made female gatherings of more than five illegal. Then on 22 August came the new Constitution with its definition of the good citizen as a 'good son, good father, good brother, good friend, or good husband'.

It was written confirmation that the Revolution had brought women neither *Liberté, Égalité* nor *Fraternité*.

IV

In the Musée du Nouveau Monde (Museum of the New World) in La Rochelle, on the Atlantic coast of France, there are two very revealing works of art.

The first is a painting by Léon Cogniet, an artist who was born in 1794 and who specialized in historical subjects. He painted several canvases about the Revolution – one depicts the National Guard valiantly marching through Paris on their way to repel the foreign invaders in 1792, admired by swooning ladies proffering flowers. It could almost have been a recruitment poster. The picture in La Rochelle is just as romanticized – it shows Jean Sylvain Bailly being sworn in as leader of the first Assemblée in 1789. He too is surrounded by swooning admirers, though his are all male, because women were not allowed to hold political office. In the painting, there are two spectators who should not be in the parliamentary chamber, and who weren't there in 1789 when the scene took place. They are bare-footed, shirt-sleeved black men gazing up at Bailly in gratitude for having broken the chains that lie at their feet. The implication is, of course, that the Revolution ended slavery, and freed the hundreds of thousands of men, women and children who were being worked to death in France's colonies in the Caribbean. This, as we shall see, was not entirely true. (Not that Britain or 'all men are born equal' America were any better, of course.)

The second work of art in La Rochelle is a Sèvres porcelain statuette, made in 1793, of a slave couple pointing to a *bonnet phrygien*, the revolutionary cap, again in thanks for being freed. The caption on its base, written in pidgin French, is racist but well intentioned: it reads *'Moi égal à toi, moi libre aussi'* – 'Me equal to you, me free too'. It was obviously designed to adorn the mantelpiece of a rich urban household that hoped to prove its revolutionary credentials.

It was true that some of the original members of the Assemblée wanted to free slaves and give equal rights to all human beings, regardless of their race, gender or religion. But at the end of the eighteenth century, slavery was a huge source of income for France, and ending it would have been like closing down all of Britain's cotton mills in the 1880s, or America's car factories a century later. At the time of the Revolution, Haiti, or Saint-Domingue as the French called it, produced as much sugar as all the British-held Caribbean islands put together. France's navy was almost entirely devoted to holding on to it, and some very rich, very influential French families depended on Saint-Domingue for their wealth and status. In other words, a few uppity slaves and trendy Parisian politicians were not going to mess things up so easily.

Abolitionism had started in France before the Revolution. Earlier in the century, Diderot had predicted that 'as forceful as floodwaters, the [slaves] will leave the indelible traces of their just resentment'.

In 1785, in her play *The Lucky Shipwreck*, Olympe de Gouges made her escaped slaves speak like philosophy lecturers:

MIRZA We are human, just like them. Why do they make such a great distinction between their race and ours?
ZAMOUR The difference is very slight. It is only about colour. But their advantages over us are immense. Art has set them

above Nature. Education has made them gods. And we are only human. They use us in these climates like they use animals in theirs.

In February 1788, the Société des Amis des Noirs was set up in Paris by a group of idealists who wanted not only to free slaves but to educate them in preparation for the time when all French people would enjoy *Liberté*. It was a sort of Parisian branch of a British organization, the Society for Effecting the Abolition of the Slave Trade, created a year earlier in London. When the Revolution began, the Société des Amis des Noirs had about 140 members, including prestigious names like Mirabeau, Sieyès, La Fayette, Condorcet and La Rochefoucauld. They immediately began lobbying the Assemblée to stop the slave ships, give citizens' rights to free people of mixed race in the colonies, and abolish slavery.

But they encountered stiff and organized opposition from a group of men who started meeting in August 1789 in a Paris mansion called the Hôtel de Massiac, home of a *marquis* of the same name. The group started out with 70 members, mostly slave owners, slave shippers and colonial administrators, and grew to an imposing 400 over the following two years, as battle was waged in the Assemblée. One of the founders was a Martinique-born landowner and Assemblée delegate called Moreau de Saint-Méry, who had written a theoretical treatise on the colonies, listing the nine 'degrees' of mixed race, and setting out a minutely detailed recipe for levels of discrimination.

These slave owners saw France's first *Declaration of Men's and Citizens' Rights* (article 1: 'All men are born and remain free and equal in law') of 1789 as a serious threat to their business, so they went on the offensive, lobbying to exclude their slaves from this equality, as well as the theoretically free mixed-race citizens in the colonies, who outnumbered the whites.

At first, the *esclavagistes* were successful. When the subject was debated in parliament in March 1790, they shouted down abolitionists, and the Assemblée issued a decree saying that it 'put colonists and their properties under the protection of the nation, and declares it a criminal offence towards the nation to stir up insurrection against them'.

This was despite a heroic performance by Mirabeau who thundered:

> 'I plead before you the cause of a race of men who ... live, suffer
> and die as slaves beneath the most detestable tyranny that history
> has ever known ... I will not degrade this Assemblée or myself
> by trying to prove that *les nègres*[6] have the right to freedom. You
> have already settled this question by declaring that all men are
> born and remain free and equal.'

Condorcet commented ironically, 'Let's add a word to the first article of the *Declaration of Men's and Citizens' Rights* – all *white* men are born free and equal.'

The colonists went even further, and organized a minor *coup d'état* in Haiti, replacing the official royal administration with their own assembly, and setting up a private militia. They even lynched the local army commander, a certain Colonel Thomas-Antoine de Mauduit. In April 1790, when the mixed-race freemen demonstrated to demand equal citizens' rights, they were massacred.

A free *homme de couleur*, of one-quarter African origin and three-quarters white French colonist, took up the baton. Vincent Ogé was a Bordeaux-educated son of a Haitian family that owned a coffee plantation. He made his living importing French products into the Caribbean colonies, and was in France on business in July 1789. He began to attend meetings of the Société des Amis des Noirs and to campaign for equal rights for free men like himself. When all calls for *Égalité* were ignored, he

---

[6] I leave this in the original French because to translate it would make Mirabeau sound politically incorrect.

decided to go back to Saint-Domingue and take matters into his own hands.

In October 1790, he wrote a polite letter to the white administrators of the north of the island, saying that he only wanted his rights under the Constitution – 'My claims are just, and I hope you will respect them' – with a mild threat added on at the end: 'Before resorting to other means, I will exercise restraint, but if, contrary to my hopes, you do not agree to my request, I shall not be answerable for the disorder that my just vengeance may cause.' When this too was ignored, Ogé assembled about 300 free men and attacked the local white militias.

They weren't looking to cause an outright slave rebellion, and retreated to the Spanish half of the island when about 2,000 regular soldiers arrived. But the Spanish handed them over, and on 25 February 1791, Ogé and his fellow militant Jean-Baptiste Chavannes earned the sad distinction of being two of the last Frenchmen to be put to death on the wheel[7] – the medieval punishment whereby the victim had his arms and legs smashed with an iron bar and his chest caved in, before being left to die. Several dozen of their supporters were hanged. Predictably, this did little to quell the rising tide of discontent amongst the island's slaves and disenfranchised free men.

Meanwhile back in Paris, a delegate at the Assemblée, the Abbé Henri Grégoire, mounted a fierce campaign against the slavers, who were bombarding the country with propaganda about the dangers of freeing 'savages'. He wrote an impassioned rebuttal of their lies in a *Letter to Philanthropists* in 1790, defending the rights of some 40,000 mixed-race people who met the requirements of age, gender and wealth to be considered 'active citizens' – voters, in fact – although none of them were even allowed to call themselves *Monsieur* or *Madame*, and the men were not allowed to carry swords (ironically, some of these mixed-race

---

[7] See Chapter 16 for the last man to suffer this punishment on the French mainland.

people were themselves slave owners). Abbé Grégoire delivered a philosophical broadside: 'Men have the right to exercise their freedom, as they have the right to sleep, eat, etc.'

But still the slavers held their ground, and when the Assemblée returned to the question of slavery for a five-day debate in May 1791, it fudged the issue yet again. This time La Fayette gave the most memorable abolitionist speech, saying: 'Free men, landowners and taxpayers in a colony are colonists. And yet it is disputed that people of colour can be landowners, farmers, taxpayers or free men. Are they men? I think so.'

But the spokesman for the slave owners, Antoine Barnave, played a subtle political game. He warned his colleagues that France might lose its valuable colonies if it acted rashly. He agreed that equal rights for all (or at least, for free people of mixed race) would be ideal, but that it was best to leave the timing of all this to the people who knew best – the colonists out in the islands. So on 13 May 1791, the Assemblée decreed that 'No law on the status of non-free[8] people can be passed for the colonies except by a formal, spontaneous request from the colonial assemblies' – which was simply a message to the slave owners that they could carry on as usual. Robespierre was furious, and gave one of his most idealistic speeches, lambasting his colleagues: 'You talk to us all the time about human rights, but you believe in them so little that you have just legalized slavery ... If the colonists want to threaten us into passing laws that suit their interests, let the colonies perish.'

In August 1791, the slaves in Saint-Domingue rebelled – not all of them, only a few tens of thousands out of the almost half a million in the colony, but they were enough to kill hundreds of slave masters, destroy more than 150 sugar refineries

[8] Partly at Robespierre's insistence – he had made a late entrance into the anti-slavery debate – the word *'non-libre'* was used instead of *'esclave'*, because he thought that to write the word 'slave' into a law would recognize its validity. A good philosophical argument, but it didn't help the slaves much.

and burn 1,600 coffee plantations across the west of the island. The slaves had several leaders, but the most famous is François Toussaint (later nicknamed 'Louverture', or 'Opening', either because of his skills in battle or a gap between his front teeth). He was a freed slave who took up arms, but he also tried to negotiate with the French colonists, seeking a political solution to the problem. The Spanish (who controlled the eastern end of Saint-Domingue) intervened on the side of the slaves, offering freedom to anyone who fought with them against France. Toussaint accepted the offer and was made an officer in the Spanish army.

These developments worried the Assemblée so much that they finally agreed to give voting rights to free men of mixed race in the colonies, and they sent out a delegation to try to pacify Haiti – and, of course, get the plantations working again. Its head was a member of parliament called Léger-Félicité Sonthonax. As befitting his first names – 'Light Happiness' – he was an abolitionist, and quickly understood that nothing could be done if the hard-line racists were left in charge. He joined forces with the freed men, disbanded the whites-only local assemblies, and exiled some of the worst racists from the island. He also matched the Spanish offer – freedom for any man who would join the French army. When Toussaint Louverture brought his men over to Sonthonax's cause, these tactics began to bear fruit and, finally, Sonthonax went the whole hog and took the personal initiative to abolish slavery in the north of the island (in exchange for a return to work), with the promise to 'prepare gradually, without violence and without confrontation, the total freedom of the slaves'.

And Sonthonax was true to his word. He ordered the *Declaration of Men's and Citizens' Rights* to be displayed across the island, declaring, 'It is high time that it was published in every part of the Republic.' He also issued an order that: 'All *nègres* and people of mixed blood currently held in slavery are declared free to enjoy all the rights attached to the status of French citizenhood.'

Over the next few months, Sonthonax extended abolition to the whole of French Haiti, despite ferocious opposition from pro-slavery lobbyists in Paris who were accusing him of treason and subversion – Robespierre had now changed sides and, this being the Terreur, decided that the abolitionists were being anti-revolutionary, and that the slave revolt was exactly like the uprising in the Vendée.

Finally, however, the Convention had to bow to the realization that they had been completely hypocritical about the issue of racial equality and slavery over the previous four or five years. On 4 February 1794, the parliamentarians decreed, bluntly for once: 'The Convention nationale declares that the enslavement of *nègres*, in all the colonies, is abolished; in consequence, it decrees that all men, without distinction of colour, living in the colonies, are French citizens and will enjoy all the rights guaranteed by the Constitution.'

In Saint-Domingue, this was quickly put into practice. Sugar plantations that had been abandoned by their owners were declared 'national assets' and run by an early form of commune, with a third of income kept for investment, a third paid to workers, and a third given to the state in tax. Meanwhile, freed slaves began to take over uncultivated land and set themselves up as farmers. They still lived in the semi-abject poverty they shared with the peasants on mainland France, but now no one was whipping them, raping them or selling their children.

Even so, the law of 1794 did not mention slave *trading*, which meant that French shippers could continue filling their boats with human cargoes and selling them to America, Britain or anywhere else that had not yet abolished slavery. And in fact, the slave wars raged on throughout the Caribbean, as French slave owners joined forces with the British and tried to re-establish the old colonial regime. In Saint-Domingue, Toussaint Louverture was forced to fight a continuous battle to hold off the British, the Spanish and incursions by white French slavers. In 1796, French plantations on Grenada, Saint Lucia and Saint Vincent were captured and returned to slavery.

However, another work of art – this one in the château de Versailles – seems to confirm that the battle had at least been partially won. In 1797, an artist called Anne-Louis Girodet (a man despite his first name) painted a portrait of Jean-Baptiste Belley, a member of both the Convention and its successor, the Conseil des Cinq-Cents, who had been elected to represent the northern zone of the colony of Saint-Domingue. Dressed in the black coat and white sash of his office, holding the feathered top hat and leaning against a marble sculpture of a revolutionary thinker and abolitionist called Guillaume-Thomas Raynal, he embodies all the calm self-assurance of his status. The unusual thing about the painting is that Belley is black – the first black man to be portrayed in a position of power in France.

A freed slave who fought in the French army, Belley was voted into political office in September 1793, but soon found out the difference between theoretical and real freedom. En route to France, he was threatened by colonists who objected to a non-white man holding a position of power. He apparently replied: 'When one knows how to save whites and defend them, one may have power over them.' Arriving in Brittany, he was arrested, and only freed when the Convention wrote and confirmed that he had been elected to parliament.

In 1797, Belley returned to Saint-Domingue as a commander of its *gendarmerie*. But by then, the political winds were changing back in France. In 1802, a new military governor of the island arrived from Paris, and he had Belley deported back to France and imprisoned in various Breton jails until he died in 1805. Meanwhile, Toussaint Louverture was tricked into giving himself up to the new governor, shipped back to France, and died in a Burgundy prison in 1803.

The abolitionist Sonthonax suffered a similar fate. He too served as a member of parliament for Saint-Domingue, and he too was arrested and exiled – in his case to his home town Oyonnax, in the Jura mountains of eastern France.

The cause of this change in attitudes to slavery was the arrival on the political scene of a certain Napoleon Bonaparte.

A sentimentalist with individuals, but ruthless when it came to sending whole armies to their deaths or imposing his rule over whole populations, Napoleon saw the economic need for slavery. On 20 May 1802, he issued a brief decree to the effect that 'slavery will be maintained according to the laws and regulations in force before 1789' and 'the trading of blacks and importing them into the colonies will continue, according to the above-mentioned laws and regulations pre-dating 1789.'

In short, despite its ideals, the Revolution took several years to live up to its promises of equal rights for all its citizens (well, the males at least), and even then, its work was undone less than a decade later. Slavery would not be abolished by the French government until 1848.

Chapter 22

THE REVOLUTION
SMOULDERS ON

'Dans les révolutions, il y a deux sortes de gens: ceux qui les font et ceux qui en profitent.'
'In revolutions, there are two types of people – those who make them, and those who take advantage of them.'

Napoleon Bonaparte (1769–1821) revolutionary
soldier turned emperor

I

Even if it failed to revolutionize the lives of some of France's least privileged citizens, the Revolution did open the way for one class of person – the ambitious alpha male.

We saw this with the rise, and subsequent fall, of people like Mirabeau, Marat, Danton and Robespierre, who battled like gladiators and killed each other off in the factional fighting of the early Revolution. But as the conservatives and reactionaries of 1795 published their woolly, compromising Constitution, there was a younger man, a product of the Revolution, waiting to step into the vacuum. It wasn't exactly a power vacuum – the 1795 Directoire was a vast, well-organized parliament surrounded by an intricately structured civil service. But after years of fiery speeches, riots and public executions, there was a political lull that must have felt a tad boring, even to people who were relieved that they weren't having to watch detached heads being brandished every day.

Into this lull stepped a young hothead called Napolionne di Buonaparte.

He was a product of aristocratic privilege – he had been given a free place at France's École militaire because his family was of Corsican noble stock. At the age of 16, he joined the royal army as a second lieutenant in an artillery regiment. At 19, during the first days of the Revolution, he successfully put down a food riot in Auxonne in Burgundy, where his regiment was stationed.

A few days after the invasion of the Tuileries palace in summer 1792, a shaken Louis XVI presided over a ceremony at which Bonaparte (who had now gallicized his name) was made a captain.

Captain Bonaparte rode the transition from constitutional monarchy to republic smoothly, and it was as a young patriotic officer in late 1793 that he seized his opportunity for major advancement. The port of Toulon had rebelled against the Revolution, and was being supported by a small British fleet. The commander of the French forces there was a bumbling former painter, who was happy to hand over control of the operation to the 24-year-old Corsican. Napoleon had cannons brought in from all over the south of France, built a huge artillery battery out of 100,000 sacks of soil, and pounded the town into submission.

His next exploit was to put down another rebellion, this time in Paris itself. In the summer of 1795, the British landed an army of 3,500 royalists in Brittany, hoping to join up with the remains of the Chouans rebels in western France. The invasion foundered, and almost all the invading royalists were either killed in battle, imprisoned or put before a firing squad. But not wanting to admit defeat, and with a conservative government in power, Parisian royalists assembled an army of 30,000 men and marched towards parliament. However, the MPs had got wind of the attack and drafted in the young Captain Bonaparte to organize its defence, at the head of only 8,000 troops.

Repeating his Toulon trick, Bonaparte had 40 cannons brought into the city from the western suburbs, and posted them on all the roads leading to the parliament building. When the insurgents appeared, he blasted them with grapeshot (small pieces of metal that are much more murderous than cannon balls when fired into a crowd). Keeping up this barrage for some 40 minutes, he killed about 300 men and frightened off the rest. Rebellion over.

Predictably, Bonaparte was made a general at age 26, and given command of a disheartened, badly equipped army on the border with Italy. Within a few months, he had roused them and won more victories over Italian armies than any other commander for three centuries. He even invaded the Vatican and requisitioned a vast collection of priceless artworks that he shipped back to the new national museum at the Louvre.

All this made him a national hero, and he was greeted in Paris with a victory ceremony worthy of Caesar returning to ancient Rome.

After an excursion into Egypt that was spoilt by another rising star of the times, Horatio Nelson, Bonaparte arrived back in Paris in 1799 to find the government in crisis. The Directoire had weeded out troublemakers from parliament (in one case by rigging an election), but it had failed to reboot the economy, and the Parisians were demonstrating again. The situation had become so unstable that parliament was forced to move around so that potential rioters and conspirators would have to guess where to stage their rebellion.

One veteran revolutionary, Emmanuel-Joseph Sieyès, decided to use these evasion tactics to stage a *coup d'état*. Announcing that the upper house, the Conseil des Anciens, needed to take refuge out in the suburb of Saint-Cloud, he arranged a military escort for them. This was to be organized by the military man of the moment, Napoleon Bonaparte (whose brother, Lucien, was president of the lower house, the Conseil des Cinq-Cents).

It was therefore not a surprise when, on the morning of 9 November 1799, 10,000 soldiers surrounded the Tuileries palace, where the Anciens were sitting. The surprise only came when Napoleon harried them out to the former royal palace of Saint-Cloud, treating them more like prisoners than esteemed members of parliament.

Having understood that this was a *coup d'état* in the making, all the next day in the château de Saint-Cloud's Orangerie, the parliamentarians stood firm and swore allegiance to the Constitution. They accused Napoleon of wanting to impose a dictatorship, and managed to prevent him from addressing them with their usual tactic of shouting down opposition (and in this case, allegedly threatening to stab him). Using the supposed threat of violence as an excuse, in the late afternoon, Napoleon marched into the chamber with a gang of bayonet-toting soldiers and physically chased the Anciens out of the building. Some of them leapt out of the windows.

On 13 December 1799, it was announced that France now had a new style of government – a 'consulate', ruled by three consuls, of whom only the first (Bonaparte, *bien sûr*) had real power. In any case the other two, fairly anonymous members of parliament called Charles-François Lebrun and Jean-Jacques-Régis de Cambacérès, would soon be eclipsed.

In exchange for his help, Abbé Sieyès, the former defender of the poor, received 200,000 *livres*, a large château just outside Paris and (a few years later) the aristocratic title of count.

Two days after his coup, Bonaparte's early Christmas present to the nation was an announcement: a new Constitution, introducing powers that would be 'strong and stable, as they must be to guarantee the rights of citizens and the interests of the state'. His declaration included the historic statement: 'Citizens, the Revolution has been settled according to the principles that started it. It is over.'

Napoleon's actual words were *'elle est finie'*, which was ambiguous. Did he mean that the Revolution was now complete, that it had reached perfection, like a brightly polished new sword? Or that it was finished, over, like a play after the curtain falls, so that there would be no more rioting, no more protests, no more change?

The implication was, of course, that it was the former. The reality was the latter. Using Robespierre's favourite tactic, Napoleon brutally crushed any domestic opposition by inventing assassination plots (though he did also suffer a few real attempts) and executing the culprits. In 1804 he organized an 'election' and was chosen by a miraculous 99 per cent of voters as the Emperor of France. His coronation at Notre-Dame cathedral in December 1804 was as lavish as anything imagined by the Ancien Régime. He took over the royal palace, the Tuileries, and replaced all the royal *fleurs-de-lys* in the decorations with his own symbol, the bee. He began to elevate his allies to a new French aristocracy, installed his brothers as Kings of Holland, Naples, Westphalia and Spain, and gave his sisters the title of *princesse*.

The Revolution really was over.

II

Or rather, the Revolution was over *for now*. As we all know, Napoleon's reign did not last, and thanks to his warmongering – and most particularly his disastrous incursion in Russia in 1812 and his constant attempts to outdo France's oldest enemy, Britain – his empire came crashing down in 1814, and Louis XVI's brother Louis Stanislas was crowned Louis XVIII.[1] Napoleon returned from exile and regained power in early 1815, only to lose it (for the last time) 100 days later at Waterloo.

In fact – and this is France's key problem – the Revolution did not really end until after 1871. It had created so many unresolved issues that resentment, revenge and ambition simmered just beneath the surface of French society for decades, costing countless lives and periodically wrecking the economy.

---

[1] Louis XVI's son, Louis Charles, was nominally Louis XVII when he died in prison in 1795.

To give the briefest summary of the chaotic period after 1815:

France underwent two more monarchies, under Charles X and Louis-Philippe, both of which ended in a *coup d'état*, in 1830 and 1848. It then became an empire again, under Napoléon III (Bonaparte's nephew), who provoked an invasion by the Prussians in 1870. This ended in the siege of Paris, after which the city declared itself an independent, revolutionary-style Commune, governed by the so-called 'Communards'.

In February 1871, parliamentary elections were held, and, incredible as it may sound, a majority of seats (396 out of 675) were won by overtly royalist candidates. The only reason the monarchy was not restored yet again was that the royalists were divided into two factions – the *légitimistes* (anti-republican supporters of the Bourbon royals) and the *orléanistes* (those in favour of Philippe Égalité's purported ideal of a post-revolutionary monarchy). Henri d'Artois, the grandson of Charles X, the last surviving descendant of the Bourbon line, would probably have been crowned King Henri V if only he had agreed to accept the tricolour flag. When he held out for the white, pre-revolutionary emblem, his bid for power fizzled out.

Meanwhile, in spring 1871, all the unresolved issues of 1789–95, all the vengeful rage of the monarchists who had seen Louis XVI executed and two other kings, Charles X and Louis-Philippe, ousted, burst like a massively swollen appendix. More than 70 years after Napoleon Bonaparte had declared the Revolution *'finie'*, Paris descended into civil war.

With the city in uproar, the official French government based itself out in the former royal capital of Versailles, a neat piece of historical symmetry. From March to May 1871, more than 150,000 troops of the French army attacked Paris, which was defended by around 50,000 men and women behind their improvised barricades of paving stones, carts and bits of furniture. More than 6,000 Parisians were killed on the barricades. During the fighting, the Communards burned down the Hôtel de Ville (with all its archives) and the palais des Tuileries, a symbol of royalist and imperial power. The final pocket of Communards, holed up in the Père Lachaise cemetery, were overrun, and 150 of them, many wounded, were lined up against a wall and shot.

Once all resistance in the city was broken, a repeat of the Chouans massacres of Le Mans and Nantes in 1793 began. Government soldiers searched houses, killing anyone who smelt of gunpowder, finishing off the wounded and arresting thousands. Kangaroo courts were set up, one of them in the palais du Luxembourg, Louis XVIII's former home, where death sentences were pronounced on anyone who was thought to have fired a weapon. The 'guilty' were immediately taken out to face a firing squad. It was like a mirror-image reprisal for the *tribunaux révolutionnaires* of the 1790s.

About 40,000 people were taken prisoner, including more than 1,000 women, and marched out to Versailles – again, a perverse repetition of a key revolutionary event, the 'women's march' of 5 October 1789. Some didn't make it that far. One particularly murderous officer called Gaston de Gallifet got a reputation for thinning out prisoner numbers by shooting all those with grey hair, on the grounds that they had probably taken part in the 1848 revolution against King Louis-Philippe. Between French royalists and republicans, it was never too late for political revenge.

Of the 40,000 prisoners who made it to Versailles, about 100 would be executed, 4,500 transported to France's prison camps in the tropics (a virtual death sentence), and about 5,000 sent to jail in France.

Still the old issues weren't resolved. Even after Henri d'Artois accepted defeat, in 1873 a royalist president, Patrice de Mac-Mahon, was elected, and set about trying to restore the monarchy yet again. It took another six years of wrangling between royalists and republicans in parliament before the Troisième République was stabilized under a republican president (Jules Grévy), and the royalists finally accepted that they weren't going to be able to put a king back on the throne.

In essence, it had taken almost a century for the Revolution of 1789 to produce a stable republic, proving that the idea of sudden *Liberté, Égalité* and *Fraternité* is a complete myth.

And one could argue that even that stability was precarious. The bloodiness of this long revolutionary process had left such deep scars that when the Nazis invaded in 1940, it was almost inevitable that France would again divide into two violently opposed factions. Yet again, French militias began arresting French resistance fighters. French kangaroo courts sentenced French patriots to be shot. After the Liberation of 1944, there were lynchings, reprisals, show trials and executions. Admittedly, it was not royalist versus revolutionary, but it was proof of how easily France could be split like an atom into two murderously opposed halves.

Today, almost no citizen of France would say that they want a return to their old monarchy. After Louis XVI, their kings were spectacular failures. But that is not the question – or at least, not in this book.

I have not tried to answer a theoretical question about whether France needs to be a republic or a monarchy, whether one political system is inherently 'better' or 'fairer' than the other, or whether the French would currently like to see a descendant of Louis XVI showing off Bourbon family babies to the world's media.

The question that this book has tried to ask is whether, if France had contented itself with the 1789 Revolution, and had been able to nurture its constitutional monarchy beyond 1792, it would have been a more peaceful, stable, happy, unified country for the following 200-odd years.

Some will say that 1789 was not *the* Revolution, that it was a partial reform by and for the elite, and that the real Revolution came after Louis XVI had been guillotined and the country was finally free from the chains of monarchy.

And in theory, a republic does seem to offer more opportunity for true democracy. The problem with this theory is that the first French republic was born in such conditions of violence and social conflict, and created such bad blood in the population while benefiting relatively few people, that the country underwent approximately one new revolution or *coup d'état* per decade until 1871.

Today, the myth endorsed by the French education system that the storming of the Bastille resulted almost immediately in *Liberté, Égalité* and *Fraternité*, along with the hero status accorded to some very dubious populist politicians, seem to be France's way of denying that there was any other option than to guillotine everyone who disagreed with the most radical republicans.

But the contention in this book has been that if public discontent about the flaws in the constitutional monarchy of 1789–92 had been harnessed democratically instead of dictatorially, France might have been able to grow harmoniously, and relatively quickly, into a country that offered true *Liberté, Égalité* and *Fraternité* (and, who knows, perhaps *Sororité* too) – led by probably the most popular man in France.

And that regime would have been a constitutional monarchy headed by Louis XVI. Which, even on Bastille Day 1789, was almost certainly what the vast majority of the French population wanted.

EPILOGUE

WHY MODERN FRANCE IS SUFFERING FROM 'REGIS ENVY'

～

So how are *Liberté, Égalité* and *Fraternité* faring in France today?

Well, the modern République française certainly offers a good deal of *Liberté*, though no more than monarchies like Britain, Belgium, Sweden or Tonga. French citizens enjoy democracy, relative freedom of speech, and more or less equal opportunity (in theory at least).

Even so, for a country that claims to be a secular state that liberated its people from the tyranny of the clergy in 1789, it came as something of a surprise during the French presidential campaign of 2017 to see mainstream politicians disputing the rights to gay marriage and adoption by gay couples – liberties that a post-revolutionary, non-religious republic should surely recognize without batting a political eyelid.

Similarly, there was the rumpus in the summer of 2016 about women on French beaches wearing swimsuits that covered up *too much* bare flesh. It took centuries for women to win the freedom to strip off on the beach *if they wanted to*, and now there was pressure in France to make naked arms and legs compulsory. Admittedly, the rule was confined to a few beaches in the politically sensitive south of France, but it was frankly bizarre – and not very libertarian.

In short, the battle for France's fabled *Liberté* goes on.

As for *Égalité*, modern France may not have a House of Lords (its upper house is an elected senate), but the country is still full of aristocrats merrily marrying their cousins, moaning about the upkeep of their châteaux, and looking down on anyone whose surname doesn't have a noble 'de' in front of it. Meanwhile, the moneyed bourgeoisie are every bit as snobbish as their pre-Revolution aristocratic predecessors towards people who don't have an apartment in the 'right' part of Paris or can't afford the best business school or fanciest wedding for their children. Inequality is everywhere.

As for *Fraternité*, France is one of the most politically divided countries in Europe. Its bosses and unions are constantly at war, and its extreme left- and extreme right-wing parties are exceptionally strong thanks to their 'us and them' politics. There is one party in parliament, La France Insoumise ('France that has not given up', subtext: since 1789), demanding a new Constitution and a new republic. Its members want a revolution. And in 2017 their leader was only 2 per cent away from making it into the final round of the presidential election. The conflict never ends.

All this is without even touching on the frightening rift in French society that partially caused, and has since been exacerbated by, the most recent series of terrorist attacks in France and the shocked realization that many of the attackers were home-grown.

In short, despite the Revolution, France has by no means shrugged off the social divisions of its monarchist past.

Far from it – today's ruling class revels in pre-revolutionary luxury. The country's lower house of parliament, the Assemblée nationale, is based in the palais Bourbon, the former home of Princess Louise-Françoise de Bourbon, a daughter of King Louis XIV. Given that the Bourbons were France's former royal family, you'd think that someone would have suggested renaming the parliament building since 1789. After all, post-revolution Paris renamed many of its 'royal' streets. In Soviet Russia, they renamed cities; they renamed the whole country.

Similarly, the French President's residence, the 365-room palais de l'Élysée, was once home to a mistress of King Louis

XV, and was later the residence of Emperor Napoléon III. Hardly a chandelier, armchair or dinner plate has been changed since, and French Presidents live almost literally like kings, surrounded by eighteenth-century-looking liveried servants and enjoying 20,000 square metres of gardens in central Paris, where most people struggle to find a park bench to sit on.

The French Prime Minister (who, by the way, is not elected, but appointed by the President) also lives in a palace, the hôtel Matignon, which was formerly owned by the Emperor Napoleon Bonaparte and King Louis XVIII. Its decor, like that in the Élysée, tends towards marble, gold and chintz, and apart from the new phones, computers and lightbulbs, it would feel very much like home to an eighteenth-century monarch. Matignon is smaller than the Élysée, but possesses the largest private park in Paris – 30,000 square metres.

By comparison with both of these palaces, 10 Downing Street is a garden shed.

As for the leaders themselves, France seems to have an innate preference for the regal type. Charles de Gaulle and François Mitterrand, two of the most authoritarian and long-lasting of recent presidents, are still revered by many voters. On the other hand, presidents who tried to introduce the common touch, like Nicolas Sarkozy (who used to swear like a Parisian taxi driver at hecklers) and François Hollande (who declared that he wanted to be *'le président normal'*) were both considered vulgar and/ or mediocre. What France really seems to yearn for is an aloof, emperor-like figure – another Louis XIV or Bonaparte (though without the absurd wigs and catastrophic wars).

Several financial scandals that arose during the 2017 presidential election campaign proved that modern French politicians possess all the bad habits that earned so many of their eighteenth-century predecessors a rendezvous with the guillotine.

Just like the old royal family, today's MPs have been dishing out jobs to their relatives, some of whom have received small fortunes for doing virtually nothing. One 2017 presidential contender allegedly paid his wife more than half a million euros of public money over about nine years – more than double the average salary in France in all of that period – as a 'parliamentary assistant'. (At the time of writing, there has still been no proof that she actually did any work to earn it.)

Despite a stream of scandalous revelations, this candidate did not withdraw from the election, and eventually polled 20 per cent. He was able to do so because, shockingly, when most of his payments were being made, it was *perfectly legal* for a French MP to hand out huge sums of taxpayers' money to members of his or her family *without declaring it*. Now, at last, it has become compulsory to publish salaries paid to relatives, but pre-revolutionary cronyism has not been totally forbidden.

These modern French politicians enjoy plenty of other legal, regal privileges. During the 2017 campaign, it was revealed that a certain minister's wife had *three* chauffeurs at her disposal. And that minister was a socialist, so who knows how many chauffeurs she would have had if her husband had not possessed a social conscience.

Meanwhile, it has been revealed that while President Hollande was in office, he kept a personal hairdresser on a retainer of 9,895 euros a month – almost exactly the salary of a government minister. Who would have thought that a socialist with so little hair would have so much in common with Marie-Antoinette?

But then in modern, post-Revolution France, politicians of all persuasions have been following in the footsteps of their pre-Revolution forerunners.

The French will argue that these are just aberrations, that monarchies are *inherently* over-privileged regimes, and that almost no one wants to see the return of the French royal family. Politically this is true, but in that case, why is it that, whenever a British prince marries, or even gets a new fiancée, the whole of the French media comes charging across the Channel to cover the story?

If a British royal baby is due, French TV crews, some of them paid by the republican state, are happy to camp for days outside the hospital alongside their monarchistic British colleagues. And when ordinary French tourists travel to London, they are just as royally obsessed. If you're queuing to visit Buckingham Palace or the Crown Jewels, you're bound to hear French being spoken all along the line – and not only by Belgians, Swiss and Québécois Canadians.

This French fascination with British royalty seems to stem from two things: first, dissatisfaction with their own political elite for the above-cited reasons; and secondly, a feeling that their country's identity is somehow incomplete. France possesses several of the most famous historic monuments on the planet, and yet there's something lacking. Perhaps it all feels too recent. The Eiffel Tower is little more than a century old. The Louvre has only been a museum for about 200 years. Versailles dates back to the seventeenth century, but it is a shell – its former life is over. The same goes for the medieval castles and prehistoric cave paintings.

In short, France possesses no living, continuous entity that identifies it to the rest of the world as an ancient civilization that existed for a millennium before the Revolution. Britain, on the other hand, has the Queen, who (if you don't look too closely) can trace her ancestry back to the eleventh century, or even beyond. And once she has departed the throne, there are already three generations in line to take up the royal reins. Whether one agrees with the principle of monarchy or not, this notion of historical continuity gives Britain a certain old-school cachet that France has lost.

Britain has its divisions, of course – Scotland keeps threatening independence, Northern Ireland will probably never solve its religious problems, Northern and Southern England are at constant cultural war, and Brexit has split the nation in two (at least). But the French don't really see all this, and retain a romantic view of *Angleterre* (they often use the name to describe the whole of Britain) that is largely based on the continuity of the monarchy.

The French republic has nothing to replace its royals. The President never unites the country in the same sentimental way that, for example, the better British monarchs can. A new president is elected every five years, and occasionally he (there has still never been a *Madame* President) is carried into office by a wave of optimism, but within weeks this usually collapses and France sinks back into its distrust of the authorities, its profound conviction that nothing will ever get better, and its impatience to see a new leader – all throwbacks to its turbulent revolutionary past.

And yet, if the reformed constitutional monarchy of 1789 had been allowed to develop into a true democracy, then just over two centuries later, at little or no extra cost to the taxpayer, France could be attracting the world's media and millions of extra tourists per year to royal jubilees, weddings and baby brandishings, and its politicians might be less prone to behave like monarchs.

Instead, the French complain about elitism dividing their society, spend a disproportionate amount of working days organizing 1789-style political marches, and regularly turn for their illicit royal thrills towards Britain.

Even if they would never admit it, deep down, the French are suffering from acute regis envy.

A TIMELINE OF THE FRENCH REVOLUTION

~

1733: Voltaire publishes his book *Lettres philosophiques*, in which he praises Britain's constitutional monarchy.

1770, Apr 19: Louis XVI is married by proxy to Maria Antonia Josepha Johanna, Archduchess of Austria, who takes the name Marie-Antoinette. Some French people are against the marriage to a foreigner and dub her *'l'Autrichienne'* – literally, 'the Austrian woman', but *chienne* means bitch.

1774, May 10: Louis XVI becomes King of France.

1785, Aug: Marie-Antoinette is implicated in the 'necklace affair', which confirms the general opinion of her as an exorbitant spender of public money.

1787, Feb–May: during the Assemblée des notables at Versailles, selected national bigwigs examine France's disastrous accounts.

1787, Aug & Nov: the Paris parliament (of aristocratic judges) blocks tax reforms.

1788, summer: the harvest fails.

1788, Dec: Louis XVI doubles the number of representatives of the *tiers état*, the commoners to be elected to the États généraux, an undemocratic, and occasionally convened, form of royal consultation of the national mood.

1789, Jan: Emmanuel-Joseph de Sieyès publishes *Qu'est-ce que le tiers état?*, a call for increased commoners' rights.

1789, Jan: Louis XVI commissions the *cahiers de doléances*, the complaints books to be written by every community in the country. (Or its male citizens, anyway.)

1789, Apr 27–8: a Paris mob ransacks the wallpaper factory of Jean-Baptiste Réveillon. This is the first major riot of the Revolution.

1789, May 5: the États généraux open in Versailles, bringing together the three 'estates' – the aristocracy, the clergy and the *tiers état*, the commoners.

1789, Jun 17: the *tiers état* revolts, and declares the creation of the Assemblée nationale, a permanent single house of parliament.

1789, Jun 20: meeting in a tennis court (the *Jeu de paume*) in Versailles, the Assemblée declares that it will install a constitutional monarchy.

1789, Jun 27: Louis XVI orders the aristocrats and clergy to join the Assemblée nationale.

1789, Jul 9: delegates at the Assemblée vote to draft a *Déclaration des droits de l'homme et du citoyen*, the basis of France's new Constitution.

1789: Jul 12–14: food riots in Paris turn violent, culminating in the storming of the Bastille.

1789, Jul 17: Louis XVI is taken into Paris for the day, and wears the tricolour *cocarde* (rosette). His brother Charles (the future King Charles X) had escaped to Savoy the previous day.

1789, Aug 13: first issue of *Le Journal d'Etat et du citoyen*, founded by Louise de Kéralio, the first Frenchwoman to publish and edit a newspaper.

1789, Sep 12: first issue of *L'Ami du peuple*, written and published by Jean-Paul Marat, probably the most bloodthirsty of the revolutionary thinkers.

1789, Oct 5–6: rioters march from Paris and storm the château de Versailles, forcing the royal family to move into the palais des Tuileries in Paris.

1789, Oct 9: Docteur Joseph-Ignace Guillotin proposes humane execution for all, regardless of rank.

1789, Nov 2: Church lands and properties are confiscated. About 90 per cent of these will be bought by rich bourgeois.

1789, Dec 19: a new currency, the *assignat*, is created, based on the value of the confiscated Church lands.

1790, May 21: Paris is divided into 48 *sections* – district councils that will become hotbeds of insurgency. The general council of Paris is now the Commune.

1790, Jul 14: Louis XVI is guest of honour at the *fête de la Fédération* in Paris, in commemoration of Bastille Day.

1790, Oct: slaves revolt in Saint-Domingue (French Haiti).

1790, Nov 27: the Assemblée rules that clergymen must now say an oath of allegiance to the state, and must be elected by the people.

1791, Feb 28: an eventful day – a riot at the château de Vincennes west of Paris; an attempt on the life of La Fayette, head of the National Guard; and 400 armed nobles convene at the palais des Tuileries to protect Louis XVI (he sends them away).

1791, Jun 20: the royal family flee Paris, getting as far as Varennes in the northeast of France. They are captured and escorted back. Louis XVI's brother, Louis Stanislas (the future King Louis XVIII), leaves separately, and escapes.

1791, Jul 17: a riot at the Champ-de-Mars in Paris is repressed; around 50 protesters die in the shooting.

1791, Aug 22: full-blown revolution breaks out in Haiti as slaves, freed former slaves and freeborn citizens of mixed race demand equal rights.

1791, Aug 27: Austria and Prussia issue the Declaration of Pillnitz, calling on all European monarchies to restore the monarchy in France (not that it has ended – the constitutional monarchy is functioning).

1791, Sep 3: the new French Constitution is officially published, prefaced by the *Declaration of Men's and Citizens' Rights*. Louis XVI signs it on 14 September.

1791, Sep: the playwright Olympe de Gouges writes her *Déclaration des droits de la femme et de la citoyenne*, to be included in a booklet about women's rights addressed to Marie-Antoinette. She hoped it would be read out before parliament, but this never happened.

1791, Nov 9: the Assemblée orders all émigrés (some 140,000 people, mainly aristocrats, will leave France between 1789 and 1800) to return. Failing this they will be dispossessed and sentenced to death *in absentia*. (Louis XVI will use his royal veto on this decree.)

1791, Dec 14: Louis XVI threatens war against foreign powers who intervene in France (though under the new Constitution he no longer has the right to declare war).

1792, Mar 25: Louis XVI signs the decree legalizing the use of the guillotine. It will be used a month later, on a murderer called Nicolas Jacques Pelletier.

1792, Apr 20: France declares war on Austria and its ally, Prussia.

1792, Apr 25–6: during the night, an army captain called Claude Joseph Rouget de Lisle writes the '*Marseillaise*'. (In 1814 he would write a royalist song, '*Vive le Roi!*' with less success.)

1792, Jun 20: a Parisian mob storms the palais des Tuileries but is evicted.

1792, Jul 11: the Assemblée declares '*la Patrie en danger*' – the homeland is in danger of foreign attack and counter-revolution at home.

1792, Jul 25: the Prussians issue the *Brunswick Manifesto*, threatening carnage if the French royal family is harmed.

1792, Aug 10: the Paris mob storms the Tuileries again, this time ransacking the palace, taking the royal family into custody and putting an end to the constitutional monarchy.

1792, Sep 2–6: the Terreur begins with massacres of around 1,200 inmates in Paris's prisons. Marie-Antoinette's friend the Princesse de Lamballe is killed and mutilated, and her head is carried to the Temple prison, where the royal family are being held. Revolutionary leaders fail to condemn the massacres.

1792, Sep 21: Parliament renames itself the Convention nationale.

1792, Sep 22: France is now a republic.

1792, Oct 2: création of the Comité de sûreté générale (Committee of General Security) to oversee the police and enforce revolutionary justice.

1792, Nov 20: a hidden safe is found in the palais des Tuileries containing documents that reveal Louis XVI's dealings with foreign counter-revolutionaries.

1792, Dec 3: Maximilien Robespierre tells the Convention: *'Louis doit mourir pour que la patrie vive'* ('Louis must die so that the homeland can live').

1792, Dec 11: Louis XVI hears the accusations against him at the Convention. To most of them, he answers (rightly) that what he did was allowed by the first Constitution.

1792, Dec 26: Louis XVI's lawyers present his defence.

1793, Jan 14: Louis XVI's trial begins, and will mostly involve 12-hour daily sittings.

1793, Jan 16 – 17: members of the Convention debate possible punishments – death, imprisonment or banishment; 387 vote for death, 334 for other punishments, including imprisonment with death if France is invaded, or imprisonment until peace is restored, followed by banishment.

1793, Jan 20: the verdict is guilty, and 380 vote for death within 24 hours, 310 against. Louis XVI's cousin, Louis Philippe, now calling himself Philippe Égalité, votes for death.

1793, Jan 21: Louis XVI is guillotined in the place de la Révolution, now the place de la Concorde.

1793, Feb: uprisings in the west of France, mainly in the Vendée and Brittany, will soon develop into a full-blown rebellion. Only partially inspired by royalists, it is mainly a revolt against army conscription and a revolution that has done little to raise peasants out of poverty.

1793, Mar 10: creation of the Tribunal révolutionnaire, the court that needs only flimsy evidence of counter-revolutionary sentiment to condemn someone to death.

1793, Apr 6: creation of the Comité de salut public (Committee of Public Salvation), to guard against the enemy within. Its most famous heads would be Georges Danton and Maximilien Robespierre.

1793, Jun 2: moderate Girondins (so-called because many of them came from southwest France) are ousted from the Convention by Robespierre and his allies, backed by a Parisian mob that invades parliament. More than 20 MPs are condemned to death as traitors.

1793, Jul 13: Marat is stabbed to death by a Norman woman called Charlotte Corday. She is guillotined on 17 July.

1793, Sep 17: the *loi des suspects* is passed. Now, merely being suspected of opposing or criticizing the Convention is punishable by death.

1793, Oct 24: the revolutionary calendar is implemented, backdated to the declaration of the republic on 22 September 1792 (24 October 1793 is now *3 brumaire an II*).

1793, Oct 14: Marie-Antoinette is tried before the Revolutionary Tribunal.

1793, Oct 16: she is guillotined.

1793, Dec 12: the town of Le Mans, occupied by anti-revolutionary rebels, the so-called 'Chouans', is captured. Around 1,000 are massacred, including women and children. Fugitives are hunted down and killed; about 9,000 are taken to prison in Nantes, where from December 1793 to January 1794 at least half of them will be shot, drowned, stabbed or beaten to death.

1793, Dec 19: a rebellion in the port of Toulon is crushed by a young artillery captain, Napoleon Bonaparte.

1794, Feb 4: slavery is abolished in French colonies.

1794, Feb 15: the tricolour becomes the flag of the French republic.

1794, Apr 5: Danton is guillotined after becoming 'too moderate'.

1794, May 10: Louis XVI's sister Élisabeth is guillotined.

1794, Jun 10: a law is passed taking away a suspect's rights to a defence or a hearing if accused of treason.

1794, Jul 27: moderate members of the Convention oust Robespierre from power. He is arrested at the Hôtel de Ville while trying to organize an uprising by the Paris mob. He is guillotined the following day.

1795, Jun 8: Louis XVI's son, Louis Charles (now, according to royalists, officially Louis XVII) dies in prison, probably of tuberculosis, aged ten.

1795, Aug 22: a new, very conservative, Constitution is published. The Convention becomes a bicameral system, headed by a five-man committee, the Directoire.

1795, Oct 5: Napoleon uses his cannons to crush a royalist uprising in Paris.

1799, Dec 13: Napoleon leads a *coup d'état* and declares that the Revolution is *'finie'*.

1802, May 20: Napoleon reinstates slavery in the French colonies.

1804, May 18: Napoleon declares himself Emperor of France (or rather, he is voted as such by 99 per cent of the electorate).

1814, Apr 6: Napoleon abdicates, and the monarchy is restored, under Louis XVIII (Louis XVI's brother Louis Stanislas).

1815, Mar 20: Napoleon escapes from exile on the island of Elba and returns to power.

1815, Jun 22: after 100 days, Napoleon abdicates again, and Louis XVIII returns. He will reign until 1824, and be succeeded by his brother Charles X.

1830, Aug 2: after days of rioting by the Paris mob, Charles X flees and the monarchy ends again. Or rather, a new one starts, as Louis-Philippe, the son of Louis XVI's cousin Philippe Égalité, takes the throne.

1848, Feb 24: a *coup d'état* ousts Louis-Philippe, and Louis-Napoléon Bonaparte, nephew of the Emperor, becomes President of France.

1852, Dec 2: Louis-Napoléon declares himself Emperor Napoléon III.

1870, Sep 4: after a disastrous war against Prussia, Napoléon III is overthrown when a mob invades parliament, and a new republic (the 'third') is declared. When the Prussians invade and besiege Paris, the government takes refuge in Bordeaux, then Versailles.

1871, Feb 8: in parliamentary elections, of 675 seats, 396 are won by the two main monarchist movements, the *légitimistes* (anti-republican supporters of the Bourbon royals) and the *orléanistes* (those in favour of Philippe Égalité's purported ideal of a post-revolutionary monarchy). It is only disagreements between these two factions (especially about whether to have a white or tricolour flag) that prevent a restoration of the monarchy.

1871, Mar 18–May 28: when the siege of Paris is lifted, the city declares itself a semi-autonomous Commune in the spirit of 1789, and is invaded by the French army. There is fierce street fighting, and tens of thousands of Communards are either killed on the barricades, massacred after surrendering, or marched out to Versailles and executed after a trial. Some of the most ruthless army commanders are overt royalists.

VICTIMS OF THE REVOLUTION

The Guillotine by Numbers

According to surviving city records, 2,918 people were guillotined in Paris between 14 July 1789 and 21 October 1796. Of those, 2,518 were men and 370 women (with 30 victims of unspecified gender).

By age

Under 18: 22
18–20: 45
20–25: 336
25–50: 1,669
50–60: 528
60–70: 206
70–80: 103
Over 80: 9

By profession and status

Aristocrats (who were not politicians, soldiers or members of the clergy): 381
Members of the Assemblée nationale: 39
Members of the Convention: 45

Members of the Paris Commune (city council): 73
Magistrates and ex-politicians: 245
Bishops and archbishops: 6
Other clergy: 319
High-ranking royal civil servants: 25
Members of the professions (bankers, doctors, lawyers, solicitors, etc.): 479
Merchants and shopkeepers: 275
Craftsmen: 391
Soldiers: 365
Writers: 25
Artists: 16
Servants, gardeners, coachmen, etc.: 129
Peasants: 105

Outside Paris, about 14,000 people were guillotined (around 3,500 of them in the west of France during the rebellion there). The approximate social breakdown was:

Workers: about 30%
Bourgeois: about 25%
Peasants: below 25%
Aristocrats: about 10%
Clergy: below 10%

Other causes of death

Estimates as to the numbers who died during the Revolution for other unnatural and/or unnecessary reasons vary hugely. Predictably, republican sources play them down, royalist sources bump them up. It is generally thought that the French people who died of poverty, firing squads, mass drownings, lynchings, cannon fire or in civil-war battles between 1789 and 1796 probably numbered almost 300,000.

SELECT BIBLIOGRAPHY

⁓

I have deliberately not added source references in the body of the text, along the lines of: Louis XVI replied 'Oui'[75] – the number 75 referring to a note 'op. cit., p. 362' at the back of the book, obliging the reader to scan the list in search of the first mention of the book to which the 'op.cit.' refers, by which time they have forgotten what they were originally reading.

I can understand why modern academics should want to cite a reference for every single piece of information they provide, and thereby prove to their colleagues that they have actually done their research. But it is a relatively recent habit. You can read (if you have the time and the energy) the seven highly conversational volumes of Jules Michelet's *Histoire de la Révolution française*, published between 1847 and 1853, and you will find that most of the superscript numbers in his text refer the reader to suggestions for further reading, justifications for using a particular word, apologies for not being more precise about figures, and similar notes from author to reader that would interrupt the flow of his main narrative. Rarely are they used simply to give sources for his facts or quotations.

As a constant reader of history books, I find the incessant use of source reference numbers intensely distracting while I am trying to follow an often complex course of events. I find it much more useful when an author explains in the main text where a quotation comes from by saying something like 'in the memoirs of Madame Campan, one of Marie-Antoinette's ladies-in-waiting, we are told that ...' or 'according to the parliamentary archives for 6 October 1789 ...' As an ordinary reader, I don't really need anything more precise, so that is the policy I have adopted in this book.

Of course, giving exact references at the back of the book would prove that I am not just making everything up (though who knows whether the quoted source didn't invent the event or quotation in the first place?). But I take the view that either you believe me when I tell you I've found a reliable piece of information, or you don't. If you don't, why bother reading my book?

In any case, reading a history book is a leap of faith, because even the best referenced and documented history books can omit information, or use strategically selected sources to prove whatever the author wants to prove. This is how we have ended up with impeccably researched but (in my view) inaccurate books presenting the French Revolution as a swift, heroic switch from monarchist tyranny to republican dreamland. I have found plenty of sources, many of them eyewitness accounts, that prove the contrary.

Below is a list of my main sources, more or less chapter by chapter. This method means that there will be some repetition, because key texts like the parliamentary archives or the memoirs of central figures during the Revolution will crop up more than once.

There were mountains of sources to choose from. However, many of these posed serious problems.

Modern French history books often assume a sort of folk knowledge, and contain sentences along the lines of: 'As we now know, *fructidor* failed because the Girondins rejected the Montagnards' call for a Comité de sûreté entirely independent from the Comité de salut.' You need a history degree just to understand the preface.

Many French books on the Revolution are devoted to one single event, and have titles like *What Exactly Happened Between 9 a.m. and 9.30 p.m. on 14 July 1789?* Interesting, but exhausting.

Then of course there is the *Poor Marie-Antoinette* and *Hail Robespierre* school of biography.

All this explains why, as much as possible, I went back to the original sources, especially the speeches, the minutes of meetings, newspaper articles, and the eyewitness accounts of people who lived through the Revolution (or whose careers, and memoirs, were cut short by the guillotine). The memoirs are often exercises in self-defence, but fascinating nevertheless.

My view is that we can only understand history if we go back and look at what people were saying and writing during the events in question. For obvious reasons, during the French Revolution, most of those people were not writing in English, so apologies to any reader who does not understand French, because my list of sources won't be of much use unless translations for these old, often out-of-print, texts are available.

French-speakers will certainly enjoy reading some of these original sources as much as I did. The parliamentary archives in particular are very revealing. They show that fair-minded stenographers were busily noting every word spoken, more or less seven days a week, 365 days a year, during the whole of the revolutionary period. Whatever one might think of the politicians of the time, they destroy the myth of the work-shy Frenchman (at the time, all elected politicians were male). And they certainly put modern France's overpaid, chauffeur-driven, scandal-surfing, long-lunching political elite to shame.

The vast majority of pre-twentieth-century texts are available online via the website of the Bibliothèque nationale de France, *gallica.bnf.fr*. For translations of their titles, and information about their contents, see the main body of this book, where they are quoted.

All French quotations taken from these books were translated into English by the author.

Introduction

Mopinot, Antoine Rigobert, *Adresse à l'Assemblée nationale: Observations et propositions sur l'emplacement des statues* (1792).

Chapter 1

Anon, *Château de Versailles, site officiel*, chateauversailles.fr.

Levron, Jacques, *La Vie quotidienne à la cour de Versailles au XVIIe et XVIIIe siècles* (1965).

Louis XIV, *Manière de montrer les jardins de Versailles* (1689–1705).

Michelet, Jules, *Tableau chronologique de l'histoire moderne de 1453 à 1749* (1825).

Ogg, David, *Louis XIV* (1933).

Sandras, Gatien de Courtilz de, *La vie de Jean-Baptiste Colbert, Ministre d'État sous Louis XIV roi de France* (1696).

Chapter 2

Anon, *Château de Versailles, site officiel*, chateauversailles.fr.

Académie des sciences, *Mémoires* (published 1833).

Bruyère, Jean de la, *Les Caractères, ou Les Moeurs du siècle* (1688).

Saint-Simon, Louis de Rouvroy, duc de, *Mémoires complets et authentiques du duc de Saint-Simon sur le siècle de Louis XIV et la Régence* (1856 edition).

Sourches, Louis-François Du Bouchet, marquis de, *Mémoires du marquis de Sourches sur le règne de Louis XIV* (1882 edition).

Visconti, Primi, *Mémoires sur la cour de Louis XIV 1673–1681* (1988 edition).

Chapter 3

Ainsworth, William Harrison, *John Law: The Projector* (1864).

Maurepas, Jean-Frédéric Phélypeaux, comte de, *Mémoires du comte de Maurepas* (1791 edition).
Michelet, Jules, *Histoire de France au XVIIIe Siècle: la Régence* (1863).
Saint-Simon, Louis de Rouvroy, duc de, *Mémoires complets et authentiques du duc de Saint-Simon sur le siècle de Louis XIV et la Régence* (1856 edition).

Chapter 4

Argenson, René-Louis de Voyer, marquis d', *Journal et mémoires du marquis d'Argenson* (1859 edition).
Delavault, Hélène, Darton, Robert and Pavy, Claude, *Quand la chanson défait le pouvoir, chansons de rue parisiennes, 1748–50* (conference given in 2011).

Chapter 5

Académie des sciences, *Histoire de l'Académie royale des sciences* (1784).
Beaumarchais, Pierre-Augustin Caron de, *Oeuvres complètes* (1809).
Bougainville, Louis-Antoine de, *Voyage autour du monde par la frégate La Boudeuse et la flûte L'Étoile* (1771).
Diderot, Denis et al., *L'Encyclopédie, ou Dictionnaire raisonné des sciences, des arts et des métiers* (1751–72).
Diderot, Denis, *Lettres sur les aveugles à l'usage de ceux qui voyent* (1749).
Louis XV, *Déclaration du Roi, pour la discipline du Parlement* (1756).
Montesquieu, Charles Louis de Secondat, baron de la Brède et de, *De l'esprit des lois* (1748).
Montesquieu, Charles Louis de Secondat, baron de la Brède et de, *Lettres persanes* (1721).
Sade, Donatien Alphonse François, marquis de, *Aline et Valcour* (1795).

Sade, Donatien Alphonse François, marquis de, *Dialogue entre un prêtre et un moribond* (published 1926).
Voltaire, *Dictionnaire philosophe portatif* (1764).
Voltaire, *Éloge funèbre de Louis XV* (1774).
Voltaire, *Lettres philosophiques* (1733).

Chapter 6

Anon, *'Le Godemiché royal'* (1789).
Anon, *Les Amours de Charlot et Toinette* (1779).
Breton, Guy, *Histoires d'amour de l'histoire de France*, volume 10 (1991).
Campan, Henriette, *Mémoires sur la vie privée de Marie-Antoinette, Reine de France et de Navarre; suivis de souvenirs et anecdotes historiques sur les règnes de Louis XIV, de Louis XV et de Louis XVI* (1823 edition).
Genlis, Félicité de, *Mémoires inédits sur le dix-huitième siècle et la Révolution française, depuis 1756 jusqu'à nos jours* (1825).
Hézecques, Félix d', *Souvenirs d'un page de la cour de Louis XVI, par Félix, comte de France d'Hézecques, baron de Mailly* (1895 edition).
Louis XVI, *Journal* (1873 edition).
Mercy Argenteau, Florimond de, *Correspondance secrète entre Marie-Thérèse et le comte de Mercy-Argenteau: avec les lettres de Marie-Thérèse et de Marie-Antoinette* (1864 edition).
Rousseau, Jean-Jacques, *Émile, ou De l'éducation* (1762).
Séguret, Joseph-François-Régis de, *Les Mémoires de M. de Séguret, secrétaire de la cassette et premier commis des petits appartements de Louis XVI* (1897 edition).

Chapter 7

Anon, *L'Autrichienne en goguettes, ou L'Orgie royale* (1789).
Fleischmann, Hector, *Les pamphlets libertins contre Marie-Antoinette: d'après des documents nouveaux et les pamphlets tirés de l'enfer de la Bibliothèque nationale* (1908).

La Motte, Jeanne de Valois-Saint-Rémy, *Mémoires justificatifs de la comtesse de Valois de la Motte* (1789).

Montbarrey, Alexandre Marie Léonor de Saint-Mauris, prince de, *Mémoires autographes de M. le prince de Montbarey [sic]: ministre secrétaire d'état au Département de la guerre sous Louis XVI* (1826).

Radier, Jean-François Dreux du, *Mémoires historiques, et anecdotes sur les reines et régentes de France* (1827).

Soulavie, Jean-Louis Giraud, *Histoire de la décadence de la monarchie française* (1803).

Vaublanc, Vincent-Marie Viénot, comte de, *Mémoires sur la Révolution de France et recherches sur les causes qui ont amené la Révolution de 1789 et celles qui l'ont suivie* (1833).

Young, Arthur, *Travels During the Years 1787, 1788 & 1789: Undertaken More Particularly with a View of Ascertaining the Cultivation, Wealth, Resources, and National Prosperity of the Kingdom of France* (1792).

Zweig, Stefan, *Marie-Antoinette, The Portrait of an Average Woman* (1932).

Chapter 8

Anon, *L'Autrichienne en goguettes, ou L'Orgie royale* (1789).

Anon, *'Ode à la Reine'* (1789).

Bluche, François, *La Vie quotidienne au temps de Louis XVI* (1980).

Campan, Henriette, *Mémoires sur la vie privée de Marie-Antoinette, Reine de France et de Navarre; suivis de souvenirs et anecdotes historiques sur les règnes de Louis XIV, de Louis XV et de Louis XVI* (1823 edition).

Chastelet (fils), Paul Hay du, *Traité de la politique de France* (1669).

Malouet, Pierre-Victoire, *Mémoires de Malouet* (1868 edition).

Maurepas, Jean-Frédéric Phélypeaux, comte de, *Mémoires du comte de Maurepas* (1791 edition).

Parny, Évariste de, *Poésies érotiques* (1778).

Turgot, Anne-Robert-Jacques, *Œuvres de Turgot et documents le concernant* (1913 edition).

Vergenne, Charles-Gravier de, *Réflexions sur la situation actuelle des colonies anglaises et sur la conduite qu'il convient à la France de tenir à leur égard* (1776).

Verneilh Puiraseau, Joseph de, *Statistique générale de la France* (1807).

Chapter 9

Brienne, Loménie de, *Discours de réception de Loménie de Brienne* (1770).

Brienne, Loménie de, *Simplification et généralisation des finances, suppression de l'arbitraire dans l'impôt* (1789).

Calonne, Charles-Alexandre de, *Réponse de Monsieur de Calonne à l'écrit de Monsieur Necker, contenant l'examen des comptes de la situation des finances rendus en 1774, 1776, 1781, 1783 & 1787* (1787).

Caraccioli, Louis-Antoine de, *Lettre de M. le marquis de Caraccioli à M. d'Alembert* (1789).

Castries, René de la Croix, *Le Maréchal de Castries 1727–1800* (1979).

Hézecques, Félix d', *Souvenirs d'un page de la cour de Louis XVI, par Félix, comte de France d'Hézecques, baron de Mailly* (1895 edition).

Howard, John, *State of the Prisons* (1777).

Louis XVI, *Déclaration du Roi concernant le timbre, donnée à Versailles le 4 août 1787* (1787).

Loysel, Antoine, *Institutes coustumières, ou Manuel de plusieurs et diverses reigles, sentences et proverbes tant anciens que modernes du droit coutumier & plus ordinaire de la France* (1607).

Necker, Jacques, *Compte rendu au Roi* (1781).

Necker, Jacques, *De l'administration des finances de la France* (1784).

Necker, Jacques, *Institution, règles et usages de cette maison* (1780).

Necker, Jacques, *Mémoire au Roi sur l'établissement des administrations provinciales* (1776).

Vovelle, Michel, *La Chute de la monarchie 1787–1792* (1975).

Chapter 10

Argenson, René-Louis de Voyer, marquis d', *Journal et mémoires du marquis d'Argenson* (1859 edition).

Beaumarchais, Pierre-Augustin Caron de, *Le Mariage de Figaro* (1784).

Bézout, Étienne, *Arithmétique de Bézout, à l'usage de la marine et de l'artillerie* (1770).

Bluche, François, *La Vie quotidienne au temps de Louis XVI* (1980).

Fénelon, François, *De l'éducation des filles (1687).*

Franklin, Benjamin, *Report on the Montgolfier Balloon* (1783).

Laclos, Pierre-Ambroise-François, Choderlos de, *De l'éducation des femmes* (1783).

Lambert, Anne-Thérèse de Marguenat de Courcelles, marquise de, *Avis d'une mère à sa fille* (1728).

Malesherbes, Guillaume-Chrétien de Lamoignon de, *Remontrances* (1771–75).

Meister, Jacques-Henri, article in *Correspondance littéraire, philosophique et critique* (1776).

Mercier, Louis-Sébastien, *Tableau de Paris* (1782).

Pasquier, Étienne-Denis, *Histoire de mon temps* (published 1893–95).

Reyre, Abbé Joseph, *L'École des jeunes demoiselles* (1786).

Saint-Font, Faujaus de, *Description des expériences de la machine aérostatique de MM. de Montgolfier* (1783).

Thiéry, Luc-Vincent, *Guide des amateurs et des étrangers voyageurs à Paris* (1787).

Various, *Journal de Paris* (NB 1777–87 issues freely available on gallica.bnf.fr).

Young, Arthur, *Travels During the Years 1787, 1788 & 1789: Undertaken More Particularly with a View of Ascertaining the*

Cultivation, Wealth, Resources, and National Prosperity of the Kingdom of France (1792).

Chapter 11

Anon, *Cahier des représentations & doléances du beau sexe* (1789).

Bailly, Jean Sylvain, *Mémoires d'un témoin de la Révolution, ou Journal des faits qui se sont passés sous ses yeux, et qui ont préparé et fixé la Constitution française* (1822 edition with notes and corrections by Saint-Albin Berville).

Bluche, François, *La Vie quotidienne au temps de Louis XVI* (1980).

Hézecques, Félix d', *Souvenirs d'un page de la cour de Louis XVI, par Félix, comte de France d'Hézecques, baron de Mailly* (1895 edition).

Louis XVI, *Lettre du Roi, pour la convocation des États généraux à Versailles, du 24 janvier 1789* (1789).

Michelet, Jules, *Histoire de la Révolution française*, tome 1 (1847).

Mounier, Jean-Joseph, *Rapport du comité chargé du travail sur la Constitution* (1789).

P ..., Mademoiselle, *Cahier des doléances des demoiselles* (1789).

Réveillon, Jean-Baptiste, *Exposé justificatif* (1789).

Sieyès, Emmanuel-Joseph, *Essai sur les privilèges* (1788).

Various, *Archives parlementaires de 1787 à 1860: recueil complet des débats législatifs et politiques des Chambres françaises* (1884 edition – search by date available at https://frda.stanford.edu/en/ap).

Various, *Cahiers de doléances* (1789).

Chapter 12

Bailly, Jean Sylvain, *Mémoires d'un témoin de la Révolution, ou Journal des faits qui se sont passés sous ses yeux, et qui ont préparé et fixé la Constitution française* (1822 edition with notes and corrections by Saint-Albin Berville).

Campan, Henriette, *Mémoires sur la vie privée de Marie-Antoinette, Reine de France et de Navarre; suivis de souvenirs et anecdotes historiques sur les règnes de Louis XIV, de Louis XV et de Louis XVI* (1823 edition).
Godart, Félix, *Camille Desmoulins d'après ses œuvres* (1889).
Le Bas, Philippe, *Dictionnaire encyclopédique* (1842).
Pottet, Eugène, *Histoire de Saint-Lazare* (1912).

Chapter 13

Bailly, Jean Sylvain, *Mémoires d'un témoin de la Révolution, ou Journal des faits qui se sont passés sous ses yeux, et qui ont préparé et fixé la Constitution française* (1822 edition with notes and corrections by Saint-Albin Berville).
Matossian Mary, *Poisons of the Past: Molds, Epidemics and History* (1989).
Morris, Gouverneur, *The Diary and Letters of Gouverneur Morris* (1888 edition).
Various, *Archives parlementaires de 1787 à 1860: recueil complet des débats législatifs et politiques des Chambres françaises* (1884 edition – search by date available at https://frda.stanford.edu/en/ap).
Various, *La Déclaration des droits de l'homme et du citoyen de 1789* (1789).
Vovelle, Michel, *La Chute de la monarchie 1787–1792* (1975).
Young, Arthur, *Travels During the Years 1787, 1788 & 1789: Undertaken More Particularly with a View of Ascertaining the Cultivation, Wealth, Resources, and National Prosperity of the Kingdom of France* (1792).

Chapter 14

Bailly, Jean Sylvain, *Mémoires d'un témoin de la Révolution, ou Journal des faits qui se sont passés sous ses yeux, et qui ont préparé et fixé la Constitution française* (1822 edition with notes and corrections by Saint-Albin Berville).

Gorsas, Antoine, *Le Courrier de Versailles à Paris et de Paris à Versailles* (1789 issues available on gallica.bnf.fr).

Louis XVI, *Journal* (1873 edition).

Marat, Jean-Paul, *L'Ami du peuple* (1789–92 issues available on gallica.bnf.fr).

Mounier, Jean-Joseph, *Exposé de la conduite de M. Mounier, dans l'Assemblée nationale, et des motifs de son retour en Dauphiné* (1789).

Various, *Journal de Paris* (NB 1777–87 issues freely available on gallica.bnf.fr).

Chapter 15

Campan, Henriette, *Mémoires sur la vie privée de Marie-Antoinette, Reine de France et de Navarre; suivis de souvenirs et anecdotes historiques sur les règnes de Louis XIV, de Louis XV et de Louis XVI* (1823 edition).

Louis XVI, *Journal* (1873 edition).

Various, *Archives parlementaires de 1787 à 1860: recueil complet des débats législatifs et politiques des Chambres françaises* (1884 edition – search by date available at https://frda.stanford.edu/en/ap).

Chapter 16

Anon, *La Confession de Marie-Antoinette* (1790).

Anon, *Soirées amoureuses du général Mottier et de la belle Antoinette par le petit épagneul de l'Autrichienne* (1790).

Blaizot, *Almanach de la ville de Versailles*, 1791 (1790).

Lavaux, Christophe, *Les Campagnes d'un avocat, ou Anecdotes pour servir à l'histoire de la Révolution* (1816).

Marat, Jean-Paul, *L'Ami du peuple* (1789–92 issues available on gallica.bnf.fr).

Marat, Jean-Paul, *Le Moniteur patriote* (1789).

Proyart, Liévin-Bonaventure, *La Vie et les crimes de Robespierre, surnommé le tyran, depuis sa naissance jusqu'à sa mort* (1795).

Various, *Archives parlementaires de 1787 à 1860: recueil complet des débats législatifs et politiques des Chambres françaises* (1884 edition – search by date available at https://frda.stanford.edu/en/ap).
Various, *La Constitution française* (1791).

Chapter 17

Campan, Henriette, *Mémoires sur la vie privée de Marie-Antoinette, Reine de France et de Navarre; suivis de souvenirs et anecdotes historiques sur les règnes de Louis XIV, de Louis XV et de Louis XVI* (1823 edition).
Ferrières, Charles-Élie de, *Mémoires du marquis de Ferrières* (1822 edition).
Lenôtre, G. (real name: Louis Gosselin), *Le Drame de Varennes, juin 1791, d'après des documents inédits et les relations des témoins oculaires* (1908).
Louis XVI, *Déclaration de Louis XVI à tous les Français à sa sortie de Paris* (1791).
Louis XVI, *Journal* (1873 edition).
Various, *Archives parlementaires de 1787 à 1860: recueil complet des débats législatifs et politiques des Chambres françaises* (1884 edition – search by date available at https://frda.stanford.edu/en/ap).
Various, *Le Journal des clubs* (also known as *Journal des amis de la Constitution*) (1790–91).

Chapter 18

Brunswick, Karl Wilhelm Ferdinand, Duke of, (signatory), *Manifeste de Brunswick* (1792).
Caron, Pierre, *Les Massacres de septembre* (1935).
Danton, Georges Jacques, *Discours de Danton* (1910).
Louis XVI, *Correspondance politique et confidentielle inédite de Louis XVI* (1803 edition).
Marat, Jean-Paul, *L'Ami du peuple* (1789–92 issues available on gallica.bnf.fr).

Robespierre, Maximilien, *Discours et rapports de Robespierre* (1908 edition).
Tourzel, Louise Élisabeth, duchesse de, *Mémoires de madame la duchesse de Tourzel* (1883).
Various, *Archives parlementaires de 1787 à 1860: recueil complet des débats législatifs et politiques des Chambres françaises* (1884 edition – search by date available at https://frda.stanford.edu/en/ap).

Chapter 19

Benard, Alfred, *La Marseillaise et Rouget de Lisle* (1907).
Millin, Aubin-Louis, *Annuaire du républicain, ou Légende physico-économique: avec l'explication des trois cents soixante-douze noms imposés aux mois et aux jours* (1793–4).
Various, *Archives parlementaires de 1787 à 1860: recueil complet des débats législatifs et politiques des Chambres françaises* (1884 edition – search by date available at https://frda.stanford.edu/en/ap).
Various, *Bulletin de la Société de l'histoire de Paris et de l'Île-de-France* (1889).
Various, *Bulletin du Tribunal criminel révolutionnaire, établi au Palais, à Paris, par la loi du 10 mars 1793, pour juger sans appel les conspirateurs* (1793–5: 441 bulletins available on gallica.bnf.fr).

Chapter 20

Beauchesne, Alcide de, *La Vie de Madame Élisabeth, soeur de Louis XVI* (1869).
Garambouville, Louis Marie Turreau de, *Mémoires pour servir à l'histoire de la guerre de Vendée* (1796).
Kléber, Jean-Baptiste, *Mémoires politiques et militaires: Vendée, 1793–1794* (1989 edition).
Lafue, Pierre, *Louis XVI* (1941).
Launay, Arsène, *La Terreur en Anjou, correspondance et journal de Benaben, commissaire civil du Maine-et-Loire auprès des armées républicaines* (2007).

Lenôtre, G. (real name: Louis Gosselin), *Les Noyades de Nantes* (1914).

Marat, Jean-Paul, *L'Ami du peuple* (1789–92 issues available on gallica.bnf.fr).

Mounier, Jean-Joseph, *Recherches sur les causes qui ont empêché les François de devenir libres, et sur les moyens qui leur restent pour acquérir la liberté* (1792).

Various, *Archives parlementaires de 1787 à 1860: recueil complet des débats législatifs et politiques des Chambres françaises* (1884 edition – search by date available at https://frda.stanford.edu/en/ap).

Various, *Décret du 17 septembre 1793 relatif aux gens suspects* (1793).

Various, *Le Procès de Louis XVI, roi de France, avec la liste comparative des appels nominaux et des opinions motivées de chaque membre de la Convention nationale* (1814).

Chapter 21

Blanc, Olivier, *Olympe de Gouges* (1981).

Diderot, Denis et al., *L'Encyclopédie, ou Dictionnaire raisonné des sciences, des arts et des métiers* (1751–72).

Donnadieu, Jean-Louis, *Toussaint Louverture – Le Napoléon noir* (2014).

Gouges, Olympe de, *Déclaration des droits de la femme et de la citoyenne* (1791).

Gouges, Olympe de, *Les Trois Urnes, ou Le Salut de la patrie, par un voyageur aérien* (1793).

Gouges, Olympe de, *Lettre au peuple, ou Projet d'une caisse patriotique* (1788).

Gouges, Olympe de, *Zamore et Milza, ou L'Heureux Naufrage* (1788).

Grégoire, Henri, *Lettre aux philanthropes* (1790).

Kéralio, Louise-Félicité de, *Le Journal d'État et du citoyen* (and *Mercure national*) (1789–90).

Michelet, Jules, *Les Femmes de la révolution: Mademoiselle Kéralio* (1855).

Palm d'Aelders, Etta, *Appel aux Françoises sur la régénération des moeurs et nécessité de l'influence des femmes dans un gouvernement libre* (1790).

Rimbaud, Arthur, *Œuvres complètes* (2009 edition).

Rousseau, Jean-Jacques, *Émile, ou De l'éducation* (1762).

Various, *Archives parlementaires de 1787 à 1860: recueil complet des débats législatifs et politiques des Chambres françaises* (1884 edition – search by date available at https://frda.stanford.edu/en/ap).

Various, *Constitution du 24 juin 1793* (on website http://www.conseil-constitutionnel.fr/).

Various, *Déclaration des droits et des devoirs de l'homme et du citoyen: 1795* (preface to *Constitution du 5 fructidor an III* on website http://www.conseil-constitutionnel.fr/).

Voltaire, *Dictionnaire philosophe portatif* (1764).

Chapter 22

Bourgin, Georges, *La Guerre de 1870–1871 et la Commune* (1939).

Lentz, Thierry, *Le 18 Brumaire* (1997).

PICTURE PERMISSIONS

Plate Section 1

1. Versailles. De Agostini Picture Library / Contributor
2. Louis XIV. Heritage Images / Contributor
3. Louis XV. Français : Collection de Louis XV
4. Madame du Pompadour. Photo Josse/Leemage / Contributor
5. Donatien Alphonse François De Sade. Heritage Images / Contributor
6. 'Down with the taxes'. DEA / G. DAGLI ORTI / Contributor
7. King Louis XVI. Heritage Images / Contributor
8. Jacques Necker. Culture Club / Contributor
10. Belle Poule hairstyle. Heritage Images / Contributor
12. Opening of the Estates General. Photo Josse/Leemage / Contributor
13. Jean Sylvain Bailly. Photo Josse/Leemage / Contributor
14. The sacking of Saint-Lazare in Paris. DEA / G. DAGLI ORTI
15. Le Serment du Jeu de Paume. Photo RMN
16. Louis is welcomed by the Paris council. DEA / G. DAGLI ORTI

Plate Section 2

4. Mirabeau. PHAS / Contributor
5. The Revolutionary constitution of 1791. ullstein bild Dtl. / Contributor

6. Portrait of a Parisian sans-culotte. Leemage / Contributor
7. Georges-Jacques Danton, Jean-Paul Marat and Maximilien de Robespierre. GEA / G. DAGLI ORTI / Contributor
8. The Marat newspaper. Photo 12 / Contributor
9. Massacre of women at La Salpêtrière. Photo 12 / Contributor
10. Louis XVI inspects the guillotine. ullstein bild Dtl. / Contributor
12. Former French Queen Marie Antoinette On The Way To The Guillotine. Keystone-France / Contributor
13. Olympe de Gouges. Heritage Images / Contributor
14. The drownings in the Loire during The Terror. Universal Images Group / Contributor
16. The coup of 18 Brumaire. Universal History Archive / Contributor

The author and publisher have made all reasonable effort to contact copyright holders for permission and apologise for any omission or error in the credits given. Corrections may be made to future reprints.

INDEX

Assemblée des notables, 211–13, 214, 246, 288
Assemblée nationale see National Assembly
Augeard, Jacques-Mathieu, 361
Augustus III, King of Poland, 110
Austria, France declares war (1792), 415
Austrian War of Succession, 74, 75

Baillaud-Varenne, Jacques-Nicolas, 431
Bailly, Jean Sylvain: National Assembly delegate, 295–7, 299, 303, 315; elected Mayor of Paris, 316; support for Louis XVI and continuation of the monarchy, 315–20, 397; and royal family's removal to Paris, 350, 358; and the *Dames de la Halle*, 341–2; horror at mob violence, 327–30; on Louis XVI's attempted escape, 403; role in 17 July 1791 massacre, 408–10; execution, 463; painted by Léon Cogniet, 500
balloons *see* hot air balloon, invention of

Balzac, Honoré de, 170*n*
Banque Générale, 53–5
Barnave, Antoine, 407–8, 463, 505
Barrière, François, 184
Barry, Jeanne du, 98–9, 103–4, 105, 111, 116, 132–3, 139, 156, 464
Bart, Jean (female mariner), 77
Bastille Day, first celebrations of (1790), xii, 365–8
Bastille prison, 72, 87–8, 96, 101, 104, 126, 158, 200, 218, 284, 304–5; storming of the, xii, 304–5, 306, 312–18, 518
Beauharnais, Vicomte Alexandre de, 332–3
Beaumarchais, Pierre-Augustin Caron de, 103, 149, 201, 208, 364; as watchmaker to Louis XV, 79; rise and literary career, 79*n*, 92, 96–100; acts for Louis XVI in American War, 201; *The Marriage of Figaro*, 243–5, 246–7
Beaune, Jacques de, 7
Beauvais, Bishop of, 297
Belley, Jean-Baptiste, 508
Benaben, Commissaire, 471, 474
Benoist, Antoine, 38*n*

Berry, Marie Louise
Elizabeth, duchesse
du ('Jouflotte'),
49–50
Berthoud, Ferdinand, 78
Bertier de Sauvigny,
Louis Bénigne François,
327–9
Besenval, Pierre Victor de,
312
Besnard, François-Yves,
169–70
Bézout, Étienne, 239
Bicêtre prison hosptial,
massacre in, 427
Blaizot (bookseller to Louis
XVI), 370–2
Bluche, François, 169
Böhmer, Auguste, 156, 158
Bonnay, Charles-François de,
367
botany, Louis XV's promotion
of, 79–80
Boucheporn, Claude-François
Bertrand de, 182
Boucher, François, 68, 69–70
Bougainville, Louis-Antoine
de, 77–8, 80, 239
Bouillé, François Claude
Amour de, 167–8, 388–9,
390–1, 398, 400
Bourbon, Louis Henri de, 331
Bourbon, Louis Joseph de,
330–1

Bourbon, Palais de, 520
Bourbon dynasty, 14
Bourbon whiskey and biscuits,
14*n*
Bourbon-Conti, Louis
François de, 97
Bourbotte, Pierre, 446
bourgeois, 164–5, 167–8
Breteuil, Louis Charles
Auguste Le Tonnelier de,
389
Brienne, Etienne Charles de
Loménie de, 213–16, 217,
218, 220, 224
Brienne military academy,
237–8
Brissac, Duc de, 113
Brissot, Jacques Pierre, 414,
458
Britain: and the American
war, 201–2; industrial
goods, 208–9, 484 *see also*
England
Brittany: Chouan uprisings,
469–76; invaded by Britain
(1795), 511; revolt (1718),
58–9
Broglie, Victor-François de,
330
Brunswick, Karl Wilhelm
Ferdinand, Duke of,
420
Brunswick Manifesto, 419–20
Byron, Lord, 231

Cottereau, Jean, 470, 476
Courrier de Versailles, Le
(newspaper), 339, 342
Couturelle, Comte de, 131
Crédit municipal, 198*n*
currency, revolutionary, 373,
483

Damiens, Robert-François,
72–3, 85
Dansard, Claude, 492
Danton, Georges Jacques:
background and political
activities, 382–4; *The
Marriage of Figaro* and,
244; role in 17 July 1791
massacre, 408; flees to
England (1791), 409; as
Minister of Justice in
the *Convention Nationale*,
426, 428; votes for the
death penalty for Louis
XVI, 451; and the
Revolutionary Tribunal,
456; crushes the
Girondins, 457; physical
deformities of, 463*n*; political decline and execution,
466–8
Daujon, François, 433
David, Jacques-Louis, 386,
465*n*
*Déclaration des droits de
l'homme et du citoyen*

[Declaration of Men's and
Citizens' Rights], 297–8,
333–4, 349, 497
Delalande, Michel Richard, 22
Delfaud, Guillaume-Antoine,
427
Desmoulins, Camille, 306–8,
463–4
Destez, Jacques, 401
destruction of historic build-
ings, 374–5
Diderot, Denis: *Encyclopédie*,
76, 80–6, 89, 96, 106, 248,
249, 250, 464, 490–1;
imprisoned in the Bastille,
393; on slavery, 501
Dillon, Théodore, 415
Directoire (1795), 487, 510,
512
Dreux-Brézé, Henri-Évrard
de, 295–7
droit de remontrance, 48, 101
Drouet, Jean-Baptiste, 401
Duhem, Pierre Joseph, 456
Dupuys, Jean, 6
Durosoy, Barnabé Farmian,
442–3
Duval-d'Esprémesnil, Jean-
Jacques, 217
Duverney, Joseph Pâris, 97

economy, after the Revolution,
484
education system, 224–30

Lamballe, Marie-Thérèse de, 143, 149, 359, 428–9, 433

Lambert, Marquise de, 227–8

Lamoignon, Chrétien François de, 216

Launay, Bernard-René Jourdan de, 312–14, 318, 328, 344

L'Autrichienne en goguettes, ou L'Orgie royale (play), 148–9, 176

Lavaux, Christophe, 384

Lavoisier, Antoine-Laurent de, 236–7, 464

Law, John, 52–6

Le Bas, Philippe, 314

Le Breton, André, 86

Le Brun, Charles, 29

Le Mans, battle and massacre at, 471

Le Normant de Tournehem, Charles François Paul, 66

Le Nôtre, André, 19, 71

Le Peletier, Louis, 310

Le Roy, Pierre, 78, 123

Le Vau, Louis, 15–16

Lebrun, Charles-François, 513

Legendre, Louis, 417

Lenoir, Jean-Charles-Pierre, 242

Léon, Pauline, 495

Léonard (hairdresser to Marie-Antoinette), 135, 143, 358, 359, 400

Léopold, duc de Lorraine, 110

Leopold II, Holy Roman Emperor, 390–1, 398, 404, 415

Lepeletier de Saint-Fargeau, Louis-Michel, 451n

life expectancy (1789), 175

Limon, Jérôme-Joseph Geoffroy de, 419–20

literacy rates, pre-Revolution, 224

longitude, calculation of, 239

Lorraine, Charles-Eugène de, 330

Louchet, Louis, 468

Louis, Antoine, 440–1

Louis, Dauphin of France (son of Louis XV), 82, 110

Louis, Grand Dauphin (son of Louis XIV), 34

Louis Antoine, Duc d'Angoulême, 286

Louis Antoine, Duc d'Enghien, 331

Louis XI, King, 104

Louis XIII, King, 10–12

Louis XIV, King (the 'Sun King'): absolutism of, 5–6; during his mother's regency, 12–13; builds the

412–13; confronts mob at Tuileries, 417–18; leaves Tuileries to take refuge with the National Assembly, 422–3; imprisoned in the Temple prison, 423, 433; correspondence with royalist émigrés, 443–5; 'suspended from office,' 423; trial, 445–51; execution, 451–3

Louis XVII of France (Louis-Charles, son of Louis XVI), 399, 460–1, 514

Louis XVIII, King (*formerly* Louis Stanislas), 93, 286, 331, 357*n*, 396; lack of issue, 116; character, 121; extravagance of, 206; flees France (1791), 404; plans invasion of France from Koblenz, 413; as monarch, 438, 514

Louise-Françoise de Bourbon, Princess, 520

Louis-Philippe I, King, 123–4, 374, 458, 515, 516

Louis Philippe (father of Louis–Philippe I), see Orléans

Loysel, Antoine, 161, 219

Lully, Jean-Baptiste, 28, 33

Lumières, Les, 76, 84, 86, 227, 240, 333, 390, 435, 489

Luxembourg, Palais de, 50, 396, 516; gardens, 50

MacMahon, Patrice de, 516

Macron, Emmanuel, 177, 379

Maillard, Stanislas, 344–5

Maine, Louis-Auguste de Bourbon, Duc de, 59

Maintenon, Marquise de, 27, 38

Maison royale (school for girls), 227

Malesherbes, Guillaume-Chrétien de Lamoignon de, 247–8, 464

Mallet du Pan, Jacques, 419

Malouet, Pierre-Victor, 179–80

Manuel, Pierre-Louis, 446

Marat, Jean-Paul: background and political ideas, 380–2; revolutionary tracts and journalism, 395, 397–8, 409, 419, 426, 442–3, 456–7; opposes military action (1791), 414; and September massacres, 428; and Louis XVI's trial, 446; votes for the death penalty for Louis XVI, 451; skin disease, 463*n*, 464–5; death, 464–6

Maria Giuseppina of Savoy, Princess, 116

Maria Josepha, Archduchess, 110

Mercy Argenteau, Florimond
Claude de, 114, 115, 116,
122, 130, 143, 152
Metz, 171, 331, 348, 388, 416,
418
military academies, 237–8
Miomandre de Sainte-Marie,
351
Mirabeau, Honoré Gabriel
de: National Assembly
delegate, 296; support of
constitutional monarchy,
377–9; works as spy for
Louis XVI, 296, 378–9,
383n, 384; loses aristo-
cratic title, 364; physical
deformities of, 296, 463n;
on slavery, 503; impris-
oned in the Bastille, 393;
death, 396–7
Mitterand, François, 240, 521
Molière, 15, 47, 242, 249
'monarchiens,' 380, 387, 406–7,
411, 414
Montagnards (political faction),
455, 456, 457, 465, 486, 536
Montbarrey, Prince de, 142
Montespan, Madame de, 59
Montesquieu, 86–7, 90
Montgolfier, Joseph-Michel
and Jacques Etienne, 233–6,
281
Mopinot, Antoine Rigobert,
xii–xiii

Morande, Charles Théveneau
de, 98–9
Morris, Gouverneur, 264, 327
Motteville, Madame de, 39
Mounier, Jean-Joseph:
National Assembly dele-
gate, 292, 294, 304; on the
Constitution, 297–8, 303;
support for the constitu-
tional monarchy, 316; per-
suades Louis XVI to
accept the Constitution,
345–6, 347–9; on the
removal of the royal family
to Paris, 353; flees to
Switzerland and con-
demns the Revolution,
464
Mozart, Wolfgang Amadeus,
245
Mur des Fermiers généraux,
207, 214, 308

Nantes, Brittany, 59–60,
472–3
Napoléon Bonaparte, 237,
238, 240, 364n, 461; on
Louis XVI, 126–7; rise and
seizure of power, 510–14;
reinstates slavery, 508–9
Napoléon III, Emperor, 51n,
357n, 364n, 515, 521
National Assembly: formed at
Versailles, 292–4; renamed

National Constituent
Assembly, 297
National Constituent
Assembly, 299, 311, 323,
425; abolishes hereditary
status, 364; draws up
*Declaration of Men's and
Citizens' Rights*, 333–4;
draws up the Constitution,
297–8, 307, 322, 332–4;
Louis XVI submits to,
315–17; moves to Paris,
358–9; publishes the
Constitution (1791),
410–11; reforms of, 332–5,
362; supports Louis XVI,
352
National Guard, 367–8, 377,
382, 387, 388, 393–4, 403,
417, 486; formation of, 349
National Legislative
Assembly, 411, 413, 421,
423, 425
navigation, 77, 78, 239
Necker, Jacques, 190–205,
206, 207, 208, 209,
210, 211, 212, 213, 214,
215, 220, 224, 231, 253,
264, 267, 273, 289–90, 293,
306, 307, 308, 310, 318,
327, 330, 373, 404
Nelson, Horatio, 512
New Orleans (La Nouvelle-
Orléans), 56

newspapers: under Louis
XVI, 245–7; revolutionary,
415
Nouailles, Adrien de, 48
Noyon, Bishop of, 36

Oberkirch, Baronne d',
143–4, 145
Ogé, Vincent, 503–4
Ollières, Louis Nicolas Victor
de Félix d', 181
O'Murphy, Marie-Louise,
69–70, 74, 111
Order of the Holy Spirit, 140
Orléans, Louis Philippe, duc
d': good looks of, 121;
present at first balloon
flight, 235; disloyalty to
Louis XVI, 217, 228,
274–6, 350–1; at the *États
généraux*, 287, 289; and the
'Réveillon affair,' 282–3;
joins National Assembly,
297; and the *Dames de la
Halle*, 340; as 'Philippe
Égalité,' 374, 424–5; votes
for the death penalty for
Louis XVI, 451; execution,
458
Ormesson, Henri-François d',
178, 205–6

Palais-Royal, Paris, 13, 49,
261, 275, 307, 314, 340

Reyre, Abbé Joseph, 226
Richelieu, Duc de, 232, 240
Richelieu, Maréchal de, 127–8
Ridicule (film, 1996), 23
Rimbaud, Arthur, 481–2
Robert, Anne-Jean, 233
Robert, Hubert, 150–1
Robert, Nicolas-Louis, 233, 235
Robert, Pierre-François-Joseph, 493
Robespierre, Augustin, 468–9
Robespierre, Maximilien de: rise of, 385–7; role in 17 July 1791 massacre, 407, 408; opposes military action (1791), 414–15; denounces the monarchy and National Assembly, 421; assumes office in the Convention Nationale, 426; and Louis XVI's trial, 445; votes for the death penalty for Louis XVI, 451; and the Reign of Terror, 461, 462–3; Danton opposes, 467–8; arrested and executed, 468–9
Rochambeau, Jean-Baptiste de, 202
Rohan, Louis-René de, Bishop of Strasbourg, 155–8, 160, 169
Roland, Jean-Marie, 432, 445
Romme, Gilbert, 435

Rouget de Lisle, Claude Joseph, 436–8
Rousseau, Jean-Jacques, 92, 123, 124, 150, 225, 347, 490
Rouyer, Jean-Pascal, 465
Rozier, Jean-François Pilâtre de, 234, 236

Sade, Marquis de, 92–6, 393
Saint-Cloud, Château de, 360, 397–8, 512–13
Saint-Domingue *see* Haiti
Saint-Germain-en-Laye, royal palace, 6, 13, 14, 124, 183
Saint-Lazare, Convent of, 308–9
Saint-Méry, Moreau de, 359, 502
Saint-Paul-des-Champs church, Paris, 374–5
Saint-Simon, Claude de Rouvroy, duc de, 10
Saint-Simon, Louis de Rouvroy, duc de, 23, 24, 29, 32; on the French banking crisis, 54, 56, 57; on Philippe d'Orléans, 49, 51; on the Poncallec Conspiracy, 59
Salpêtrière prison hospital, massacre at, 428
salt tax, 7, 48, 173
sans-culottes, 431, 433, 468

PILLGWENLLY

04-06-18.